THE MAKING OF THE NEW DEAL

The Making
OF THE
New Deal

THE INSIDERS SPEAK

Edited by

KATIE LOUCHHEIM

With historical notes by Jonathan Dembo

Harvard University Press

Cambridge, Massachusetts, and London, England

1983

Library of Congress Cataloging in Publication Data
Main entry under title:

The Making of the New Deal.

Includes index.
1. New Deal, 1933–1939. 2. United States—Politics
and government—1933–1945. 3. United States—Economic
policy—1933–1945. 4. United States—Officials and
employees—Interviews. I. Louchheim, Katie, 1903–
II. Dembo, Jonathan, 1948–
E806.M275   1983   973.917   83-10867
ISBN 0-674-54345-9

To Donald Klopfer

Contents

ILLUSTRATIONS

Foreword

BY FRANK FREIDEL

The decade of the 1930s, despite the privations of the Great Depression and the threats of global war, was a time of national reaffirmation and the laying of the foundations of modern America. This was the era of Franklin D. Roosevelt and the New Deal. Roosevelt and his administrators were receptive to new ideas, and so were at least part of the leaders in Congress and members of the judiciary.

Zealous in serving them, both in Washington and throughout the United States, were hundreds, indeed thousands, of men and women still in their twenties and thirties. The young New Dealers, trained in the law, economics, public administration, or new technical fields, brilliant and dedicated, brought their energy and creativity to the federal government. Nurtured on progressive ideals, schooled in the improved universities of the 1920s, they possessed both the knowledge and the vision to engage in the restructuring of government and society.

The New Deal was one of those occasional periods in American history when suddenly large numbers of opportunities opened for young people of talent to fill roles of importance. That had been the case in the American Revolution and the establishment of the federal government. Jefferson, Hamilton, Adams, and many others performed remarkable services before they reached the age of forty. Young leaders of both the blue and the gray during the Civil War dominated politics for a generation afterward. So too, the top leaders of the New Deal had been seasoned in the progressive movement and the First World War.

While the New Deal would not have been possible without the vision and receptivity of Roosevelt and other key figures, it owed much of its shape and substance to these resourceful, indefatigable youthful

New Dealers. It was they who helped propose new programs, draft legislation, and put the new agencies into operation. They were active in the Administration, Congress, the courts, and the news media. They were, to borrow the title of Dean Acheson's autobiography, "present at the creation," and many of them went on to long and resplendent careers in the new America they had helped create.

Much has been written about Roosevelt and his lieutenants. Now here, a half-century later, thanks to Katie Louchheim, who interviewed and gathered reminiscences from many of her old friends, are the New Dealers' memories of the times when they were young and the age of Roosevelt was in the making.

Katie arrived in Washington in 1934, the wife of Walter Louchheim, a young philosopher turned New Dealer. She became renowned for her wit and observing eye, and was soon fast friends with many of those contributing most during the Roosevelt era. They continued to be her friends and associates as she rose from a first assignment with the United Nations Relief and Rehabilitation Administration to vice-chairman of the Democratic National Committee, Deputy Assistant Secretary of State for Cultural and Educational Affairs, and U.S. representative on the Executive Board of the United Nations Educational, Scientific, and Cultural Organization, with the personal rank of Ambassador. She has been both a poet and a public servant of distinction. As one of the New Deal generation, she has captured their excitement, attitudes, and contributions.

There was irony in Roosevelt's advent as President, for the Great Depression marked the antithesis of opportunity for millions who were unemployed or helplessly mired in lowly, ill-paying jobs. The new President had not only pledged himself to rigid economy, but actually slashed employment in the established federal departments and agencies. Even a large part of the 1933 graduating classes of Annapolis and West Point were unable to go on active duty.

Along with the contraction came a sudden expansion in new directions, since the nation's top talent was Roosevelt's to command. In the prosperous 1920s there was a dispersal of the best minds through business, finance, the great law firms, and academia. There could have been no such full assemblage of talent in the government as took place in the New Deal had it not been for the diminution of opportunities elsewhere. There were other factors too. Some talent that largely had hitherto gone to waste obtained New Deal employment. Conspicuously, there were the brilliant Jewish lawyers that the prestigious, old-line firms were reluctant to hire, who came to win acceptance and fame in Washington. Less conspicuously, there were skilled women and blacks who filled responsible government positions in unprecedented large numbers. Even for those who had obtained promising positions elsewhere, there was the lure of the New Deal, with its excitement and opportunities to build a better nation.

Into many of the top openings went, of course, the nominees of the patronage-hungry Democrats; never had patronage been so important as during these depression years. Yet the President himself chose those academics and experts of established reputation who had already served him as members of the Brain Trust—Raymond Moley and Rexford G. Tugwell, for example, who while aiding Roosevelt became secretaries in the Departments of State and Agriculture respectively.

In the lower echelons and in the new agencies, young people found employment, often with considerable power and responsibility. Some already were in place, such as the economist Mordecai Ezekiel in the Department of Agriculture and the lawyer Thomas Corcoran in President Hoover's new loan agency, the Reconstruction Finance Corporation. In turn, Corcoran recruited Milton Katz in the summer of 1932. "I discovered a group of young lawyers who were wholly oriented toward government and public service," says Katz in his interview later in this book. "It was a spawning ground for those who eventually wound up all over Washington when Mr. Roosevelt came in." The presence of Ezekiel and a number of experts in the Department of Agriculture who had already gathered data and planned machinery made it possible for the new Agricultural Adjustment Administration to put into operation its crop control program with remarkable speed in the spring of 1933. Corcoran that spring became involved with Benjamin Cohen and James Landis in drafting the new securities legislation for Representative Sam Rayburn—and Cohen and Corcoran went on to become the most notable bill-drafting team of the New Deal years.

For the most part the young New Dealers came to Washington for their first experience in government, such as Walter Louchheim, who laid aside his doctoral thesis in philosophy to help put into operation the Securities and Exchange Commission he had so strongly favored. Wilbur Cohen, only twenty-one in 1934, went from his studies at the University of Wisconsin to assist Professor Edwin E. Witte in the planning of a social security system. He stayed on in Washington, rising ultimately to become, in the Lyndon B. Johnson Administration, Secretary of Health, Education, and Welfare.

Able young lawyers were particularly in demand. Charles A. Horsky remembers here: "In those days, there was a sense that you could get better results if you hired first-class young men. Older people couldn't be attracted by the salaries that were then paid. My first job paid $3,600 a year. That to me was a damned good salary, but for a practicing lawyer who was experienced and mature, that was peanuts. I think FDR and . . . all the rest of them, believed that what you do is get good young people."

Some of the brightest of the young people had been serving apprenticeships in Washington as clerks to Supreme Court Justices. There for a year they helped research or even draft decisions or dissents for the particular Justice to whom they were assigned. Several enjoyed the remarkable experience of spending a year serving the aged Justice Oliver Wendell Holmes, that living embodiment of the American legal tradition. Felix Frankfurter, as both friends and foes acknowledge, was the most indefatigable recruiter of legal talent for Washington. For years he had supplied Brandeis with clerks; he knew of an able person for every opening, whether it be to draft securities legislation or to serve as counsel in one of the agencies. Most of these fledgling lawyers went on to the new agencies, but David Riesman, not enthusiastic about the New Deal, ultimately became one of the nation's most renowned sociologists.

Roosevelt was receptive to the fresh ideas and the zeal of these early New Dealers. He had no prejudice against either the seasoned old-timers or the tyros. When he needed a securities bill, he had first commissioned the seventy-four-year-old Samuel Untermyer, who had been counsel for the famous 1912 Pujo Committee investigation of the "money trust," and next a former head of the Federal Trade Commission—thus paying off political obligations. But when difficulties ensued, Moley, with Roosevelt's knowledge but technically acting for Congressman Rayburn, turned to Frankfurter, who sent his three brilliant protégés. Roosevelt soon had Cohen and Corcoran working directly for him, and ultimately appointed James Landis chairman of the Securities and Exchange Commission. The oldsters were rigid and often could rally strong support among senior congressional leaders to reinforce them in positions Roosevelt did not relish. The younger men were more supple and innovative. Cohen and Corcoran, although trained by Frankfurter in the Brandeis tradition, moved well beyond it to take into account the changes in corporate and financial structures that had taken place during the First World War and the 1920s. A bit uncertainly at first, they were devising new techniques of securities regulation. They and untold numbers of others on different assignments had one other immediate advantage as well, the vitality of youth. They could—and did—work well into the night, sometimes seven days a week. They could outlast the old-timers, with whom they were sometimes in competition. Corcoran reputedly did not want married men working for him because it was difficult for them to keep such long hours. He himself did not marry until 1940. Cohen never married. Those who did not relish either their enthusiasm or their hours soon left.

Among them there was inevitably rivalry and a grasping for power, especially if they were seeking the President's ear. Yet Frank Watson, who left a Boston law office to come to work for Corcoran, tells in his recollections that among that group "none of us was particularly interested in power because we all felt we were going to leave just as soon as things got back to normal. We were quite cocky about our ability to accomplish great things in the outside world. Tom encouraged this. He told us not to have any concern about our later years. We were all brilliant. So none of us was fighting for power, and I think this was one of the great strengths in our group."

The friendly cooperation among Corcoran's group sometimes helped further the New Deal overall. Watson remembers "several occasions when Harold Ickes, Secretary of the Interior, and Jesse Jones, head of the RFC, were at sword's points. Some of us were writing memorandums for each of them to send the other. We'd call each other to smooth things out, never letting our bosses know that we were engaged in such activity."

Sometimes the senior officials gave invaluable guidance to the beginners. David A. Morse, at twenty-six, fresh to the field of labor law, found himself trying to negotiate a settlement to an oil refinery dispute and became well aware of that. "I had never seen a labor dispute," he recalls here. "I got myself three books on labor relations and collective bargaining. I took the train from Washington to Oklahoma." After two weeks, in desperation he called his superior, William M. Leiserson, who counseled him, "Be fair and persist and settle it." In the end, Morse succeeded. "There's a lot to be said for bringing young people into service," he believes, "and there's a lot to be said for putting them under the supervision of more experienced people."

There was a camaraderie that extended beyond working hours. Corcoran rented a large, rather run-down house in Georgetown which had once served as the summer White House for President Grant, and shared it with about a half-dozen men. Cohen, preferring quiet, lived elsewhere, but spent so much time at the Little Red House that he ultimately moved into it. Other young men also shared living arrangements. Throughout these reminiscences there are numerous accounts of the partying and the bonds of mutual interest and friendship extending through New Deal Washington.

One of the most renowned of the houses was Hockley, where Edward Prichard, who late in the New Deal clerked for Justice Frank-

furter, then became an assistant to the President, shared a room with
Philip Graham. "We had a lot of parties," he remembers. "Mint juleps
during the warm weather, toddies during the less warm weather. We
had Sunday morning parties, with fried chicken and ham and biscuits.
The Frankfurters would come, and the Reeds and the Achesons and
Adlai Stevenson and others."

Not everyone looked back upon the house with enthusiasm. Riesman, in particular, gives a different perspective. "I lived in a Washington house of dedicated New Deal activists. To their parties there came
many talented young men scattered throughout the government, mostly
lawyers along with a few economists. Some of these young visitors had
in my judgment too much contempt for ordinary Americans. They
thought it hopeless to try to persuade the country, or even to persuade
Congress. Clever and ingenious, they were therefore tempted to use undemocratic means. I was the 'house Tory' and I'm one of the few people
who have become less conservative as I've grown older, I guess."

A number of the young New Dealers were of poor, sometimes immigrant background and full of compassion for the less fortunate. When
Morse received a government appointment, he had to borrow $50.00 to
live on for the first two weeks before he received a paycheck. Roosevelt
was his inspiration. "Somehow in his fireside chats and his articulation
of the problems that confronted the country, he inspired us as young
people to reach out to help."

The dispossessed were a prime concern of a considerable part of the
young officials, many of whom came from a social-work background.
They worked for Harry Hopkins's relief agencies or for the Resettlement Administration and the Farm Security Administration. Tex
Goldschmidt and his bride, Elizabeth Wickenden, who had been working in New York for an organization that promoted barter among the
unemployed, came to Washington in the fall of 1933 to join the Federal
Emergency Relief Administration. "Wickie" Wickenden began by writing a report on transients, then soon was involved in establishing camps
for transients. Later, among many activities, she supervised the FERA
mailroom, which received three thousand letters a day, many of which
had been addressed to the President or Mrs. Roosevelt. She saw to it
that some of the most interesting of these went each week to Hopkins
and Mrs. Roosevelt. Most of them read, she remembers, "Dear Mr.
President, I have four children and all I have in the pantry is such and
such. Please send me help right away."

The gulf between these underprivileged, to whom Roosevelt offered a distant glimmer of hope, and the young people of power in
Washington was an enormous one. Those in power sometimes could

participate in decisions that affected the welfare of millions; they could feel that their proposals were of some consequence. Horsky suffered the frustrations of working on briefs for the Solicitor General, Stanley Reed, to use in arguing New Deal cases before the Supreme Court. He tells how, somewhat to his dismay, he had to miss the fiftieth anniversary dinner of the *Harvard Law Review* to accompany Reed, Cohen, and Corcoran to the White House to thrash out a problem with the President: "The debate was whether the Fair Labor Standards Act should set a national minimum, 25 or 35 cents an hour, or whether it should make the rate flexible and allow for differences between occupations. The great problem was the pecan pickers in Texas, who would all be put out of work if the minimum was fixed, because they weren't getting anywhere near that much. Roosevelt listened to all this for a while with his cigarette sticking out of his mouth, and he finally said, 'Let's have a flat minimum.' So we all went back and drafted a flat minimum statute that was passed and has worked all right."

The New Dealers formed a network, not only sharing views but upon occasion helping each other move among the departments and agencies. There were also subnetworks. Most important was a woman's network, extending from Eleanor Roosevelt, Frances Perkins, and Mollie Dewson of the Democratic National Committee, on down through the echelons. Women reporters also rallied around Mrs. Roosevelt, who aided them by establishing her own press conferences. There were sufficient blacks in the New Deal for them to form their own group. As Robert C. Weaver recalls, Mary McLeod Bethune brought them together in 1935 in what the black press referred to as the Black Cabinet. It had no direct access to the President except through Mrs. Bethune, who had Eleanor Roosevelt's ear. They met when problems arose in order to develop potential solutions. A subgroup of younger blacks came to meet frequently in Weaver's recreation room, where, according to a *New York Times* reporter, sessions "swung from feverish rounds of poker to even more feverish discussions of how faster progress could be made in achieving equal opportunities for Negroes."

Throughout the country, many thousands of other young people became involved in the New Deal, and for them too it became a training ground for the future. Lady Bird Johnson recalls in her interview here "a busy and wonderful year" when her husband, Lyndon B. Johnson, headed the National Youth Administration in Texas. "Lyndon learned a lot and made friendships that lasted all his life." A generation later when the Johnsons came back to dedicate a job-training corps at San Marcos, they looked about the platform. "There was a judge who handled the guest of honor, the governor, and on up to the President.

All of them had been with the National Youth Administration . . . So it was a breeding ground for learning and achievement."

Some of these New Dealers from the hinterland went on to Washington, as did Lyndon Johnson in 1937, when he was elected to Congress. "It was a yeasty, exciting time," Mrs. Johnson remembers, "and the people really felt that they could roll up their sleeves and make America great. Lyndon had an expression about that: 'You feel like charging Hell with a bucket of water.' There were very few times in our country's life when so many good minds gathered together in that city intent on raising the level of living and the safety of the American people. I'm so glad I got to be a part of it."

This book, as no other, captures that spirit and that time.

Preface

One day in 1977, in the midst of a noisy political gathering, a friend was asking me questions. "You're the pro," he kept repeating, delivering a barrage of inquiries about the financial policies of the politician we were celebrating. Finally, we found a quiet palm tree. "You take the Whitney case," I began, feeling myself on solid ground. "The Whitney what?" he came back. Had he forgotten the man whose elegant credentials defied suspicion but who in the end turned out to have stolen stocks from every upper-class, middle-class, and plain Joe acquaintance, friend, or relative, escaping detection for years? "Never heard of him." So the Whitney case of 1938 was unremembered. My friend was middle-aged, educated, prosperous. Was there no link between his generation and those eventful years? Was that triumphant recovery known as the New Deal lost? Had we, as a nation, forgotten that we have to share every turn and every curve in history's road?

I recalled an article I had written in 1976 on Ben Cohen and Tom Corcoran, the two almost invisible mechanics of that era, whose Damon and Pythias relationship had long fascinated me. I looked up that article and the big black notebook containing all the research for it. I had asked Ben and Tom to lunch to talk about the New Deal. They tried to recall the names of all the young men who had lived and worked with them then in what was called the Little Red House, a five-story Italianate mansion in Georgetown. The radical right had inferred that the house was a Communist hideaway and gave it that newsmaking name. A caustic reporter described the residents as "up and coming young lawyers, economists, and specialists . . . on call day or night to help draft measures," and he alluded to Plato's *Republic* as he interviewed the household. They included Gerard Swope, son of the General Electric giant; Frank Watson and Merritt N. Willits, roommates at Harvard, both helpers at Hoover's Reconstruction Finance Corporation; Charles Stuart Guthrie, a Bull-Moose Republican; Richard E. Guggenheim, Republican from San Francisco; Richard Quay, the quiet Rhodes Scholar; Tom's brother Howard Corcoran. They came and went, and the overflow took to the porch. Ben Cohen reported: "So many of these young men thought they were working for the Lord, although they never saw him."

Ben and Tom became legendary. In one of the press clippings collected in my notebook, a Tammany Hall figure is quoted: "As it is Corcoran and Cohen are beyond the political rules. They are engaged in writing them." Ben's fealty to Tom was clear when someone attributed Tom's entrée to the White House to his entertaining accordion playing. Ben angrily countered with: "It was his agile mind and the lilt he could put in his language that drew FDR's attention." Tom, on his part, regretted Ben's modesty: "Presidents, even the greatest of them, need the unbiased support of persons they regard as their peers." Ben worked behind the scenes because he could count on Tom to deliver the legislation right on to the floor of the House and into the offices of those who voted pro and con.

Time limitations were not allowed to interrupt the young New Dealers; they were too preoccupied with saving their country. I know because my husband was one of them. I married a Wall Street broker who had a seat on the Stock Exchange. After the stock market crash of October 1929, the family firm dissolved. "There are no rules," my husband said. The words "Stock Exchange" protected no one. Walter decided to go to graduate school and studied at Columbia University with Professor Richard McKeon for a doctorate in philosophy. One morning in the early fall of 1934, the *New York Times* arrived late. I ran up two flights of stairs, paper in hand, and fairly shouted at him: "Look they are going to reform Wall Street!" He glanced at the headline—"SEC in Process"—grabbed the paper, and followed me back downstairs. I knew so little about the rights and wrongs, except there were too many of the latter. But Walter knew all about that. He was immediately hired by Judge Ferdinand Pecora and became the thirteenth employee at the Securities and Exchange Commission. "He came aboard," as they described the hiring process. And so did I.

I kept reading that heavy black notebook, realizing all that has been left out in the story of the New Deal. When I had finished, I knew what I must do; find all those New Deal friends and acquaintances who were still around and persuade them to tell their stories. What follows describes those exhilarating days.

To help the reader understand the chronology and some of the more technical allusions of the recollections, Jonathan Dembo has added short headnotes at the beginning of each chapter and occasional footnotes explaining specific acts, court cases, and so forth. Brief descriptions of some of the persons mentioned in the text may be found in the section of Biographical Notes at the end of the book, following the Biographies of Contributors.

It is customary to express one's thanks to those who help put a book together. In my case there is just one basic fact. There would not have been a book without Lorraine Brown and Becky Byrne, who accompanied me on interviews and ran the tape recorder; Theresa Egan, who turned the taped conversational exchanges into readable documents; and typists Rhoda Dyrkin, Elizabeth McGehee, and Steve Brockman.

My appreciation of the bright, gifted personnel at Harvard University Press—Aida Donald, Executive Editor, Nancy Clemente, and Elizabeth Suttell—would fill another book. Arthur Rosenthal, publisher, gave me confidence right from the beginning, telling me how much he liked the first draft. My personal publisher—Chairman Emeritus of Random House and my husband, Donald Klopfer—encouraged me as we moved along.

To all those who granted me interviews, you are now safely between covers. I thank you for contributing to this new and enlightening form of transmitting our generation's contribution to the New Deal.

K.L.

THE MAKING OF THE NEW DEAL

CHAPTER 1

The Campaign Trail in 1932

In the summer of 1932, the Great Depression that followed the stock market crash of 1929 showed no signs of ending. President Hoover, a pathetically shy, dour, uncommunicative man, was unable to deal with the situation. His popularity plummeted. Nevertheless, the Republicans renominated him. They had little choice: expecting defeat, no other prominent Republican wanted the job.

The only ray of light and hope for the millions of unemployed, destitute, hungry, and homeless men, women, and children who looked to government for some kind of relief came from the Democratic party. In Chicago, the Democrats nominated as their presidential candidate Franklin Delano Roosevelt. As governor of New York, FDR had established a record of social concern and political activism. A patrician, he seemed a genial, good-hearted man. But was he up to the task? Could he overcome his physical disability? Did he have the intellect to deal with the crisis? W. B. Ragsdale, a gifted young reporter on the Roosevelt campaign train in 1932, and Dorothy Rosenman, a close family friend, give emphatically affirmative answers to these vital questions.

WARNER B. RAGSDALE

Franklin D. Roosevelt wheeled his chair through a circle of light out the back entrance of the Albany governor's mansion. A car waited at the edge of the shadows. Gus Gennerich, his husky bodyguard, lifted him into the automobile. The Democratic candidate for President tugged the brim of his "good-luck" hat, waved at three reporters, and rode across town to the railroad yards where a private car waited.

Roosevelt said good-bye to friends assembled to see him off. Gennerich helped him up the steps into the car. The governor's staff settled into the car adjacent; newsmen sprinted for their allotted space farther along. Just before midnight, the cars lurched forward and the train crept out of town.

It was 11 September 1932 and the nation was deep into the third year of the Great Depression. The popular song "Brother, Can You Spare a Dime?" was approaching the importance of a national anthem. Both parties were so short of money that they met, ten days apart, in the same convention hall and even shared the same decorations. Democratic advisers had decided that travel in the country would show the voters that Roosevelt, a man crippled by polio, did have the physical strength to handle the presidency. A majority of the delegates at the Chicago convention had little knowledge of his lack of mobility. When he appeared to accept the nomination, he had stood alone, only a strong torso, broad shoulders, and a grim face showing above the reading stand.

Many who had seen him at Houston in 1928, dragging himself on crutches to the microphone to nominate Alfred E. Smith, his Happy Warrior, noted he stood without crutches in 1932. A side view from the press rows showed trousers dangling loosely about his legs and knuckles white from his tight grip on the reading stand. But his voice was clear and mellow as a French horn. His promise of a New Deal for the American people aroused such a roar of applause that the 200 delegates from big eastern states who had fought to the end against him forgot Al Smith. What to do about Al Smith's bitterness would remain a problem, but first he must put down the whispers that the times demanded an able-bodied man in the White House. The more vicious suggested that polio affected both the legs and the brain.

Two months of careful planning had gone into the arrangements that would take the candidate through 12,000 miles of travel: whistle-stops, back platform talks, automobile parades, and major speeches. During eight weeks his physical endurance surpassed that of any politician in American history. He shook thousands of hands, was heard by hundreds of thousands, and was seen by more than a million.

Tucked away on the special equipment provided by the New York Central were speech writers, political advisers, money men, secretaries, and radio and mimeographing equipment. Advance men were already in the field.

Raymond Moley of Columbia University, a member of the Brain Trust, and Joseph P. Kennedy, a link with the financial community, were also aboard. At every stop of more than ten minutes someone would be in touch with Louis M. Howe, Roosevelt's alter ego, or James A. Farley, the campaign chairman, at the New York headquarters. Four other cars housed telegraph men to assure that copy flowed quickly to papers, a man from the Washington press galleries to arrange accommodations for reporters following in automobiles, others to make sure halls where major speeches would be made were ready, and railroad officials to keep the train moving. Reporters stowed baggage and typewriters and matched coins for lower and upper berths. Experienced campaigners chose uppers, preferring swaying motion to up-and-down jouncing.

During that first night the train paused for water and fuel at Syracuse. Small crowds at early morning stations in Ohio found James Roosevelt trying to substitute for his father, who was having a comfortable breakfast in his bedroom. Roosevelt spent most of his first day on the train working with Moley on a farm speech to be made at Topeka the following day. Crowds at small stations in Ohio, Indiana, and Illinois got no more than a wave from his window. He was hurrying toward a test of strength.

His first real test came on 13 September at Jefferson City, Missouri. State Democrats adjourned a meeting to hear him. They had arranged a platform with a wooden ramp leading to the back platform—an easy walk for a man with two good legs. For a man walking with steel leg braces it was an ordeal. As the train drew to a stop beside the ramp, Roosevelt locked his braces at the knees. With James in front and Gus following, he began to walk along an untested ramp. On either side he clasped the railings. Midway, one of the rails crumpled. We saw him straining to keep his balance, tottering forward in a losing struggle. Gus grasped Roosevelt by the waist and literally lifted him upright, holding him until he reached the speaker's stand.

Ignoring the fact that he had almost fallen, Roosevelt smiled, grasped the lectern and spoke as if nothing had happened. He emphasized the need for change, gestured bravely with his head, and was applauded with ringing cheers. Then he turned and walked back alone, with Gus and James guarding every step.

That experience, if shown on television, would surely have raised questions. He trod no more untried ramps. When the New York Central train was turned over to the Union Pacific the next day, instructions carried this notation: "There will be a ramp in the N.Y. Central baggage car. It will require four men to handle. Give this matter careful attention."

Each time the candidate left the train from Jefferson City on, the stout ramp that had been tested in advance was put in place. He would walk behind Gus, gripping the rails. The transfer to a car was made so fast that only intimates realized he was being lifted in.

Before he left Albany, the governor had promised that he would make "look, listen, and learn" trips that would give him a broad glimpse of how the depression was being felt. Even at that first important stop at Jefferson City he heard a question that would rise again and again; "Are you going to make us sleep on benches like Hoover did?" Roosevelt ignored the question.

The candidate was also well aware of the wild cries of alarm. Spokesmen for the rich were saying that trains ran better under Mussolini and were calling for a dictator. Will Rogers was writing that the Communists had some "mighty good ideas." Important churchmen were urging employers to abandon the profit motive, and powerful industrialists warned that if business did not take care of the workers the government would have to do so.

In this atmosphere of doom the candidate moved through his "look and listen" campaign. Before the campaign was over Roosevelt had made three of these "learning" trips, which gave him a broad glimpse of the depression as it affected thirty-eight of the forty-eight states in the country. He saw every region, from Maine to California and Illinois to Georgia, talking with all kinds of people and bolstering his personal observations with the views of hundreds of local politicians who moved in and out of his car.

On the very first day he saw shacks built of tin and packing boxes, called "Hoovervilles," huddled near the railroad tracks. In these hundreds, perhaps thousands, of men and women found shelter. They were warmed in the bitter winter of 1931–32 by coal tossed from passing freights by soft-hearted brakemen. In big cities he saw men and women sleeping in parks, teenaged girls man-hunting on the principal streets, people selling apples, scrounging for food, queued in lines in front of soup kitchens.

That first day also took him through the rich corn belt of Indiana and Illinois, where farm houses were unpainted, fences crumbled, and crops rotted in the fields. Corn was selling for fifteen cents a bushel, too little to pay for harvesting; it would be burned for fuel. It was cheaper than coal. On the second day, the train passed through Kansas, where a farmer, refusing to sell his wheat for twenty-five cents a bushel, opened the back gate of his truck and let grain spill into the road. Later he would see men panning for gold in Colorado streams, hoping to get enough "color" to buy a meal. By the thousands, hard-eyed men and anxious women gathered at market towns in the farm belt to hear his hopeful words.

At Kansas City John Nance Garner, his vice-presidential running mate, came aboard to talk to people in his earthy language. Speaker of the House of Representatives, lawyer, small-town banker, and ranch owner, Garner knew the needs in West Texas. He had put through a bill to provide relief and public works—but the bill had been vetoed by President Hoover.

On 14 September Garner rode with Roosevelt through eastern Kansas and along the streets of Topeka. In the Kansas capital, he told the people crisply he had neither horns nor hooves, as some antagonists had suggested. Then he went back to Uvalde. Little more was heard from him during the campaign.

At Topeka, speaking from the top of the marble steps of the capitol, under a hot Kansas sun, to the thousands spread across the grounds into nearby streets, Roosevelt promised help for farmers.

In Denver, on 15 September, the group got their first baths. Lorena Hickok of the Associated Press had been lucky. She had a room at the Brown Palace. Reporters stood in line outside her room waiting for their chance at her bath. The next real cleansing for reporters would come ten days later on the return trip from California. The railroad cars were luckier; they got a rubdown at important stops.

While in Salt Lake City from 17–18 September, Roosevelt occupied a seat in the Mormon Tabernacle that was usually filled by Senator Reed Smoot, apostle of the church, staunch conservative supporter of President Hoover. Roosevelt hammered Republicans, and the applause shook the rafters. The great Tabernacle choir sang, and the pipe organ thundered "Happy Days Are Here Again." In a few weeks Utah would vote against Hoover and strip Smoot of his seat.

At all stops there were people, small groups clustered about the stations just to catch a glimpse of the train. With the first sign of day-light, crowds multiplied at road crossings and along the tracks. At small towns at which no stop was scheduled, the crowds often ignored the warnings of the trainmen and edged so close that we marveled that none were hurt. They were clamoring for a sight of the candidate.

When possible, Roosevelt slept until 8:00 A.M. His black valet, Irvin McDuffie, brought breakfast to his bed. McDuffie, who had been an At-lanta barber, gave him his shave, during which the governor went over the day's schedule with Marvin McIntyre, his press aide, and the night's speech with either Moley or Farley when the latter was on the train.

In the Rocky Mountain states, as the train crept carefully through the trackside crowds, Roosevelt would lock his braces and be helped to a standing position by James. When the car came to a full stop, he emerged from the rear door on his son's arm. "I'm glad to see you fine people," he would say, taking a firm stance at the rail. Then he would introduce his daughter Anna and his daughter-in-law Betsey Cushing Roosevelt, the wife of James. Next, he would look up at his towering son and say: "This is my little boy, Jimmy." As the crowd laughed, he would add: "I have more hair than he has." After a few days, James found the joke thinner than his hair, but he would grin on cue. Mrs. Roosevelt joined the party in Arizona on the return trip. She often appeared with him on the platform.

Roosevelt dealt easily and gracefully with crowds, his voice ringing with hope and assurance. He had none of the stiffness of Herbert Hoover and lacked the strident combativeness of Harry Truman. After FDR's first sentence people forgot his aristocratic accent and accepted him as one of their own. While the candidate spoke, reporters jotted down notes. They wrote their stories on paper propped against the side of the private car, and handed them to the telegraph men as they sprinted back to the train.

Roosevelt's family and aides crowded about to help ease him back into the car. A local politician would step forward to wave as the train crept slowly out, its bell clanging.

Roosevelt's doctrine of a new liberalism flowered as he moved west: he talked of national planning for farmers, reordering economic life, government regulation of utility holding companies, using federal power projects as "yardsticks" for utility rates, and reciprocal tariffs. His friendly, uninhibited press conferences held daily in his private car allowed him to give the press an intimate glimpse of his plans. Such relationships have become impossible in these days of campaign planes, press buses, and television.

In Sacramento, on 22 September, it came as no surprise when he praised Senator Hiram Johnson, the maverick Republican, in his hometown. The next day, at the Commonwealth Club in San Francisco, he told industry flatly that if it did not accept the responsibility that went with power the federal government would have to protect the public interest. With a hint of prophecy he warned business that if concentration continued "we shall have all American industry controlled by a dozen corporations and run by perhaps a hundred men." His bid for the support of liberal Republicans became clearer on the return trip.

In Los Angeles, on 24 September, after several brief stops in suburbs, the candidate was met by war veterans and a drum and bugle corps whose banner proclaimed: "Welcome to Roosevelt from the Forgotten Men." (This was a phrase used in a radio speech on 7 April 1932.)

The procession passed City Hall, where he was stopped by the mayor, John C. Porter, who had declined to welcome him. Then, seeing the outpouring of fellow townsmen, Porter changed his mind and came running after the candidate's car, hatless and breathless.

Two days later, on 27 September, at Lamy, New Mexico, Roosevelt continued his pursuit of liberal Republicans. In the crowd was Republican Senator Bronson Cutting, who, like Roosevelt, was an alumnus of Groton and Harvard. He applauded Roosevelt and joined him on the platform.

From Lamy, the train climbed into the arid highlands of Colorado and Mrs. Roosevelt became a regular member of the back platform group to greet crowds at Trinidad, La Junta, and Pueblo. The party spent the night at the Broadmoor Hotel in Colorado Springs and reveled in the hot water of the first tub bath any had felt in ten days.

The next day, in McCook, Nebraska, Roosevelt shook hands with another Republican, Senator George W. Norris of Nebraska. Norris had already announced his support and he presented Roosevelt to 16,000 of his friends, some of whom had driven a hundred miles to hear him.

Then, two hard days of platform talks, parades, and informal speeches, from 29–30 September, took us through Nebraska, Iowa, and Wisconsin, where farmers, threatened with foreclosure of their homes, were ready for rebellion. Later, Nebraskans would talk of burning the state capitol, an Iowa judge would be smeared with tar and feathers, and prospective bidders on foreclosed farms would have nooses dangled in their faces. They cheered when he urged support for the Wisconsin La Follettes.

In Chicago, on 30 September, Mayor Anton Cermak, who later died from an assassin's bullet intended for Roosevelt, arranged a triumphal reception. Streets and windows were jammed, and confetti sprayed down. The next day, Mr. and Mrs. Roosevelt gave a luncheon for the twenty reporters and ten photographers who had made the entire trip.

When Roosevelt told listeners in Detroit, on 1 October, that 6 million children did not have enough to eat, the opposition called his programs "paternalistic"; he replied, "All right; I am a father."

After twenty days, seventeen nights, and 9,000 miles on the train, we reached Albany. We had written unnumbered thousands of words on folding tables that were always a little too high, in speeding automobiles, and on jerry-built racks in baseball parks and halls. Sometimes the copy was written in the midst of a crowd where a member of the audience read the words aloud to bystanders as we wrote. The entire party was bone-weary from too much work and too little sleep.

Two weeks later the party boarded the train again in a pouring rain for eight more days of travel into the Midwest and South. In Pittsburgh, on 19 October, we saw hundreds of millions of dollars worth of steel plants standing idle. In city parks men and women were pitching tents in the nippy October weather. That night Roosevelt promised to cut 25 percent from the nation's $4 billion budget, a promise that would haunt him in the future.[1]

The Middle West and South saw Roosevelt at his best, waving jauntily from open cars, talking bravely to bent and grimy miners. Farmers and sun-bonneted wives stared from cotton fields; at five cents a pound, a bale would bring them $25, and two bales could represent a year's work for one person on an upland farm. The crowd in Atlanta, on 24 October, was called the greatest the South had ever seen.

In a formal speech at Baltimore the next day, the candidate described the four horsemen of the Republicans as "Destruction, Delay, Deceit, and Despair." We rolled back into Albany on October 26 and began preparations for a swing through New England. Soon the party piled into a dozen limousines and set out through the drab remnants of a colorful autumn. Roosevelt spent the night of 30 October at his old school, Groton. Then we moved through narrow streets of crowded towns to Portland, lunched on sandwiches, and turned down the coast to Boston.

There was no New England chill about his welcome. Even a cold and steady rain did not discourage the crowds that shouted and scrambled for a glimpse of Roosevelt. On that day, Hoover called the roll of Democratic proposals and said that if the tariff were reduced "the grass will grow in the streets of a hundred cities, the weeds will overrun the fields of millions of farms ... churches and schoolhouses will decay." Roosevelt replied before a crowd that filled every inch of space in the Boston Arena, tearing into Republicans with the sharpest speech of the campaign. "They threaten American business and American workers with dire destruction," he said as the crowd roared. "They crack the whip of fear over the backs of American voters. Five thousand men who control industry are joining the chorus of fear."

On election night, 8 November 1932, we saw new faces around Roosevelt. Secret Service men had moved in to protect him, just as they had come to Palo Alto in 1928 to protect Herbert Hoover.

No pictures of the candidate being lifted into an automobile had been allowed. One such picture had been killed and did not find its way into print until years later. A year later the wife of one reporter wept when she saw him walking so laboriously at the White House.

1. FDR's promise to cut the budget resulted in passage of the Economy Act of 1933, which saved an estimated $243 million.

Not until 1 March 1945 did Roosevelt acknowledge that he was tired. He mentioned his crippled legs for the first time since his 1928 campaign for governor of New York. Appearing before a joint session of Congress to give a report of his conferences with Joseph Stalin and Winston Churchill at Yalta, he said: "I hope that you will pardon me for this unusual posture of sitting down . . . but I know that you will realize that it makes it for me a lot easier not to have to carry about ten pounds of steel around on the bottom of my legs."

DOROTHY ROSENMAN

The only person who ever called me Dot was President Roosevelt. He called my husband "Sammy the Rose," a name he invented. I remember the all-night session during the 1932 convention when it didn't look as though Roosevelt was going to be nominated at all. We were all up in Albany at the governor's mansion, and some of us were lying on the floor. I was leaning against Sam and fell asleep. I claim to be the first person who snored at the President-to-be.

That summer of the convention, Roosevelt asked that we rent a cottage near him. We had a farmhouse in Wappingers Falls, which is not far from Hyde Park. He asked Sam to be with him in Albany the week before the convention started and then, characteristically, he said, "Tell Dot to come up the day the balloting starts." Eleanor, Johnny, Elliott, Mama, and the two secretaries, Missy LeHand and Grace Tully, were in Albany. James and Anna were out in Chicago. Mama was so disheartened by the fact that her son wasn't being nominated and that people of her own class, like James Gerard, voted for Smith rather than for Roosevelt, she left the next day and went back to Hyde Park.

Roosevelt had a direct line to Chicago to the convention. He had a long cord connected to the phone and he brought it in to the dining room table. While we were at dinner the phone rang. He took a message and clammed up completely, which caused Missy to say, "You look like the cat who swallowed the canary." When the balloting started again, we realized what had happened. That's when we got the signal that Garner and McAdoo had given him their votes.

When Roosevelt was nominated, there was no security such as there is today. The press just came screaming in. The reporters knew that a plane was waiting at the airport, and they suspected it was waiting to take him to Chicago. They asked about the plane and who was going, and he mentioned the members of his family and his two secretaries and Gus Gennerich and Al Miller, who were his bodyguards. Then he said, "and Sammy the Rose," whereupon Sam's secretary, an elderly lady, came dashing over: "Oh, Mrs. Rosenman, you're not going to let your husband fly, are you?" In those days very few people flew. I burst out crying, not because I didn't want Sam to go, it was the emotion of the moment. Somebody told Eleanor that I was crying because I didn't want Sam to fly. She dropped everything and got me into a corner and said, "I must tell Franklin he cannot take Sam with him. Love is more important than anything in the world."

I kept boohooing and saying, "But I want him to go." However, she did speak to Roosevelt. I went to Sam and he said, "We'll wait until the governor goes upstairs." When they went up, Sam took me with him and I told Roosevelt that I definitely wanted Sam to go, that my crying had nothing to do with not wanting him to go. Roosevelt felt that I might be nervous, so he made me promise not to drive down to our farmhouse until the plane landed in Chicago. Well, there were headwinds and they had to stop in Buffalo. Then they had to stop at Detroit. They were hours late. The President had also given me a mission; he asked me to get in touch with Judge Bernard L. Shientag, who was an old friend of Al Smith's and a very good friend of ours, and ask him to go up to Harman. Al Smith was coming home by train and all trains stopped at Harman to change engines. He wanted the judge to try to keep Smith from making an angry statement when the reporters met him at Grand Central Station.

There I was wandering around that big mansion by myself. Finally I saw that if I didn't leave to drive to our Wappingers Falls farmhouse, I wouldn't get there before dark. So I disobeyed and left. When I passed the governor's house at Hyde Park, I stopped in. Mrs. Roosevelt, in the tiny radio room listening, said, "They haven't reached Chicago yet." So I sat there a little while. When I got to our place, my mother, who had been there with our children while I was away, came out on the porch and said, "They're just landing."

We didn't want to go to Washington and we only went later on when Roosevelt asked Sam to get off the bench. Sam said he knew New York state affairs, but he didn't know Washington affairs and didn't want to get embroiled in what was called Potomac Fever. His ambition was to go on the bench and there was a vacancy and Roosevelt appointed him to it. He was thirty-six years old.

Sam coined the term "New Deal." On that night in 1932 when it didn't look as though Roosevelt was going to be nominated, Sam went into another room and wrote a peroration he hoped Roosevelt was going to be able to deliver. He used the term, "the New Deal." The cartoonist Roland Kirby picked up that phrase, and the next day there was a picture of a plane flying from Albany to Chicago and on its wings were emblazoned "The New Deal."

There never has been anything like that era because everyone who could lend their talent gravitated to Washington. People gave up lucrative jobs, and government salaries in those days were absurdly low. But they thrived on living in Washington and enjoying their work, and they worked long hours. The amount of partying was relatively insignificant because everybody was working. We didn't live there in those days because Sam was on the bench, but we went down frequently when Roosevelt would ask Sam to do certain special things. We always stayed at the White House.

The President had a tremendous feeling for people, individuals and people as a whole. Those who gathered around him imbibed that spirit and acquired some of it within themselves. So it was a period when people were searching for a solution to those terrible times and were giving whatever they could to contribute to it.

Roosevelt, you know, reacted to people. Many a time, for instance, when we were in Hyde Park, he would go out in his specially built car, which he could operate by hand. He would stop to talk to farmers, and he'd chin along and talk about what they were doing and how it was going. The same thing was true in Warm Springs. It was a personal thing.

When he talked on the radio, his sentences were short. He never used big words because he was talking to the average man. He had an affinity for that average man. He always talked simply, and this I think was the magic of Roosevelt, that he had an empathy for everyone, for people on the whole.

My husband and I were typical examples. We were far from the types that Roosevelt had grown up with or mixed with in the Hudson Valley or at Harvard. But we were close and we always felt he enjoyed us as we enjoyed him. He was our friend.

CHAPTER 2

The President and the Press

FDR's relationship with the press was a tumultuous love-hate affair. He loved the give and take of press conferences and performed brilliantly. He also used the press with unparalleled effectiveness. Reporters responded to his warm and genial personality as most people did, with sympathy and affection. Yet, FDR believed that 85 percent of the publishers opposed the New Deal. The press's essential task, he felt, should be to act as a channel through which the government could transmit the facts to the people. Although reporters suspected that FDR's interpretations and his "facts" occasionally covered up politically embarrassing information along with imperfect analysis, they generally went along with his many restrictions of their coverage. FDR's press conferences were intended to bridge the gap between what they wanted to know and what he wanted the public to know. Reporters also greatly appreciated his long background, off-the-record discussions, which helped them understand the issues. When the United States abandoned the gold standard in 1933, the reporters, having failed to report the event intelligibly, appealed to the White House for assistance. The President responded by sending a government economist to help them prepare their reports. From that moment, the traditional adversary relationship between the President and the press broke down and FDR had the upper hand.

RICHARD LEE STROUT

When Roosevelt took over, the banks were closed, the people had almost lost hope. We were desperate. In those days, the new President did not take over until March, a gap of four months after the November elections.[1] In those months we almost went into panic. Then Roosevelt came, a cripple. I was against him myself; I think I voted for Norman Thomas. But then I was enthralled by him as almost everybody was. He began by making that magnificent inaugural address, "We have nothing to fear but fear itself." Immediately afterward, he made his first radio address to the nation, his fireside chat.

Roosevelt made radio his medium—his voice, calm, beautifully modulated, came right into the living room with you. You felt he was there talking to you, not to 50 million others, but to you personally. Those were happy, happy days when gasoline cost fourteen cents a gallon and milk thirteen cents a quart.

Roosevelt started off having two press conferences a week. He continued that until the war came; then he had one press conference a week. Altogether, I think he had a thousand press conferences. I was present at practically all of them. One press conference was held in the morning for the afternoon papers, one in the afternoon for the morning papers the next day. We'd gather outside and there'd be anywhere from fifty or more reporters. At big times, 200 reporters might be there. We'd go in and stand around his desk. It was covered with dolls, totems, and knick-knacks. It was like a meeting of a club.

Television has destroyed the press conference as we knew it, destroyed the old freedom, the intimacy, the lack of inhibition, and that jocular familiarity between two antagonists that we had then. We were antagonists, but we liked each other and we laughed and we had a perfect understanding of what each was trying to do and there was a certain degree of affection.

The publishers of papers were generally hostile, but the reporters were won by his personality. We might not have agreed with his politics, but we had a symbiotic relationship. He got everything he could from us and we got everything we could from him. We nearly always got a good story. He would sit behind the desk with his long cigarette holder and his glasses. He had one curious trick which I haven't seen reported before. He would bring his right hand around and scratch his left eye while he was dangling his glasses or his cigarette holder in the left hand. He talked to us informally and unconventionally. He had little jokes. One day everybody crowded in at one time, and someone said he couldn't see. Roosevelt said, "That great big Fred Storm, he's right in front. Fred, here's a chair. You sit right here." From then on Fred always had a special place right in front of the desk. Mostly, I was an in-

1. The Twentieth Amendment to the Constitution, the Lame Duck Amendment, which changed Inauguration Day from 4 March to 20 January, went into effect in 1933. Thus, FDR's first inaugural was the last to be held on 4 March.

conspicuous second- or third-rate reporter and watched things from a distance.

In Roosevelt's four elections, the majority of the editorial pages were against him. In two cases, it was up to 60 or 65 percent. Some reporters got orders—they had to direct their columns. It wasn't a free press. At that time journalists took it for granted that if their publishers were biased, they either agreed with the publisher or they retired.

People often ask me why Roosevelt's being crippled was concealed from the public: "Why didn't you say so when you wrote a story about him? Why didn't you say he was in a wheelchair? Why didn't you say he was heaved up or heaved down?" We just took it for granted. Everybody knew it. It was common knowledge. Occasionally, he wore braces to walk, or he would appear in a wheelchair, or he would be supported by someone until he had his hand on a rail. When he was President, again and again during a campaign, he had to show his dependence and the fact that he was crippled. There would be an utter silence in the crowd; the old proverbial pin was dropping, and then he'd reach his microphone. He would wave and there'd be a great cheer. That had nothing to do with politics.

The Cabinet members were more accessible than at any other time that I've known. All Presidents start by saying they are going to have press conferences. But then they encounter the questions they have to answer. It's a strain. Roosevelt could reply to hostile questions and then quip with reporters.

I don't understand how Roosevelt and Harold Ickes got along so well. It's really to the credit of both men. Ickes would come and cry on Roosevelt's shoulder; he needed to be reassured; he would complain; he'd have fault to find with everyone else in the Cabinet. But Roosevelt was patient with him and he'd listen to him. He saw his value and he knew Ickes was absolutely honest and doing a superb job in the Department of Interior.

Senator Borah was an isolationist, but I loved him. There was never anyone quite like him. He knew everything and yet at heart he was modest. When the reporters in the press gallery heard "Borah's up," that meant he was speaking, and if Borah was up, there was a story. We were like fish attracted by bait. He was a complete isolationist, and in a press conference he had the audacity to tell Cordell Hull, Secretary of State, that he knew better.

Mrs. Roosevelt was the President's eyes and ears. Recently I visited the Hyde Park museum. I had forgotten what affection I had for Mrs. Roosevelt; for Franklin, too, but particularly for Mrs. Roosevelt. I saw that big plain, strongly marked face. There was magnificence in her and

The campaign train, 1932

FDR with the press on the campaign train, 1932

yet she was extraordinarily commonplace. It was all summed up in a *New Yorker* cartoon. Two miners were underground in a shaft in a coal mine. Another figure is there. One miner says to the other, "It's Mrs. Roosevelt." She was everywhere; that's the way we felt about her. I don't know that any President's wife went down into coal mines before.

Roosevelt extricated us and then bang, bang, bang, the Hundred Days. The country was saved in those First Hundred Days. Then people of wealth and the corporations, who had previously run things, felt that their privileges were being encroached upon. They turned venomously against the President.

What Roosevelt did in a period of a little over twelve years was to change the form of government. Washington had been largely run by big business, by Wall Street. He brought the government to Washington. He made the government responsible for the economy and for the welfare of the people.

He was the greatest President of my lifetime. Still, I can criticize him. There was a vein of extraordinary deviousness in him. He was not only the lion but the fox; there was a slight strain of—perhaps cruelty. He enjoyed setting some of his own subordinates against each other and then he seemed to enjoy their division. He was stimulated by it.

Roosevelt, on the record, would say things that sounded so harsh but then the smile would nullify what he said. When I reviewed Ernest Lindley's book,[2] I called Ernest. There is an incident in which Roosevelt said three times, "Ernest, you lied." Those are fighting words. He did use the word "lie." I said to Ernest, "I can't understand this." He admitted some recollection of having an altercation with the President. Ernest had taken offense, decided he wouldn't go to the Christmas party. Then Mrs. Roosevelt called up and said, "Ernest, the President didn't mean that. You come to the Christmas party." Ernest came.

The spirit of the New Deal could be recreated, but it would take a catastrophe to bring that about. You'd have to have the beginning. There are always ambitious and able and burning individuals who come to work in government. They're on tap for a President who has the political authority to use them. The basic thing about Roosevelt was said by Oliver Wendell Holmes, that he had a second-rate intellect but a first-rate personality. His personality was first-rate.

2. Ernest Kidder Lindley is the author of *The Roosevelt Revolution* (New York: Viking, 1933), *Halfway with Roosevelt* (New York: Viking, 1936) and *The New Deal for Youth* (New York: Viking, 1938).

KENNETH CRAWFORD

The New Deal was so abruptly different it was startling. Suddenly Washington was alive. The White House became the hub not only of the United States but of the world. The people who were brought in were exciting; Brain Trusters from the Ivy League, men like Ben Cohen and Tom Corcoran; characters like Hugh Johnson, who was head of the National Recovery Administration, which was to restore prices to a reasonable level and fight deflation. We felt that something was being accomplished. We felt a part of it. It was a great time to be a journalist in Washington.

There were two echelons of correspondents in Washington then. There were the old-timers, who had by that time been there for twenty-five years or more, a group who wore spats and who did not think of stepping out without their canes. The great majority were youngsters, usually from the sticks like me. There was a camaraderie that's been lost, unfortunately. There's no central area for correspondents anymore. They're spread all over town.

President Roosevelt had two press conferences a week, and they too were informal. We streamed into the Oval Office and stood in front of his desk. He sat there with a cigarette in his holder and answered off the cuff. He called on almost all of us by name.

The press wasn't invited to the White House, except once a year the Roosevelts gave a beer bust and a dance. These parties were great fun. There was a lot of leaking going on because the place was so wide open. What was going to happen next was never a secret. They'd come out with one big scheme for raising farm prices, for example, and that would be the big story for the day. But on its heels would come plans for something else and what it was, you could almost always find out. President Roosevelt did not play favorites too much, although there were some insiders. Ernest Lindley, for example, had covered Roosevelt in Albany. He was very good on what was going to happen a week from now or three days from now. Then he was on the *New York Herald Tribune*.

My wife and I went to the White House for dinner when the American Newspaper Guild was being organized. Heywood Broun, the New York columnist, was president. When he died suddenly, I was elected to take his place. The Guild had the same trouble other labor unions were having, only more so, from Communist infiltration and disruption. The Roosevelts's daughter Anna was then copublisher of a paper on the west coast. She had written her mother saying she was having a hard time running the newspaper because the Communist-dominated Guild unit in her town created constant disruptions. Mrs. Roosevelt herself was a member, because she was also a newspaper columnist. She came to our meetings and sat in the front seat knitting.

My wife and I got our dinner clothes and drove to the White House. We found ourselves in the small dining room having dinner with President and Mrs. Roosevelt, Harry Hopkins, and Admiral and Mrs. Richard Byrd. Admiral Byrd was just back from an expedition to the South Pole. The President had obviously agreed with Hopkins that they were not going to be bored by long accounts of Byrd's travels to the South Pole. Every time Byrd started a travelogue, they interrupted. We had a very big evening full of political talk. Mrs. Roosevelt invited me upstairs to question me about her daughter Anna's letter. I had to tell her that Anna was telling the truth, that there probably was Communist infiltration. The Guild fought for four years until the Communist influence was overcome.

Mrs. Roosevelt wanted to help the female journalists. There were not very many of them, and they were just getting a toehold in the Washington press corps. She had her own little circle of women correspondents, all devoted to her and all good journalists. The most prominent were May Craig of the Maine newspapers and Doris Fleeson of the *Daily News.* These two women broke precedent by getting invited to cover Roosevelt on a trip that involved transportation by the Navy. The Navy staff was baffled because they had no toilet facilities for women so they got them. Subsequently, they did the same thing for the press galleries of the Capitol.

Tom Corcoran and Ben Cohen were good sources of information. They wrote so much of the legislation and knew so much about what Roosevelt was thinking. They were always available, but they weren't quoted. They were protected. We never put the finger on the source of the leak. Harry Hopkins was so much a Roosevelt favorite that he eventually moved into the White House and lived there. Hopkins was trusted with diplomatic missions, bargaining with the Soviet leaders. If there was such a thing as an assistant President, toward the end of Roosevelt's life he was it. After that White House dinner, my wife said she was in love with Harry Hopkins, and I told her to get in line. He was enormously appealing to women, to everybody. He was bright, quite funny, and he ran what became the biggest federal agencies, the Federal Emergency Relief Administration and the Works Progress Administration, and did it well without any big scandal. He couldn't have weighed over 125 pounds. He was ill, but there was a vitality about him that was palpable. The agencies had press people by that time, but it wasn't impossible to get to Hopkins.

FDR once told John O'Donnell of the *New York News* to go sit in the corner with a dunce cap. The *Daily News* was an early Roosevelt partisan, but had become one of the New Deal's bitterest critics, and Roosevelt took it out on John. John and his wife, Doris Fleeson, had been New Dealers but they cooled after that episode.

The atmosphere was very free and easy in Washington. We could descend on any Cabinet officer. Almost all of them had regular press conferences, and between press conferences you could walk in and talk with them. The conferences were successful because the New Deal had a great deal to sell to the public. The press was the go-between between the government and the governed.

We could get at Senators very easily too. We also worked in the Capitol, sending pages onto the floor and calling members off the floor to what was the "President's room."

Congress responded to Roosevelt through the First Hundred Days of the New Deal. Then the resistance started, when the Supreme Court questioned the constitutionality of some of the early measures. The Supreme Court thus became the greatest source of news in the city.

The Treasury was experimenting with gold, doing things which most journalists were not equipped to understand, although we gradually learned. A professor from Cornell, George Frederick Warren, was varying the gold content of the dollar. He was varying it from day to day, feeling that the amount of gold the paper dollar stood for was a key factor in market pricing. I don't think it was, as it turned out, but for a while the Administration thought so.

The depression was not felt in Washington as it was in other places. For a part of that time, I was transferred to Buffalo where I watched the depression and the start of the New Deal. The impact was more obvious there. I remember the first Blue Eagle parade in Buffalo to celebrate the institution of the codes that lifted wages and changed price levels.[3] It was all very exciting in the industrial cities, more so than in Washington, where government employment was a stabilizing factor. The downturn wasn't felt there as it was in New York and other cities in the countryside.

The national disease was deflation. Everything had slowed down and it was thought that the answer was to get things moving again with prices high enough to make it worthwhile to be in business and in manufacturing, to get some return on investment. During the depression, there was so little money in circulation that it was almost impossible for

3. A blue American Indian thunderbird with outstretched wings was the symbol of industrial recovery. Those who supported the National Recovery Administration's codes of fair competition were allowed to display the emblem.

enterprise to sustain itself. But we didn't really get out of the depression during the early days of the New Deal. What the NRA did was to institute codes of conduct for various industries and free the labor unions to organize more completely, which was a measure for raising prices and getting a better distribution as well. That was the difficulty. There wasn't a reasonable distribution. These codes were designed to correct that, to get more money into circulation, thus more goods and services, and to correct the price structure to the point where a farmer or a business industrialist could make a reasonable profit. It wasn't simply raising prices. But that was one of the things that was most obvious about it.

CHAPTER 3

Clerks of the Court on Justice Holmes

Civil War hero, lawyer, professor of law, author, orator, judge, and renowned Justice of the United States Supreme Court, Oliver Wendell Holmes, Jr., was heir to an illustrious tradition of service, achievement, and loyalty to the nation. He left an equally brilliant legacy. Born in 1841 in Boston, the son of the famous author, poet, and physician Oliver Wendell Holmes, Sr., he fought for the Union in the Civil War and was wounded three times. By the end of the war, he had risen to the rank of lieutenant colonel on the staff of Major General Horatio G. Wright. In 1866, Holmes obtained his law degree from Harvard Law School and for the next few years practiced law in the Boston area. Later, he was an instructor and professor of law and edited the *American Law Review.* In 1882, he became Associate Justice of the Massachusetts Supreme Court, and from 1899 to 1902 served as Chief Justice. Finally, in 1902, he was appointed an Associate Justice of the United States Supreme Court, where he served until 1932, when, at the age of ninety, he retired.

While on the Supreme Court, Holmes became the leader of its liberal wing and a frequent dissenter from the decisions of its conservative majority. He favored broader interpretations of the Commerce clause of the Constitution so as to regulate trusts; he opposed restrictive interpretations of the Fourteenth Amendment to the Constitution which limited civil rights; he protested the overturning of the federal Child Labor Act. In *Schenck v. U.S.* (1919), he formulated the "clear and present danger" doctrine to protect freedom of speech, even while warning against malicious uses of speech. He constantly sought to apply the common law to the conditions of the present and to free the law from the bounds of mere precedent.

THOMAS CORCORAN

When I met Justice Holmes he was eighty-five years old. That was in 1926. He and Mrs. Holmes had led a rather gay social life, but by the time I got there, they had cut down on that completely. I don't remember that they ever had a dinner party or that Mrs. Holmes ever went out.

I had an office adjoining his on the second floor of the house. Holmes never would use the Supreme Court Building, and he was absolutely right. He kept his étude, as they said, in his house. Mrs. Holmes read things that were amusing to him; he said they were French novels.

One of the reasons I came back to Washington was to be with Holmes after his wife died in 1929. When I first visited him after she died, he was sitting playing solitaire. That was not unusual, but it had a certain symbolic significance. I expressed my sorrow; she had been very good to me. He held out a card and said just one thing. "She made life poetry for me. She was very lovely."

I was the first Irish Catholic law clerk he'd had. He wondered how the hell a practicing Irish Catholic from Boston could have gone to a place called Brown University, where the president was a Baptist minister, and then to agnostic Harvard Law School. He was very interested in what went on in my mind.

I graduated from Harvard Law School in 1925. We were one of the most remarkable classes they ever had, as they've always said in the law school. That class could have done anything. It included Adlai Stevenson and J. Lawrence Fly, who was later the head of the Federal Communications Commission and decided newspapers shouldn't own television stations.[1] He also saved the Tennessee Valley Authority from going under when David Lilienthal got into all kinds of trouble.

At that time they decided at Harvard to develop a new faculty to succeed a very brilliant faculty of men who were getting old. I and eight other fellows were selected to be part of the new faculty. We became teaching fellows and I was under Felix Frankfurter because I was interested in utilities and he taught certain courses in administrative law. I was sent down to New York to find out why the district attorney's office wasn't working with the Prohibition law, and I found out why.[2] Every-

---

1. The Federal Communications Commission was established by the Communications Act of 1934 to regulate interstate and foreign communications by telegraph, cable, radio, and television.
2. The National Prohibition Enforcement Act of 1919 (Volstead Act) was passed over President Wilson's veto and, effective 16 January 1920, implemented the Eighteenth Amendment to the Constitution, which forbade the sale of alcoholic beverages.

one was asking for a jury trial and there wasn't enough money in the world to give them all a jury trial. So anybody who violated the Prohibition law could get off for $5.00 if he'd plead guilty to anything at all.

The next year, 1926, I took my doctor's degree, and it was a real doctor's degree, an SJD. Then I tied up with Joe Cotton's law office in New York; Cotton and Franklin was the great liberal office there. The head of the office at that time was William G. McAdoo, who had been Wilson's son-in-law. Before I actually joined the firm, I was asked if I'd work for Holmes. I think it was sheer accident that I was picked. I suspect some nice Boston boy with good Boston manners was supposed to succeed Charles Denby, and the Boston boy decided that it wasn't worthwhile working for an eighty-five-year-old man.

I've never forgotten what Mrs. Holmes said to me when I arrived. She was quite aware that I was a Boston Irishman and a Catholic. So when the door opened and I came in, Mrs. Holmes said to me, "You're going to see the Justice, and I want to talk to you first. Mr. Corcoran, you come from Boston and you're an Irishman. We know all about you. What do you know about us?" I said, "Why, Mrs. Holmes, I've heard all there is to say about the Justice. I'm excited, very excited." "Well," she said, "that's important. I just want to know, Mr. Corcoran, do you know what a Unitarian is?" I said, "Oh yes. I think I know what a Unitarian is. A Unitarian is a kind of refined Congregationalist." "Well," she said, "that will do if you want to put it that way, but if you want to put it very simply, a Unitarian in Boston was the least you could be. We were Unitarians." And so I went up to meet the old man. I think she was a very remarkable woman. She took her problem and bounced it on me right away.

At that time I was in a very lucky situation. All we made at that time, and this was supposedly a prized job, was $3,600 a year. Nowadays one of those guys gets $45,000 a year. But unfortunately I had a deal with my younger brother Howard who is now a federal judge. You see, our ancestors were seamen, and we had a crazy idea that we had to follow my grandfather, so I had to split my $3,600 with my brother because he had to finish out the family dossier. So he went down to Callao, Peru, and from Callao he went over the Andes. He went down the Amazon tributaries on a little boat and arrived months later at Harvard Law School. He damned near flunked out.

It was a wonderful time in 1926 and 1927. There was a resurgence of Coolidge prosperity. We had just had Mr. Harding and the girl in the closet and the Secret Service men outside. And Mrs. Harding had poisoned him, and Coolidge had succeeded. It was the time when some of the old hotels were being built, when the Mayflower Hotel was being built, when the Wardman Park was being built. It had the atmosphere that these inaugural balls have. But I had to live very, very lean in my bed for $4.00 a month in a garret up on 18th Street. My fare was completely intellectual. I never lived so intellectually in all my life. Every night I'd go to my room and I'd read everything Holmes had ever written, all his old opinions, and I'd read everything he told me to read: Montaigne and Burke and Lord Acton, who said, "Absolute power corrupts absolutely." I had a wonderful education.

Holmes always exercised in the afternoon. He'd come home from the Court, he'd make little notes of what he had heard, and then we went for a walk. During the walk, trying to probe my mind, he'd say, "You've read the New Testament, of course? Have you ever read the Old Testament?" Every night he gave me three chapters of the Old Testament he wanted me to read. The next day when we walked, we went over it. We used to walk down as far as the Pension Building. That was the Grand Army of the Republic Building, you know. We'd talk about the Civil War, and then we would go back. We passed the Civil Service Building and we would watch the employees come out. He used to say, "You know, little boy, do you think the Lord God really intended every one of those civil servants should be fertilized?" He had a lovely sense of humor.

Holmes was never very interested in the purposes of the Civil War. It was for just one thing, to save the Union. As far as he was concerned, the war ended at Antietam, 17 September 1862, which is when the war really ended because that's when the British decided they were not going to recognize the Confederacy.

Holmes would say, "You know, up in Massachusetts it was a white feather, and if you were an aristocrat you didn't go to war. So we all went to war. Most of my friends got killed in the war, and most of them got killed in the war not really believing in it." When his enlistment was over, which was for three years, he did not reenlist. By this time he'd risen from being a lieutenant to being a lieutenant colonel on the staff of Major General Horatio G. Wright. Even though most of his companions had been killed, his regiment was called a "copperhead regiment," that is, a regiment that was for making peace with the southerners now that it was clear they weren't going to win. And Copperheads were for McClellan, not for Lincoln.

Holmes was like all Yankees. He was a capitalist. I will always remember what a friend said: "One of my contemporaries lost his capital. He might as well be dead." Holmes had his father's house at Beverly Farms, and he owned his house in Washington, a very decent house with a lovely garden that Mrs. Holmes took care of.

About 1865 Holmes still wanted to be a law professor, and he became a professor at Harvard Law School. He wanted to reorganize the then-existing law as a response to a concrete need. He bought himself a black book, and, being a prudent Yankee, he kept that book till he died. He put down in it not only notes he took for *The Common Law* but a list of every book he read. They're listed according to the year published and go way back into the 1800s.

After Mrs. Holmes died, I would sometimes have supper with him. Then we'd sit down and I'd read. My first year with him was just an introduction to the wonder of him. When I returned to Washington to work for Stanley Reed at the Reconstruction Finance Corporation, I would occasionally have a chance once again to read to the Justice after dinner. The wonder I had first felt was still very much present.

Among other things, I used to take care of his checkbook. Believe you me, it was quite a business making sure the checkbook exactly balanced, that it was not one cent or five cents off! We'd go over it and we'd go over it and we'd go over it. One day I went into a pharmacy and bought a package of Life Savers. I came back and offered him a Life Saver and he took one. Then he said, "Son, do you know what you've done?" I said, "I bought a package of Life Savers." "Do you know how much you paid for it?" "I paid five cents." He said, "Do you know how much you really paid? You paid out the interest on $1.00 for a year."

Once, Mrs. Holmes worked for a week to get him to take me to a lecture. But it cost five bucks—too much. He went alone. I overheard the conversation the next day. "It wasn't worth $5.00. I'm glad I didn't take the boy."

Holmes had one of the old-fashioned desks, a stand-up desk. He wrote his opinions standing up because he said it was conducive to brevity.

One of the last things we read was *The Education of Henry Adams.* We often talked about Henry Adams and his relationship to the government. He was always waiting to be called because every other Adams had been in government. Holmes always said to him, "You can't just sit outside and do nothing but criticize. You've got to be down in the arena where you're working with the actual problems of government." We read *Mont-Saint-Michel and Chartres.*

There's a chair out in my office, the chair in which he used to sit. His things were disposed of at auction when he died, and I should have picked it up, but Hugh Cox did. Then Hugh left it to me in his will with the understanding I'd leave it to Jim Rowe in my will. The old man would sit there half prone and I'd be reading to him and the lights would be down. All of a sudden we'd be talking about the Norman knights in the melee. Ye gods! He was still in the Civil War. To this day I can't forget Holmes.

ALGER HISS

Each of us clerks to Justice Holmes was chosen by Felix Frankfurter. We didn't know about it, didn't even know we were being considered, until we got a letter from the Justice. My letter simply said, "Felix Frankfurter has selected you to come and serve me next year. I will expect to see you on the Friday before the first Monday in October." Then there was a sentence which said, "At my age I must of course reserve the right to resign or die." He was ninety when he retired from the Court. It was signed: "Very sincerely yours, O. W. Holmes."

So, scared to death, I reported on Friday at 1720 I Street, and from then on I had a love affair with this great man. I am certain this was true of every secretary. It was probably the greatest emotional, intellectual experience any of us had, and our memories are pretty good about what happened because (a) we were young and (b) it was so important.

None of the Justices had offices in the Court. I reported in October 1929, the fall after my graduation from Harvard Law School, and served with him until the following October. I can claim a couple of special accomplishments, special privileges. I was the first secretary to serve him during the summer. It was one of the perks of the job that you had the summer off after you'd served all year. The Judge went up to Beverly Farms in Massachusetts to his father's house, his own house by then, and the secretary had the summer off. But his wife had died in April, before I came, and he was lonely. I knew I could help, and it was a great privilege to be with him. So I persuaded him, when the time came to think about a vacation, to allow me to go up. My wife and I and Timmy, my oldest boy, took a house for the summer nearby, and I went to work for the Judge every single day.

The other thing I can claim as a special distinction is that I was the first secretary to read aloud to him. Again this was because of the death of Mrs. Holmes; she used to read aloud to him at night. He would play solitaire while he listened. I would see him reading in the late afternoon, and sometimes he would doze off and drop the book. I had been brought up in a family where there was a lot of reading aloud. I liked reading, thought I did it pretty well, and so I suggested to him that I do so. He discarded my suggestion, saying that it would remind him of his wife.

So I entered into a benign conspiracy with Sir Esme Howard, who was then the British ambassador. He had come to know Holmes, and called quite frequently. I knew that Sir Esme's son was acting as his private secretary and read aloud a great deal to him. Sir Esme enjoyed it and found it relaxing. I suggested he tell Holmes how much he liked being read aloud to. At first Holmes paid no attention to him, brushed him off. But he did mention to me that Sir Esme had suggested this. It must have been November or December when he said, "You still willing to try reading aloud? I've been thinking about it." I said, "Certainly." "I don't think it'll work, but go ahead and try." And it worked. We read all the Walpole letters that were in print, seven volumes. Later, when the New Deal started, a number of us clerks came back to Washington. We picked up the reading aloud to spell the then secretary, and one or another of us read to him practically every night. Until the end his mind was so clear that if you were reading a book and you'd only got a third through and you'd come back the next week to finish, it made no difference. You'd pick that book up where you left off.

The most astonishing thing about the Judge, aside from his own longevity, was how his family's longevity fits into the history of the country. He told all of us that when he was a small boy his grandmother told him of seeing the British enter Boston before the Battle of Bunker Hill. This man spanned the entire history of his country, personally or through a forebear. His house on Beacon Hill had been occupied by Lord William Howe, the British commander, as his headquarters. I own a Queen Anne mirror that hung in his house. I prize it because it reminds me of his puckish, almost boyish humor. It hung in the downstairs living room. He would peer into it occasionally when he was going by and say, "Sonny, when you look into that mirror, do you sometimes think you see the bewigged visage of Lord Howe? I do."

Within the first week or ten days that I was with him, he casually referred to Harry and Will James. I'd never heard Henry James called Harry. William James was certainly never Will in my thoughts. It was not that Holmes dropped names; they were related to something he was talking about.

His working habits were very definitely old-fashioned. No newspapers were allowed in the house. He said, "If anything important happens, my friends will tell me." There was no typewriter; everything was done in longhand. I persuaded him to let me fill in his checks when he had bills to pay; all he had to do was sign. I also persuaded him to let me answer a lot of the idle mail he got that didn't require any thought on his part. Until then he had answered every letter personally; somewhere very valuable letters must be floating around.

On the second floor there was a series of rooms. One was his bedroom. He could stay on that floor except when he went down in the elevator for meals. It was a big, open room, with sliding doors, which I
never saw closed, where the secretary sat. That room and the next room,
his actual study, were both lined with bookshelves all around the four
walls. He had a big, flat-topped, lovely desk beside a window that faced
on a little garden. In the western corner was a standing desk. I think it
had belonged to a grandfather of his. In those days people wrote standing at a desk. He frequently stood at that desk, which was in front of the
other window facing his garden. Aesthetically speaking, it was remarkable to see this beautiful man, with his heavy mane of completely snow
white hair and handlebar moustaches, his ruddy color, standing slightly
stooped contemplating the surroundings. He regularly received boxes of
Havana cigars from S. S. Pierce. They were almost as long as the Churchill cigars. To see him at his writing desk, facing the garden, the clouds
of white smoke as he puffed and worked resembled the halo of a sainted
character.

I never heard him use a word of profanity except once. Something
was going wrong; he suddenly said, "Shit!" and then was embarrassed.
Yet remember, this was a man who'd served in the Army and had
learned Army talk.

In terms of the most important influences in his life, I would put the
Army high. He learned democracy, as he was frank to say, and as a
Boston Brahmin he was very much of an elitist and knew it. He has said
in my hearing, and must have said it to many others, that when he discovered young men of his precise age but not of his social background
and found them to be first-class fearless leaders in the Army, he realized
that they were every bit as manly and deserving of respect and affection
as he was. Every time the calendar rolled around to one of the major
battles in which he'd participated, he would remember it the way people
remember birthdays. There are notations in the well-known black book.
He would mark the appearance of a crocus or a violet, a rare bird, and
occasionally a reference to dates of the famous battles.

His feeling toward the "lower classes," the poor, the working folk,
was "upper-class romantic." I remember driving around with him north
of Boston. We were going through Salem on a warm day; a woman was
leaning out of one of the small milltown houses with her elbows on the
window sill. She could be clearly seen from her second-floor window,
and she had her sleeves rolled up. Holmes said, "Sonny, see what beautifully formed arms that woman has. That's one of the advantages of the
working class." To me this comment was indicative of a generous-
minded, sophisticated man.

William James was a close friend, and he admired Charles Pierce. He went into the law, perhaps, more because his family felt he ought to have a degree in that profession than because it lured him. He may have preferred philosophy, but unless you were going to teach, you couldn't be a professional philosopher. I always thought the phrase, to quote from a speech, "One can live greatly in the law as elsewhere," was a bit of a protest. I don't think he felt that it was as big a world as that of the philosopher or the writer. But he did philosophize, not just in his correspondence, but occasionally in his opinions, and he did write beautifully. Early in my service with him, he made this remark: "A man is like a tree that grows in a cleft in a rock, bent by its location. To straighten it or him is at the peril of its life," perhaps meaning that circumstances confine us.

Besides being useful in a procedural way, such as entering the cases in the docket, the secretary's chief duty was to study the petitions for *certiorari*.[3] That is how the bulk of the Court's jurisdiction gets to it. It has discretionary jurisdiction. It does not have to accept cases to consider unless it finds that they fit into its own special requirements of a constitutional issue, a conflict between different Circuit Courts of Appeal, or a matter of very great general importance. Otherwise, to transfer an appeal to an intermediate court is all that is required. The Justices are there simply to supervise the overall judicial system.

We would stand by the Judge's flat-topped desk with the briefs record. We'd pile them up beside us because we'd do five or six cases at once, each of which we would study carefully. He held an unlined white pad, on which he wrote, in the tiniest, almost illegible hand. He would write the number of the case and its name. Then we would recite the facts that we had carefully distilled from the record. He would write down the facts as we stated them. We would repeat the chief arguments pro and con and make a tentative recommendation. He would then reach for the papers and make sure that he agreed with our report.

As for the major cases, he seldom discussed them with his clerks. Brandeis was quite the opposite. Brandeis sent his clerks to the library to do research. I think the extent of our help on major opinions would be to get cases for him, not to summarize them. "Sonny," he would say, "see if you can find the *Massachusetts Reports*[4] by my favorite author," always referring to himself. He would say: "Why not that? I have a right to suit myself. If I don't like it, I change it, so naturally I like it the way I write it."

3. Requests for a superior court to call up the records of an inferior court case for review.
4. The printed opinions of the Massachusetts Supreme Court.

He seldom conferred with his colleagues except at the Saturday morning conference when votes were taken on *certiorari* and on the major cases that had been argued. He did infrequently confer by telephone with Brandeis and Stone. They would send their opinions and particularly their dissents to him. I was with him when the conservatives ruled the Court, and he, Stone, and Brandeis most frequently dissented. They did confer a great deal largely by sending drafts back and forth, and sometimes by telephone.

I was present when Cardozo and he met for the first time at Beverly Farms the summer I was with him. Cardozo was brought to see him by Felix Frankfurter. Although they had not met before, they had corresponded, and obviously they had the highest respect for each other. Cardozo said, "All the way up I've been trying to think of the appropriate thing to say. All I can think of is what Heine said when he came to see Goethe. All he could think of to say was, 'How beautiful the cherry trees are.'" Well, Holmes was touched. Such a gracious, lovely thing to compare him to Goethe.

When I discuss Holmes I always insist on telling students that Holmes is famous in the books as a positivist, and I quote what he has said: "The law should be clear," inferring that morality, a sense of compassion, "should not enter into it." This is certainly true in a basic, philosophic, and technical sense, but like every other man of nobility, Holmes was a man of sentiment and compassion.

At one of the lunches during the summer Walter Lippmann, Felix Frankfurter, and Learned Hand came. As the secretary I was privileged to be present. A decision had just come down from the New York Court of Appeals. The case was a mortgage and bonding case affecting a very valuable piece of real estate in New York. Two very experienced investors, not speculators, who had dealt with each other often and knew each other's families, were involved. In this particular instance, one of them was the mortgagor and one was the mortgagee. A payment was due three weeks after the mortgagee was going to leave on a trip to Europe. He called the mortgagor and said, "I have put aside the payment in escrow, but naturally I want to get the interest up until the last minute. My faithful secretary, whom you know, has my power of attorney, and on the due date she will transfer the payment to you." The faithful secretary, for the first time in her life, forgot. No bad reason; she just forgot. The moment the payment didn't come the mortgagor foreclosed. It was then, he said, too late, even though he knew all he had to do was call up.

Judge Morgan J. O'Brien of the Court of Appeals had said, "A bond is a bond. They were experienced, sophisticated men who had dealt with each other. This is the risk you take. He has to give up the property." Cardozo had said, "There was no damage to the mortgagor. All he had to do was pick up the phone. If the law is as strict as that, then equity should step in." All the way up that day from Cambridge, Felix and Learned Hand had debated this issue. Learned Hand said, "A bond is a bond. That's what we lawyers believe." Felix said, "No, Cardozo's quite right." Finally they said, "We'll leave it to the great man, the Judge. We're going to have lunch with him. Let's stop arguing with each other." Apparently Walter Lippmann had kept quiet and just listened.

They were so full of this that when they came into the sitting room, they were still talking about it. The Judge was obviously annoyed. He had looked forward to a nice lively general conversation at lunch, picking up news of this one or that one at Harvard. But they kept saying, "What do you think?" He said, "I don't know anything about it." He thought of every excuse: "It might come before me. It's not impossible, surely, a New York state case—how can I—I haven't seen the record. It would be just foolish offhand to think—" They said, "These are the facts and no other facts. It's as simple as this." Even after we sat down at lunch they were still pestering him, and he was really annoyed. Finally, as he was spooning up the soup, he muttered more to the soup than to them, "I sure would have tried to help the fellow." Now this indicates to me the compassion of Judge Holmes. It's quite true he was always a strict positivist, and I'm sure that Learned Hand was furious that his idol had softened.

The only intimate personal memento of any kind that Holmes left behind was the so-called "black book." It's simply a nicely bound copy book, nineteenth century, that any student who could afford such a nice copy book might use. Holmes originally used a black book in preparing his notes for *The Common Law*. His readings went through all the books on common law from Roman times on. He would copy out what he would want to quote, with page references, and of course would give the date of publication of the book itself, its whole title, just what a scholar would want to refer back to. In later years he kept track of the books he read and commented on seasonal events.

He was one of the great historians of the time. He was in close touch with Frederic W. Maitland and with Sir Frederick Pollock. And there's no question that Holmes was a master of the history of the common law. But the black book was his research compendium, a compendium of the research he'd done. The front page is rather flowery, sort of like Holmes, and has "O. W. Holmes, Jr." written in it. That is a rather personal page because he adds on that page his father's and mother's birthdays and his own marriage date to Fanny Dixwell. But any sentimentality or sentiment he had was buttoned up.

One of our duties as secretaries was to burn the handwritten drafts of his opinions. As I said, he didn't have a typewriter in the house. Everything was handwritten. He did not want memos being passed around. "What I wish to leave as my work is the printed opinions and the printed articles and speeches. These are preparatory matters, nobody else's business." So he would watch; I don't know that he thought we weren't reliable, but he actually would watch when we went to the fireplace, lighted each page, burned it up. The same thing was true of the proofs of his printed opinions, printer's proofs. So this black book is of special significance because of its sentimental aspects.

When *The Common Law* was published, it seems to me clear that he must have anticipated a second edition, because for the first year or two after *The Common Law* appeared almost all that he read was legal in nature.

The black book contains every book Holmes read for fifty years, and since he was a man of wide culture, it's a marvelous cross section of the intellectual nourishment of a great American. He would say as he came home from Court, for example, "Well, son, shall we read a bit? What'll it be? Shall we improve our minds or shall we have a little murder, but not Agatha Christie." You will see from going through the list that there are a number of mysteries. He loved Lord Peter Wimsey.

I think Holmes was the greatest single influence on me. I, and I'm sure others, idealized him. Certainly his patriotism was as admirable in our sight as other characteristics he had. When Holmes died, he left most of his estate to the government. Today that sounds whimsical, but of all the people I have known, it was Holmes who said, "I pay my tax bill with pleasure because with it I buy civilization." In Holmes's world it was easy to explain it: fire department, police department, all the civilized amenities, education, and what the government did in terms of national protection and of foreign policy came as a result of the taxes he paid. Since his income as a judge from fifty years or so, first in Massachusetts and then in Washington, was all from a public source, he felt it only appropriate that most of what he had saved as the result of shrewd investments should go back where it came from. In fact this was a nuisance, a drop in the bucket. It took a long time for that modest sum to be properly spent. I served on the committee that was set up. They finally decided to fund the writing of a history of the Supreme Court, of which Paul Freund was the chief editor.

Holmes suffered many hostile criticisms. In Boston he was considered a radical, a dangerous radical. In fact, Holmes almost took a delight in accosting, deliberately braving, the strictures of narrow-mindedness. He would sometimes say that he liked to make the monkeys howl.

This may seem like a touch of arrogance, which he certainly had.

But he was subjected to criticism in Massachusetts for the courage with which he defended the rights of labor and freedom of speech as a dissenter from the conservative members of the Court. He and Brandeis and Stone were constantly under attack. I think Holmes taught all of us, certainly me, that your own judgment and your own integrity have to be your guiding rule, your lodestar, and that you can't tailor your views according to fashion, style, or what conservatives want you to do. You can think for yourself and if you can't be proud of your own opinion, then something is wrong.

I should add that his skepticism, which many people have worried about, also affected us. Holmes had to be convinced. He never accepted lightly somebody else's thought.

I have mentioned the influence of his formative years on him. For example, Holmes grew up at a time when intellectuals, particularly free-thinking individuals, found the conformity of the Catholic Church, especially in Europe, a horror. Remember, Maryland was founded by Catholics. Some of my close friends were Catholics. This seemed to me an exaggeration on Holmes's part. For example, we once drove to a monastery, where he got out of his car and walked through the rose garden. He said, "Isn't it astonishing that people who have such benighted ideas can appreciate such beauty as these roses?" I understood it better when he read aloud a couple of poems that I had not studied in college. One is called "The Bishop Orders His Tomb at St. Praxed's," the other is "Bishop Blougram's Apology."

DONALD HISS

In September 1932, just three months after I'd graduated from Harvard Law School, I reported to Justice Holmes at his Beverly Farms home in Massachusetts. Holmes had left the bench, retired in January of 1932, so that I had no court experience with him. When I took over, we stayed at Beverly Farms until mid-October and then came down to Washington.

Let me give a brief summary of our usual day. I arrived at nine o'clock and worked a seven-day week. I took care of bills, other matters of immediate concern, certain household affairs, and any letters he received, particularly those from Sir Frederick Pollock or Harold Laski, who were his most frequent correspondents during his retirement.

I'd start the day by asking if he wanted me to read to him, or whether he wanted to look at some of his engravings or do other things on his own. Usually around 11:30 I would read to him, and the selection was a joint effort. He received numerous books. I remember one that Laski had sent him, *Love on the Dole,* by Walter Greenwood. It was a depression book set in England and very touching.

His tastes varied from Giorgio Vasari's *Lives of the Painters,* which we read continuously with very few interruptions, to E. Phillips Oppenheim. In between we read Bertrand Russell and Alfred North Whitehead. Occasionally he would observe, "Sonny," as he called all of his secretaries, "at ninety-one, one outlives duty. Let's read E. Phillips Oppenheim." He was very fond of Oppenheim and the lighter things. But the reading and the discussion were always varied.

At one o'clock we had lunch down in the dining room. His visitors ranged from Owen Wister, Benjamin Cardozo, and Tom Corcoran, to Felix Frankfurter, but most of the time we lunched alone. His interest in politics was limited. He never read the newspapers, regarding them as foolish. He did read the *New Republic* and the *Atlantic Monthly,* and he read legal periodicals and philosophical tracts. His newspaper reading was limited to what I read to him when I found an article I thought would be of interest. His interest in law politics was limited compared to present-day Washington, but it was still a general interest.

He was interested in individuals and in talking of the Civil War, which he did only on occasions when an anniversary of one of the battles in which he had been injured would occur. The clerks made a practice of sending him flowers or a book to commemorate the day. Then he would talk about the Civil War. I remember the anniversary of the Battle of Antietam, where he had been wounded. That night as he was going to bed, I walked into his dressing room to help him. He started to talk about having been wounded and how he waited, not knowing whether they ferried wounded to an island or whether they took them to another place nearby. As his company sergeant walked by, Holmes sighed. He sighed with wonder, not with anything else, and the sergeant said, "What's the matter, Holmesy?" And he said, "I don't know where I go from here," meaning whether he went to the island or to another place for the wounded. The sergeant misunderstood and said, "Oh, what the hell, Holmes, you believe in Jesus Christ; you're all right, whichever way you go." As Holmes was leaving his dressing room he said, "Sonny, if sixty years ago someone had said, 'Holmes, sixty years from now you'll be telling a bright young lad from the Harvard Law School about your experiences today,' I'd have said, 'Don't be an idiot, man.' But here I am and I enjoy it."

There isn't any question that Holmes's experience in the Civil War made a lasting impression on him. His entire outlook as a Brahmin, a great friend of William and Henry James, and an admirer of Ralph Waldo Emerson changed to one with a broader reach and a great respect for what we call the common man. Of course "The Soldier's Faith," one of his Memorial Day speeches, is famous.[5] But throughout his speeches there is frequent reference to a soldier's faith and the Civil War.

After lunch he would go upstairs and drop off for a very few minutes' nap, sometimes while I read to him and other times without my reading to him. We always took a drive in the afternoon. He referred to his chauffeur not as an employee but as a private contractor. This probably was Holmes's way of limiting his liability in case of an accident. Charlie Buckley, who drove badly, was a poor risk. We drove everywhere from Fort Sumner down to Mt. Vernon, all around the countryside. I can recall another independent contractor, Timmy O'Brien, who drove us when the foliage was at its height on Beverly Farms in early October. In the middle of October in Virginia, the foliage was much more somber and Holmes would observe that it was extremely difficult to choose between the brilliance of New England and the quiet autumn foliage of Virginia and the Maryland countryside. There was a contrast between them, but he could not decide which he preferred.

He always wore his swallowtail coat when he was driving. When he came in he had an old alpaca coat that he shifted to. After the drive we would read. At six o'clock I would leave and at seven o'clock he would have his supper, with Mary Donnellan in attendance. Except for a few instances when old friends such as the head of the Agassiz[6] were in town, he dined alone. I would come back at 8:30 and read to him for an hour or so. This was the general routine, interspersed frequently with discussion of what we were reading or of almost any subject, because his interests were extremely wide. There was nothing that did not interest him except athletics. He still found an interest in the Court but cared little for the details of Court operations. When he retired he had finished with that, but we would occasionally read opinions when I found one that I thought would be of interest.

Brandeis was a frequent caller. Early in October Holmes said he wanted to be reminded of Brandeis's birthday. He'd missed it the year before, and he didn't want to miss it this year because this was Bran-

5. Delivered 30 May 1895 at a meeting called by the graduating class of Harvard University.
6. The Harvard Museum of Comparative Zoology at Harvard, founded in 1859 by Jean Louis Rodolphe Agassiz.

deis's seventieth. That morning when I came in I reminded him of Brandeis's birthday, and I asked him if he wanted me to order flowers. "No," he replied. "Just give me an arm and help me over to my chair." He wrote briefly and handed me a note. "Sonny, do you think this will do?" The note read: "Dear Brandeis, Congratulations on your seventieth birthday. Young fellow, guard your youth well. Once lost it's impossible to recapture." He wrote with ease and flair, as his opinions show, and as his speeches and collected legal papers confirm. He had a knack with the pen; he had a knack in conversation.

He was a magnificent man, over six feet when he stood up straight, with beautiful light hair, ruddy complexion, and light blue, penetrating eyes with thick eyebrows and a white moustache. Mary would occasionally help him. She would shave him; he had been accustomed to being shaved. When he got out of his chair, he'd want an arm to help. But he was entirely capable of dressing himself. Someone always held his coat, which I guess had been his custom even when he was a much younger man.

There was only one relative, Edward Jackson Holmes, a nephew who was then director of the Boston Museum of Fine Arts. He and his wife were childless, and when he died that was the end of the Holmes line. He called on Holmes several times in Washington but more often when he was up in Beverly Farms.

From the Court, Brandeis was the most frequent caller. Chief Justice Hughes came in several times, as did Stone and McReynolds, which is surprising. McReynolds visited on at least two occasions and I remember the first time he came. We sat in the library, which was on the second floor. There was an elevator from the first floor to the second floor that had been installed some years before. The visitor was shown into the living room or parlor, as they called it in those days, down on the first floor, and then I would go down and escort them up. In the case of McReynolds, he would call to say he would like to come. The servants were afraid of him. They did not like him. By reputation he had a temper. It was amazing how they got on, and I gathered from the Justice that McReynolds had been a great admirer of Mrs. Holmes. His observation to me as I brought him upstairs the first time was, "I'm so glad to see that nothing has been changed in the living room; it's just as Mrs. Holmes left it."

He told an amusing story to Holmes about a minister reading the Bible on a train. Some drunk sat down beside him and nudged him. "What are you reading?" "I'm reading the Bible," the minister replied very politely. He nudged him again, "Do you read it often?" "Yes, I read it every day." Later he nudged him again and said, "Don't you get bored with it?" The minister had finally had enough and said, "Young man, can't you go to hell quietly?"

Later I said to Holmes, "It's amazing that McReynolds can be so pleasant." McReynolds, whom we all knew at the law school, was anti-Semitic; we thought he was anti-everything. He always dissented in any liberal vote, and he was a mean curmudgeon. It amazed me that he could be so pleasant and yet so limited in his views.

McReynolds was responsible for Holmes's closeness to Brandeis in a sense. McReynolds had been appointed to the Court just before Brandeis. At that time it was the custom to make an annual New Year's Day call at the White House, entering according to seniority, after the Chief Justice. Holmes was then a very senior member of the Court, having survived since 1902. When they were lining up outside the White House, having come there in their carriages, he overheard McReynolds cursing and saying, "I have to go in with that damned Jew." Holmes offered to change places. So he walked beside Brandeis. Observers have always attributed this action on Holmes's part to be the start of an extremely warm friendship. It might have developed anyway because of their interest in Court matters, but they became close friends. In the summer months they wrote to each other. Brandeis went to Chatham on Cape Cod and Holmes to Beverly Farms.

The regular callers were Brandeis, McReynolds, and Stone. Other visitors were members of the U.S. Court of Appeals for the First Circuit, Judge Learned B. Hand, Judge Augustus N. Hand, and Judge Billy Hicks. Holmes once observed after Hicks left, "Billy Hicks, he's funny as a billygoat." Hicks remarked that the subject of my brother Alger's marriage during his year with Holmes was taboo. He is also the one who had a case before the Court of Appeals in which there were two North Carolina couples who had gone to Reno to get divorces. While there they switched. The new couples got married but when one of the marriages ended in divorce Judge Hicks wrote the following opinion: "This Court will not recognize with impunity parties who litigate by day, copulate by night, *indente lite intercesse,*" a witty remark often quoted in other opinions. Translated from the Latin it means "Parties in litigation may not go to court in the daytime and sleep together at night while the litigation is going on between them."

I recall Holmes's ninety-second birthday on 8 March 1933. Felix had arranged that the President would call on the Justice that afternoon. It was to be kept from the Justice. The Secret Service sent two men over to examine the elevator to be sure it would operate properly for the President to get up from the first floor to the second floor, and to be certain the steps would have a ramp for his wheelchair. There was no inquiry about the servants or who they were. There was no checking of anything or anyone or of the danger from sharpshooters.

Felix Frankfurter and Tommy Corcoran came for lunch. I had gotten a bootlegger to sell me champagne but told Holmes that the British ambassador had sent it to him. Holmes referred to it as "fizzle water," of which he was fond. He no longer had any champagne in his cellar. We had a delicious luncheon. Holmes would take a sip of the champagne and say, "This stuff feels good to your face, doesn't it, Sonny?" Tom Corcoran told the story of Holmes's eighty-fifth birthday, when the British ambassador had sent quite a bit of champagne and Chief Justice Hughes came to call while they were finishing lunch. Holmes had said to the Chief, "Mr. Chief Justice, gaze on me with awe. Before you stands a vessel that contains eight glasses of that not-yet-forgotten champagne." The luncheon was very, very exciting. Frankfurter had been called to the telephone several times, so before luncheon he told me to give strict instructions that no matter who called, they were to be told that he was not available. So I gave instructions to the servants that that's what they were to tell anyone who asked for Frankfurter while we were at lunch.

After lunch we went upstairs. I told Frankfurter that there had been a call from the White House. As he was going out he did make his telephone call, which I didn't hear. I have since noticed in Frankfurter's published letters a reference to Holmes's luncheon. Frankfurter obviously kept numerous memoranda, hoping that he would be a historical figure.

We didn't take our drive that day. The streets were crowded, and it was not a very pleasant day. I didn't want Holmes to get too tired. I had read to him, but he had nodded off to sleep. I kept going back and forth between the library on the second floor and the bedroom where he slept to be sure that we knew when the President arrived, because Holmes was then in his old alpaca coat. When I saw the open car drive up and a crowd gathering immediately, I said, "Mr. Justice, I think the President of the United States is outside." He woke up and said, "Don't be an idiot, boy. He wouldn't call on me." And I said, "I'm pretty sure it is." "Well, we'd better not take any chances. Give me your arm. Get this coat off." So I got his alpaca coat off and got him into his swallowtail coat. Then the doorbell rang and I said, "It is the President. He's coming up."

I went downstairs and escorted the President. The wheelchair came right into the elevator, along with Jimmy Roosevelt, the President's son, and the Secret Service men. The President was able to maneuver from the elevator to the chairs I had set up. Mrs. Roosevelt and Felix came up by the stairway. The four of them sat, Mrs. Roosevelt, Frankfurter,

Jimmy, and Holmes, and I just hovered to see if I could be of any assistance.

The conversation was very animated. Holmes had a pair of swords, which his grandfather, Charles Jackson, had used in the Indian wars; they hung over the fireplace. The President noted that they were very handsome. Holmes told him that they were his Grandfather Jackson's, who later went on the Massachusetts Supreme Court of Appeals. Holmes then remarked, "I remember that my governor told me that he was having lunch as a young student and his father came home for lunch, as he frequently did, with a friend. And the friend said, 'You know, I saw that little West Indian bastard downtown today,' referring of course to Alexander Hamilton." Holmes added, "That takes us way back to Alexander Hamilton." The President remarked, "Well, my grandmother goes back as far as the Revolutionary War, but not as far as the Indian wars."

The conversation was very easy, and Mrs. Roosevelt's voice was clear. I remember as they started to go, the President said to Holmes, "You've been very helpful, anything I can do for you?" He said, "No, Mr. President. Well, you could do one thing. You could let retired Justices—don't make it all Supreme Court Justices, just retired Justices—have some cash to pay their servants. I haven't been able to pay my servants this month." And they laughed very heartily.

"Have you got any final advice to give me?" the President asked. "No, Mr. President. The time I was in retreat, the Army was in retreat in disaster, the thing to do was to stop the retreat, blow your trumpet, have them give the order to charge. And that's exactly what you are doing. This is the admirable thing to do and the only thing you could have done."

The President left. Holmes said to me afterward, "You know, I haven't seen Frank Roosevelt for years, but this ordeal of his with polio, and also the governorship and the presidency, have made his face much stronger than it was when I knew him, when he was Assistant Secretary of the Navy during the war."

The Justice always used to tease me because I had been born in Baltimore and must have been a Rebel. During the Civil War, as the Union forces came south, they had to change trains in Baltimore. They left the Union Station, which is as far as that line went, and then went to the Baltimore and Ohio Station across town. Holmes said that he had been in one of the groups that had crossed from the Union Station to the Baltimore and Ohio, and that people lined the streets and threw cobblestones at the soldiers, and some had been bruised because the shots really hurt. "Some of your forebears, I'm sure, cast cobblestones at us as we walked," Holmes said, but it was all said in jest.

We read Paul De Kruif's book *The Microbe Hunters,* and toward the end of the book he tells about the discovery of the cause of puerperal fever, childbed fever. De Kruif gave credit to a Viennese doctor, Ignaz Semmelweis, for the discovery that this disease was carried by physicians who did not wash their hands before going from one patient to another. Holmes interrupted me: "Sonny, I always thought my governor was the discoverer. I'm sure he was. Maybe he did it later, maybe he borrowed, but look it up in the *Massachusetts Medical Association Journal."* He told me exactly where it was. He knew where every volume was in his library. He was quite good at it. Sure enough, there it was, and he told me to look in the index and find an article by O. W. Holmes on puerperal fever. The date was earlier than the date De Kruif had given for Semmelweis, so he said, "Well, I'm glad to see this, he didn't steal the credit. I always thought my governor would have done much better if he'd just limited himself to medicine and not gone into writing silly books like *The Autocrat of the Breakfast Table."* We finished *The Microbe Hunters* and the story of puerperal fever and a footnote said, "At or about the same time Dr. O. W. Holmes of Boston was making a similar discovery."[7] And Holmes said, "I don't think he gives my governor enough credit. I think that's rather short shrift."

The interesting thing is that Holmes's feeling toward his father was not exactly friendly. It was not a warm feeling at all. He had a great feeling of warmth toward his mother but not toward his father. His father, I think, according to everything I've heard and read, dissuaded him from following William James and going into philosophy. He ordered young Holmes to go into medicine and the compromise reached was law school. But be that as it may, Holmes told of going home one night from either a Massachusetts 20th Reunion or a club dinner at Harvard at which he'd imbibed too much, and he did not reach the stairs but passed out in the vestibule. That's where he was discovered early the next morning by his father. He said, "Sonny, my father never let me forget this for weeks. My mother, being a much wiser woman, never said a word. That hurt me much more than my father did. My father just got my back up, my governor," so he always said. There was rivalry between them, but he also had respect for his father. If others criticized, Holmes would then defend him; Holmes reserved the right to criticize and praise.

He would say, "But you know, the southern troops had beautiful faces. I remember once I was carrying a message and it was at dusk. I was given a horse to ride and I was to go at a galloping speed down a certain road until I reached the commander of another regiment and

7. Doctor Holmes proved statistically that the disease was spread by contagion. Semmelweis's work, published eighteen years later in 1861, confirmed this conclusion.

gave him this message. And as I passed, I looked up and I saw this lovely face of a Confederate, and I heard his gun click. He'd seen me before I had heard him. I remember seeing the wounded and the dead. And the southerners, we know, gave up the flower of the South. It showed in their faces."

Then he would shift and remark that they had some horrible, disagreeable habits. "I had a good friend who was headmaster of the Episcopal high school, and he'd been an officer in the Confederate Army. He used to come calling and in return I would call on him. He was a charming man, very well read, very literate, a wonderful conversationalist. But occasionally he would lapse. 'Now Holmes, you knew So-and-So in Charleston, South Carolina, didn't you?' 'No, I didn't.' 'Oh, too bad; she was gently born. You knew So-and-So in Richmond, didn't you?' 'No, I'm afraid I didn't.' 'Oh, too bad; she was gently born. You knew So-and-So in Charleston, didn't you?' 'No, no.' 'Well, he was gently born.' Finally I would explode. 'Did every even-numbered house in Charleston and Richmond have a Van Dyke and every odd one a Rembrandt? Everyone was gently born? Down in the South don't they have any whores and muzzle loaders?' Gently born! What a bawdy expression! My God, Sonny, were you gently born in Maryland?" I said, "No, I was not. I was a muzzle loader." All this came from his Civil War experience. He was a Brahmin but he did not like southerners who carried on about their gentility after the Civil War when nothing else was left.

He told me that on his honeymoon he and Mrs. Holmes went to Niagara Falls. He said every morning he would go down to the Falls, where there were fish swimming in the pool and if you raised your hand the fish would immediately disperse. And there were flies there that would get on you and you would have to kill them to get rid of them. "There was a charming looking southerner with a top hat and lovely moustaches and a gold-headed cane. I think he was in a morning coat and striped trousers, and he was obviously a southerner. The southerner explained to me one morning about the fish. He said to me, 'You see those fish in there?' 'Yes.' 'You know, it's very much like life. If you raise your hand when they're young—they have a period of several months, as I understand it, before they evolve into the fish that we have here—they dart. They want to live, they want to carry out their function in life. On the other hand, when flies evolve, they're like old people. Good heavens, you can't get rid of them. They don't care whether they live or not. It's very much the way you and I are, young fella. You're like these young fish and I'm like these old flies.' "

Holmes said, "It was a very charming story, and one morning as he left he said, 'Well, I guess I'll be off on my morning walk. Young man, will I see you at Darby's this afternoon?' 'No, sir, I'm afraid we weren't invited.' 'Oh, too bad. The finest blood in America will be there.' And he walked on and then he turned around to see my face drop. 'Sir, I referred to horses' and went on." The finest blood in America. I thought it was a lovely story.

One day the Justice made an observation when we were reading about some tycoon and a banker, one of the muckraking books we were reading. He referred to the fact that J. Pierpont Morgan or one of the steel people, Charles Michael Schwab, had been an intellectual giant. I remonstrated. I said, "Intellectual giant?" "Yes." "Why intellectual? What has he written? What has he done?" Well, he had taken the steel industry from nothing and made it into a great industry. So had the bankers. "I think that's an intellect." As I kept interrogating him, he found that his patience was coming to an end or he pretended it was. He wanted to dispense with this conversation and he turned to me and said, "Sonny, I am not an anvil on which you can beat out your impressions of life," whereupon I roared and stopped my interrogation. It's an example of his incredible use of phraseology in conversation. He was really a charming man.

I saw Washington briefly under the Hoover Administration when I first came to Justice Holmes in October of 1932, and then of course I saw it after March under the Roosevelt Administration, from March until June when we went to Beverly Farms for the summer. But the situation in Washington when I first came there was tragic. I had come to Washington in the summer to see General Douglas MacArthur lead the Bonus Marchers[8] out of Washington, force them out on his horse with the troops. The situation in Washington was desperate. There was no leadership, there was no hope, there was nothing except a forlorn atmosphere of real defeat. After the election, when Hoover had been so badly defeated, this was exacerbated. It was a lonely and quiet city without hope or ambition. Immediately after the New Deal came, there was a basic change from Inauguration Day on. You sensed it immediately, because there had been work with the Brain Trust earlier and the change of atmosphere was very rapid. The action by FDR during the First Hundred Days was just incredible. It was an amazing performance. It reminded me in a rather limited and colloquial way of Cambridge, Massachusetts, being changed for a Harvard-Yale game. The morning of the inauguration was like Cambridge the day of the Harvard-Yale game. All the shops were on display, everyone was joyous,

8. An organization of World War I veterans who demanded early payment of their promised overseas service bonuses.

crowds moved excitedly. There was something in the air that had not been there before, and in the New Deal that continued throughout. It was not just for the day as it was in Cambridge. It was in the inaugural speech that the President made his remarkable statement about one-third of the nation being ill-fed, ill-clothed, ill-housed.

It was a thrilling sight to see him at Justice Holmes's when he called four days later on Holmes's birthday. When his car drove up at 1720 I Street the crowds surrounded him just as dusk had settled. When he left it was dark, the street lamps were on, but you could see in their illumination as the President got into his car.

Mrs. Roosevelt said she would walk and she went along with the crowds, all applauding, shouting as he got into his car. It was an open car and Felix Frankfurter got into the back. I'd come down to the doorway to watch him, and I heard this loud voice in the background. "Hey Felix!" It was Felix's colleague at the Harvard Law School, Thomas Reed Powell, who spotted Felix and shouted at him. The crowd was really thrilled with Roosevelt. You found them cheerful and you found them hopeful, and they all ran out and praised and applauded as Roosevelt got into his car and drove off.

Washington began to be filled with people who were interested in government and some of them called on the Justice. I had dinner with a number of them—Jerome Frank, Charlie Wyzanski, Tom Eliot. There was an enthusiasm that was extremely exhilarating and bright.

I went up to Beverly Farms with the Justice that summer of 1933. We went up on the Federal and got to the station an hour and a half early. I went in and had to get the stationmaster out. We got into our drawing room more than an hour before the train was to leave, and I said, "Mr. Justice, did you ever miss a train?" He said, "No, Sonny, but Fanny did once and she never forgot it. This is the way to travel."

JAMES H. ROWE, JR.

In 1934 and 1935 I was Justice Holmes's clerk. At that time he was off the bench, but he still took law clerks. There was not much difference whether he was on the bench or not because he used law clerks more as companions. There is a famous story. One day, one of his law clerks was reading a novel, and he said, "Young man, if I could disturb your cultivated leisure, would you mind going to look up a case for me?"

I stayed with Holmes until he died. I read to him a lot, and we went

Oliver Wendell Holmes, Jr.

James H. Rowe, Jr.

driving every afternoon. We talked quite a bit. I kept his books, I wrote his checks, I did his income tax, that sort of thing. I was there every day. I worked seven days a week, at night too, unless I could get one of the former law clerks to take over. At that time in Washington there were Alger and Donny Hiss, and once in a while Tom Corcoran. They would come in sometimes in the evening and read to him, giving me a night off. I preferred Alger and Donny because when they said they would come at a certain time they came. You didn't really feel you should leave the Justice until the substitute arrived.

He had a housekeeper named Mary Donnellan, who is still alive. When Mrs. Holmes broke her hip she decided she was not going to live forever. So she trained this young Irish girl, who must have been about eighteen or nineteen when she started. She'd just come off the boat from Skivereen in Ireland. The first morning on the job she served the Justice. In those days they wore frock coats, and he was on his way to court all dressed up magnificently. She was so nervous she spilled scrambled eggs all over him. He looked up and smiled and said, "Don't worry," went upstairs, changed, came back, and ate his breakfast. From that time she was his slave.

Mary was very bright. She took care of him and ran the house and the law clerks with an iron hand and stayed with him until he died. In his will he left her $10,000, which was a lot of money in those days. She immediately married a carpenter, a red-headed Irishman named Coakley. They went back to Ireland, bought a farm, and had a number of children. One by one the children started coming back. Coakley was a citizen; she was not. She wouldn't take out her "first papers," as we called them. But because he was a citizen the children could come in fairly easily, and I used to handle all their papers. They were all bright. One of them was a stewardess for Aer Lingus, another one went to Georgetown and then to Princeton. When I last heard of him he was in the Department of Commerce. Two grandsons played football at Landon School in Washington. When Mary has a problem she calls me. Donny Hiss was always her favorite among the clerks.

They had a number of other servants who were all Irish and very ancient. Some of them had worked for his father, for instance, and he promised to take care of them.

Madeira was one of Holmes's favorite drives. The Justice was very fond of the city, which was much more rural then. When you drove out to Madeira there was practically nothing on the way. He had five or six preferred places; we drove to the Arlington National Cemetery, where his wife was buried, about once a week. We drove to Fort Lincoln, the fort where the Confederates came in north of Washington. Jubal Early's cavalry swung around. They were starting to press toward Washington, and Holmes was out there. President Lincoln had come out to see the fighting. He stood up on the ramparts and Holmes saw him there. Holmes was a lieutenant, and he said, "Get down, you damned fool!" Lincoln did. He was not shocked.[9]

Justice Holmes was quite an eater, even at lunch. He got all the food from Magruder's (an expensive grocer) for himself and his five or six servants. After his death, his executor, Mr. Palfrey of Boston, cracked down and said, "Rowe, get your food in"—whatever was the equivalent of the supermarket. He cut our food bill to about one-third of what it had been.

Holmes lived in a huge four-story house at 1720 I Street. There was an elevator, and his study and library and bedroom were on the second floor. The third floor was for the servants. The house has only recently been torn down. There's a high-rise office building there now. I can remember when they were first remodeling it I went in to look at it; I could have bought some marvelous marble fireplaces. To place it, the Hay-Adams houses were on 16th and H. The Holmes house was on 17th and I. He knew the Adamses. He was very fond of Mrs. Adams, but he couldn't stand Henry.

The Court Justices came to see him often. He was the popular man on the bench. Justice Brandeis came about three times a week. They called and said they'd like to come, and they were always welcome. James Clark McReynolds came a great deal, Chief Justice Charles Evans Hughes came, Harlan Fiske Stone came—they all came, but what they chattered about I do not know. They went in and sat in the study with him, and we closed the doors. I assume they gossiped about the Court. But he never told me, and I was sufficiently intimidated that I didn't ask.

His correspondence was limited by the time I got there. I used to answer the letters. Harold Laski wrote a great deal; Felix Frankfurter would write. Some of Holmes's papers are at the Harvard Law School, and some are in the Library of Congress. A former congressman from Connecticut, John Monagan, is writing a book about Holmes. During his research he found something quite interesting. Holmes often went to England in the summer. Mrs. Holmes didn't always go with him. There he met an Irish countess, whom he grew very fond of. He wrote to her and she would write him, and at the end of every letter he said, "Please

9. This is an apocryphal story, but was told for generations by Justice Holmes's intimates. See John Henry Cramer, *Lincoln Under Enemy Fire: The Complete Account of His Experiences During Early's Attack on Washington* (Baton Rouge: Louisiana State University Press, 1949).

destroy this letter. I destroy yours." He did, but she didn't. She kept them, and when she died her brother sold them to the Harvard Law School. This congressman has found them and says they're very interesting. Holmes wrote good letters; he wrote very well.

He liked to talk about the Civil War. After all, it was *the* big experience of his life. He was a Yankee, but he was much tougher than many Yankees because he fought for three years. In those days they did fight every day or every other day. The fact that he was wounded three times made him take a rather stern view of life. His sympathies, by inclination, were not against the South. He didn't like the abolitionists that much, and said so. He rather admired the Confederates because they went through what he went through. He knew they were getting shot at every day too. One of his great friendships on the Court was with Chief Justice Edward Douglass White, a Confederate. They were great friends, mostly because they fought in the war against each other.

Although he was not enthusiastic about abolitionists, he did feel that if your country is in a war you should go. A fairly large number of his contemporaries bought substitutes.[10] He was rather huffy about that. Most of those people turned out to be businessmen; he really didn't like businessmen very much, and I suspect that's where his prejudice came from. He had felt it was his duty. Two-thirds of his Harvard class went to war right away. Most of them ended up as officers. A lot of them were killed. Some of his best writing is quite warlike, but he also talks about his friends who died. He tells the story of a lieutenant, one of his best friends, who was ordered to swing around a corner where he knew he'd be killed. Holmes could still see him jauntily swaggering along with his sword, his troops behind him. He got about twenty feet, and that was the end of him. It was the bloodiest war in history. I'm told the battles were very well fought, and they are still studied. The British come over to study them. Most professional soldiers come to study the terrain where the battles were fought.

His former law clerks used to come and see him when they were in Washington. Francis Biddle, who became Attorney General, was a law clerk. I remember Katherine Biddle. The first time I saw her she was about twenty-eight or thirty years older than I was. Holmes was dying, and Biddle had just come to Washington. He had come to check up. It was a winter night, and they were down on the first floor. A big fire was blazing when I walked in. There stood this absolutely beautiful woman in a red dress, leaning against the fireplace. I can see it now. For years

10. The Conscription Act of 1863 made all men aged twenty to forty-five subject to conscription into the military but allowed them to avoid service by paying $300 or by obtaining a substitute who would enlist for three years.

she ran a salon. I remember spending evenings with people like Robert Frost.

Holmes was definitely the intellectual leader of the Court. Most people still regard him as the best Supreme Court Justice we ever had, with the possible exception of Judge John Marshall. Holmes too had great influence on the Court; he was the leader of the Court for a long time. He was known as the Great Dissenter, but he didn't like that. Nowadays Holmes still has great influence. He was relatively liberal. Even during the Civil War he believed in free speech. On the other hand, he reminded us, "You cannot shout 'Fire!' in a theater."[11] He insisted on limits to what liberalism condones.

He left an estate of $500,000. Family papers and a bequest went to his nephew, Edward Jackson Holmes, who lived in Boston. They were not close. He had no close relatives. He left gifts to all of his servants, including Mary. He gave Harvard his collected opinions and $25,000 for the law library and his books went to the Library of Congress, where they were catalogued by David C. Mearns, the Lincoln expert.

I recall especially on March 15th he always used to say, "Taxes are the price you pay for civilization."

The last book I read to the Justice was Thornton Wilder's *Heaven's My Destination.*

11. In his classic opinion in *Schenck v. U.S.* (1919), Justice Holmes exempted nonpolitical speech from protection under the First Amendment and said that even political speech could be limited in time of war if "the words are used in such circumstances and are of such a nature as to create a clear and present danger."

CHAPTER 4

Clerks of the Court on the Justices

During FDR's first Administration, the Supreme Court was the scene of bitter conflict. The conservative majority of Justices Willis Van Devanter, James McReynolds, George Sutherland, and Pierce Butler, joined frequently by Chief Justice Charles Evans Hughes, clearly dominated the Court. In case after case, the conservatives overturned New Deal legislation to the point where, as FDR protested, they had created a "no-man's-land," where no government, state or federal, could function properly. The Court's liberal Justices, Harlan Stone and Benjamin Cardozo, were usually joined by Brandeis and occasionally joined by Hughes and Owen Roberts, but they still formed a permanent minority. Although aging, the conservative Justices seemed intent on riding out the New Deal and denying FDR the opportunity to nominate any of his own candidates to the Court.

When he won reelection in 1936, FDR moved swiftly. In the climactic Court-packing plan, the Judiciary Reorganization bill of 5 February 1937, he proposed to expand the Court by one new Justice for any present Justice who was over seventy years old. The plan aroused a storm of protest from all sides of the political spectrum. The fight lasted until late July, when the Senate sent the bill back to committee. The Court's conservatives, however, got the message. First, Van Devanter announced that he would retire at the end of the 1937 term. This led FDR to withdraw his proposal, since it meant he could shift the majority with a new appointment. Even more significantly, Justice Roberts, who had usually supported the conservatives, shifted sides and gave the liberals a five-to-four majority. FDR's first three appointments to the Court, Justices Hugo Black, Stanley Reed, and Frank Murphy (who replaced Van Devanter, Sutherland, and Butler, respectively) added to the liberal majority. When Cardozo and Brandeis died, FDR replaced them with Felix Frankfurter and William Douglas, men who shared their predecessors' enthusiasm for social reform. By 1941, FDR had appointed seven Justices.

As law clerks to the Justices at this epochal period in American history, Herbert Wechsler, Joseph L. Rauh, Jr., Edward F. Prichard, Jr., and David Riesman had ringside seats while history was made. Far from being mere bystanders, however, they often had a real impact on the judicial process.

HERBERT WECHSLER

I graduated from Columbia Law School in the early summer of 1931. Justice Stone had been dean of the Law School, had practiced law in New York, and had then become Attorney General in the Coolidge Administration, after the scandals of the Harry M. Daugherty attorney-generalship. He was a cleanup man. After a little over a year there was a vacancy on the Supreme Court, and Coolidge appointed him. Stone then inaugurated the practice of taking his law clerks from Columbia graduates each year, following the example that Holmes and Brandeis had set in taking their clerks from Felix Frankfurter at Harvard.

My first contact with Washington and the Supreme Court came when I was interviewed by Justice Stone in New York in the late spring of 1931. I'd been first in my class at law school and editor-in-chief of the *Law Review,* so I was a natural candidate. However, there were two of us; the other was Walter Gellhorn, a classmate, who had been very high in the class, too, and secretary of the *Law Review.* Stone hired Walter, with whom he had very friendly connections because Walter was an Amherst alumnus and so was Stone. Stone was very apologetic about it but said quite frankly that he had personal reasons for wanting Walter, which seemed very understandable to me. However they both had a certain sense of guilt, because when I had just begun to teach at Columbia in the spring of 1932, I got a telephone call from Stone asking if I'd like to come as his clerk for the following year, which meant doing somebody in the class of 1932 out of the clerkship. But that didn't seem to bother him, and I guess it didn't bother me. Of course I accepted.

In the summer of 1932, therefore, I found myself headed for Washington as law clerk to Justice Stone. In those days, there was a collection of law clerks who had established housekeeping arrangements together—Tommy Austern, an earlier law clerk to Brandeis, Henry Hart, then law clerk to Brandeis, Walter Gellhorn, and H. Chapman Rose, who was with Holmes. Of that group, the only one who remained in Washington was Tommy Austern, who went into the firm of Covington, Burling. Our menage consisted of Tommy Austern, Paul Freund, who was my contemporary and clerk to Brandeis, and Milton Katz, former clerk to Judge Julian Mack, who had come to Washington to work for the Reconstruction Finance Corporation under Stanley Reed. So there were four of us. Cardozo's law clerk, Mel Siegel, lived practically around the corner and appeared steadily in our living room.

We had one of those ancient-looking, highly conventional houses out near the Cathedral with a porch around the outside. I guess those houses were built in the early twenties. They almost all had three or four bedrooms and a downstairs consisting of a living room, dining room, servant's room, and usually a quite suitable kitchen.

In those days I didn't go to the Court. The Court as we know it now hadn't been built, and the Justices all had their chambers at home, except for Chief Justice Hughes, who had an office in the Capitol on the Senate side. Stone had his chambers in his home on Wyoming Avenue, a beautiful house that he had built right across the street from the home of the journalist Mark Sullivan, who had quite an elaborate establishment. Sullivan was a great friend of Hoover and that was a close bond. I used to see him all the time in Stone's study. One whole wing of the Stone house was the study, a beautiful room three stories high with a secret door. It was an interesting place to work because there was this huge area with Stone's desk and an easy chair and a few chairs for visitors. The secretary's perch was a balcony that you got to by climbing a circular iron staircase. There was a platform with a desk and a lamp and a small bookcase and a railing that looked out over the library. If Stone had a visitor you could hear the conversation, but unless the visitor knew about the arrangement, he wouldn't be aware that you were there. One of the most interesting parts of the job was eavesdropping on Stone's conversations, particularly in the early part of 1932 when his visitors included practically everybody who was anybody in the Republican party and a good many who hoped that Stone might be the presidential candidate. He toyed with them like a cat with a mouse, enjoying every minute of it. I don't think for a moment he had any thought of taking it seriously. He was a very good politician and knew that the Republican party was dead or at least dormant.

When there was a particularly interesting case to be argued, Stone would often invite me to come to the Court and listen. His routine was quite simple. He got up very early, as most New Englanders did. He had a New England farmer's breakfast and then went out and took a short walk. He was a great walker; he practically walked my legs off, but his didn't seem to suffer at all. He liked to talk while he walked. He was a very easy person and very relaxed. After all, he'd been a law teacher and a law dean, and he was used to people of my age. He was usually at work in his study by eight o'clock. The Court convened at noon. They'd hear argument for two hours and then take a thirty-minute recess for lunch. They would come back and hear argument from 2:30 to 4:30. Stone would always leave the house about 11:15 or 11:30. He had a car and a chauffeur, and he sometimes invited me to go up with him.

Mrs. Stone always gave him his lunch in a little lunch box, the kind that bricklayers take on the job, with a thermos of hot soup, tea, or coffee. Sometimes the Justices ate together, sometimes they didn't. The robing room was their main common room and also their conference room; the facilities were nothing compared to those they're in now. Later Stone derided the new Supreme Court Building as "the great marble palace." He claimed not to like it, but that may have been New England talk. In the very beginning I think they were very suspicious of it. I guess it was Cass Gilbert's best government building.

From September on, all the visitors to the house discussed politics and Mr. Hoover's low place in the polls. Stone was very pessimistic about the Republicans' chances. He was a staunch Republican and was totally unimpressed by the Democratic hopefuls, particularly the governor of New York. Mrs. Stone, in a nice, amateurish way, was also interested in politics. Her main concern was the then talked-about possibility that if FDR were elected, he would appoint Al Smith as Secretary of State. Since she had many social contacts with diplomats, she simply couldn't see how anybody with Al Smith's Brooklyn accent could maintain the position of the United States in the world as Secretary of State. When she had nothing else to talk about, she would mention this to me, because she knew that I was from New York and a Democrat and an admirer of Al Smith. I used to delight in elaborating on this possibility.

I don't remember many of the names of people who came to see him. The exception is Ned Bruce, an artist who in the Roosevelt days became quite a figure in the artists' program.

Progressives were riding high. In the labor field there was the Norris-La Guardia Act,[1] cutting down the federal courts' interference

1. The Anti-Injunction Act of 1932 (Norris–La Guardia Act) limited the use of injunctions against strikers, picketers, and boycotters. It also had a clause that outlawed yellow-dog contracts, employment contracts between a worker and an employer in which, as a condition of employment, the worker is forced to give up the right to join a union.

with labor organization, the yellow-dog contract, the nomination to the Supreme Court of Judge John J. Parker, who was defeated by one vote in the Senate. He came from North Carolina and the key vote against him was cast by Senator Kenneth McKellar. He voted against Parker, not because of the antilabor decisions attributed to him by the labor people, but because he was damned if he would vote for a southern Republican for anything. Parker was lynched, really. But I guess it's probably true that people like Senator George Norris of Nebraska or Burton K. Wheeler of Montana or David Walsh of Massachusetts really did think Parker was antilabor. The labor movement was just beginning to come out of its chrysalis. After Parker's defeat, Hoover nominated Owen Roberts, a more conservative man than Parker had been.

At that time Holmes had just retired, and his place had been taken by Cardozo. Hughes was Chief Justice. The Court was Sutherland, Butler, Van Devanter, and McReynolds in the conservative bloc. Then Roberts became a swing person along with Hughes, with Holmes, Brandeis, Stone, and later Cardozo in what was referred to as the "liberal" bloc. The Court was highly polarized. The liberals had to pick up both Roberts and Hughes to prevail, which they sometimes did.

As for the social relationships among the liberals, Stone, as I recall, didn't call on Brandeis, but the Brandeises were not very social people. Tommy Austern, who had been Brandeis's clerk, remarked that if you were invited to dinner at the Brandeises', you had the wonderful opportunity of watching someone carve up the sardine. I was there only once. The sardine was a bird, but it was not much larger than a sardine. I remember that Mabel Walker Willebrandt was there. She had been Assistant Attorney General in charge of Prohibition enforcement. Brandeis's daughter Elizabeth, her husband, Paul Raushenbush, and the law clerk, Paul Freund, were there. One went to dinner and when Mrs. Brandeis stood up, one left.

It was very austere, but Monday open house was quite different. The Justices would have what were called "teas" every Monday afternoon. People connected with the Court were all invited, as well as other people. It was interesting to go to the Brandeises'. Whenever I wasn't on duty at the Stones' I would go. Somewhat different kinds of people came to the Stones', who were very social. One would meet Washington dowagers and businessmen, whereas at the Brandeises' one tended to meet academics or public officials.

I remember particularly meeting the chairman of the Interstate Commerce Commission, Joseph Eastman, there. He was a protégé of Brandeis. He had revived the Interstate Commerce Commission, made it into a great, pliable, effective organization dealing with the railroads.

Established back in the 1880s, it had not really amounted to anything until perhaps the Wilson period. I think that's when Eastman came in. He had a great career as chairman of the Commission. In the thirties there were so few independent commissions in Washington compared to the myriad that exist today. But the ICC was the prize exhibit. We had, for instance, the ICC, the Federal Trade Commission, and the Federal Radio Commission, established in the twenties, the ancestor of the present FCC.[2]

Once when I was driving with Stone up to Court, Mrs. Stone had given him an errand to run, which she often did—stopping at Magruder's to order some groceries or taking a rug to be cleaned, for example. He would dutifully get out of the car and attend to this chore. We were parked waiting for him opposite the Mayflower Hotel when I saw Justice McReynolds standing at the curb on Connecticut Avenue waving his malacca walking stick, trying to get a taxicab to get up to Court. There were three of us sitting in the car waiting for the judge, the chauffeur, Edward, the messenger, and myself. Edward and the chauffeur were in the front, I was in the back. I said to Edward, "There's Justice McReynolds obviously having trouble getting a cab up to Court. Wouldn't it be nice to ask him if he wants a ride up with us?" Edward turned and looked at me and said, "Well, Mr. Wechsler, if you tell me to do that, I'll do it. But if you're asking me if I think Justice Stone would want me to, I have to tell you that I don't think he would." So I said, "You'd better not then." As soon as Stone came back I told him this story. Meanwhile McReynolds had gotten a cab. Stone said, "Well, Wechsler, it's perfectly clear that Edward has a lot more sense then you have." That's an indication of what the relationship was between Stone and McReynolds, and I dare say that probably it was the same with practically all of the Justices and McReynolds.

Even in the quartet, I don't think that there was much affection for him. For example, I don't think Hughes liked him. There is a story about Hughes and McReynolds. Once McReynolds went to a barbershop at the Capitol to get a haircut, and the time was approaching for the Court to convene. Hughes sent his messenger down to the barbershop to remind Justice McReynolds it was ten minutes to twelve.

2. The Interstate Commerce Commission, created by the Interstate Commerce Act of 1887, is a seven-member board that supervises and regulates all public carriers, except airlines, engaged in interstate commerce. The Federal Trade Commission, established by the Federal Trade Commission Act of 1915, is a five-member bipartisan board whose function is to investigate and prevent illegal corporate practices in interstate commerce such as price fixing, boycotts, mislabeling, fraud, monopolies, and adulteration of commodities. The Federal Radio Commission, established in 1927, was empowered to license radio stations and assign radio frequencies. It was replaced by the Federal Communications Commission in 1934.

McReynolds said to the messenger, "You go back and tell the Chief Justice that I don't work for him."

Van Devanter was a very reserved, almost remote, tightly disciplined, inner-directed person who by the time I was there was having trouble on the Court because he had suffered from what is technically called a "writing block." He was very effective orally in conference, but he couldn't write. Term after term he didn't carry his weight as far as turning out opinions was concerned. He became more and more withdrawn. The others simply accepted the situation, understanding it. In those days the volume of cases in the Court was small compared to what it is now. It wasn't so serious, but it did tend to be rather scandalous that term after term the others would each have eighteen or nineteen opinions and Van Devanter would turn up two or three.

Sutherland was a very genial, twinkly kind of man. I had a chance to talk to Butler only once. But Norris Darrell had been his law clerk, and I later worked closely with Darrell when he was president of the American Law Institute, and I got to know more about Butler in that indirect way. Darrell and Butler had both come from Minnesota. Butler seemed a very human person as one got to know him. Between Stone and Butler there was such an intellectual dissonance that Stone didn't have any respect at all for Butler. He thought Butler was too soft in dealing with criminal matters. Curiously, since he's always thought of as a right-winger, he was the only member of that Court who had strong feelings about the protection of defendants in criminal cases, which has come to be accepted as part of the liberal creed. He'd been a railroad lawyer and an arch-conservative in economic matters.

McReynolds was an army without any troops. He was the only member of the Court in this century who was nasty to other Justices. He's the fellow who, when Cardozo came to the Court, was heard to mumble quite audibly, "Well, these days to be appointed to the Supreme Court, one not only has to be a Jew but the son of a crook." His father was a crook. People who think that that was an important factor in Justice Cardozo's life are right.

Stone was a very happy and effective man. He played a great role in persuading Hoover to appoint Cardozo. Hoover was under pressure from people like Senator Borah to appoint Cardozo to the Holmes vacancy. He was unresponsive at first and concerned that there was already one Jew on the Court (Brandeis), and there were two New Yorkers on the Court in the persons of Hughes and Stone. Geographically and ethnically there were, from the politician's point of view, strong arguments against the appointment. Borah said to Hoover that Cardozo belonged to the country and not first to New York. But Stone really put all of his influence on the line when that vacancy existed, including offering to resign himself so there would not be three people from New York on the Court simultaneously. He did this with the utmost sincerity. I came just after that, but I heard some of the story from Stone. He was rather proud that he had played this role in bringing Cardozo to the Court.

Stone was a member of what was called the "medicine ball cabinet" in the Hoover period, a group of people who met at the White House about seven o'clock in the morning once or twice a week and played medicine ball with the President for an hour. A medicine ball is a very heavy leather ball, larger than a basketball but, unlike a basketball, you'd think it was full of lead. Between the weight and the effort taken to propel it at one another, it really was quite a heavy siege of exercise. After the game they all had breakfast at the White House. Obviously Stone was thus very close to the Administration. The Hoovers and the Stones were close. Hoover was a great fisherman, and so was Stone. The Hoovers still maintained the presidential yacht, and Mrs. Hoover and Mrs. Stone were good friends.

At the time when I was clerk, Stone did not have a happy relationship with Chief Justice Hughes. He resented what he felt was discrimination by Hughes in the assignment of opinions. He felt that he was getting the unimportant, junky cases whereas Hughes was courting Roberts by giving him more important material. There was quite a genuine hostility, at least on Stone's part. I don't know that there was on Hughes's part. Stone was really a disaffected member of the Court. He was excessively critical of the Four Horsemen and very, very critical of Hughes and Roberts, and not without reason. Of course attitudes change and I'm talking about 1932–33. Some eight years later, when Hughes retired in the summer of 1941, Stone was appointed Chief Justice to succeed Hughes. He served as Chief Justice until his death in 1946. I saw a good deal of him then, partly because of the legal business that I had in the Court. Since I was the only one of his clerks who was incumbent then in the Justice Department, he would very often ask me to come up and see him and he would tell me what was on his mind. Then I'd take it back and tell the Attorney General and try to work out whatever it was. I don't mean that this happened often, but it did happen. In his later years his view of Hughes softened considerably.

The same thing happened with Frankfurter vis-à-vis Hughes. In the Alphaeus T. Mason book you'll find the Frankfurter-Stone correspondence dealt with at length. If you look at a later book by Max Freedman, the Frankfurter-Roosevelt letters, you get much more of it.[3]

3. Alphaeus T. Mason, *Harlan Fiske Stone: Pillar of the Law* (New York: Viking, 1956); Max Freedman, ed., *Roosevelt and Frankfurter: Their Correspondence* (Boston: Little, Brown, 1967).

Frankfurter was about as critical of Hughes as it was possible to be of a man in public life in the mid-thirties. But by the early forties, after Frankfurter had served with him on the Court and Hughes had retired, Frankfurter wrote that he was the greatest Chief Justice since Marshall.

When Mark Sullivan came to see Stone, as he did very frequently during that October as the Republican news got worse, I remember sitting on my balcony and overhearing Sullivan say: "Do you think we can draft a telegram that avoids the word 'congratulate'?" Stone did suggest some words, but I don't believe that they were actually used when the election turned out as they anticipated.

Near the end of Hoover's administration, he gave a formal white tie dinner party at the White House, mainly for the medicine ball cabinet and their wives. I was working late that night, and Stone came in from the living room and walked to the door that opened from the chambers to the side street. It was a beautiful evening. As soon as he came in, that was my signal to pack up and get the hell out because my perch was right opposite the door to their bedroom. I could work there at night only when they were out. He stood there in his full dress with his top hat cocked just looking out at the moon and ruminating. So meanwhile I sneaked down my staircase to go home and said, "Good evening." He looked very reflective. I wondered what he was thinking about. "Well," he said, "what I'm thinking about mainly is that I guess we won't be dining very much at the White House any more." "You view that with regret?" I asked. He said, "Yes, I do. But not with surprise. If I told the President once I told him many times, he was in danger of forgetting that it was the common people of this country who elected him." And those were Stone's final words about the Hoover-FDR contest.

JOSEPH L. RAUH, JR.

I graduated from Harvard Law School in 1935. I had been with Felix Frankfurter only one year at the law school, when I took his course in federal jurisdictions. Professor Frankfurter taught Frankfurter law, not any particular subject, so I don't remember anything about federal jurisdictions, but I have a lively memory of the professor. In that year, 1934–35, the anti-Roosevelt corps started fighting. It was the first of three years of that battle, and our task in that course was to read Supreme Court decisions. This was an exciting and wonderful experience because the professor was one of Roosevelt's chief advisers and at the same time he was a great student of the Court. One day the advance sheet of the Court's opinions had the *Tom Mooney* case in it. Felix called on me, as he almost always did. I'd been out the night before and I hadn't read anything, so I started to fake. "You know, Professor, you've got to remember how the times were out in California at that particular period when Mooney was accused." Frankfurter hit the table with his fist. I'd never heard anything like that. "You don't know where I was in 1916?" I started to shrivel up and said, "No, I'm terribly sorry, I don't know where you were in 1916, sir." He said, "President Wilson sent me out to investigate the Mooney case." So I've never forgotten that he ran the Mooney case. That was the kind of class we had.

Tom Mooney was alleged to have thrown a bomb into the Preparedness Day parade of 1916. He was convicted, and "Free Tom Mooney" became a major slogan of the left for many years. The case created a great deal of unrest, especially in plants that were gearing up for war, so Wilson sent Frankfurter out to investigate. The case that was in the Supreme Court was a part of the long history of the litigation, but in that particular case the Court said the prosecution was wrong because it had knowingly used perjured testimony against Mooney. But he didn't get out on that basis. He later got out, I believe, on a commutation from Governor Olson of California.

That course with Frankfurter was a wonderful experience. I'm a total product of Justice Frankfurter, because if it weren't for him I would be a fat corporate lawyer in Cincinnati, Ohio. He changed the course of my life. I gave the second Francis Biddle lecture at Harvard on Justice Frankfurter and I commented on the impact that he had had.

In 1935, I was to be Justice Benjamin Cardozo's law clerk, but Bill Stroock, his then law clerk, stayed an extra year. So Frankfurter said, "Well, you just go work for the New Deal for a year and then you can be Justice Cardozo's clerk," which is what happened. I was Justice Cardozo's clerk from 1936 until July 1938, when he died. I became Justice Frankfurter's law clerk for a period after he went on the Court in January 1939.

In the year 1935–36, and in the few months between Justice Cardozo and Justice Frankfurter, I worked most of the time with Ben Cohen, who is one of the great law teachers of all time. You wouldn't think he could teach such firm and strong tactics because he was a very soft, lovely human being. I was with him in 1935–36 when he and Tom Corcoran were "running the government." I've always thought that was a somewhat overstated position, but they did have a serious influence on the Administration. I worked for Ben for a year on defending the Public

Utility Holding Company Act.[4] He taught me more about how to win a case that's unwinnable than anyone else could have. If you had asked anyone in 1935 if the Supreme Court would uphold the Public Utility Holding Company Act, you would have been laughed at. Well, that's what Ben accomplished. He was a magnificent lawyer and a brilliant human being.

Justice Cardozo was a saintlike human being. I wrote a piece for the Yeshiva University *Cardozo Law Review* remembering him.[5] It was hard to think of anything that he ever did that wasn't perfect. Justice Cardozo led a very private life, but his law clerk became his son. He worked in his apartment and his clerk was there all day with him. He knew everything about the cases, but he would ask your opinion and then say, "That's brilliant!" to some half-witted answer that you had given him. If he had a fault, it was that he overflattered everyone. For example, he autographed pictures with inscriptions that were beyond any semblance of truth. A writer whom I had never seen in the two years I was with Cardozo appeared the minute he died. He wanted to write a potboiler about the Justice. I said to him, "Well, you weren't that close. I don't think you're the right person to write the book. You're not a lawyer, you can't know anything about his work." He pulled out a photo that Cardozo had inscribed to him with the most syrupy language. He said, "You're saying I wasn't close to him?" I was licked. He did write the book and it's absolutely dreadful. He didn't have any feeling for this remarkable human being.

Usually I would stay there on Saturday afternoons because in those days the Court held conferences then. They sat every weekday hearing cases and on Saturday afternoon they'd have a conference and decide the cases they'd just heard. If I went out on a Saturday afternoon with my wife, I'd go back, because Cardozo would be disappointed if I wasn't there. He'd have nobody to talk to. He'd come home, this beautiful figure, to an empty apartment. Empty but for three servants. There was a cook, a maid, and a housekeeper. He never had a wife. No member of his family, brothers or sisters, ever married. There's always been a great question whether that resulted from the fact that his father resigned in

4. The Public Utility Holding Company Act of 1935 (Wheeler-Rayburn Act) gave powers to the Federal Power Commission to regulate interstate shipment of electricity, to the Federal Trade Commission to regulate natural gas shipments, and to the Securities and Exchange Commission to regulate the financial practices of public utility holding companies in order to prevent monopolistic tendencies, and imposed a "death sentence" clause on those holding companies that did not divest themselves of their subsidiaries within five years (unless they proved that they were efficient).
5. Joseph L. Rauh, Jr., and others, "A Personal View of Justice Benjamin N. Cardozo: Recollections of Four Cardozo Law Clerks," *Cardozo Law Review,* 1 (Spring 1979), 5–22.

the scandal of the Tweed Ring judges, who were found guilty of accepting bribes and doing what the Tweed Ring wanted done. I never knew whether that caused the family to be so reclusive, but it is not impossible. He was the last of the brothers and sisters. So he was all alone. He did have a hundred first cousins. Two of these cousins were rather famous. One was Annie Nathan Meyer, the writer, and the other was Mrs. Frederick Nathan, whose son is a famous writer. It was a very talented Sephardic Jewish family.

He'd come home bubbling to tell what had happened at the conference. If I wasn't there, he was disappointed. Miss Tracy, his housekeeper, once told me, "Oh, Mr. Rauh, it was awful. The judge looked all over the apartment for you." Sometimes I went to the Court and did some work while the conference was going on. Then I rode back with him. But most often I was sitting there waiting for him, and he would tell me all about the cases. I remember when he came back after the Wagner Act had been upheld in the *Jones and Laughlin* case.[6] He said, "Oh, Mr. Rauh, you won't believe what happened. Roberts and Hughes switched without even saying why they were switching." He referred to the fact that in the *Carter Coal* case the year before the Court had ruled out a law very similar to the Wagner Act.[7] Everyone knew why. It was because Roosevelt's Court-packing plan had the Court scared stiff. I still remember the wonderment with which Cardozo said, "You know, judges ought to explain their actions. They have a right to change, but they oughtn't to pretend that they're not changing." He had such a wonderful time when things like that happened. Of course, it was a vindication for him because he'd written the Carter Coal dissent and now that was the law of the land. This happened in 1937. It came after the Court-packing plan, which was in February 1937.

He always called me by my last name. When he asked me to stay a second year, I said, "Yes, sir, but there's one condition. I'd feel so much better if you'd call me by my first name." He said, "Well, I will," but he had great trouble doing it. I never held him to it because he was not formal in a haughty sense. It was just that he had been brought up to use a certain degree of formality.

After he became ill in December 1937, he didn't go back to the

6. The National Labor Relations Act of 1935 (Wagner Act) created the National Labor Relations Board, with powers to determine appropriate collective bargaining units, to supervise union elections, to certify duly chosen unions, and to hear complaints of unfair labor practices. The Supreme Court not only upheld the Wagner Act but also agreed to allow use of the Commerce clause as a device for bringing about economic recovery in *NLRB v. Jones and Laughlin Steel Corp.* (1937).

7. In *Carter v. Carter Coal Co.* (1936), the Supreme Court had overturned the compulsory extension of the labor provisions of the Bituminous Coal Conservation Act of 1935 (Guffey-Snyder Act) to unwilling minorities in union elections as an unconstitutional delegation of legislative powers to the Executive.

Court. He did not resign; he was never well enough to do so. When the press would call I'd simply say, "He's going to get well." I have to admit to some white lies because the doctor had said he probably wouldn't get well.

Judge Irving Lehman and his wife, Sissy Strauss Lehman, were the closest of the Cardozo friends. Every two months they came from New York to see him. In a sense I considered them the relatives, the ones who would make any decisions that had to be made. Justice Cardozo's last months were spent in their house in Westchester County. The Judge died up there, and I think he was as contented as a very sick person could be. He was with his closest friends.

Cardozo had no close relations with the other Justices on the Court. Justice Brandeis wrote him once. That letter happens to be on my wall. Stone wrote him once. In an article I wrote about Justice Cardozo after his death I pointed out that he had no close associates on the Court. Stone wrote me a vicious letter protesting my article. I wrote back that I was sorry, I had not meant to hurt his feelings, but it happened to have been true. They did meet every Friday afternoon when Cardozo and Stone would go to Brandeis's apartment for a caucus to decide what they were going to do the next day at the conference. Brandeis was the senior, so they would go to his house. It was only two blocks away, but both Stone and Cardozo rode in their chauffeur-driven cars to Brandeis's apartment on California Street. They would then talk over the cases for the next day and decide how they were going to vote. When they didn't agree, Cardozo would come home very perturbed. I had to wait for him on Friday nights because he wanted to tell me the results. Cardozo was without any doubt the most liberal of the three. Brandeis had grown more conservative in this period, and Stone was never as liberal as Cardozo. Even when they did agree, they knew that they were usually going to lose. They held their own caucus because the four conservatives—Pierce Butler, Willis Van Devanter, George Sutherland, and James McReynolds—had a caucus every day as they drove to work together in a big car. Charles Evans Hughes and Owen Roberts had the deciding votes, which inspired a cartoonist to show those two as the men on the flying trapeze.

When Cardozo was the chief judge of the Court of Appeals in New York, the judges lived near one another in Albany, they talked together, they worked together. It was the happiest period of his life. I'm sure if he were here and could tell us, he'd say he made a mistake when he came to Washington. I don't ever remember his saying that to me because he was never harsh about his colleagues, but I believe that he never was happy.

The first Jew on the Court was Brandeis. He was appointed by

Woodrow Wilson in 1916, and all the conservatives in the Bar Association opposed his appointment, but he won out in the end. When Oliver Wendell Holmes retired in 1932, Cardozo was so clearly the greatest judge in America that even though he was sixty-two, quite old for a Supreme Court appointment, Hoover chose him. It was one of the few acts that Hoover got kudos for. Cardozo, while known as a liberal, had such distinction as a judge that he was accepted as the proper person to succeed Holmes.

President Roosevelt sent the Court-packing plan to the Congress in February 1937. Cardozo was opposed to it because one couldn't be a judge and be in favor of a plan to alter decisions by putting additional people on the bench. He took a negative but rather calm and understated position. He was not so violent about it as many others were. What's more, he was angrier at Hughes and Brandeis for writing supporting letters to Senator Wheeler, the leader of the opposition, than he was at Roosevelt for sending up the plan. He felt that Hughes and Brandeis had no reason to get involved. This was a matter for the Congress to decide. I think it's because Brandeis and Hughes were fighting the plan that he got so much pleasure when Hughes reversed himself in some of the controversial cases. It gave him satisfaction to realize that Hughes was fighting the Court plan in a different way. He enjoyed the dilemma in which his colleagues found themselves. He liked Roosevelt's speeches, because Roosevelt praised the decisions that he, Cardozo, hoped to have rendered and denounced the decisions that were actually being rendered. He was tremendously excited every time President Roosevelt called him. That would make his day. He was devoted to the President, and at that time I think he was the only Justice who really believed in what Roosevelt was trying to do. Brandeis and Stone supported the President because they didn't think judges should tell the Executive or the Congress that they couldn't do something. Stone and Brandeis were restrained judges. Cardozo liked the New Deal; he really believed in it. He had more feeling for the poor and the underprivileged than anyone else on the bench. Therefore, his votes were less "Let Congress decide, let the Executive decide" than "It's right." When he got to write his first important decision, on the Social Security Act, I could feel how much he was for it.[8] He wasn't pulling any of this "Well, I'm a judge and I can't say whether it's good or bad." He was openly writing that it was good.

If Cardozo hadn't been a judge, he'd have been a New Deal senator

8. Cardozo wrote the Court's five-to-four majority opinion in *Charles C. Steward Machine Co. v. Davis* (1937), which upheld the employers' tax and the conditional federal grant-in-aid to the states of the Social Security Act of 1935.

or a New Deal executive. He was more like the later liberals, Douglas and Black, than he was like the later Frankfurter, who made so much of the restraint of the law and thereby angered the liberals. I've always felt that if Cardozo had lived, he would have become the leader of the liberal bloc of Black and Douglas, Robert H. Jackson, Wiley B. Rutledge, and Frank Murphy. It was a shame that he was taken from us at the age of sixty-eight. He had only two months with Black, October and November 1937. One can't tell how they would have gotten along, but in my opinion Black would have deferred to Cardozo. In fact, Cardozo might have been appointed Chief Justice rather than Stone, who was appointed a couple of years after Cardozo died.

There were other law clerks before me who became his friends: Bill Stroock, Ambrose Doskow, and Mel Siegel. As for other real friends, there were a few. Bob Marshall was a very wonderful human being, who lived with the Alaskans and wrote books about them. He was a really funny guy, and Cardozo just loved him. He came to the door one day and as I opened it he somersaulted all the way down the hall. Cardozo just loved stunts. He heard the ruckus and came out to watch Bob. He loved C. C. Burlingham, the man who got him started as a judge. Burlingham asked him to run for the Court of Appeals, so he did. When Cardozo won, he said, "It was easy to get elected; everybody thought I was an Italian." Mr. Burlingham died at 101. He was the head of the Good Government party. Burlingham and Cardozo had a marvelous correspondence. Felix was always after us to call on Mr. Burlingham, so one day when I was in New York, and I had a few minutes, I called him. The nice lady who ran his apartment said, "You're invited for lunch." Burlingham was then ninety-nine, blind, and pretty deaf, but he was a wonderful talker still. At the end of the lunch he said, "Joe, I'm going to give you something. Follow me." He felt his way to a file cabinet and pulled something out of it. "Is this my correspondence with Cardozo?" I said, "No, sir." "Is this?" And then finally it came out, and I said, "Yes." He said, "It's yours." I said, "Well, I don't deserve it. There's no possible reason why." He got very angry and at ninety-nine when a man gets angry it's a temper tantrum. I was so scared I said, "Well, if you'd like me to have it, I'd love to have it." I read the letters and they were marvelous. I gave them to Harvard Law School. They belong there.

Cardozo loved Felix, and there are great letters between them. He also loved the people on the court in New York. When Judge Pound died, President Roosevelt personally called Cardozo to tell him saying, "I don't want you to read about this death in the paper." Pound was the judge who succeeded him on the New York Court of Appeals. The President of the United States thought enough of Cardozo to call him when a mutual friend died. It was just beautiful. The call from the President shows the depth of their relationship. It was not the kind of thing that someone might have told Roosevelt to do. I don't imagine there was anyone around who knew that the President and Cardozo had this friendly relationship. Cardozo was also a great admirer of Alfred E. Smith. He liked to describe the dinners the Court in New York had once a year with the governor. He would come and tell stories. One evening Al Smith stopped in the midst of a story; he said, "Hey, you guys, I've got to make a fifteen-minute talk somewhere, but don't anybody go away because I'm comin' back. I'm havin' too good a time." Cardozo loved Smith.

So very little is known of Cardozo. There may never be a good book about him because his was such a private life. His closest relationship was with his sister Nellie. Cardozo wrote to her from Albany often. I've never seen one of the letters, but naturally when there's such a close family relationship there's bound to be gossip. There was some, but Cardozo's private papers are mostly lost. I don't know what was in the letters, and today they probably wouldn't even provoke a yawn.

All I know about his father, who was a judge in New York, is that he resigned in a public scandal involving the Tweed Ring. Tweed was the then Tammany boss. He ran a pretty corrupt system; he told judges what to do. I am somewhat skeptical that his father's disgrace was the basic reason for the family's abstaining from marrying. It was never discussed. The closest we got was on one morning when he was a little tense. He said, "Mr. Rauh, have you read *The Nine Old Men?*"[9] I said, "Uh, yes sir." And he said, "Well, what's it say about me?" Well, I almost died because what it said about him was that Cardozo was so saintly because he was working to live down his father's disgrace. I believe he knew this was in the book, because he pressed me on it. I told him all about the part that was very favorable. I had the feeling later, as I thought about it and talked to my wife about it, that he would have been ready to talk if I'd had the courage to say, "It's about your father and the Tweed Ring." Maybe I made a mistake in not doing that and letting him express himself, because why else did he bring it up? In retrospect it might have been a more loyal act to have told him the truth, thereby giving him a chance to talk with me about it. He did make one great crack. He said, "Mr. Rauh, is it true that in the book they say Brandeis is going to put up a statue of Hitler because he did so much for Palestine?"

Felix succeeded Cardozo. My relationship with Felix as a clerk was

9. Drew Pearson and Robert Allen, *The Nine Old Men* (Garden City, N.Y.: Doubleday, 1936).

more general and of shorter duration. Most people don't appreciate the gigantic influence Felix had in the early New Deal days. Hugh Johnson, the head of the National Recovery Administration, once wrote of Felix, "He was the single most influential man in the United States." Johnson meant that as an attack, and there may have been some anti-Semitism involved, but there was a good deal of basic truth in what he said. When Felix came to Washington, I was working for Ben Cohen and Tom Corcoran. They were pretty important guys, but when Felix walked in the door there wasn't any question who was boss. "Felix is in town." He'd come down once a week, or once every two weeks. He would see Roosevelt and then he would see Tom and Ben. I'd be lucky if I saw him. Dozens and dozens of young people down here had come from his classes at Harvard. He really was an incredible figure. It seemed to me he was a useful Barney Baruch; for me Baruch was always a big bag of wind. But Felix would sit and just let people talk. He'd move around and find out what people were doing and be helpful. He always could be helpful to Roosevelt. I regret there is no biography of him. The fact that no one has written well about our greatest Justices continues to shock me. There are some books about Felix. None of them are worth the powder to blow 'em to hell.

The whole story of his relationship to the New Deal has remained untold, although the letters Felix wrote to Roosevelt have been published. I've glanced through them, and Felix's are very sycophantic. They are not a credit, and neither are the diaries that Joe Lash located in the Library of Congress.[10] Lash wrote an essay of 100 pages and added excerpts from the diaries. This is still the best biography of Frankfurter, even though it's very short. It caught the spirit of Frankfurter. The diaries reflect rather badly on Justice Frankfurter. They are quite unfair to his colleagues on the Court. In reading the diaries carefully, I found this absolute inconsistency, which indicates that Felix wasn't really being venal. He just didn't understand. He talks about how terrible it was that Douglas had done something political that morning, and then he says, "I had dinner with Ambassador Casey, and some other people to decide who should be our envoy to the Middle East." He simply did not realize that such a decision was political. It was for the public good. But what Bill Douglas was doing he judged to be an infringement of his office. He could feel his acts weren't political because he was not actually in politics. There is this difference, Bill Douglas ran for President of the United States from the Court. He didn't make it, but there isn't any question he was running in 1948. Felix always thought of Douglas as a

10. Joseph P. Lash, ed., *From the Diaries of Felix Frankfurter* (New York: Norton, 1975).

political figure. So did Roosevelt. Roosevelt wanted Douglas to leave the Court and work in the Administration; he would never have thought of asking Felix to do that. So I guess Felix's justification, if I can make it for him retroactively, was that what Douglas did was for his own political future, while what he did was for the good of the country. But that doesn't absolve Felix of some of the things he said in his diaries.

When Felix went on the bench in January 1939 he had such stature as a professor, an adviser to Presidents, an articulate writer, and a liberal that he was assumed to be the leader of the liberal wing. At first I think his leadership was accepted. In 1940 he did something that caused the liberals ultimately to desert him, and he became an island unto himself. He wrote that a child has to salute the flag in school, and he took all the new liberals, Douglas, Black, and Jackson, with him.[11] Stone was the only dissenter, and I guess they didn't consider Stone a part of their group. Young liberals were offended that a child had to salute the flag. It was a terrible decision; no real thought had been given to it. One night Ed Prichard came to see me. He was all excited. He said, "Read this." He handed me the galley proofs of the flag salute case. I said, "Oh my God!" He replied, "That's what I said. I've been begging Felix not to do this. If he does he will throw away his liberal credentials on the very first case." Prichard then said to me, "Joe, you've got to tell him not to do it." "Well, Prich," I said, "could you explain just how I'm going to know about this case? Somebody would have had to tell me." Prichard said, "Oh no! I don't want to be the person who told you." So that was the end of that chapter. The case duly came down a week or two later, and there never was a decision received with such hostility by liberals as this one. Every law review, every liberal spokesman, attacked it. Mrs. Roosevelt took a crack at it.

A year later, in a different state, the same kind of case came up.[12] Felix stood firm. The others went the other way, and the case was reversed. An entry in Felix's diary tells us that he went to see Douglas and Black to ask them what they were going to do. Douglas said, "We're going to say that the child doesn't have to salute the flag." When Frankfurter asked Douglas whether Hugo Black had any new insight into the case, Douglas said, "No, but he's read the papers." Felix thought that was terrible! I never did see what was so wrong about reading the

11. In *Minersville School District v. Gobitis* (1940), the Court upheld the Pennsylvania state law requiring students to pledge allegiance to the flag.
12. In *West Virginia State Board of Education v. Barnette* (1943), the Court reversed its ruling in the *Gobitis* case on the grounds that the state law infringed the citizens' rights under the First Amendment.

papers. For me each judge has to act according to his own experiences. If it was true that there had been a public outcry against the case, this fact should not have been overlooked.

I believe what happened in those two cases had a tremendous effect on Felix's leadership. He had led them, but he had led them astray in this particular case. Felix felt they had deserted him, and there was great bitterness. He wrote an opinion dissenting on the second flag salute case. He stuck by his first decision. From then on it was a downhill relationship. There were many cases where he went with the conservative crew. It seems to me that one can make an argument for Frankfurter that he was bound to do what he did because of his belief in judicial restraint. All the liberals jumped on Frankfurter saying he had changed. I think he was wrong, but I don't think he changed. My own philosophy is Black's and Douglas's, but I can still say that I loved Felix and agree with Black and Douglas. I do say this to people who ask me about the three of them. I think they were right and he was wrong, but he didn't change. He honestly believed in allowing the local legislatures and the Exeutive to make certain decisions. This was perfectly natural when he was attacking the anti-Roosevelt Court. All you had to say to the anti-Roosevelt Court to be liberal was, "Leave Congress alone." But when our Congress starts passing anti-Communist, Joe McCarthy acts, it shouldn't be left alone. Frankfurter's philosophy of "Leave the Congress alone" made perfectly good sense for liberals when they were fighting the antiliberal majority of the Court that was upsetting congressional actions. It made no sense for liberals when they were fighting loyalty-security programs, the disciplining of people without letting them confront their accusers, or statutes to register Communists. The liberal position then was "Don't let Congress do it." The only rationale for believing as Stone, Black, Douglas, and others did was that civil liberties are different from property rights. In the 1930s judges were dealing with rights higher than the right of property, which does not have the importance of the right of free speech in the Bill of Rights. Felix rejected that, and I discussed this in my Francis Biddle lecture about him. He rejected the idea of higher rights in the civil liberties area. He believed in an equality of rights. This explains the philosophy of Black and Douglas, who would certainly have agreed that Congress should be deferred to in the area of regulation of business, but they wouldn't say Congress should be deferred to in the area of free speech.

My wife and I saw a great deal of the Frankfurters. We were very close. My wife got them their house, their maids, and everything they needed when they moved from Boston to Washington. We both loved him very much despite all our differences. The former law clerks had

dinner with him a couple of times a year. For the first few years Butch
Fisher, Phil Graham, Ed Prichard, and I talked to him as if he were one
of us; we would tell him when we thought he was wrong. The flag salute case was over with, so we would say what we wanted to about that.
One night we were having dinner and there were just five law clerks and
Felix. One of us said, "God, that was a stupid opinion!" I remember the
case, the United States against some monopolist. The issue was whether
the United States could get triple damages from the company. Felix had
written that the government couldn't get triple damages. All of us were
having fits! Here was this goddamned monopolist getting away with
murder. We let Felix have it, and he got mad. There were no more dinners like that. We could kid around, we loved him, and we did have
some rights, but we could no longer tell him he'd been stupid. After that
the law clerks' dinners got larger and very formal, but for the first several years they were riotous.

Throughout his life, however, he would call me once a week and
talk, usually on Sunday morning. He'd call and approve or disapprove,
as the case might be, of something I had done that had been mentioned
in the papers. He would say exactly what he thought. It wasn't always
complimentary. When Felix first had his heart trouble the doctor told
him he had to stop telephoning. He'd get all excited over the telephone.
Our telephone conversations diminished, but I still received notes. The
one call I remember as the most exciting was on the Sunday morning
when the *Washington Post* printed two reviews of Max Lowenthal's attack on the FBI.[13] Max had written it at the height of the McCarthy period. The *Post* editors worried about how to handle this book. They did
not want just to attack the FBI. So they got Father Walsh, who thought
the FBI was the greatest organization that ever existed, to write one review. My review of course attacked the FBI. At about seven or eight the
phone rang: "My, that's the greatest thing I've ever read." Felix kept repeating that remark. Max Lowenthal, the author, was a friend of his, but
he also kept on praising my review. He hated J. Edgar Hoover's guts; he
had cross-examined Hoover during the Palmer Red Raids in 1920, when
Attorney General Palmer wanted to deport all aliens. Felix had represented the aliens in a case up in Boston; he called Hoover "the biggest
liar ever." That morning he was in seventh heaven. Someone had finally
given it to Hoover.

Felix was so human and so incredibly bright! But he did get a lot of
people mad. He could be very sharp. He was never subtle, and if you
were wrong, you got it! Once he had taught you at Harvard, he would be

13. Max Lowenthal, *The Federal Bureau of Investigation* (New York: Sloane, 1950).

your teacher for life. If you were arguing a case in front of him, he would still act as if he were your professor. Joe Loftus of the *New York Times* was reporting at the Court when I was arguing a case. Joe wrote a piece about the Supreme Court argument between the professor and his former student. Many felt he handled lawyers badly because he asked more questions than the rest of the Justices put together. The arguments became too heated.

Basically he was a lovable man. One of the saddest things in my life was his break with Ben Cohen and Tom Corcoran. Both became vicious about him. As I understand it, this is what happened. Tom wanted to be Solicitor General. He had been a great servant of Roosevelt's, but in doing his job he had cut up a lot of people. He became a political liability, yet he wanted to be Solicitor General. He had done all this dirty work, and he wanted recognition. He drafted a letter to Roosevelt from five members of the Court. He obtained four signatures, probably from the four most liberal men, but Felix would not sign it. Felix had two reasons, one was that the Court shouldn't interfere, which was an anachronism since he interfered in everything. The second was that Roosevelt was now gearing for war and a confirmation fight over Tom might make that more difficult for him. A third reason may have been that he simply did not want Tom to have the job. This was a worrisome time for all of us. We didn't give a damn about anything but stopping Hitler. Someone told me that Tom said to Felix, "I put you there; now produce." Felix never mentioned that Tom said that, so I don't know whether he actually did. Ben took Tom's side, and that broke up their relationship. Felix and Tom never spoke again.

EDWARD F. PRICHARD, JR.

I finished Harvard Law School in the summer of 1938 and returned to Kentucky for what I thought was going to be a summer vacation before going back to Harvard in the fall to work with Professor Frankfurter. Early in the summer I got a call from him ordering me to report to Senator Bob La Follette in Washington immediately. Senator La Follette was then conducting investigations of violations of civil liberties. The subcommittee of the Senate Committee on Education and Labor was holding the hearings. That summer they were investigating the steel strikes in Chicago, where some people were killed during the so-called Little Steel strike, the strike of the employees of Republic

Steel, Inland Steel, and a couple of the other companies that were not part of United States Steel.[14]

Bob La Follette was delightful. He was very down to earth, unpretentious, direct. He had a splendid sense of humor. He did not have the eloquence and charisma of his father and his brother Philip, but he was a very astute legislator. Politically, he was well to the left of center in the Senate, but he knew how to get along with the Senate club, and he was very effective in the investigations. He did a splendid job and had an able staff. That's when I first met Joe Fowler. He was general counsel for the committee during a part of that summer. One of the pleasures I had was when Tom Girdler of Republic Steel was on the witness stand and Senator La Follette cross-examined him in a very rigorous way. Girdler got excited and lost his temper. I was on Senator La Follette's right, suggesting questions and conferring with him. Years later, Tom Girdler bought a farm in Bourbon County, Kentucky, where my parents lived and where I was raised. I was home one time, met the Girdlers at a party, and he said, "I still remember you, sitting up in that white suit next to Senator La Follette, slipping those questions to him to embarrass and humiliate me." I was delighted that he remembered me.

In the fall of 1938 I went back to Harvard on a research fellowship to work with Felix in his classes and seminars. That was heaven for me because I got paid and my duties were just to work with him. I helped him a little bit on a long article he wrote on Justice Cardozo, and then I helped him a little bit in his labor law class and a little bit in his seminar on federal jurisdiction. We were having a great time. But around Christmastime Roosevelt nominated him to replace Justice Cardozo on the Supreme Court, so he left. I went to Washington for his confirmation hearing, and was with him when he was grilled by the Senate Judiciary Committee. Dean Acheson was his counsel, and I enjoyed that. He jousted with Senator Patrick McCarran particularly, but of course he was confirmed without difficulty. Then I went back to Cambridge and helped Jim Landis, who had taken over Felix's Harvard courses for the rest of that academic year. In the summer of 1939 I started to work for Felix as his law clerk.

At that time, the Justices were Hughes, Roberts, McReynolds, Butler, Black, Reed, Stone, and Brandeis. Shortly after Justice Frankfurter went on the Court, Douglas was appointed. Ironically, Frankfurter was

---

14. The Little Steel strike occurred during May 1937 against Bethlehem, Republic, Youngstown Sheet and Tube, and Inland Steel companies and collapsed by the middle of the year. Eventually, the NLRB and the courts forced the companies to recognize the union.

very enthusiastic about the appointment of Douglas and looked forward to a great association. It turned just as sour as it could be. There was no love lost between them.

Felix would ask me to write a memorandum about a case, which never found its way into his opinion. He would study the briefs. I would study the briefs. Then we would sit down and, after he had digested my memorandum, he would start to dictate to me. I would just type with two fingers, and we would talk, discuss each sentence in the opinion. They were his sentences, not mine, but we'd argue about them, discuss them, and he might make changes or transpose things. It was an editing process. As soon as I finished typing with my hunt and peck system, I would give the opinion to Esther Austern, Tommy Austern's wife, who was his secretary. She was probably his favorite secretary. She'd been his secretary at the law school before she married Tommy. She would type it up, and then we'd go over it again, and he'd edit it and make changes in it. That would be done two or three times, and then it would go to the printer.

To a great extent, Felix was still active politically. He was constantly in touch with the White House, with various Cabinet members, Secretary Ickes, Tom Corcoran, Ben Cohen, Dave Lilienthal, and Henry Morgenthau. Felix was the prime mover in the appointment of Henry Stimson as Secretary of War. He regarded that as a great triumph.

When I was Felix's law clerk, he and Tom had not broken up yet. The first breach that occurred was when the Justices decided they needed an administrator. A new position called the administrator of the courts was created in the late thirties. The administrator was supposed to police the district courts and their dockets. Tom was very much dedicated to seeing his friend Stuart Guthrie get the job. Felix made a pass at that, but never was able to get enough votes to see Stuart Guthrie named. Tom thought that Felix had not been persistent enough in holding out for Stuart Guthrie, and he was very angry. Felix said, and I think he was right, that the drafted position didn't amount to a hill of beans. Tom could be pretty obdurate about these things, but I don't think that caused an irreparable breach. I think Felix's proper reason for not supporting Tom for Solicitor General was that he thought this was a priestly task, and that it involved dedication to being Solicitor General and nothing else. Felix repeatedly said, to me and to others, that if he thought Tom was going to dedicate himself to the job of Solicitor General, he would support him cheerfully and go to bat for him, but he felt that Tom viewed the Solicitor General's position as just another post from which he could operate politically. Felix felt that the Solicitor General's post was not appropriate for that. I think, way down underneath, Felix had some apprehensions about the general direction Tom's life was taking—he was becoming more reckless.

I can remember what I think was the beginning of his breach with Justice Douglas. It was a case in which an Indian had brought a suit against a state taxing district alleging that he was immune from taxation because he was an Indian and a ward of the federal government.[15] The Indian won the suit, and the question was whether the Indian was entitled to interest on his judgment. That was the case that came to the Supreme Court. The underlying issue of law there was whether the right to interest in a case of that sort derived from federal law or from state law. Justice Frankfurter's opinion in this case came nearer to being my opinion than any that I can think of while I was his law clerk. I suggested to him that the proper answer was that the Indian's right—whether or not he got interest—was a matter that referred to federal law, but that federal law would accommodate itself to the law of the state as a matter of comity. Felix was convinced and wrote the opinion that way. Every judge, including Douglas, wrote an endorsement. Douglas said, "This is a splendid opinion. I agree wholeheartedly." But Black decided to dissent because Black did not believe in interest. He went back to the Middle Ages and believed that interest was a sin. At the last minute Douglas concurred in Black's dissenting opinion, and in effect said to Felix, "I went with Black's dissenting opinion because I just didn't want Hugo to feel by himself out there." That attitude irritated Frankfurter tremendously. That a Justice would change his vote just to keep another Justice from feeling bad upset him.

Felix thought Black was a judge of tremendous intellect, tremendous qualities, but that he had a little bit of the demagogue and the absolutist in him. He never felt the same personal hostility toward Black that he did toward Douglas, and indeed, after Felix retired from the Court he and Black became greatly reconciled. Black came to visit with him frequently when he was ill and out of commission. I heard him say repeatedly that God Almighty gave Black the best brain in our Court. They disagreed and fought and clashed a good deal, to some degree personally, but there wasn't the same hostility and even viciousness between Frankfurter and Black that there was between Frankfurter and Douglas.

Frankfurter had thought Hughes was a swine before he went on the Court. He was very bitter about Hughes's treatment of Cardozo and Brandeis, and he was very critical of Hughes's performance during the Court-packing plan. But as soon as he got on the Court, he was totally captivated by him, and came almost to venerate him. I think Hughes

15. *Board of County Commissioners et al. v. Seber et al.* (1943).

was hard on Cardozo and Brandeis because of ideological differences. I don't think he was anti-Semitic. I'll tell you this, Frankfurter was bedazzled by him. Hughes scared me to death. He's one of the few people in the world who ever really scared me. Once Felix was sick and missed a couple of days on the Court, and I got a message that the Chief Justice wanted to see me. Well, I'd never done more than pass the time of day with him. He was not a fellow you got very intimate with, from a law clerk's vantage point. I went in there just shaking in my shoes. I thought, my God, have I said something indiscreet? Have I done something I shouldn't have? I came in, and he sat up there with that beard and that distinguished presence, and he said, "I just wanted you to tell Justice Frankfurter that for those cases where he was not able to hear the oral arguments, he need not recluse himself. He may feel himself perfectly eligible to participate in the decision. Thank you very much." Well, I walked out feeling relieved! He was the most impressive, the most godlike person that I ever saw. I think he was a casuist. He could reconcile opposites and make things that were inconsistent consistent more easily than almost anyone. When he had a flaming red beard he looked like a hippie, and he was thought to be kind of wild and radical. But when his beard turned snow white he was impressive. He and his wife once had dinner at the French Pavilion at the World's Fair, and as they entered every person in the room automatically stood up.

Felix thought of Stone as a poor Chief Justice, a poor administrator of the Court's business, and he would poke a little fun at him. When Stone first went on the Court, Felix spoke in a very ugly way about him, but he came to have much greater respect and admiration for Stone as a judge—for example, in the flag salute cases, where Frankfurter incurred all kinds of hostility. The first case was decided in the year that I was his law clerk. Stone was the lone dissenter. In his conversations with me Frankfurter showed great respect for Stone's position and his opinion. There was no put-down. He said that he thought Stone's dissent in that divided flag salute case was a noble affirmation of the spirit of freedom. But he had great contempt for Murphy, Black, and Douglas, because they voted with him in the first case and then changed their minds. He always said he didn't believe they had reread the Constitution, they had just read the newspapers.

The case involved the question of whether a pupil could be expelled from school for refusing to salute the flag. Frankfurter wrote an opinion saying that it was constitutional to expel the student, that the flag was a great symbol of our unity and our nation, and that even though it might be unwise, it was not unconstitutional. Stone dissented. Then, three years later—when the composition of the Court had changed with the appointment of Jackson—Murphy, Black, and Douglas changed their minds and the Court overruled the *Gobitis* case. In the *Barnette* case the court held that it was unconstitutional to compel students to salute the flag if it was against their religious convictions, and Frankfurter dissented. This was not an indication of the political character of the Court. I would say that it reflected their emotional views and the value systems of the judges. It was the beginning of Frankfurter's continual reaffirmation of his philosophy of judicial restraint. He believed that the Court should abstain from interfering with other organs of government, whereas Black, Douglas, Murphy, and, later on, the Warren Court, took a much stronger view of the role of the judiciary in protecting individual liberty against incursions by other organs of government.

Felix could be combative at times. He was extremely generous and loving with those he was close to, but at the same time, that love was certainly connected with the desire to dominate, to feel they were his boys. I don't say he never tolerated deviation from his own views, but one had to be rather careful in how one expressed deviation. He and I got into long harangues about several legal issues. I soon found, however, that the best thing to do was let it drop. He was going to do what he wanted to do, which was exactly right. After all, he was on the Court. I wasn't.

Felix didn't have all that much success on the Court. He never was able to hold Murphy and Black and Douglas. I would say Felix's only successes were Roberts and Jackson. I don't think Jackson was flattered by Felix; they just became close and intimate and liked each other and agreed with each other. Even before he went on the Court, Felix had utter contempt for Roberts, but when he found that the rest of them were leaving him, he formed an alliance with Roberts and began to reestimate him.

At the end of my year as his clerk, Felix called Jimmy Byrnes, who had been his colleague on the Court. I had met Justice Byrnes several times and was pleasantly acquainted, but I am sure he would never have put me in the White House if it hadn't been for Felix. I was there all during the war, except for a brief period when I was in the military. I was involved in all kinds of economic matters: wages, prices, rationing.

I remember the first day I went to work at the White House. Ben Cohen was there. I looked through the window and there was Lord Halifax getting out of his car to come in the back way to see the President. I said, "There, Ben, there's Lord Halifax coming in." Ben said, "I don't want it recorded that on your first day in the White House you were seen peeking through the window at notables."

Once when I was working in the White House I got a telephone call from Felix who said, "You must come up here right away. It's terribly important." That was one of his favorite phrases, "terribly important," so I grabbed a cab and went to the Court. Felix was in his chambers having lunch with Frank Knox, Secretary of the Navy, and Felix said, "Prichard, it's terribly important. I'm so glad you came up here. Secretary Knox and I were having lunch, and I just wanted you to do your imitation of John L. Lewis for him."

During this time a group of young men shared a house called Hockley. Graham Claytor,[16] Adrian Fisher, Phil Graham, and others lived there. I knew Phil first in law school. He was a year behind me, but we met each other on the *Law Review*. In his senior year he was president of the *Law Review*. He and Felix and I became very close. I can remember Felix saying to me, "I think Phil Graham ought to be dean of the Harvard Law School right now." He was then a third-year student. While Phil and I lived at Hockley, we shared a room and saw each other all the time. I was with Phil and Kay Graham all through their courtship, I was the best man at their wedding, and Phil was the best man at Lucy's and my wedding. Everyone who ever knew Phil Graham realized that he was a person of unusual brilliance and gifts.

We had a lot of parties. Mint juleps during the warm weather, toddies during the less warm weather. We had Sunday morning parties, with fried chicken and ham and biscuits. The Frankfurters would come and the Reeds and the Achesons, and Adlai Stevenson would come occasionally. I can remember one occasion. A bunch of bankers were there, and I don't know who all of them were. One of them was Harry Morgan, J. P. Morgan's son, and there was a lot of vicious political talk, appeasement talk, suggesting we might as well deal with the Germans. Phil and I—we'd had several drinks—got tired of this, and finally we stood up. As we walked out of the room I said, "All who love democracy, follow us." Some did. Some didn't.

Henry Reuss lived at Hockley, and he was a very close friend of Jane Ickes. Henry and I saw a good deal of the Ickeses. Many times we had Sunday lunch with them. Ickes was always threatening to resign, and he was always firing his under secretaries. I remember when Charlie

16. Claytor once called Adrian Fisher, his successor as clerk to Justice Brandeis, at what he knew to be "nap time," when the Justice could not be disturbed. In a heavy German accent he demanded to speak to the Justice about the Palestine problem. Fisher anguished over what to do; Claytor finally confessed. When a call came the next day at the same time and a voice said, "This is President Roosevelt. I'd like to talk to the Justice about Palestine," Fisher immediately suspected Claytor. When the President repeated his request, however, an appointment was promptly made.

West was his under secretary. Ickes wanted to get rid of him but he couldn't get him to resign, so he finally had his furniture moved out and locked his office door.

DAVID RIESMAN

When I was Justice Brandeis's clerk late in his life I had extremely limited personal relations with him. I had an office on the sixth floor, and he had his offices on the fifth floor where he lived. We would communicate by his slipping under the door each day (he used the printer as a typist) an opinion that he was working on. I was to "improve" it, but I rarely felt that I did. We never discussed cases; he had already decided them before I saw them. I was not to discuss cases with the other law clerks, even the clerks of such allies as Justices Cardozo and Stone. It was a monastic existence, and the only times I saw Justice Brandeis personally were when I brought someone to meet him, such as William Bullitt, who was a family friend, or Harold Laski, whom I knew. Of course, I also saw Brandeis at the Sunday teas which I "managed." We never argued about anything, except once, when I said to him very early on that I thought Zionism was Jewish fascism. He was furious, and he said in his austere way, you don't know Jewish history, and this is a subject we should not discuss again.

I had the impression from my predecessors, such as Paul Freund, who praised Brandeis so highly and appeared to have closer relations with him, that the fault lay with me; according to some biographers, I am the only clerk who has been critical of the Justice. I felt torn between my criticism of him and my sense of futility, the feeling that I was of no use to him because I couldn't contribute to opinions that had already been decided. Since it didn't matter whether I agreed or not, I could only embellish them, and I didn't do very well in that respect. At the end of the year, in May, I got jaundice and left him. I felt guilty about that, but not too guilty because I hadn't been that much help. He knew what he wanted, and all I did was to add some citations from New Zealand or wherever.

His intransigence increased with age. I did meet him late in life and therefore at a more rigid point, but with all people, not only me, his attitude was purely instrumental. I could see this at the teas. Bruce Murphy[17] cites from an interview with me an exchange that was sup-

17. Bruce Allen Murphy, *The Brandeis/Frankfurter Connection: The Secret Political Activities of Two Supreme Court Justices* (New York: Oxford University Press, 1982).

posed to have occurred at a tea. It was not at a tea but in Brandeis's office, for he would never have said publicly what is reported. I took William Bullitt down to meet him, and Brandeis asked him: "What is the cotton production in Turkestan?" Bullitt replied, "I haven't the faintest idea." And Brandeis dismissed him contemptuously, because Brandeis was a Southern Agrarian. That's what mattered, the cotton production in Turkestan. If he met somebody at the teas who wanted to talk to him, let's say a law clerk or Tom Corcoran or Benjamin Cohen, he'd take them aside. Jim Rowe was an exception. Every time Jim Rowe came, and I brought him regularly to the teas, the Justice would say: "Jim, when are you going back to Montana?" To me he would say that he didn't want me to go back to Boston; I should go to Tupelo, Mississippi, perhaps in connection with the TVA, and do legal work for the deprived. But I did go back to Boston, and in his view I shouldn't have.

Brandeis was not concerned about civil rights; the Southern Agrarian in him led to his concern with the South, with the Tennessee Valley and the poverty-stricken South generally. Brandeis became many other things, but he was in his origins a southerner, with a sympathy for Southern Agrarians. I shared this sympathy because I read some of the Nashville "Fugitives" when I was in college. On many issues I did not share Justice Brandeis's views, but I did on decentralization.

I lived in a Washington house of dedicated New Deal activists. To their parties there came many talented young men scattered throughout the government, mostly lawyers along with a few economists. Some of these young visitors had in my judgment too much contempt for ordinary Americans. They thought it hopeless to try to persuade the country, or even to persuade Congress. Clever and ingenious, they were therefore tempted to use undemocratic means. I was the "house Tory" and I'm one of the few people who have become less conservative as I've grown older, I guess.

Let me give an example of a judgment I had, which I may never have expressed because it seemed so outré, concerning the Public Utility Holding Company Act and, to a lesser degree, the Securities Exchange Act.[18] Both seemed to me motivated by animus against Wall Street. I recognize that both acts, especially the Securities Exchange Act, were intended to prevent—and have in the case of the latter—real abuses in frauds against investors, securities dealings by corporate officials with inside knowledge, and so on. But I regard the price paid for curbing these abuses as too high. The Holding Company Act transferred power

18. The Securities Exchange Act of 1934 established the Securities and Exchange Commission, with powers to investigate and reform unfair securities practices, to license exchanges, and to regulate stock transactions.

from sophisticated bankers (such as Lehman Brothers or Lazard Frères or Maurice Wertheim or people like that) and from Wall Street lawyers (who often sought, contrary to what is generally thought, to keep their clients honest) to Akron tire-makers and rubber-makers, and to steel-makers in Gary and Birmingham, to people who were really going to shoot strikers. This shift of the locus of industrial power was a mistake. We can see this now vis-à-vis Japan, France, or Germany. We do not have investment bankers who are helping to manage the economy. We don't go to the investment banks to decide where money should go. We have congressional investment banking. I also think that the Securities Exchange Act, which has provided enormous sums for lawyers and accountants, has made it difficult for small business to get equity capital. The Holding Company Act and the Securities Exchange Act were anti-Wall Street, antibusiness acts, which have turned out to be self-defeating because they put power in the hands of the most benighted industrialists rather than the more cosmopolitan in Wall Street.

I had great respect for Ben Cohen; I regarded him as a very thoughtful person and not given to the undercurrent of arrogance. What I have said concerning the arrogance of many bright lawyers is an over-generalization, and many lawyers escape it; many lawyers, in spite of it, outlive it, to think in broader terms. Tom Corcoran was attractive and affable, but probably less engaging than Cohen.

The New Deal ran out of ideas very quickly. I was never one of Franklin Roosevelt's great admirers. It was good what was said of him: he had a first-class temperament with a second-rate mind. That's about the impression I had. I also thought he was something of a joker. When he ran out of ideas, he attacked the Supreme Court and finished any possibility of further political leverage. Then he became Dr. Win-the-War. Here I found myself in strong opposition. Long before Hiroshima I was against the mass bombings of German and Japanese cities. In these bombings, which left 800,000 citizens of Hamburg homeless, and destroyed Tokyo in a firestorm, we were using means of warfare which any theory of "just war" would outlaw as disproportionate to any possible military gains. Indeed, the mass bombings of civilians, as the later bombing surveys showed, paradoxically helped the German war effort because it concentrated the workers in the factories. It was a prelude to later disparities between ends and means, whether the atom bomb or Vietnam or Beirut today. Some of the ways in which the war was conducted showed the limitations of the New Deal.

What I regarded as great about the New Deal is suggested by the stupidity of the people who were avowed Communists and who thought that there would have to be a revolution in America. Thanks to Franklin

Roosevelt, however, this country had hope; he gave people hope even in the midst of the Great Depression. I think that was the great thing he did; his buoyancy was in some ways more important than the particular tasks of reform he attempted, often against great difficulty.

Let me tell you one experience I had. I got so fed up with my rich friends saying that anybody who wants a job can get one—friends who had not suffered from the depression, who still had their country places, their yachts, and whatever—that I decided I would try it for myself. I did something quite foolhardy. I went out to Detroit with what I thought would be a worker's equipment, in what I thought was a worker's uniform of blue jeans, with a poncho slung over my shoulder. I went and stood at the factory gates, the Ford River Rouge Plant, for instance, where every day they might take five of the many dozens of unemployed lined up. My way of going about it was ridiculous: I could only go to one place at a time by public transport, whereas most of the other workers had cars. Nobody in a personnel office would hire me anyway. I got sick and went to a Federal Transient Center, meeting there people who had been on the road for years, as artisans; they had pictures of their families in their wallets. I became convinced that these people would not make a revolution; they did not lose hope.

CHAPTER 5

The Solicitor General

The Office of the Solicitor General was created in 1870 at the same time that the Justice Department was established. It was set up to provide assistance to the Attorney General, who had been inundated with cases arising out of California land claims. The Solicitor General himself, or one of the Assistant Attorney Generals who headed the five functional divisions of the Justice Department, assumed the principal responsibility for arguing cases before the Supreme Court. This allowed the Attorney General to concentrate on his administrative duties and to provide legal advice to the President. By the 1930s, official opinions, which appeared under the name of the Attorney General, were actually prepared by the Assistant Solicitor General. During the 1930s, probably the most important of the five divisions was the antitrust division, created in 1903 to enforce the growing body of federal antitrust legislation. This division was also responsible for arguing cases arising out of the Commerce clause of the Constitution, such as the National Labor Relations Act and the Public Utility Holding Company Act cases.

From 1933 to 1945, four Solicitor Generals argued the Administration's cases before the Supreme Court. The first, J. Crawford Biggs, who served from 1933 to 1935, lost ten of his first seventeen cases. He was succeeded by Stanley F. Reed, an affable and uncontroversial Kentuckian who was a faithful New Dealer. He kept his job from 1935 to 1938. Reed, who was later appointed to the Supreme Court, successfully managed the legal defense of the New Deal at its most critical moments. Robert Jackson replaced Reed as Solicitor General and followed Reed to the Supreme Court. As the Assistant Attorney General in charge of the antitrust division, he had revitalized the government's role in antitrust prosecution with a vengeance. When FDR appointed Jackson to the Supreme Court in 1941, he named Charles Fahy Solicitor General.

ROBERT L. STERN

In November 1932 I joined the legal staff of the Petroleum Administrative Board. John F. Davis and John H. Hollands, who had been on the *Harvard Law Review* with me, also came down. Nathan Margold, solicitor of the Interior Department, was the chairman of the Petroleum Board, and Charles Fahy, associate solicitor of the Interior Department, was the vice-chairman. The Board's function was to administer the National Recovery Administration code for the petroleum industry. Margold and Fahy had joined the Interior Department because of their interest in Indian affairs, not because they had any special knowledge of the petroleum industry.

Shortly after we began work, Davis, Hollands, and I were told to write the first draft of the brief in a case called *Panama Refining Co. v. Ryan,* subsequently known as the Hot Oil case.[1] This was the first brief on the constitutionality of the National Industrial Recovery Act. It involved the constitutionality of the Petroleum Industry code, which forbade the production of oil in excess of quotas for each well in the East Texas oil field where the price of oil had gone down to 5 cents a barrel. The three of us divided up the constitutional topics, and I took the Commerce clause. I went down to the Library of Congress and read all the cases on the power of Congress under the Commerce clause; I also read everything I could find on its constitutional history.

When the case finally reached the Supreme Court, the Department of Justice sent over a somewhat older lawyer named Moses Huberman to take charge. We initially resented the appearance of this outsider, but discovered that he had also been on the *Harvard Law Review* and indeed had written briefs before, which was more than the three of us had done. We soon became good friends, and within a few months I was asked to join the Department of Justice's antitrust division, headed by Harold M. Stephens. At that time it was handling all cases involving the regulation of business under the New Deal statutes. It had not been necessary for me to get any political clearance to join the Interior Department under Harold Ickes, who was nonpolitical and was not concerned about Democratic endorsements. But when I was invited to join Justice, I was asked to obtain political clearance if possible. I called Tom Corcoran and also my uncle, Arthur Garfield Hays, in New York. They both contacted

---

1. In *Panama Refining Co. v. Ryan* (1935), the Hot Oil case, the Supreme Court overturned a section of the National Industrial Recovery Act that authorized a code to govern the petroleum industry. In its eight-to-one ruling (only Justice Cardozo dissented), the Court said that it was an undue delegation of legislative powers to the Executive.

Senator Robert Wagner, and within a day or two I had the necessary political clearance.

The antitrust division contained a number of very able lawyers. Those involved in the constitutional litigation included Stephens, Carl MacFarland, Huberman, Charles Weston, and Abe Feller. It was Huberman who, by checking the original in the State Department of the Executive Order establishing the Petroleum code, discovered that a paragraph of the code containing the crucial language had been unintentionally deleted when a section was amended. We felt obligated to call this to the Court's attention, although the omitted provision was immediately reinstated in the code. The result was that after we wrote an exhaustive and exhausting brief of 195 pages, mainly on the constitutionality under the Commerce clause of federal regulation of the production of oil, the Supreme Court was able to duck the question on the ground that it was not really presented.

The *Panama* case was decided by the Supreme Court in January 1935. The Court held that a small section of the National Industrial Recovery Act was unconstitutional because it lacked standards to guide the President in determining whether to make operative a prohibition on the interstate transportation of hot oil (produced in excess of state quotas). This clearly foreshadowed a similar holding of invalid delegation on the rest of the National Industrial Recovery Act, which was even more vulnerable on that ground.

Charles Weston and I have the distinction of being the only lawyers in 190 years who managed to write losing briefs for the government on the question of delegation of powers. Only in the *Panama, Schechter,*[2] and *Carter* cases has the Supreme Court held statutes unconstitutional for that reason. Thereafter, I was more successful on that subject and others, although not because I had learned how to write better briefs.

When the *Schechter* case came along the lawyer in the antitrust division who had handled it below, Walter Rice, urged that the government join in consenting to the review by the Supreme Court in part because the 1,500-page record contained a great deal to show how interstate commerce was affected by unfair practices in the kosher poultry industry in New York city. Partly as a result of that, the government agreed to *certiorari.* By then the antitrust division had been told to clear everything with Stanley Reed, who was general counsel of the Reconstruction Finance Corporation; Paul Freund was his assistant. That

2. In *Schechter Poultry Corp. v. U.S.* (1935), the Sick Chicken case, the Supreme Court unanimously overturned the National Industrial Recovery Act on three grounds: it was an excessive delegation of legislative powers to the President; there was no constitutional authority to delegate legislative powers to the President; and it regulated businesses wholly in intrastate commerce.

meant submitting everything to Reed through Freund, with whom I was living at the time in the house on Q Street. We were all very happy to have him review anything we did. While this was going on I was reading the 1,500-page record in the *Schechter* case. I soon reported to Freund and Reed that there was practically nothing in the record that supported the government's position under the Commerce clause. I was told that it was too late for the government to change its position. And so the *Schechter* case proceeded on an accelerated schedule, even though, if the government had let it take its regular course, the statute would have expired long before the case would have been argued. It was argued by Reed and Donald Richberg, by then head of the National Recovery Administration and a well-known and able Chicago labor lawyer. Those on the brief included MacFarland, Freund, Weston, Huberman, and me. On May 27, 1935, the Court unanimously held the NRA unconstitutional both under the Commerce clause and as an invalid delegation of power.

In order to deal with the special and serious ills of the bituminous coal industry, the Guffey Coal Act was passed a few months later; it sought to raise prices and wages and encourage collective bargaining in that industry.[3] Immediately a test suit challenging its constitutionality was brought by the officers of the Carter Coal Company against the corporation itself, as well as government officials. I was the junior member of the trial team that tried the case in the District of Columbia trial court for a few weeks. The then head of the antitrust division, John Dickinson, was in charge of the case and argued it in the Supreme Court. Feller, Weston, and I wrote the Supreme Court brief. The government had proved that strikes in the bituminous coal industry would close down all of the railroads and most of the industries that shipped by rail, thus affecting the major portion of interstate commerce in the country. The Supreme Court held in May 1936 that such effects on interstate commerce were merely indirect and not sufficient to justify federal regulation of labor relations in the coal industry. Justices Brandeis, Stone, and Cardozo dissented.

After that I began to work on Railway Labor Act cases in the antitrust division under Leo F. Tierney. In 1937, eleven months after the *Carter* decision, the Supreme Court in the Labor Board cases held that the federal government did have the power to regulate labor relations in large and small companies producing goods for interstate commerce, a

3. The Bituminous Coal Conservation Act of 1935, named for its cosponsor Senator Joseph Guffey, a Pennsylvania Democrat, sought to regulate the bituminous coal industry as a public utility, with clauses protecting labor, controlling prices, allocating production, and retiring marginal lands from production by government purchase. It was financed by a tax on the industry.

stand completely inconsistent with the *Carter* case. Hughes and Roberts changed their positions, swinging over to the side of the Brandeis group. No one can be sure that FDR's Court-packing plan, announced shortly before, had anything to do with their shift in position—or that it didn't. The Labor Board cases were argued by Reed, J. Warren Madden, chairman of the NLRB, Charles Fahy, general counsel of the NLRB, and Charles Wyzanski, of the Solicitor General's office. I did not work on those cases, but wrote the government's brief in a companion case, *Virginian Railway Co. v. System Federation No. 40,* under the Railway Labor Act, which was argued at the same time; it asked whether Congress could regulate the labor relations of railroad shopmen who did not themselves travel in interstate commerce.[4]

In 1938 Congress passed the Fair Labor Standards Act which regulated wages and hours in industries producing goods for interstate commerce. Like the NLRA, this statute was an offshoot of the National Industrial Recovery Act. My job was to defend the constitutionality of the statute in the lower courts and to write the briefs for the Supreme Court. In the trial court I handled the *Darby Lumber* case, which became the test case in the Supreme Court and was argued there by Attorney General Francis Biddle.[5] By the time of the decision in 1941, all four members of the Court's right wing had died or retired, and the Court had no trouble in accepting the same Commerce clause arguments that had been so unsuccessful in the 1935 and 1936 decisions. The opinion upholding the statute in that case was written by Justice Stone, who later became Chief Justice. He gave a number of great opinions on the Commerce clause and other subjects as well. Stone does not have the recognition that I think he deserves as one of the great Supreme Court Justices. This may be because he was not renowned as a Chief Justice (after Hughes, whom he replaced in 1941) because he was not a very effective judicial administrator. But his opinions, particularly on constitutional issues, were among the very best. This is not surprising, since he had been a professor and dean of the Columbia Law School shortly before he became Attorney General of the United States and then a member of the Supreme Court in 1925.

There was life outside the law in Washington as well. I roomed

4. In *Virginian Railway Co. v. System Federation No. 40* (1937), the Supreme Court upheld the right of employees of a railroad to be represented by nonemployees, that is, by officers of a national railroad union.

5. In *U.S. v. Darby Lumber Co.* (1941), the Supreme Court unanimously upheld the constitutionality of the Fair Labor Standards Act of 1938 (also known as the wage and hour law or the minimum wage law). The Court held that commerce was a complete function controllable by Congress to the point of prohibition and repudiated the doctrine of mutually exclusive federal and state jurisdictions over commerce.

with John F. Davis for a few months until both of us joined the house on Q Street where Paul Freund, Arnold Raum, and other law school friends such as Samuel H. Levy, Harold Rosenwald, and Melvin Siegel resided. Siegel's marriage to Felix Frankfurter's secretary left room in the house for me.

The most memorable social events in my life during this period were the teas given by Justice Brandeis on Monday afternoons. I remember that my reaction on meeting Justice Brandeis was that this was about the closest I was ever going to get to meeting God in person.

In August 1935, Paul Freund and I were invited to a party by Nathaniel Nathanson, who had followed Paul as a Brandeis law clerk. Nat's sister invited to the party a girl from Wisconsin named Terese Marks. Since then I have not had a date with anybody but Terese, whom I married the next year at the house on Q Street. The marriage was performed by Harold Stephens, my former boss in the antitrust division, who by then was a judge on the United States Circuit Court of Appeals for the District of Columbia.

I stayed in the antitrust division, working largely on New Deal commerce cases, not antitrust, until 1941 when Charles Fahy became Solicitor General. He immediately brought me up to the Solicitor General's office, with which I had been working pretty steadily in the preceding years. Paul Freund by that time had gone back to Harvard Law School to teach, but during the war he came back to the office.

I left the Solicitor General's office for strictly financial reasons. The work, as law work, could not be beat. But I was not sure whether my income would be sufficient to pay for straightening the teeth of my three sons, much less eventually sending them to college. I was probably the best paid nonpolitical lawyer in the government, but that amounted to only $12,000.

Most of what I have recalled concerns details of litigation of great national importance. I cannot easily reconstruct the economic distress of the country, the need to try to do something about it—or the effect of the pre-1937 Supreme Court decisions holding that the national government lacked constitutional power to make that attempt, when no other body or persons possibly could. The causes of the depression, which came close to destroying our economic system and the interstate commerce of which it largely consisted, were national not local, and not remediable by the separate states.

I started in the Solicitor General's office at the instance of Judge Augustus Hand. I had been clerking for him when he got a call from Stanley Reed, the Solicitor General, saying that he had some vacancies in his office and did Judge Hand have any suggestions? I was interviewed by Mr. Reed and got the job, starting on the first of August 1935. At that time the office was deeply involved in the defense of New Deal legislation, although not all of it had yet been passed. The great issue for Paul Freund was the Tennessee Valley Authority, the *Ashwander* case.[6] Alger Hiss was defending the Agricultural Adjustment Act, and I was assigned to Alger's team, working with him on the brief in *U.S. v. Butler*.[7]

It was a relatively small office, and we worked damned hard. In fact, it was a kind of crusade. Everybody I knew or met in Washington was out to save the world.

Lawyers from other agencies would gather for parties. There was a house on Q Street called "Paradise" where Paul Freund and Arnold Raum and Bob Stern and others lived. They had numerous dinners and parties. When you went to a party, you didn't talk sports, you didn't talk women. You talked about the case you were on or what the problem was with the conservative Supreme Court. I remember working straight through many nights in order to get things printed at the Government Printing Office and to the Supreme Court on time.

The results were mixed. We lost the *Butler* case and Triple-A was declared unconstitutional. Paul won the *Ashwander* case and the TVA was sustained. Then along came the National Labor Relations Act. I was put in charge of those cases. Stanley Reed, quite properly, thought that one of the ways to get the cases before the Supreme Court was to get involved in them before they got there. So he and I would travel to the Sixth Circuit and the Fifth Circuit and participate in or listen to or help with the briefs on our cases in the Courts of Appeal. Finally we got to the point where the Supreme Court agreed to review five National

6. In *Ashwander v. TVA* (1936), the Supreme Court upheld the TVA's power to build dams as a legitimate exercise of the federal government's power to control navigable streams and to provide for the national defense.
7. In *U.S. v. Butler* (1936), the Hoosac Mills case, the Supreme Court invalidated the Agricultural Adjustment Act of 1933 on the grounds that the processing tax it imposed was not really a tax but a part of a system for regulating agricultural production and thus not within the Welfare clause of the Constitution.

Labor Relations Board cases, the *Associated Press* case, the *Jones and Laughlin* case, and a few others.[8]

The National Labor Relations Act was an outgrowth of earlier New Deal legislation that had tried to bring in the federal government as mediator in conflicts between labor and management. It provided a machinery for collective bargaining with penalties for failure to bargain by either side. Its stated justification was that strikes and other disputes between labor and management interfered with interstate commerce. Therefore, the Interstate Commerce clause of the Constitution gave the federal government jurisdiction to deal with what might be regarded as essentially a local problem, a strike in a steel mill. The strike would interrupt the flow of steel, and therefore the federal government had an interest. This was a rather extreme position for the federal government to take. It had not, up to that time, asserted very much power under the Interstate Commerce clause; the great problem was to determine the extent of that authority. If the federal government could intervene in a strike in a steel mill because interruptions would affect interstate commerce, could it also control the price of haircuts because the scissors came across state lines to get to the barber? The problem was to present the matter to the Supreme Court in a fashion that would not completely destroy the power of the states or completely expand the power of the federal government.

The team that worked on those briefs included Abe Feller, who was then a lawyer in the antitrust division of the department, Charlie Wyzanski, who was in the Solicitor General's office, Steve Farrand, and myself. We worked literally day and night for a period of some weeks, almost months, getting out the briefs in the five labor cases. The procedure, in rough fashion, was that we would sit around and try to decide, point by point, what kind of position we ought to take. Then I would spend the afternoon and usually most of the evening trying to put that on paper. Then we would meet again in the morning and look it over, and we'd tear it all apart and try to do it over again. This went on and on, later with participation by the Solicitor General himself and considerable participation by Charles Fahy, who was then general counsel of the National Labor Relations Board.

We did get the cases out and the Supreme Court upheld the act by a five-to-four vote. Justice Roberts turned around, as the phrase went, and the National Labor Relations Act was declared constitutional. I think

8. In *Associated Press v. NLRB* (1937); *NLRB v. Jones and Laughlin Steel Corp.* (1937), *NLRB v. Fruehauf Trailer Co.* (1937); and *NLRB v. Friedman-Harry Marks Clothing Co.* (1937), the Supreme Court upheld the constitutionality of the National Labor Relations Act of 1935 (Wagner Act).

the position the Supreme Court ultimately adopted is a perfectly rational position, one that has worked very well. It doesn't mean that the federal government has to exercise the power, but if it needs to, then the Commerce clause is available to give it that authority.

Then other New Deal statutes came under attack. Old-age benefits under the Social Security Act were attacked as improper uses of the taxing power. We wrote briefs in those cases, and the Supreme Court sustained us.[9] Then came the minimum wage law (the Fair Labor Standards Act of 1938), the law that controlled how little a person may be paid. This was being drafted by Corcoran and Cohen, and Stanley Reed was asked for help, so I worked on the original drafts.

I remember with some dismay that I planned to attend the fiftieth anniversary of the *Harvard Law Review,* of which I had been an officer. The day before I was to leave for Boston, Stanley Reed said, "The President wants to see us tomorrow evening at seven o'clock to talk about a controversy that has arisen with respect to the drafting of the Fair Labor Standards Act." "I was going to go to Boston," I said. "Well, which do you think is more important, your going to Boston or your going to see President Roosevelt at his request?" "Well, I suppose the answer is pretty obvious."

So I went over to the White House with Tommy Corcoran and Ben Cohen and Reed, and the debate was whether the Fair Labor Standards Act should set a national minimum, 25 or 35 cents an hour, or whether it should make the rate flexible and allow for differences between occupations. The great problem was the pecan pickers in Texas who would all be put out of work if the minimum was fixed, because they weren't getting anywhere near that much. Roosevelt listened to all this for a while with his cigarette sticking out of his mouth, and he finally said, "Let's have a flat minimum." So we all went back and drafted a flat minimum statute that was passed and has worked all right.

I stayed on for two years, handling other labor cases as they came along, working with Charlie Fahy. Then I joined the firm of Covington, Burling for a year. Stanley Reed went to the Supreme Court and Bob Jackson became Solicitor General. By the time I got a second invitation, from Solicitor General Jackson, I was eligible to become a member of the bar of the Supreme Court. He called me up and said, "If you will come back for a year, we have a vacancy. I'd like to have you back. After a year you'll be eligible to argue cases in the Supreme Court, and I'll be assured of having some arguments." So I went back, and during that year the sit-down strike cases came along. We briefed and argued the cases out in Detroit and won.

9. In *Steward Machine Co. v. Davis* (1937) and *Helvering v. Davis* (1937), the Supreme Court ruled five to four in favor of the Social Security Act of 1935.

I did argue some cases in the Court. I won some and lost some. On one occasion, Stanley Reed, then Solicitor General, was arguing a case involving the Bankhead Cotton Control Act, which was a supplement to the general Agricultural Adjustment Act.[10] I had written the briefs. Reed had made a good argument but obviously a losing one because the Court had already decided that the Triple-A was unconstitutional and the Bankhead Act was in the same general area. He collapsed while he was arguing. I helped him into his chair and the Chief Justice adjourned the Court and gave him some smelling salts. I was petrified for fear the Chief Justice would say, "Well, Mr. Horsky, won't you continue with the argument?" He didn't, fortunately. But this is an illustration of how hard everybody was working. Stanley Reed worked just as hard as the rest of us. The country was coming out of the depression and everything was moving along. Roosevelt was giving leadership; he had a program and we had to defend it. The Supreme Court was a serious obstacle because until the Labor Relations Act cases the Supreme Court consistently knocked everything down by five votes. They had declared the National Industrial Recovery Act and regulation of oil production in the Southwest unconstitutional before I got there. The Court was the barrier, we felt, to progress. When the Court-packing plan was announced, we were all shocked; Charlie Wyzanski was going to resign. We watched the contest in the Senate with enormous interest. All of us felt that the Supreme Court was a real obstacle, but that wasn't the way to get rid of the obstacle.

The Solicitor General's office was at the center of the New Deal legal fight. The Department of Agriculture concentrated on the Agricultural Adjustment Act. The Tennessee Valley Authority was interested in electric power. The Labor Board was interested in the Labor Act, and others were interested in Social Security. It all came together in the Solicitor General's office, where the ultimate decisions on constitutionality and interpretation would be made. It was a very important place to be at that time. I was just delighted to be part of it.

We would, of course, not start from scratch. We would get briefs or drafts or help from other parts of the government. When the labor cases came along, Abe Feller from the antitrust division helped. Larry Fly came over on the TVA case. I remember his sleeping on the table one evening while we were working. He said, "I can't stay awake any longer. Do you mind if I stretch out?"

I knew Abe Feller in the Department of Justice. He was in the anti-

10. The Cotton Control Act of 1934 (Bankhead Act) amended the Agricultural Adjustment Act of 1933 and provided for the compulsory reduction of surplus cotton crops through the licensing of individual producers who, in return, received benefit payments from the federal government for not growing their crops.

trust division, and I saw him frequently. We were good friends; I knew his wife and his children very well. He was an extraordinary man. He was a linguist; he spoke about eight languages fluently. He told me once that the only one he ever bogged down on was Finnish. He and Wyzanski and I would meet very frequently just to talk. They were the most interesting conversationalists I've ever met. We talked about anything and everything: the Restoration, the Roman Empire, problems of South Africa, exploration of the North Pole. They were very widely read, cultivated people. Obviously we talked about what was going on in the government and in the Supreme Court and the Solicitor General's office.

The thing I remember most about those times is the esprit de corps, the sense that we were doing something worthwhile, that it was important, that it was important to do it the very best way you could, and that it was important to get it done on time. Everybody had that sense. Paul Freund is not a man who exudes excitement and enthusiasm, but Paul was imbued with it, and Alger Hiss, probably more than anyone else. I never saw anybody work harder than Alger did on the cases that he had in the Solicitor General's office. The time and effort and energy and enthusiasm he put into all of those cases was just outstanding. Even my wife, who saw me very little during those days, was completely sympathetic. She was imbued with it too. This was the spirit of the New Deal. We felt we were going to change the United States and make it a better place. And we did, damn it, we did.

In those days, there was a sense that you could get better results if you hired first-class young men. Older people couldn't be attracted by the salaries that were then paid. My first job at the S.G.'s office paid $3,600 a year. That to me was a damned good salary, but for a practicing lawyer who was experienced and mature, that was peanuts. I think FDR and Homer Cummings, Stanley Reed, Felix, all the rest of them, believed that what you do is get good young people.

In those days, many of the Justices held open house on Monday, and since the Solicitor General's staff, by and large, knew the Supreme Court better than anybody else, we would generally trot around to pay respects. I recall with great pleasure going to the parties at Justice Black's after he was appointed. Felix and Stone had parties; even McReynolds had parties once in a while, although his parties were a little more Spartan than others. The Brandeis parties were by invitation only, but I did attend some of those. They were really Spartan, as if you were in a prison: bare walls, a little bit of furniture, a threadbare rug, and a little bitty sandwich. The Justice would pick out somebody and have a conversation with him, and then you'd go home. I was invited to

Cardozo's on one occasion with my wife, just the two of us. He didn't have parties, generally speaking. But they were very pleasant. It was a nice thing to do on Monday afternoon at five o'clock, to go out and have a sandwich and a cup of tea with the Justice, tell him that you didn't really agree with that last opinion of his because you'd lost it, but you could understand how he might come out that way.

I remember having a discussion with Cardozo about western slang. I had said something was haywire, and he said, "Haywire? That's an interesting expression. What does that mean?" I explained that haywire really meant it wasn't working very well; it had been fixed but not very well. So we had a long discussion about western expressions. I don't even remember what they were now, but he was fascinated with them. He was a lovely man; he was so kind and so gentle and so pleasant. You were afraid he was going to fall apart at any moment because he looked so fragile, but a hell of a nice person.

DAVID A. MORSE

I went to Washington in November 1933, a year after I graduated from Harvard Law School. I was invited to join the staff of the solicitor of the Interior Department, Nathan Margold, having been recommended by Felix Frankfurter. My job was in the area of oil conservation and development, transportation rates for oil, things that were a mystery to me. What happened that really got me into the mainstream of the FDR period came about by accident. After I'd been working for Margold for some time, Charles Fahy was appointed by Harold L. Ickes, Secretary of the Interior, to be chairman of the Petroleum Administrative Board. This office was set up to administer part of the National Industrial Recovery Act. Rather than have it administered by Hugh Johnson, who was the NRA administrator, Ickes insisted that he administer it. Because it was oil, it was Interior. By an Executive Order it was transferred to Ickes. Charles Fahy was chairman, and there was a board of three or four people. Fahy asked me to come over to the legal side, which was all within the same house anyway, because it was all under Ickes. I was appointed special assistant to the Attorney General of the United States to investigate and prosecute violators of the Petroleum code. I went to Chicago and worked with United States Attorney Dwight Green, a Republican who later became governor. I was called back to Washington because Ickes decided to set up a Petroleum Labor

Policy Board, a mini-National Labor Relations Board. The reason I was called back to work on that is interesting because it shows how youngsters' careers can develop just by accident.

When I was with the Petroleum Board before the Labor Policy Board was created, I had a secretary, Mary Satterfield, whose father was general counsel of the Bank for Reconstruction. I noticed a growing mountain of mail bags next to my office and asked Mary, "What can that be? Every day there are ten more big mail bags." "I don't know," she said. I suggested we take a look. We found that there were workers, poor families, all over the country who were writing the Secretary saying, "We've lost our home, we couldn't pay our mortgage, we've been dismissed from our jobs, we're unemployed because we tried to organize into trade unions with the protection of the Petroleum code you administer. But how are we going to be protected? We've taken advantage of rights that we have, and there's no protection, and we call on you for protection." So I said, "Mary, let's come in every night and write each one of these people and say, 'I acknowledge receipt of your letter. I'm doing this on behalf of the Secretary of the Interior. We're at the early stages, and we're urgently thinking of the kind of machinery that has to be set up to protect your interest and we will get back to you.' " I signed my name on behalf of the Secretary of the Interior.

After a few weeks, the Petroleum Labor Policy Board was set up, and Dr. William Leiserson, a labor expert from Antioch College, was appointed chairman. They didn't have a general counsel. One day I got a call to come to see the Secretary of the Interior, whom I'd never seen, never dreamed of seeing. I said, "Mary, this is it; I'm going to get fired. You remember we wrote all those letters on behalf of the Secretary? I had no authority to do it." Mary assured me that if I got fired, I could find another job.

I went in absolutely petrified. There was Ickes sitting behind his big desk with his shirt sleeves rolled up. "Are you the fellow that's been writing all those letters?" "Yes, sir." "Sit down. Why'd you do that?" "Because I reckoned that that's what you'd want done. You're responsible, and I thought it was right to let those people know they're going to be protected, that the machinery will be set up. I just assumed it as a matter of fact." "Well, I'm going to tell you something. You assumed right, and I'm going to make you the first general counsel of the Petroleum Labor Policy Board."

I didn't know the difference between a collective agreement and a patch of potatoes, but that did it. Because of this appointment, I was able to meet people like John L. Lewis, Sidney Hillman, many others, and I was just twenty-six years old.

We had to develop a whole body of labor law. The NLRB had just been formed, and Francis Biddle was then chairman. A strike had been called out in Enid, Oklahoma, against the Franklin Oil Refining Company, and there were hundreds of workers, men and women, out on the street. A request came to Dr. Leiserson to intervene and settle the dispute, and I was asked to go out and settle it. I had never seen a labor dispute. I got myself three books on labor relations and collective bargaining. I took the train from Washington to Oklahoma. I was met by a group of strikers as the "federal man" who had come in. Their saviour was arriving. This was in 1934, when life was very different. I met with them that night and listened to their grievances. I decided that the logical thing to do next would be to talk with the employer, which I did the next day. I tried to settle the matter, but it seemed there was no way I could. Finally, I called Leiserson and said, "You'd better get somebody out here who knows something about this. I'm getting no place fast. I've been here now two weeks, and I'm ashamed to face these people. I'm getting nowhere. I'm narrowing the thing, but I can't get an agreement." He said, "Now, Dave, you just stay. Be fair and persist and settle it." I said, "All right. Those are my orders."

The leader for the workers in the oil union was a fellow called Wildcat Williams. He was half Cherokee Indian and a big drinker. I got along with him very well during the course of the day, but in the afternoons he had a few drinks and got nasty. The company finally agreed that they would settle, and I got an agreement which became a model, although I had no idea of its significance then. It called for a dues check-off, which was revolutionary at that time, a closed shop—whatever the book said to get I got. The employer said, "We'll do it." I met with the committee of workers in my hotel room, and Wildcat Williams said to me, "We're not going to do it." He was drunk. He had about seven women and men on his committee. He said, "You've sold us out to management." I said, "What!" I'd checked all this, and his committee was completely behind what I had done. He made more nasty statements about selling out to management. I was so frustrated and furious, I hit him. I was young and vigorous, but he was pretty young, too. He pulled himself up and said, "Okay. You've got a deal." That was the first contract in the industry that protected the unions.

In the Enid strike, there was a question of hours and wages, but that was peripheral. The real issue at that time was recognition of the union as the representative of the workers in the refinery. At that period there was great resistance to the trade union movement and efforts to break workers' attempts to organize. What was at stake at Enid was whether the refinery would recognize the Oil Field, Gas Well, and Refinery

Workers' Union as the representative of the workers. That was why the closed shop was so important. Having a closed shop meant having a continuing treasury—through a dues checkoff—to reinforce the activities of the union. Wages were very low at that time, and we were talking about reducing the work week. But the fundamental issue was recognition.

When I came back, this was considered quite an accomplishment. Calvert Magruder, who had taught me torts at Harvard Law School, called me on the phone. Francis Biddle said, "You know, now we're setting up the NLRB. We'd like you to be our first regional attorney in New York, covering New York, New Jersey, and Connecticut. You've just done this fantastic thing in Enid; you've set up the board." I was by then an expert! "And we'd like you to go . . ." "I don't know anything about it," I said. "Well, you know more than any of us. Look what you've just done. Why don't you go to New York, set up this structure, and be the counsel for our administrator there, Eleanor Herrick. We think that you'll be able to find a case up there that may help us determine the constitutionality of the National Labor Relations Act, the Wagner Act." This was still not a constitutionally established piece of legislation.

I went to New York and set up the first office of the National Labor Relations Board in that area. I proceeded to administer the legal side of the act. We had a lawsuit involving the Associated Press for alleged refusal to bargain in good faith and dismissal of employees because they tried to organize—*Associated Press v. NLRB* (1937). The complaint was filed by the Newspaper Guild, the president of which was Heywood Broun. His lawyer was a very celebrated First Amendment expert, Morris Ernst. They came to me and said, "We want to bring action against the Associated Press and have our people reinstated and have our Guild recognized. We appeal to you."

I investigated and decided they had a model case under the act. I issued the complaint and brought the case to hearing. The examiner decided that the employees should be reinstated and that there should be recognition of the Guild for collective bargaining. The Associated Press appealed to the Second Circuit Court of Appeals of Learned Hand, Gus Hand; it was a very distinguished bench. In this case, Charles Fahy, our general counsel, asked me to participate in the argument. The lawyer for the Associated Press was John W. Davis. Imagine the consternation of a youth like me having to argue against John W. Davis. It was a straight constitutional issue, depending upon the interpretation of the Interstate Commerce clause.

Davis came into court like a king, followed by three or four associates carrying his briefcase and his papers. We argued, he argued, we ar-

gued. Fahy and I divided the arguments. We won the case. The Second
Circuit Court of Appeals decided that the act was constitutional and
that the workers had the right to organize. I made a record of the case,
and I'd gotten the decision. The Associated Press appealed to the Supreme Court of the United States. Charles Fahy argued the case and I
assisted him. Ours was one of the three Wagner Act cases that the Court
decided at the same time. The Wagner Act was constitutional. That was
a historic moment in the period of the New Deal. (Once that was done, I
decided to leave. I got married and went into private law practice.)

I lived at 1718 Q Street with Paul Freund and two or three other
young lawyers before I was married. It was then that we got to know
Tom Corcoran and Ben Cohen. They came to our house constantly to
exchange views on what should be done on legislation they were working on for the President. We were all young, full of ideals and hopes for
our country, concerned about the terrible economic and social difficulties that confronted us. We were doing a job that gave very great satisfaction. Ben was the philosopher, the scholar, the innovator of social reforms. Tom was brilliant, but he was more gregarious and had more of a
political orientation. He was able to be persuasive with the President on
issues. They were two absolutely opposite types of personalities, yet they
inspired each other, they worked well with each other, they reinforced
each other. One couldn't have done the job without the other. It was a
unique combination. Tom could not only draft and innovate but also
talk effectively with leaders of Congress and get their views and support.
He could talk effectively at the White House. Ben couldn't do that; Ben
didn't have that. So Tom became the spokesman for their combined intellectual effort. But the biggest input on the intellectual side came from
Ben.

In the Interior Department, a whole new world opened up for me, a
world of important people. One day while I was working on a draft decision for the Petroleum Labor Policy Board, Sidney Hillman came to
visit Dr. Leiserson. Hillman at that time was a giant and "Clear it with
Sidney" was often heard. He had access to the White House equal to
anyone's. I was introduced to him by Leiserson. Hillman said, "Young
man, what are you doing?" I replied, "I'm trying to draft a decision, but
I can't tell you about it because it's confidential. We're trying to find a
solution to a problem." He said, "I've had a lot of experience in my life
and remember what I'm telling you. There are never solutions to problems. Don't say that you're finding a solution. If you find it politically
useful to use that word, do it, but don't kid yourself. The best you can do
is make accommodations, and make them in good faith." Later on, that
advice helped me very much. He also said, "If you're dealing with labor
relations, don't think that your decision is the best one. It's better to

have the parties agree among themselves, even if it's not a good agreement, than to decide by yourself even if you make a perfect decision. What the parties agree upon, they've done themselves. It's much better than their having to accommodate themselves to your edict, your decision."

In that same period I first met John L. Lewis. I remember having lunch with him and Leiserson at an Italian restaurant. I remember his saying to Leiserson, "I'm finished. We're defeated, we've nothing. I have a dues-paying membership of 3,000 people, and I have a bankrupt treasury. I cannot cope with the problems of my workers." And Leiserson said, "But that's why Franklin D. Roosevelt has provided the National Labor Relations Act to give you the laws you need to protect your leadership and your people, so take hope." Of course, he did and he built one of the strongest institutions in the country and became a political factor. Later he turned against FDR.

At the same time that we were developing labor policy and social policy, we were engaging in the administration and development of the Social Security system. There are probably about two people in this country who know that the legislation for the Social Security system and the training of people to administer it were done with the technical assistance of the International Labor Organization. At the request of Frances Perkins, the Secretary of Labor, they sent teams here. They devised legislative machinery, and they trained our people. John Winant, who had been governor of New Hampshire, was the first administrator of the Social Security system. Later he became the director general of the ILO. During the war, he was our ambassador to the Court of St. James's. After the war, I became the director general of the ILO.

The American people were getting an education in social policy and labor relations. There had been no Social Security system, no employment exchanges, no occupational health and safety regulations for the protection of workers in mining or other hazardous occupations. All of these things were innovations. Europeans had these things, but they had a much longer history, a greater tradition. They had gone through the industrial revolution and periods of social conflict. Governments abroad had responded to their problems. Unions were recognized, although there was labor strife. There was a body of experience there relevant to our problems at that time which could be drawn upon. That body of experience reposed to a considerable extent in the ILO, which came into existence in 1919. The U.S. government, through the decision of FDR, became a member of the ILO, even though it was not a member of the League of Nations and the ILO at that time was part of the League of Nations. It was the only international organization that the U.S. government belonged to in the thirties.

My interest in social policy goes back to my youth. I was raised by immigrant parents in a small village in Somerset County, New Jersey. I sold newspapers, raked lawns, did all sorts of things to make a few cents. Although we were not a starving family, every little bit helped. For three summers I worked with a railroad gang of Italian immigrants. Their job was to keep the railroad ties level; I was the water boy. These workers opened a whole new dimension for me. They spoke very little English, they worked hard, they lived on the other side of the tracks, they looked after me like a baby. They shared with me; they gave me whatever they had. They introduced me into their homes, and I met their families. I got to know first hand the aspirations and problems of immigrant workers. When I went to work in the New Deal and problems came up, I saw the needs of the people against this background.

As a kid, I also worked at Johns Manville in New Jersey. I remember people becoming ill because they were breathing asbestos. They were difficult conditions, but I didn't think of them as exploitation. It was just part of the time. There was a lack of understanding of what could be done. Later in life, I could do something—when I was Under Secretary of Labor, and Acting Secretary of Labor, and director general of the ILO. So when you have the authority, if you've got that kind of background, unless something's wrong with you, it has to be translated into some positive channel.

FDR was the inspiration. Somehow in his fireside chats and his articulation of the problems that confronted the country, he inspired us as young people to reach out to help. When I took my first job with the government, I didn't know what my pay was going to be. When I was asked to come to Washington to work, I borrowed $50 because I knew I could live on that for two weeks, until I got my first pay check. This was pretty much the way the young people felt. There's a lot to be said for bringing young people into service, and there's a lot to be said for putting them under the supervision of more experienced people.

When FDR died, I was in the army. I sat down on the curbside and cried. That was the end of a period, the end of a chapter. But by then we were in our thirties.

PAUL A. FREUND

I went to the Solicitor General's office in early 1935. Stanley Reed moved there from the general counsel's office of the RFC. I stayed until 1939 when I came back to Harvard to teach. Of course those years included the dramatic constitutional crises, the Court-packing plan, the changes in the Court personnel, from 1937 on.

Stanley Reed's background as an agricultural and banking lawyer was not an obvious preparation for the Solicitor Generalship, but he possessed qualities that made him an excellent choice for that office at that time. His thoughtful judgment, painstaking preparation, and candid advocacy earned the confidence of the Court, though not necessarily a majority of its votes. When he was elevated to a place on the Court in 1938 he was succeeded by Robert Jackson, whose experience as a trial lawyer and as the head, successively, of the tax and antitrust divisions of the Department of Justice, equipped him admirably for the post of Solicitor General. But his outstanding quality was his gift of appellate advocacy. Even the members of his staff who had written the brief in a case were fascinated by the distinctive turn of phrase and thought that he fashioned in oral argument: this tribute from juniors, normally the most critical observers, is the ultimate accolade for a barrister.

The staff of the S.G.'s office was small—eight or nine youngish members—but exceptionally able and dedicated. Most had served recently as law clerks to Supreme Court Justices. Among them in the office for varying lengths of time were Warner Gardner,[11] Harold Leventhal, Arnold Raum, Robert Stern, Alger Hiss, Henry Hart, and Charles Wyzanski.

Wyzanski was the most brilliant of the government advocates. He argued the Labor Relations Act cases, or at least participated in the arguments. (In those days two hours might be allowed, so counsel could divide the time.) He also argued the Social Security Act cases. He always spoke without notes, indeed without any books on the lectern, referring to cases from memory by volume and page. It was a tour de force, but more important, the arguments were extremely cogent and persuasive. After the Social Security argument, John W. Davis got hold of Secretary Perkins and said, "In my palmiest days, I could not have touched that argument." One could hardly imagine a higher compliment.

How I felt about the Court can be best summed up in a remark attributed to Justice Cardozo, "We are no longer a court." A majority of the Justices seemed to lose their judicial temperament and become animated by aversion to the New Deal. I think the President's Court-pack-

11. When Warner Gardner was in the Solicitor General's office, he was asked to try to figure out what could be done to control what seemed to be the excesses of the Supreme Court. He came up with the idea of an enlarged Court, the Court-packing plan. As a former clerk to Justice Stone, Gardner later confessed his part in the plan to Stone. The Justice's view was, according to Gardner, "a charitable one, that I was young and foolish."

ing plan, extraordinary and almost incredible as it might otherwise seem, can only be understood in the context of the Supreme Court's behavior up to 1937. It was the behavior, excluding of course Justices Stone, Brandeis, and Cardozo, and on occasion Hughes, of political partisans.

Why the Court behaved as it did is an interesting question. What motivated Justices who consistently voted against Roosevelt it's hard to know or to separate the personal from the principled. I think that some Justices felt that the President was establishing a dictatorship, that he was running roughshod over interests of property and entrenched economic interests, that perhaps he was such a fool he was being misled by radical advisers. If you read the letters that are now available, from Van Devanter to members of his family, and the letters of McReynolds to the members of his family, you will see the depth of feeling they had about the New Deal and about FDR. McReynolds wrote in a letter that FDR was "acting like a crazy man. I really think he is."[12]

One can differ about the merits of certain decisions regarding the New Deal, but there are decisions that an impartial observer could only describe as not the work of disinterested, impartial judges. For instance, the Court held unconstitutional by five to four the Railroad Retirement Act on the ground that to give pensions to railway employees on retirement was not within the commerce power of Congress, since it had nothing to do with the efficiency of the railroad. To give money to former employees, they said, was not related to the administration of the railroad business. That was too much even for Chief Justice Hughes, who wrote a sharp dissent.[13]

Similarly, in the first Securities and Exchange Commission case, *Jones v. SEC*, where the SEC had begun an investigation regarding certain securities covered by a registration statement, and where the issuer then withdrew the registration, a majority of the Court condemned the SEC for continuing the investigation. Though one might argue about the merits of the commission's action, Justice Sutherland's opinion upsetting the SEC's order likened it to the work of the Star Chamber in England. That comparison was drawn, Justice Cardozo said in dissent, "with denunciatory fervor," adding, "historians may find hyperbole in the sanguinary simile."[14]

12. Willis Van Devanter Papers, Library of Congress, Washington, D.C.; James McReynolds Papers, Alderman Library, University of Virginia, Charlottesville.
13. In *Railroad Retirement Board v. Alton Railroad Co.* (1935), the Supreme Court ruled five to four that the Railroad Retirement Act of 1934 was unconstitutional because it violated the Due Process clause and the Fifth Amendment to the Constitution and because it involved matters (pensions) outside Congress's powers under the Commerce clause.
14. In *Jones v. SEC* (1936), the Supreme Court upheld the right of a registrant to withdraw his securities registration statement (delaying the marketing of the securities in question)

In the case of the NRA, the Supreme Court held it unconstitutional not on one ground but two. That is, the Court delivered two lethal blows, contrary to accepted judicial performance. The traditional canon is to decide on the least drastic ground, not to deliver two death blows when one will do. The Supreme Court held the act unconstitutional, not merely as an excessive delegation of power to the President, but as beyond the power of Congress under the Commerce clause, thus foreclosing efforts to amend and revise the statute by giving less power to the President. Not only would the ground of undue delegation have sufficed, it would also have enabled the Congress to take a second look and have a second opportunity to legislate on the general subject.

I think, in retrospect, Felix Frankfurter's position on the Court-packing plan was the soundest. He was roundly criticized, then being a professor at the Harvard Law School in 1937, for not taking a public stand on the plan. He was, of course, in a personal bind, because of his loyalty to FDR and his deep and longstanding devotion to Justice Brandeis, who would have been affected by the plan. But I think there was a matter of principle too that led him to maintain silence.

He wrote to Judge Learned Hand, who had strongly criticized the plan, saying, "let the misdeeds of the court be aired and at length, and then I care not what plan you propose or oppose." He furnished ammunition to FDR, by letter, in the sense that he called FDR's attention to the misdeeds of the Court, much of which Frankfurter had written about in law reviews and elsewhere over the course of years. I think he regarded the episode as one for education and enlightenment of the public, the Bar, and indeed the Court. I think he would, if forced to, have voted against the plan because it went counter to all his instincts about separation of powers and independence of the judiciary. But to have taken the position early on would have obscured the misconduct of the Court, would have been defensive of the Court; in his opinion that subject needed airing, and of course it got that airing. The Supreme Court in the spring of 1937 did change direction and the Court plan was dropped by the Senate. Though FDR lost the battle, he really won the war.

The majority of the Justices, or at any rate four of them (Hughes did not align himself with any group in the way of a caucus), the Four Horsemen, did foregather. It was understood that three of them were driven to the Court together—McReynolds, Van Devanter, Sutherland—and perhaps Roberts sometimes joined them. The relations

---

before the expiration of the twenty-day "cooling period" and thus evade an SEC order to stop marketing the securities. Justices Cardozo, Brandeis, and Stone dissented.

among the Justices were, shall I say, correct. Actually, Justice Brandeis had very warm feelings toward Justice Van Devanter and toward Justice Roberts. I'll give you an example. Justice Roberts was a guest at a Brandeis tea. When he left, Brandeis escorted him to the door and put his arm around him to say good-bye. When Brandeis came back into the living room, a woman guest said, "I don't understand your attitude toward Justice Roberts. You disagree with him and yet you seem so fond of him." Brandeis said, "Justice Roberts is a young man—he'll learn."

Van Devanter was at the other pole from Brandeis in political and economic philosophy. He was a seasoned judge and Brandeis respected him for his learning and experience, particularly in the area of federal jurisdiction and procedure. Van Devanter was willing to discern ways of avoiding drastic decisions by putting the result on some narrow jurisdictional or procedural ground, and this Brandeis strongly favored. So in a way, he encouraged Van Devanter as an ally, or a potential ally. Indeed, on Van Devanter's birthday in one of the mid-thirty years, Brandeis wrote him a congratulatory note saying, "Take the best care of yourself. The Court never needed you more." This would have shocked the professional liberals, but Brandeis saw in Van Devanter a person of limited yet open-minded vision. He could be reached and touched by appeals to his professional standards. The relations on the Court were not in every case what you might have expected them to be. There were cross-currents of feelings.

I have a particular recollection of Van Devanter in the TVA litigation. There were two big cases. The first case, *Ashwander v. TVA* (1936), had to do with one dam, the Wilson Dam in Alabama, which the TVA took over from the War Department, it having been built as a World War I facility to generate power in order to manufacture ammunition. It was a good opening case for the TVA because it concerned an existing dam, not part of the TVA building program, and the dam had been built pursuant to national defense and navigation and flood control powers. In that case, the Supreme Court ultimately ruled that the dam had been validly constructed and could be operated to convert the power which was inevitably produced by the fall of the river over the dam. The Constitution didn't require that this asset of the government, inevitably produced by a valid structure, must go to waste. This was the sort of thing that appealed to Van Devanter, a conservationist from Wyoming. Hughes wrote the opinion, McReynolds dissented.

In the other case, *Tennessee Electric v. TVA* (1939), the big eighteen-company omnibus suit, all the companies, which were part of the Commonwealth and Southern system represented by Wendell Willkie, brought suit to enjoin the whole TVA program. The lower court held in favor of the TVA and the companies appealed. In the Supreme Court the TVA argued not merely the validity of the TVA statute, but also that the companies did not have standing to challenge the TVA, since there was nothing unfair about the competition and the companies, as competitors, had no standing to challenge the authority of the TVA to operate the dams. The Supreme Court accepted the government's position. Van Devanter went along with the majority. McReynolds and Butler dissented. So one begins to understand why Brandeis saw possibilities in Van Devanter that he didn't see in the others.

I don't think the Chief Justice tried to do any arm-twisting. His relations were quite formal. He was evidently powerful in conference. Brandeis respected him enormously for his ability as a presiding officer. Brandeis said to me admiringly that sometimes the conference would last for six hours and Hughes would do almost all the talking.

There are cases where it seems to me any fair-minded person judging dispassionately would regard the Court as having used excessive power beyond the limits of judicial propriety, and it is that sort of conduct which faced the Department of Justice week after week, month after month, when they brought cases to the Court. It was that kind of conduct which it seemed to me accounted for the excessive force, in turn, that was reflected in the President's Court plan.

In the Gold Clause cases, Reed had been involved when he was at the RFC, and I had worked on that litigation there.[15] I worked rather closely with the people at the Treasury in preparing the brief, because it was to include a great deal of economic material—charts and figures—showing what other countries had done in devaluing their currency, and how our move was in one aspect a defensive one against their moves. That material we relied on the Treasury to furnish. John Laylin of the Treasury was extremely helpful in this respect.

The Supreme Court argument involved two cases: one was the so-called Private Bond case, and the other was the U.S. Liberty Bond case. Homer Cummings, the Attorney General, participated in the argument for the United States. He wanted to be the first to argue so that he would not have to take account of what others said in their arguments. He went to see Chief Justice Hughes to ask that he be allowed to speak first. Since the petitioner in the first case was the private bondholder challenging the government's position, what Cummings asked for was out of the ordinary. The Chief Justice pointed out to Cummings that the peti-

15. In the four Gold Clause cases of 1935, *Perry v. U.S.*, also called the Public Bond case or the Liberty Bond case; *U.S. v. Bankers Trust Co.; Norman v. Baltimore and Ohio Railroad Co.*, also called the Private Bond case; and *Nortz v. U.S.*, the Supreme Court, in effect, upheld the constitutionality of Congressional Joint Resolution No. 44 of 5 June 1933, which nullified the requirement that private and public contracts be payable in gold.

tioner, Norman, who was suing the Baltimore and Ohio Railroad, was himself a young lawyer who would be arguing his first case in the Supreme Court. Given that circumstance, together with the normal procedure of the Court, the Chief Justice did not feel able to grant Cummings's request. Cummings was quite miffed.

I thought privately that Hughes had shown great poise, courage, and good sense in sticking to the rules. Cummings, when his turn came, made a sweeping argument about the powers of a sovereign. He thought, on the whole, our brief was too technical, and the case needed some grander gesture, which he supplied. Stanley Reed was questioned in a close and hostile way by the Four Horsemen, or as Learned Hand called them, the Mastiffs.

There was a break in the argument overnight, and those of us who had worked on the brief gathered with Reed for his final portion of the argument, and with him we tried to bring together the threads of the case which had been rather frayed during all the questioning, and we tried to clear up some possible misunderstandings floating in the air. The result was that Reed made a very coherent, consistent, concise, and helpful statement at the end of the argument. At any rate, the cases were decided five to four for the government, a narrow squeeze.

In the Liberty Bond case, Hughes did a tour de force. He scolded the government for repudiating its promise to pay in gold, in a voice that sounded like that of a Secretary of State rebuking Latin American banana republics for their repudiations. He couldn't take any other position given his background, but ultimately he concluded that there had been no damage to the bondholders, since the devaluation had not produced a corresponding rise in the price level, and since the government had validly closed the market for gold coin and gold bullion. The bondholders, by receiving the nominal face amount of the bonds in dollars, received, in effect, the value that the gold coin would have had for them, given the closed market which the Court did uphold. So Hughes was able to have it both ways. He was able to deliver a moral lecture to the government, and it didn't cost the government a penny. Hughes was very good at that sort of thing, very resourceful.

I participated in only some of the New Deal briefs. I was not involved in the agricultural cases. I did argue in the Rent Control case under OPA[16] and in the Public Utility Holding Company case, the "death sentence" under the Holding Company Act.[17] The Holding

16. The Office of Price Administration was created by FDR under provisions of the Emergency Price Control Act of 1942 to fix price ceilings on all commodities except farm products and to control rents in defense areas.
17. In *Electric Bond and Share Co. v. SEC* (1938), the Supreme Court refused to accept the holding companies' invitation to consider the constitutionality of the "death sentence" provision of the Public Utility Holding Company Act of 1935.

Company Act was the legislative drafting product, as you know, of Ben Cohen, Tom Corcoran, and Jim Landis. It was a very tightly articulated statute. It may have gone to the verge of power, as it was then understood under the Commerce clause, but not over the brink.

A series of companies were our opponents in court, each represented by a different attorney. The ablest of the lot was Charles E. Hughes, Jr., representing, I think, the North American Company; he was extremely fair-minded in his argument. All I remember of my argument is a quip. I said that our opponents maintained that the scatteration of hydroelectric properties under a single holding company was necessary for the geographical reason that rainfall varied in different parts of the country. I said that those who had investigated the subject, like the Federal Trade Commission, concluded that it was not rainfall, but windfalls, that motivated the building of these holding companies. That may have been the decisive argument, I don't know.

I enjoyed the exchanges back and forth with the Court. The opportunity to answer questions is always something to be welcomed because it tells you what's bothering the Court. Unless, of course, it's overdone, when you really have no chance to make a coherent presentation. But a good amount of questioning, I think, is useful.

Some of the argument and questioning, especially by Justice Butler, was extremely hostile. I'm not now speaking of my own experience, but of my observations in the Court when others were arguing. He was a skillful cross-examiner in his days at the Bar. He represented utility companies, and was involved in those old cases of rate-making where expert testimony on the valuation of properties was important. He was very adroit and relentless in trying to break down witnesses, and he used the same techniques against government lawyers. In one case, involving the Bankhead Cotton Act, Reed fainted under that questioning. He had finished a long argument in the basic Agricultural Act case, then came this Bankhead Cotton case. It was a strain, at best, on an advocate to have that immediate sequence of argument, and under questioning of the most fierce kind—Pierce Butler was known in Minnesota as Fierce Butler—Reed sank back, tottered, and collapsed into a chair that was pushed forward for him.

The Court adjourned. Reed revived quickly with smelling salts kept for such occasions by the marshal's office of the Court. He wanted to go on the next day to finish the argument, but wiser counsel, including his wife's, prevailed, and the government submitted the remainder of the case on the brief.

If Butler was fierce, McReynolds was simply sarcastic. Early in an argument he might say, as he did in the *Schechter* case, "The petitioners wanted to sell their chickens on the basis of the customers selecting the chickens from the coop, but the NRA code required that they buy their chickens as they came out of the coop—they refused, and it is for this that your clients have gone to jail?" "Yes, your Honor," counsel said. With that, McReynolds stacked up the briefs, took a rubber band and ostentatiously snapped it around the briefs, dropped them to the floor, leaned back and closed his eyes. It was over.

In the Court's social life—mostly the teas—Court business was not discussed. At the Brandeis teas it never was. One could always tell when Brandeis was especially interested in someone. There was a sort of tacit recognition. For example, if someone in the House or Senate made a remarkably good speech or took a notably sound position during the week, he might receive an invitation to the Brandeis tea. It was like conferring an honor, a knighthood for something splendidly done.

I think the teas were on Sunday. Maybe it varied from year to year. I'll give you one amusing story about the teas. Mrs. Brandeis kept some sort of file on the guests; some were invited fairly regularly, once a year. One of these was a young lawyer who was a favorite of Professor Frankfurter's, Joe Fanelli. On his first visit, the Justice in his usual way asked, "Mr. Fanelli, where are you working?" "The Social Security Administration." And Brandeis, in his characteristic response said, "Don't overstay your time. Go back to your home community." The next year, the same little ritual: "Go back to your home community." The third year, Fanelli was determined to break the monotony, and so when Brandeis said "Go back to your home community," Fanelli countered, "But Mr. Justice, my home community is New York city." Brandeis said, "That's your misfortune," and walked off.

Those of us who were laboring in the vineyard were so absorbed in our daily chores, often overwhelming in weight and volume, that we didn't have the perspective of the historian or the social analyst to see the large implications of what we were doing. Obviously, we knew that we were part of a major movement, but even to call it a movement is perhaps to give it an integrated character it doesn't deserve.

There were a good many cross-pulls involved. NRA was in a sense fostering monopolistic practices, which antitrust policy was combatting. Agricultural policy, at the start at any rate, was rough on sharecroppers, perhaps unduly rewarded large-scale farmers, and was thus at odds with other aspects of New Deal philosophy. It was a time of experiment, and because the economy and the country were in such disrepair, there was a freedom of experiment that was unexampled. The atmosphere is perhaps described by a remark of Justice Brandeis when a guest at one of the teas said—this was early in 1933 at the time of the bank closings—

"The bankers are descending on Washington. They seem utterly hopeless and defeated." And Brandeis said, "Well, aren't they known as the Napoleons of finance?"

When the leaders of the established order were helpless and without any confident ideas, the field was open for young people and new ideas, some of which succeeded, and some of which didn't. We had a President who was extraordinarily open. Perhaps it was a good thing he didn't have a well-rounded, firmly disciplined philosophy and there were some elements that were disharmonious, because no one was sure what the best answer was. But it was a glorious time for obscure people because the big names and the captains of industry and the majors of public life were themselves in a quandary. I think we learned some things from the New Deal experience—what would work and what wouldn't. In a way we are in that same position now because stagflation is something new, it doesn't follow the textbook curves. Economists are at sixes and sevens over how to deal with that. It is a new and strange situation. The New Deal involved a centralization of authority beyond anything that had been foreshadowed. It was a government taking responsibility for what had been thought of as the course of nature, or the business cycle, or Adam Smith, or whatever. The government was taking responsibility for giving direction to the course of national life, to the economy, even to the spirit of our common adventure.

CHAPTER 6

The Draftsmen

Many people were surprised at the quantity and the scope of the legislation that the Roosevelt Administration pushed through Congress during its First Hundred Days in office. They would have been even more startled to learn how and by whom that legislative agenda was drafted and lobbied, for much of the basic work of the New Deal was done by a small group of uncelebrated and underpaid young lawyers who, though just out of law school, were among the most brilliant in the nation. Out of the limelight, operating from obscure offices that concealed their true importance, they put in long hours of unremitting toil, without which the New Deal could not have come to pass. After work, they lived together in cooperative bachelor quarters, where their political intimacy and camaraderie were transformed into an equally brilliant and high-spirited social life. The young men and women who drafted the new laws sacrificed the income and acclaim they might have achieved in private practice because they believed in the New Deal and what it could do for the American people. Their impressions of what it was like to be behind the scenes in those heady early days are still vivid.

FRANK WATSON

The famous Little Red House in Georgetown was neither little nor red. It was quite a good-sized mansion, a three-story building. It was previously used by Ulysses S. Grant as a summer White House during his

term as President. It was a very old structure on a large lot, really quite a
nice place, except for what the years had done to it. Tom Corcoran
found the place and arranged to rent it and have all of us move in. There
were Tom and his brother, Howie Corcoran; Dick Guggenheim, a Republican of the San Francisco Guggenheims and my classmate at Harvard Law School; Ed Burke, later chief counsel of the Securities and
Exchange Commission; Stuart Guthrie, a Bull Mooser and older than
any of us; Merritt N. Willits III of Philadelphia, my former roommate at
Harvard; and myself. People came and went. It was an open house. Ben
Cohen did not live with us. He wanted a little peace and quiet. Dick
Quay and Ed Burling, of the Covington, Burling law firm, Mike
Shaughnessy, Jules Raburn Monroe of New Orleans, and half a dozen
others whom Tom had brought into Washington lived there at various
times.

Tom was the leader of the group, and we all followed. We started
together in the RFC in 1932, but then he placed us in different departments. I went to the Treasury; Merritt Willits stayed at the RFC; Ed
Burke went to the Securities and Exchange Commission.

Tom planned our weekends. One weekend we all went to Virginia
for a golfing venture. Another time we canoed down the Potomac River.
I was in Tom's canoe, and he was going to show me how to run white
water. He dumped us both over in the second rapids we went through.
Sometimes we went to ball games. Tom wanted everybody to be happy
and he kept his eye on everybody. He was an all-engrossing personality.
I count as the most cherished years of my life those I had working for
Tom. He took a couple of us over to see Justice Oliver Wendell Holmes
after the old gentleman was retired. To be in the presence of such a tremendous person was a real experience.

I was the manager of the house for a considerable length of time.
We estimated how much it would cost, which was never quite enough,
and then we assessed everybody. The costs ran out of sight because Tom
would bring in three or four guests any night, without saying a word,
and then other nights there wouldn't be anybody but the cook would
have made a big dinner because nobody reported that he would be out.
It was a poorly managed affair.

When there were enough of us at home evenings to sit around, Tom
played the piano; he played beautifully and we sang. There was very little drinking ever, but nearly everybody had one or two highballs after
dinner. I can remember one evening when one of Tom's friends came
over and brought his own baby grand piano. A moving van arrived and
three or four fellows got the piano up the flight of stairs and into the living room. Tom and his friend played piano duets all evening. Then the
boys picked up the piano and put it back into the moving van.

None of us made big money at that time, but it was a time when everybody was broke and we made, for young fellows our age, good money. Tom set the salaries. I started at $2,400 a year and that was a fabulous amount of money to me. On my $200 a month I sent at least $50 home to help my father. We didn't have expensive tastes, but we did run a household on the most inefficient system you could think of. We had a housekeeper, one helper, and a gardener. The house was old and poorly insulated. The coal came in there by the ton, and it didn't seem to last a week to a truckload.

There was quite a quest for power going on at that time. None of us was particularly interested in power, because we all felt we were going to leave just as soon as things got back to normal. We were going out into the world to earn some real money. We were quite cocky about our ability to accomplish great things in the outside world. Tom encouraged this. He told us not to have any concern about our later years. We were all brilliant. So none of us was fighting for power, and I think this was one of the great strengths in our group.

Tom was my senior by half a dozen years. He recruited others for jobs, working very closely with Felix Frankfurter at Harvard, who fed him names of recent graduates. In January 1933 I was working in a Boston law office, and I received a call from Tom, who wanted me to come to Washington and work for the RFC. He was then working for Stanley Reed, who later became a Supreme Court Justice.

We were a team, working on bank reorganizations. For young lawyers, just a year or so out of law school, it was a very heady experience to sit down and represent the government on a transaction involving some large bank like the Detroit National and watch $15 or $20 million pass across the table to brace up the bank and meet the attorneys for the other side on an equal basis. We were able to handle ourselves because the attorneys coming in from the large law firms were frequently working on their first bank reorganization. Soon most of us were working on our tenth, twelfth, or fifteenth bank reorganization. We knew what to look for. Each attorney worked with a bank examiner, and those fellows were very knowledgeable too. Of the fifteen or sixteen banks I worked on, only one of them later collapsed.

I remember the time I was working on a bank down South, and some gentlemen representing the bank came in and wanted to have the work rushed through. One of them offered me $20 if I would speed up. That was a laughable experience. We said that was typical of the Democrats to offer little people $20 bribes whereas the Republicans would have offered large bribes to big people.

Without any particular title of authority, Tom just ran things. He assigned the work, and he gave us a little background on each bank we were working on. I remember when I went to work on the Page Bank in North Carolina. I believe Ralph Page's father was ambassador to England under Wilson. Tom warned me that there was political power there and I should watch carefully. The bank had loaned most of its money to Ralph Page or his associates in the Ralph Page Farm Machinery Equipment Company, and the Ralph Page this and Ralph Page that. Still we were able to clean the thing up and save the depositors, get the bank on its feet.

Very shortly after the bank holiday, Tom moved a group of us over to the Treasury and we began looking at banks on a broader scale. The Comptroller of the Currency and the Federal Reserve made a quick survey, and we placed banks in two categories: those that could open and stay open and those that had better stay shut until they were infused with more capital in the form of RFC preferred stock.[1] There was a third category: the Bank of America, which was left open because nobody dared do anything with it. It represented too much banking for the state of California.

I remember once working with Tom, trying to convince the Comptroller General of the United States that he should look at things differently.[2] At that time he was threatening to block many of the New Deal expenditures. We kept the pressure on him for a considerable length of time. He was coming up for retirement shortly, so the President decided to let him stay. The new man would be picked carefully. The Comptroller General was taking the point of view that certain legislation went beyond the authority of Congress and, therefore, he was not going to permit the expenditure of government money.

We did feel that we were contributing something. We were moving mountains one shovelful at a time, and every bank that reopened was a help and every insurance company that got going again was a help. I think we made a definite contribution to the Social Security Act, so the Supreme Court had something to go on and did not have to declare it unconstitutional. That was just a technical job.

To give an illustration of how the group worked: Tom would see a job that needed to be done and he'd get one of us and say, "How'd you like to try this?" If things didn't work out well, we'd be back with him again. That's the way I departed from his working group. The President had ideas on housing and Winfield Riefler had some very definite ideas on how to fix up the mortgage market. He worked out the theory of mu-

1. The Comptroller of the Currency of the Treasury Department regulates the national banks and administers the issuance and redemption of Federal Reserve notes. The decision insured that banks would have adequate resources to meet the demands of depositors when they again opened for business.
2. Comptroller General John Raymond McCarl, a Republican from McCook, Nebraska, had virtually unlimited power from his long tenure in office, 1921–1936.

tual mortgage insurance. Win wanted an attorney to help him and to do some of the writing. I had known Win and liked him and Tom suggested me. So I had the chance to write the National Housing Act and take it through Congress.[3] It wasn't the greatest thing at the time, but it was a matter of some significance and I enjoyed it. It went through about sixty-four drafts before all the congressmen and senators were finally satisfied.

I recall several occasions when Harold Ickes, Secretary of the Interior, and Jesse Jones, head of the RFC, were at sword's points. Some of us were writing memorandums for each of them to send the other. We'd call each other to smooth things out, never letting our bosses know that we were engaged in such activity.

In all this, Ben Cohen was a superintellectual. He was above the whole crowd of us. He sat quietly, smoked cigarettes, listened, and said very little most of the time. Our first introduction to him was when he and Tom were writing the Securities Act of 1933. This was a terrific struggle against Wall Street, and they were working with congressional committees. I guess Ben did most of the writing. He was, of course, a genius in that field.

It's difficult now to understand why Wall Street shook and the financial world was scared to death by a $3 billion public works program. Right now $3 billion is hardly worth spending on anything. The whole scale has changed. I remember when the total federal debt topped $30 billion and everybody thought, "We've reached the limit; we can't go any further."

My secretary at that time was Peggy Dowd, who later became Mrs. Tom Corcoran. She was a brilliant individual and a very beautiful girl. She could type so fast you could hardly see the keys move, and at the same time carry on a conversation or ask a question. During this period, I would be up on the Hill all morning, going over the act with the committees. Then I'd come back and Peggy and I would work until midnight, running off copies for the next day's meetings.

In retrospect the Brain Trusters of the Little Red House in Georgetown take on a certain amount of glamour. There was no such glamour at the time. Some columnist wrote that we had a straight line to Moscow. Nothing could be farther from the truth. Not only were we not Communists, we had no sense of what Communists were. We were kids fresh out of law school. Radio was in its infancy, there was no TV, and the daily newspapers did not then report news from all over the world.

---

3. The National Housing Act of 1934 established the Federal Housing Administration, which insured loans made by private lending institutions to middle-income families to repair and modernize their homes and to build new houses. FDR hoped to revive the housing construction industry.

In those days, I had some idea that Communism meant taking all the property there was and putting it into a pot and dividing it by the number of people and giving each person a share.

We arrived with no particular theories about remaking America or saving the world. I never heard Tom mention anything of that kind. He was in Washington to straighten out a mess, and as soon as the mess was straightened out he was going to leave. And so were all the rest of us.

Our group was not deeply involved in crusading. At the Agricultural Department they had a more radical attitude. We did work a bit on the Social Security Act, but I personally didn't have too much enthusiasm for the idea that a nation could insure itself against mass unemployment. I never heard Ben voice any different point of view. We followed the economics of Winfield Riefler because he had a better grasp of economics than any of us. His philosophy was that we had a credit mechanism that had come to a grinding halt and that it was necessary for us to get the whole mechanism going again. That is about all the wild braintrusting we did. It was a pretty modest sort of thing.

JOSEPH L. RAUH, JR.

I first met Ben Cohen early in September of 1935. By that time Ben already had three major pieces of legislation to his credit. He was the dominant figure in drafting the Securities Act of 1933, the Securities Exchange Act of 1934, and the Public Utility Holding Company Act of 1935.

Later, in the winter of 1935, I visited the Little Red House. I would go on a Sunday morning and talk to Ben. Stuart Guthrie had a dog named Red Duke, and Ben just loved that dog. That showed a side of him that I had never imagined. He is a great dog lover. Ben and Tom and Stuart Guthrie and some others lived in the Little Red House. It was very pleasant. They had a big living room on the second floor with two grand pianos. Ben made masterful contributions. He never had an office in the White House; neither did Tom. Tom was very mobile, but Ben wasn't. He was the Think Man in the Interior Department. Tom would walk in and out of everybody's office. Tom and I used to smile when he would grab the telephone in my lousy little office in the Interior Department, dial, and say, "Hello, Mr. Secretary? This is Tom Corcoran. I'm calling from the White House."

From September 1935 to September 1936 I worked for Ben and

Tom. My physical presence, though, was in Ben's office; he was the general counsel of the National Power Policy Committee,[4] a subdivision of the Interior Department. I was an attorney in the Interior Department, and my job was the defense of the Public Utility Holding Company Act. The holding companies were responsible for high utility rates, and they defrauded their stockholders. They would take operating companies and milk them for the benefit of the holding company. It was a very fraudulent process. Once the act passed in the summer of 1935, every holding company in the country brought suit to upset the law, to have it declared unconstitutional. They'd all said it was unconstitutional when Ben was putting it through the Senate, and they were carrying out their previous threats to bring these suits. If Ben took certain things out of the bill in one place because he had to make a concession, he'd just slip them in somewhere else. Ben's whole strategy was brilliant in every detail. One might have thought that the SEC or Justice would be in charge of defending the bill. But Tom and Ben were deputized as special assistants to the Attorney General in charge of defending the Holding Company Act. It was possibly as great a legal feat as was ever pulled off. The Supreme Court of 1935–36 was a very conservative Court, which would have held the Holding Company Act unconstitutional. So Ben devised a strategy of stalling, and he stalled and stalled. This was the brilliant way he handled it. He stopped the suits against the government by having the Attorney General announce they were not going to prosecute anyone for not complying with the act. This ploy made the companies mad, because it kept them from bringing suit. John W. Davis thought he had a way of getting a quick decision. A holding company in Baltimore was in bankruptcy. Davis and his friends dreamed up the idea that they would have the trustee of bankruptcy ask the Court for instructions on whether to register under the Holding Company Act but suggest to the Court, "Instruct them not to on the grounds that the bill is unconstitutional." By then Ben had closed up the normal way one would get a decision, namely, an injunction against the government. Instead the government announced, "We're not going to do anything so you can't enjoin us." A pretty high-class struggle took place between Ben Cohen and John W. Davis.

On Ben's fortieth birthday, September 23, we were in front of Judge William C. Coleman in Baltimore. John W. Davis showed up and argued for a bondholder of the bankrupt company that he didn't think they should register and that the judge should hold it unconstitutional.

4. Created in July 1934 to recommend legislation to reform public utility holding companies; its report, in March 1935, formed the basis of the Public Utility Holding Company Act of 1935.

It was pretty dramatic. Here was a former Democratic presidential candidate arguing a case against the New Deal. You couldn't get into the courtroom unless you were part of the machinery. My role wasn't bad. I was told to find the bondholder that Davis said he represented. He turned out to be a dentist. I found him in Baltimore and said, "Would you come down to the court or do I have to bring a subpoena for you?" He came. We put him on the stand and asked, "Do you have a lawyer here?" He said, "Oh yes, some guy named Davis," and he pointed to John W. Davis. It was a great act. We lost in the district court. The judge said, "It's unconstitutional. Don't register." We had failed.

Ben then appealed to the Court of Appeals for the Fourth Circuit. In January Tommy Corcoran argued that case. Ben wrote the briefs, and we lost. The Court of Appeals affirmed the district court, and that, they said, would knock out the statute. Some were saying we had to petition for *certiorari* to the Supreme Court. Ben disagreed. "We're going to be against the review by the Supreme Court." We said, "Ben, how can you possibly not review a decision of a court of appeals saying your bill's unconstitutional?" He replied that it didn't make any difference. "We want the Supreme Court not to act." He was ready with the third arrow. He had a case that he wanted to send to the Court in about two years against the Electric Bond and Share Co., a large holding company. All he did was start one civil suit against Bond and Share to make them register. It was the only case where the government said, "We're going to tell the Supreme Court not to review this, that a good case is coming on Bond and Share, a collusive suit."

Everyone feared that Ben could not possibly get the Supreme Court not to review this case. One of the collusive parties petitioned for *certiorari,* but the government of the United States kept urging the Supreme Court not to review it. Ben was angry because the Court wouldn't give him time to prepare the review. He kept rewriting it all night for three nights. We finally filed it and said how skeptical we were. That same day the Germans went into the Rhineland. Ben and his acolytes were watching the ticker. There was a flash, and we figured when we heard the bell that it had something to do with the Rhine. "The Supreme Court today denied *certiorari* in the Public Utility Holding Company case." Ben got exactly what he wanted the way he wanted it. The *Electric Bond and Share* case got there a couple of years later. The Court had changed by then and Ben won.

People would come to Ben from other agencies to get his advice. He was a Mother Superior to all the young lawyers in town. He would give advice very freely, and he very much enjoyed giving it.

Ben and Tom worked well together. Tom would come in the evenings and help Ben with his briefs. He was a very good lawyer. His capacities in this regard were often underestimated. It was the only law office I've ever been in that stayed open around the clock. A secretary came in at suppertime and stayed as long as they wanted him. If they quit at midnight or if they went through till the girls came in the next day, he stayed. We used to have jokes about the hours. The girls, Sophie Mack and Peggy Dowd, later Mrs. Corcoran, would work during the day, and sometimes Peggy would come in at night and help. Peggy was beautiful as well as a wonderful secretary. We used to kid Sophie about being in love with Ben. "The only way you're ever going to get to sleep with Ben," I would kid her, "is to go to the movies with him." He loved movies, but when the music started he went right to sleep. He would talk about how he loved movies, but I don't think he ever saw any. Another one of the jokes told was that our son, Michael, was conceived on Ben's office couch because he never let anybody go home at night. My wife would come down and spend the evening reading a book. There were times when it just seemed you'd have to get some rest. The experience with those two great lawyers was well worth it.

I left Ben in September of 1936 and went to Justice Cardozo, but I continued to see Ben all the time. My clearest memory of that period is February 1937, when President Roosevelt sent to Congress the Court-packing plan. Ben called it a most ridiculous thing. He said, "They're just doing it all wrong," and he added, "Tom and I were not consulted." Roosevelt never let anybody know the whole story.

Both Ben and Tom were burned up. They were told about the plan the day before it was announced. The bill never passed. Senator Burton Wheeler of Montana defeated it. Ben was the architect of changing it. He turned the problem around. The great speech by FDR was at least partly his. Ben and Tom made the greatest contribution to the speech in the part where FDR says, "We need a wage and hour law and we need it *now.*" And he hit the word *now.* They listed all the bills the Court had knocked out and said, "We need this and we need it *now.*" That turned it around to where it should have been. I mean, you were packing the Court to get a different result. I'm not sure to this day which side I really was on, but that's a different matter. The way Roosevelt set it up at first was dishonest because he didn't state his real reason. The real reason was to change most of the Supreme Court's decisions, and this crap about not changing their decisions and "we just want to have a few more judges because these judges are overworked" was rubbish. Whether they won or lost by doing it this way is hard to judge. Roosevelt may have lost a battle, but he won a war. The Court reversed itself.

In 1938 when Justice Cardozo died I asked Ben what he wanted me

to do. He sent me to Calvert Magruder, the general counsel of the Wage
and Hour division, who needed an assistant. I knew about the wage and
hour law because when I visited his office he would show me the different drafts of the bill—the Fair Labor Standards Act that was passed in
the summer of 1938. We consulted Ben all the time about problems at
the Wage and Hour division.

Ben started to get interested in the war in the winter of 1937–38. I
remember him coming up to visit Justice Cardozo, and I sat with them.
They were talking about Hitler, and Ben said, "The real problem now is
that most of the people in the New Deal don't have any experience in
foreign affairs." He became a real force in the foreign policy field. He
shifted around in 1938 from the domestic area to foreign policy. He also
worked on the Dumbarton Oaks conference leading to the creation of
the United Nations. He was one of the draftsmen of the whole peace
movement.

KENNETH CRAWFORD

In the early thirties "Corcoran and Cohen" entered the language of
political controversy as though the two names were one word, "Cor-
coranandcone." It was a word much used in congressional and campaign debate. In Wall Street and in big business board rooms it was pe-
jorative. Thomas Gardiner Corcoran and Benjamin V. Cohen drafted
and lobbied through Congress much of the legislation that came close to
revolutionizing American government in the early days of the Roosevelt
New Deal.

Corcoran and Cohen were among the first of the bright young
Harvard Law School alumni recommended for service in the New Deal
Brain Trust by Professor Felix Frankfurter. Both had practiced law on
Wall Street and were knowledgeable about the operations of the securi-
ties exchanges. So their first assignment was to draft the Securities Act
of 1933.

During the famous First Hundred Days in the spring of 1933, Sam
Rayburn, who was engineering the White House bills through Congress,
became concerned with the drafting of the Securities Act. He telephoned Moley at the White House, who in turn telephoned Felix
Frankfurter at Harvard, requesting help. Felix then sent Jim Landis and
Ben Cohen to Washington and called on Corcoran at the Reconstruction Finance Corporation to join them. For a while they steamed on

Thomas Corcoran

Benjamin V. Cohen

ahead but, as Ben found Landis "too serious, as if he were carrying Atlas on his shoulder," Corcoran devised a promotion for Landis to another agency. The team then forged on ahead and shoved the reform legislation through in record time. Corcoran claimed to have gained twenty pounds drinking sugar-loaded coffee to keep him awake for the night sessions. Ben remembers the hotel bill did not get paid until 1936 when the Democrats became solvent.

This collaboration went on to accomplish the Securities Exchange Act of 1934, the Public Utility Holding Company Act of 1935, the National Housing Act, the Tennessee Valley Authority, and the Fair Labor Standards Act, the wage and hour law—some of the most important and permanent of the New Deal reforms.

Cohen and Corcoran argued about where they first met, Cohen claiming it was at Harvard, Corcoran finding New York more plausible. They hit it off immediately. Both were bachelors. Corcoran, worried by Cohen's affinity to New York, leased a large Italianate house in Georgetown, at 3238 R Street, once the residence of President Grant. Frankfurter filled the house with brainy Harvard Law School graduates. After a while, Cohen ceased commuting back and forth.

To some anti-New Dealers, the Little Red House was a sinister meeting place for revolutionary plotters. It was associated with the charge made by Dr. William A. Wirt, a midwestern school principal, based on a conversation he overheard at a party, that radicals associated with the New Deal regarded Roosevelt as merely "the Kerenski of the American Revolution." The Lenin was to come later. A congressional committee solemnly investigated. It found no cause for alarm since most of Wirt's revolutionaries were known to be fairly mild reformers.

Later Corcoran and Cohen rented an apartment at 1610 K Street, as a working hideout. This in due course became known as the "Little White House." The work habits of the partners required privacy. They were capable of laboring at top speed for forty-eight hours at a stretch and of wearing out several shifts of stenographers while at it. To relax from such a session, Cohen habitually sought out a movie to sleep through. He found a sound track more soporific than silence.

In the beginning Corcoran and Cohen were said to have "a passion for anonymity" and they did, in fact, feeling that their job could better be done out of the spotlight. By cooperating with certain newspaper correspondents, they managed for a time to keep their names out of print or, at worst, on the inside pages.

Whatever anonymity they had achieved ended with the fight over the so-called "death sentence" imposed by the Utility Holding Company legislation. Senator Owen Brewster of Maine, who had been one of the supporters of the legislation, changed sides in mid-conflict. When Corcoran remonstrated with him, Brewster reported that he had been threatened with cancellation of plans for a tide-harnessing hydroelectric development in Maine—the $36 million Passamaquoddy Dam. At a congressional hearing, Corcoran denied threatening Brewster. Brewster called him a liar. "We'll see who's a liar," Corcoran replied. From then on Corcoran's cover, such as it was, was blown. That committee, like many others over the years, failed to censure or even reprove Corcoran, who had a winning way with House and Senate committees.

All pretense that the team of Corcoran and Cohen operated without White House credentials was abandoned after the Brewster uproar. At the start of their collaboration, the partners got their orders through Raymond Moley, the senior Brain Truster, not from the President himself. This changed, some say, when Corcoran began attending parties at the White House playing his accordion. Ben Cohen insists, however, that Corcoran caught FDR's attention as a gifted speech writer. "Tom put a lilt in the language" according to Ben. From then on, "Tom Corcoran calling from the White House" became an effective lobbying ploy with representatives and senators.

Shy and retiring by nature, Cohen was delighted to leave the party-livening and legislative lobbying to his associate while he got on with the laborious business of law writing. Corcoran's bluff gregariousness complemented Cohen's quiet thoughtfulness.

Cohen's first official job in the Roosevelt Administration was counsel to the Public Works Administration under Secretary of Interior Harold Ickes. Later he became general counsel to the National Power Policy Committee, another Ickes agency. Both titles could be described as covers. Cohen worked in private in an old shabby government building, while Corcoran pursued the power brokers on the Hill. Technically, Corcoran remained with the Reconstruction Finance Corporation, where he had landed late in the Hoover Administration. Both performed their official duties while at the same time operating as a task force for the White House. They were also available as speech writers for front men in the executive and legislative branches.

Corcoran, in particular, had established a reputation for catchy political phrase-making and was much in demand. He also became an invaluable Administration operator because he had forged a useful network of friends in executive departments and agencies and in Congress. He knew exactly where to put his finger on the right expert for almost any kind of job. He influenced judicial appointments. He traveled with the President on political campaigns and in one of them organized an Independents-for-Roosevelt movement headed by Mayor Fiorello H.

La Guardia of New York and Senator George Norris of Nebraska. He served as the White House expert on the politics of the Northwest. In 1938 he became involved in the ill-fated attempt to "purge" certain anti-New Deal Democrats by defeating them for reelection. Corcoran did not always agree with the President's decisions and stratagems but as long as Roosevelt lived he admitted no doubts, at least not in public. He was less than enthusiastic, for example, about the Court-packing scheme, feeling confident that time and patience would take care of the problem of liberalizing the Court's membership.

His identification with Roosevelt made him an easy target for the New Deal's detractors. Once he tried unsuccessfully to persuade Amos Pinchot, brother of Governor Gifford Pinchot of Pennsylvania, to accept a place on the board of the Reconstruction Finance Corporation. Pinchot said later that Corcoran, in the course of their conversation, had suggested scattering money from airplanes as an efficient way of priming the economic pump and sharing the wealth. The incident got almost as much notoriety as a remark later attributed to Harry Hopkins, who succeeded Corcoran at the President's right hand, that the Administration's strategy was to "spend and spend, elect and elect."

Yet when he left government in 1940, Corcoran's law office was besieged by some of the same corporate leaders who had most volubly denounced him as a government official. So many of them became his clients that his law firm, Corcoran, Foley, Youngman, and Rowe, grew and prospered through subsequent decades.

Newspapers usually identified him in his private career as a lawyer-lobbyist. He called himself a lawyer-entrepreneur and said his personal fortunes needed minding and that he wanted to get out from under the Hatch Act,[5] which outlawed political activity by government employees. Corcoran had left Wall Street with a comfortable nest egg, but not a fortune. Sizeable paper profits had been wiped out by the stock market crash, for unlike Cohen, he had not sold out before the collapse. Moreover, Corcoran and Cohen had drawn on their own funds to the tune of about $5,000 a year each at times to finance some of their extracurricular services to the New Deal.

Cohen in retirement once proposed the creation of a presidential Executive Council of five to eight leading citizens whose duty it would be to study problems of national policy and advise the President of its findings. Power of decision would remain with the Chief Executive, but the Council would be available for assistance in gathering and sorting information necessary to wise decision-making. "Presidents, even the

5. Two acts, named for Senator Carl A. Hatch of New Mexico, passed in 1939 and 1940 to regulate expenditures, contributions, and procedures in political campaigns.

greatest of them," he said, "need unbiased judgment and support from persons they can regard as peers." He once supplied a President he regarded as one of the greatest with that kind of support, though he would have disclaimed such a notion as pretentious.

These two men, although they never were elected to public office and never had impressive titles, probably influenced the recent course of American government more than most members of Congress and most Cabinet officers, past or present.

CHAPTER 7

From Hoover
to Roosevelt

On occasion, it has been argued that the New Deal actually began under Hoover and that it was merely an elaboration of patterns and programs already under way. The best example cited of Hoover's New Deal was the Reconstruction Finance Corporation. But Hoover resisted creation of the RFC, and accepted it only reluctantly under strong congressional pressure to do something to provide federal relief to combat the depression. Also, he insisted that the RFC not make loans or grants to individuals, that it make loans only to corporations, banks, and governmental agencies. The RFC was half-hearted, weakly financed, and ineffective.

The RFC Act passed early in 1932 and provided the agency $500 million in capital and authority to borrow an additional $2 billion to provide emergency loans to banks, life insurance companies, building and loan associations, railroads, and farm mortgage associations. Within six months, the RFC had made $1.2 billion in loans, yet the depression was getting worse.

Under Roosevelt, the RFC grew far beyond these limitations. The new President quickly increased its capital resources and adapted it to promote recovery. Instead of just lending money to banks, the RFC bought stock in them, thus increasing the banks' capital instead of their debt. Under its new director, Jesse Jones, the RFC sprouted a vast empire of subsidiary corporations: the federal mortgage agencies, the Commodity Credit Corporation, the Electric Home and Farm Authority, and the Export-Import Bank. Instead of directing its efforts at the top of the economic pyramid, the RFC under Roosevelt directed its resources at the base of the pyramid, funneling aid to those most in need.

FDR recognized, too, that more was needed. Thus, in June 1933 he pushed through Congress the National Industrial Recovery Act. The NIRA established the National Recovery Administration under General Hugh S. Johnson and the Public Works Administration under Secretary of the Interior Harold Ickes. Patterned after the trade associations of the 1920s, the NRA supervised the establishment of codes of fair competition in about 500 different industries with about 22 million workers and provided legal support for labor unions. The PWA began a vast program of major public works construction: dams, highways, even aircraft carriers. The PWA programs developed too slowly to help the depression immediately, but the careful planning enabled FDR to respond very quickly to the recession of 1937 with a dramatic increase in spending.

Thus, while some aspects of the New Deal may have resembled the programs of the Hoover Administration, they differed greatly in their administrative, economic, and social purposes. Where Hoover was limited by a narrow ideological vision of what the government should do, FDR was limited only by the practical limitations of what government could do to end the depression.

MILTON KATZ

Like Tom Corcoran, I went to Washington during the Hoover Administration. Contrary to Mr. Hoover's political principles, he was obliged to start the Reconstruction Finance Corporation because of the growing number of bank failures. I think Walter Lippmann once pointed out that in a certain sense the New Deal started with the RFC.

Eugene Meyer, who was chairman of the Federal Reserve Board, served as chairman of the Reconstruction Finance Corporation. A banker from upstate New York named Miller was made the president and a New York lawyer named Morton Bogue became its general counsel. Bogue was a fine lawyer of the old high-powered New York corporation law type, and he brought with him to the legal division a group of very hot young lawyers.

In June 1932, Corcoran, one of Bogue's lieutenants, recruited me for the legal division. When I arrived in July 1932, I discovered a group of young lawyers who were wholly oriented toward governmental and public service. It was a spawning ground for those who eventually wound up all over Washington when Mr. Roosevelt came.

We started dealing with the increasing number of bank failures, working on financial and legal matters to bail out banks. The usual process was to create a new bank, which would assume the obligations and take over the residual assets of the failed bank. The bank was assisted in doing so by an infusion of funds from the Reconstruction Finance Corporation, a process well known in Wall Street as "reorganization."

Nevertheless, the banks continued to fail. I recall one story. I was summoned to Morton Bogue's office. He was a dry, laconic fellow. A number of senior financial and administrative people were there. General Charles G. Dawes, who was then the head of a very large Chicago bank, was on the phone. His bank was in the process of failing, and he was announcing with great force over the phone to all and sundry that, by God, he was going to have a clean break, he wasn't going to have his reputation soiled by having depositors lose money. One of the administrative people said, "Mr. Bogue, what shall we tell him? He's very excited and insistent." And Mr. Bogue, barely looking up from the papers on which he was working at his desk, in a very quiet voice said, "Tell him to get his pecker up and face the music," and that was the end. That was one of the banks we had to reorganize.

Then came the great crisis, the closing of all the banks and the arrival of Mr. Roosevelt as President. I can only describe the change as physical, virtually physical. The air suddenly changed, the wind blew through the corridors, a lot of old air blew out the windows. You suddenly felt, "By God, the air is fresh, it's moving, life is resuming. April may be the cruelest month, but now the world is beginning over again." I had lived in a world in which, for practical purposes, there appeared to be no government, in which there was an almost demoralized people who had the feeling that there was no one to whom they could turn. There was something called "the government," but it seemed so feeble, so overrun by the forces that were loose in the land, that it seemed no one was in charge.

The days that followed, the First Hundred Days, are usually described in terms of new legislation passed at the time, some of it largely forgotten despite its then current importance, like the National Industrial Recovery Act, designed to cope with vast unemployment and collapsing industry, but also legislation which lasted, like the Securities Act of 1933, measures affecting the banking system and the Treasury.

Certain steps were taken by Mr. Roosevelt which have since been referred to in a spirit of mockery. This represents, in my opinion, a lack of historical comprehension. It is often pointed out that Mr. Roosevelt came in on a program of balancing the budget, and then of course he became the first of the great spenders. To me at that time, balancing the budget had a significance going far beyond economic terms. I saw something in it much more pointedly relevant to the nation's immediate condition.

Mr. Roosevelt did get a series of measures through that, for a brief period, balanced the budget. The reason no one had been able to cut expenditures before was that each program was supported by too powerful an organized lobby. At last we had someone who took on and beat lobby after lobby, pressure group after pressure group, and said, "We're going to have a budget which reflects the needs of the United States of America as an entity." At last the government was back in charge of its affairs and a President was in charge of the government. The fact that six months to a year later, adjusting himself as he always did to current realities, FDR began to increase expenditures was not in any deep sense a denial of his earlier action. He was still in charge when he started to spend money. There was still a government making up its mind and making decisions reflecting the needs of the United States of America as the government perceived them. And these expenditures were not being made in deference to the demands of any pressure group or lobby. They were being made by someone who said, "This is what we have to do to put the country on its feet." That whole period has been ridiculed by people who seem to have no historical perspective and no knowledge of what actually happened at the time.

When I left the RFC, I went to the National Recovery Administration, known as the NRA, which had been set up under the National Industrial Recovery Act. This was the big venture at the time. "Iron Pants" General Hugh Johnson was in charge there. He had as his general counsel Donald Richberg, who at that time was one of the leading labor lawyers of America. Hugh Johnson represented the industrial side and Donald Richberg the labor side. Bernard Baruch had been in charge of the War Industries Board[1] in World War I, and Hugh Johnson had worked with him there; he took a great deal of such wisdom as he had from Mr. Baruch. He was a very picturesque fellow; he stimulated a large part of the population and terrorized another part. In due course he was replaced by what he called a "cabal," and Donald Richberg took over.

The NRA issued codes that governed American industry and the American economy, codes that were not adequately supported by a very flimsy statute that was eventually held, in substantial degree, to be unconstitutional. But out of the NRA experience came the Fair Labor

---

1. Established on 28 July 1917 to serve as a clearing house for all the nation's war industries to aid them in reducing waste and inefficiency. After a major reorganization in March 1918, it was headed by Bernard Baruch.

Standards Act, which set wages and hours. Out of Section 7a of the National Industrial Recovery Act came the National Labor Relations Act. It was Section 7a that established the principle that workers shall have the right to organize and bargain collectively through representatives of their own choosing. One may or may not attach importance to the Robinson-Patman Act, dealing with price discrimination, but the Robinson-Patman Act also comes out of certain provisions which recurred in code after code issued by the NRA.[2] Most people will think of the NRA as an attack of fever from which we recovered. Psychologically, it served for a time as a rallying point for morale. When it was declared unconstitutional, Mr. Roosevelt purported to be quite upset. I think he was secretly relieved to have the Supreme Court do what he would otherwise have had to do himself.

One of the things that General Johnson established under the aegis of the NRA was a Capital Goods Committee. This was a committee made up of some fifteen heads of heavy industry. Their function was to decide how we could get investments started in capital goods, which in turn would get us out of the depression. They were an impressive and well-known group. General Johnson designated one of his officials to represent the NRA in its relations with the Capital Goods Committee.

As one of my duties, I was assigned to that official as his counsel. One day, he handed me a document saying: "Here is a copy of 'A Bill for the Securities and Exchange Act of 1934,' which General Johnson gave me. The Capital Goods Committee, in giving recommendations for the revival of American industry, has suggested in a memorandum that one of the most important things needed to revive American industry is to make sure this bill doesn't pass. They asked me if I would work on this to see what could be done about it. Would you mind looking this over? This is a matter of great urgency."

I read it very hastily and said, "You know this is none of my business, but I have a distinct recollection that the daily papers have made it clear that Mr. Roosevelt wants very, very much to have this bill passed. It's also my impression that General Johnson is an appointee of Mr. Roosevelt and answerable to Mr. Roosevelt. Before we start a program to undermine the bill, is it perhaps desirable for you to ask General Johnson whether he's taken this up with Mr. Roosevelt?"

Then I was asked: "Do you know Tommy Corcoran?" "I know Tommy Corcoran." "Is he a friend of yours?" "A close friend." "Have you worked with him?" "Oh, yes, I've worked with him."

2. The Federal Anti-Price Discrimination Act of 1936 (Robinson-Patman Act) forbade wholesalers or manufacturers to give preferential treatment in the form of discounts or rebates to large buyers such as chain stores.

The explanation of that is simple. Everybody knew that Tom Corcoran and Ben Cohen were two of the chief architects of the Securities Act of 1933 and of the pending bill for the Securities Exchange Act of 1934. Everyone knew that they were then up in the office of Sam Rayburn, chairman of the Interstate Commerce Committee of the House, trying to help to get this bill through. The official was being careful. Was the man assigned to him as counsel an enemy agent?

Finally I said, "Really, if you want me to do a technical analysis of this thing, I can do it for you. That's got nothing to do with the case. If it's a question of opposing this, in my opinion you'll have General Johnson opposing something that his commander in chief has decided he wants. I don't quite understand how that fits, but that's up to you. It's none of my business. I'll just lay it right before you and you deal with it as you wish."

In short order, I got a phone call from Tom Corcoran: "Come on up here." "Here" was the office of Sam Rayburn. There were Sam Rayburn and Tom and Ben, and Tom said, "Milt, you know, you've seen a copy on blue mimeographed paper of the bill that we're introducing and you've seen a long memorandum analyzing what's wrong with it that was shown to you at the NRA. We have done some careful checking. That was prepared on the mimeograph machine that is used by Roly Redmond." Roland Redmond was a member of the firm of Carter Ledyard and Milburn and he was counsel to the New York Stock Exchange. The memorandum, Tom said, had been written by Roly Redmond. "Now we've just got to lick these people. This is crucial, and we want you to work with us on it. You're in a strategic position and you can find exactly what they're up to."

I said to Tom, "You mean you want me to resign and work for you?" "Hell, no," he cracked back. "You're no use to us here. You're of use to us precisely because you're there." Then it was my turn to reply: "Tom, my present function is that of being counsel to my agency." "What in the hell's that got to do with it?" Corcoran snapped back. "I don't know, but it's my impression that as a lawyer, I have some responsibility to my clients." "Where'd you get all that nonsense? You do what you're told." "Tom, I just don't know. I don't think I can do that. I'd be delighted to come up here and work with you and fight it, I'd be delighted to fight them. But if you're asking me to go there as counsel and use the occasion to let you know what's going on, I don't know how to work that one out."

Well, he bawled the daylights out of me. He said, "You know, Milt, people are getting suspicious of you. The general view is you have the best mind among the younger crowd in Washington. That's my view of you, too. But you're not altogether reliable." At this point Ben Cohen said to me, "Milt, how about the higher loyalties? You have a loyalty to the President, you have a loyalty to the United States." "Ben, that's one I have to work out. It seems to me that if I have higher loyalties to the President, then it's my duty to resign from the NRA and to work against them. I don't know how to reconcile working against them with staying on as their counsel." So I left Rayburn's office in disgrace.

Well, the bill was passed and the Capital Goods Committee went on to its well-deserved extinction.

The Securities Exchange Act, which had been through a terrific legislative battle, was passed in 1934. In 1935 I moved to the Securities and Exchange Commission.

In the Securities Exchange Act, Congress provided for studies of certain matters that had not been dealt with when the legislation was passed. There was to be a study of unlisted trading on the Exchange, a study of over-the-counter markets. Two economists were assigned to these functions. Each wrote a lengthy report. I was in the legal division doing what general lawyers do. Chairman James M. Landis walked into my office and said, "Look, I've got these two reports and they are worthless. Sam Rayburn wants action on them. I want you to rewrite them and come up with a bill."

I was naive enough to say okay. Well, I did a long study of unlisted trading and finally wrote an amendment to the statute, which got passed. Then came the question of what to do about the over-the-counter markets, how to regulate the sale of the vast body of securities, including bank stocks and government securities, which at that time generally were not traded on exchanges. I was then beginning to learn something about what the problems of regulation are. We had a strong group in the economics and statistical division, and I asked them for figures. They gave me figures showing that if we confined ourselves to securities which were outstanding in a volume of more than a million dollars and which were not already registered on exchanges, we'd be dealing with perhaps not more than roughly some 2,000 issues. I didn't see how we could handle every company in America that issued securities traded over the counter. I said to Landis, "Would you accept an arrangement in which we dropped from our new regulatory plan every security issue which has less than a million dollars worth of outstanding securities?" He accepted it.

With that as a starting point, we worked out an arrangement under which we would require issuers of securities in large volume for over-the-counter trading to make reports as if the securities were registered on Exchanges. And that was adopted as an amendment to the legisla-

tion. In the further pursuit of what to do with the over-the-counter markets, an entity called the Investment Banking Association came in with
some plans. The members who represented it in the main were highly
intelligent and seemed responsible. They wanted the SEC to authorize
them to organize the over-the-counter markets in a systematic way.

Well, one thing led to another. Senator Francis Maloney of Connecticut got interested in the problem. He was a great friend of some of
the leading liberals in Connecticut, including William O. Douglas. Two
of us from the SEC worked with Maloney to produce a statute that provided for the creation of an organization that came to be known as the
National Association of Security Dealers, Inc., assigning to it a set of
functions roughly comparable to those of a Stock Exchange, defining
what they could do and could not do, defining their relationship to the
antitrust laws. I had written something which pointed out that the statute was designed to develop more effective competition, and it was
therefore basically consistent with the antitrust laws. Maloney said, "I
follow Senator Borah on these things. I'm going to show him what
you've written." Borah was from Idaho, a western progressive liberal,
and very powerful in the Senate. He read it and gave it the nod. So the
Maloney Act was passed, and it became a new section of the Securities
Exchange legislation.[3]

About this time, Landis had a man filling the post of executive assistant to the chairman, a charming fellow from the Wall Street community, who left him to go back to Wall Street. Landis said, "I want you in
there as executive assistant to the chairman." So I spent the rest of my
time at the SEC under Landis as executive assistant to the chairman. I
was no longer a lawyer in the legal division.

Landis was succeeded as chairman by William O. Douglas. When
the recession of 1937 set in, Douglas called me in and said, "The Stock
Exchange boys and the others up there are operating a fear machine.
They're scaring everybody by depressing the market. What we're going
to do is reorganize the Stock Exchange completely, top to bottom. You
go up there and meet with them. I want them to adopt the following
measures." He gave me a series of drastic measures. I went up and spent
three days dealing with two lawyers who were counsel to the New York
Stock Exchange, Roland Redmond and William H. Jackson. The Board
of Governors met for three days. The chairman was a man named

3. The Maloney Act of 1938 enabled the creation, under the oversight of the SEC, of voluntary associations of investment bankers, brokers, or dealers of over-the-counter stocks
   to establish rules of fair practice and enforce discipline on their members. The National
   Association of Securities Dealers, Inc., which consisted of all the major investment
   bankers and over-the-counter brokers and dealers in the nation, was established in August 1939 under the act.

Charles Gay, referred to by Douglas as Charlie McCarthy Gay. I sat in the anteroom, and Jackson and Redmond went in and out. "Will you take this? Will you take that?" I would reply, "No, I can't take that. They have to do this."

Each day I reported to Douglas on the phone: "I've got the first four of your measures. The other seven they're belly-aching about," and so on. Gradually they came down the line. I said to them, "I'm sorry. Douglas simply isn't going to accept this unless you do the whole thing." Finally I called Douglas and said, "Bill, they've adopted every single thing we want without even a change of a comma or semicolon."

He said, "Good. Call Joe Kennedy." Joseph P. Kennedy, the first Chairman of the SEC, was back in private life at the time, on Wall Street. I called Kennedy at his home. "Bill Douglas says I should read this to you." When I finished he said, "Good, good. You know, Milt, when you deal with those fellows you know what you've gotta do? You've got to force their mouths open and go in with a pair of pincers and just take all the gold out of their teeth."

The next morning a call came from Douglas. "Milt, I want the following additional things from the Board of Governors." I said, "This is difficult. I assured them in response to their direct questions and in accordance with your explicit instructions to me, that if they adopted all those things, that would be satisfactory to you. Now you're asking me to go back and make some changes." "That's right." "If you don't mind, Bill, I'll come back to Washington. Will you send someone else up to do that?" I went back and walked in. "Would you like my resignation? Here it is."

"No, I don't want you to resign from the commission, but I would prefer it if you would resign as executive assistant to the chairman. We've got to get going on the Public Utility Holding Company Act. Would you mind going there as special counsel and help get that started?"

In 1937 Mr. Roosevelt took on the Supreme Court. The Supreme Court in those days had done what the Supreme Court recently has done: reached constitutional decisions in terms involving the determination of economic and social policy. Its conservative majority were a group of conscientious Justices who profoundly believed that the main measures of the New Deal were deeply wrong. They proceeded to knock out one after another of the key New Deal statutes. Roosevelt reacted as he did to uncompromising political opponents. As he saw it, the Court had come down into the political arena against him. FDR sent Congress a bill to increase the number of Justices from nine to fourteen, the so-called Court-packing bill. That broke on all of us like a thunder burst.

None of us had had any forewarning and we were appalled. We reacted to it as a bewildering attack on the integrity and independence of the judiciary. We talked about it in such terms as "This is lunacy. What's going on?"

Well, Mr. Roosevelt turned the screws. He was furiously determined on the issue, and he was going to fight it out to the end. Everybody in Washington was going to work for it or get out. There was to be no compromise. I had worked with various people on the Hill in connection with other legislative efforts, and I sought their views on this one. Senator Bob La Follette said, "As far as I'm concerned, the President has crossed the Rubicon. I'm with him now till the death. He's absolutely marvelous. He sees the issue and he's facing it." But other senators appeared to be as shocked as we young lawyers were.

Douglas, then a commissioner at the SEC before he succeeded Landis as chairman, took on one of the main jobs of organizing the political battle in favor of the Court plan. He summoned a group of us to his office and assigned responsibility for writing speeches for different phases of the legislative battle. Then I received another summons, this time from the White House. Tom Corcoran and Ben Cohen called me in there and said, "We want you to take on a speech-writing function in all this for various people supporting the plan." Everybody was to be whipped into line to support it. I was confronted again, but at a much more complex and less obvious level, because I wasn't being asked to be disloyal to anybody.

"Would you be willing to let me off the hook to this extent? I am outraged by what the Court has done, and I'm perfectly willing to write speeches arguing that the Court has misbehaved inexcusably. I'm prepared to charge the majority with a breach of trust, in the sense that they are trustees of the Constitution and violated that trust by writing their personal views into the Constitution. But the one thing I can't do is to praise affirmatively what Mr. Roosevelt has done." They let me off the hook and said, "Okay. If you'll attack the Court, that will be enough for us." So I wrote speeches criticizing the Court for the breach of trust.

In the summer of 1938, I transferred from the SEC to the antitrust division of the Department of Justice under Thurman Arnold. It was at that time that Thurman Arnold began his transformation and revitalization of the division.

In September of 1939, on the invitation of James M. Landis, then dean of the Harvard Law School, I accepted an appointment as a lecturer on law at Harvard. I became a professor of law in 1940. That was how I left the New Deal. I returned later to further service under FDR relating first to the threat of World War II and then to the war itself.

Under Franklin Roosevelt, democratic liberalism, coming into power in the Great Depression, was fully alive to the paramount importance of economic growth, productivity, and employment. Committed also to the welfare of the ill-fed, ill-clothed, and ill-housed, it undertook to develop economic growth and social equity as mutually supporting objectives. FDR said, "Above all else, I want to restore balance to American life. We have totally neglected the people who fell behind in the process of developing America."

To me and my age group, FDR represented life, excitement, movement, growth, creation, high endeavor. This was supplemented by an intense esprit-de-corps. We were one group working under a tremendous leader, united by a set of beliefs and mutual trust and respect.

CHAPTER 8

The Trial
of Richard Whitney

One of the consequences of the stock market crash was that it brought to light much criminal activity that would, in ordinary circumstances, have remained hidden. When business was good, stock speculators found it relatively easy to borrow money from the accounts in their trust, invest the money for themselves, and return it to the proper account just before the examiners appeared. They would then pocket the profits and no one would be the wiser. When the economy deteriorated, however, those who borrowed large sums of money had to do some fancy footwork to make sure that their customers' accounts balanced. Sometimes, as in the case of Richard Whitney, they managed to borrow enough from other sources to cover up their embezzlements for many years. They had to be lucky, indeed, to escape altogether.

What made the Richard Whitney case so important was that it exposed the hollowness and pretentiousness of the financially privileged. The case showed that even the very greatest of the financial elite—Whitney had been both vice-president and president of the New York Stock Exchange and his brother, George, was a partner in the House of Morgan—those who argued the loudest against any sort of government regulation, could be found with their hands in the till. The American people no longer expected them to escape justice. As FDR put it in his speech accepting renomination in 1936: "Out of this modern civilization economic royalists carved new dynasties ... The royalists of the economic order have conceded that political freedom was the business of government, but they have maintained that economic slavery was nobody's business ... Today we stand committed to the proposition that freedom is no half-and-half affair. If the average citizen is guaranteed equal opportunity in the polling place, he must have equal opportunity in the market place." Never again would Americans so easily put their trust in the leaders of corporate America.

The Whitney affair also demonstrated that, with sufficient will and legal ingenuity, the government could bring the corrupt "economic royalists" to the bar of justice. It demonstrated that FDR meant what he had said in his second inaugural address: "I should like to have it said of my first Administration that in it the forces of selfishness and of lust for power met their match. I should like to have it said of my second Administration that in it these forces met their master."

GERHARD A. GESELL

People might not remember now that Richard Whitney was the Morgan broker on the floor of the New York Stock Exchange. He was a big, tall, imposing man who wore a gold watch chain with a Porcellian charm from his days at Harvard. His brother, George, was a partner of Morgan's. Whitney was an aristocrat; he was a snob. He'd been the president of the Stock Exchange from 1930 until 1935 and had been on its governing boards and committees. He had appeared on the Hill as the leading proponent of the Wall Street groups in opposing the SEC legislation. During the Pecora hearings in 1933 (the Senate Committee on Banking and Currency's investigation of the stock market), he had become known as the champion of Wall Street's opposition to regulation.

In March 1938, the leading people in the Stock Exchange came to Bill Douglas at the SEC and told him Whitney had been very active in the Stock Exchange and they had discovered that he was bankrupt and in default of his obligations. Both Douglas and the members of the Stock Exchange immediately recognized that there'd been a total failure in regulation of the Exchange, and that this was an opportunity to demonstrate the inadequacies of the gentlemen's club that existed on Wall Street.

Bob Kline, who was in the SEC general counsel's office, asked me if I would take over the Whitney case. I was twenty-seven years old. It was a good opportunity.

We soon learned the seriousness of his situation. Whitney had already been engaged in improprieties when he testified on the Hill opposing the SEC. As the investigation ultimately showed, he'd stolen money from his wife, he'd stolen money from his customers, he'd misappropriated funds from the New York Yacht Club, of which he was treasurer. He'd stolen securities from the pension fund of the New York Stock Exchange, of which he was a trustee, and the gratuity fund for deceased members. He was deeply in debt to a large number of people on the Stock Exchange who had given him unsecured money, sums of $100,000 or $200,000, money that he needed to cover up his difficulties. He was involved in ventures down in Florida that were failing and he kept pouring money into them. He had also borrowed, as I recall, close to $3 million from his brother, George.

The first question that arose was whether or not this matter should be disclosed. There was a desire on the part of many people in Wall Street to hush it up and to imply that this was an isolated case. A man named John W. Hanes was on the SEC. He had a Wall Street background, and he couldn't believe that the situation was as bad as it seemed. At his insistence we held preliminary hearings to make sure that the situation was as serious as it looked. When it proved to be so, we went ahead promptly with public hearings that lasted for a period of about two months.

In the meantime Tom Dewey, who was prosecutor for New York County, indicted Whitney. Whitney pleaded guilty, and later he served, I believe, over five years in Sing Sing.

When I had him under investigation, he continued to be just as arrogant as always. We had to have night hearings to get through with him before he was to go to jail, and on one occasion I returned from dinner five minutes late. He was standing there waiting. He berated me. At midnight, with the sheriffs standing by to take him away, I had one more question. I said, "Mr. Whitney, when did you first realize that you were insolvent?" He drew himself up and said, "I am not insolvent." I was so amazed. "What do you mean?" "I still can borrow money from my friends." With that remark I said, "Take him away."

Public hearings were held to determine the extent to which the management of the Stock Exchange had knowledge of these improprieties without bringing them to the attention of their own authorities or those of the Securities and Exchange Commission. We had some interesting characters on the stand, including J. P. Morgan. Today most people think they recall the trial because of the midget farce, but that took place when Morgan testified earlier in the Pecora hearings. Some self-seeking prankster placed a midget in Morgan's lap and then took a picture of the distinguished old gentleman. Morgan was not a man who'd had much contact with everyday people. He spent a lot of time on yachts and in private railroad cars. I found him a perfectly delightful old gentleman; the time I met him, he was mellow and always truthful. He bore no resemblance to anyone like Whitney. I remember asking him why Morgan's had lent money to Whitney. "I never inquired what the reason was," he said. "Well, you didn't think it was wine and women and horses, did you?" He said no, he thought it was too much money for such indulgences. There was great laughter in the hearing room.

Actually, Morgan's replies were what brought Whitney's downfall. It was revealed that a Morgan partner by the name of Francis Bartow was playing bridge at the Links Club and Whitney said he wanted to talk to him. He told Bartow that he needed money and that he was in real difficulty. They went over to see John W. Davis. Davis learned how serious the difficulties were, and he took Whitney and Bartow out to see Morgan in Great Neck, Long Island, where Morgan lived on his estate. Davis said to Morgan, "If you lend Richard Whitney a nickel, now that you know he's in trouble, it'll be the end of the House of Morgan." Morgan refused to lend him any more money, and that's when he went under. Whitney always thought that as a representative of the House of Morgan the institution would always stand behind him and no one would ever question his activities. The influence of the House of Morgan, particularly in those days but even now, was very great, and Whitney was handling transactions of enormous importance for the firm.

Richard Whitney came from Groton and Harvard, and he had all the necessary credentials. There were standards, and people who were gentlemen met these standards; you could count on them because of their family background, their education, and their wealth and lineage. Apparently he was cold-blooded enough to be able to conceal what had been going on since as early as 1926. He let his class and business associates down. I don't think they ever entirely recovered. It just all blew up.

He had put money into something called Florida Humus and it wasn't working out. They kept needing more and more money. It was the old story of sending good money after bad. The company had something to do with digging up peat in the bogs and turning it into something profitable. Other speculative investments were Colloidal Products (mining and selling mineral colloids) and Distilled Liquors Corporation. Apparently Whitney was taken by speculators. It was a typical case of someone who thought it would all work out in the end. He was like the bank teller who takes a little money to bet with and feels certain he's going to be able to put it back. He never does.

We had some very dramatic hearings. There was a man named Edward Simmons who was head of the Business Conduct Committee of the Stock Exchange, a meticulously dressed man represented by several lawyers from the firm of Davis Polk. I remember him on the stand, just as cool as a cucumber, but there were a lot of things he couldn't explain.

He had a platinum watch chain, and during the questioning he kept breaking off links and putting them in his pocket. That was the only indication he ever gave that he was under any tension. The atmosphere of the courtroom was electric. The hearings were held either in the offices of the commission in New York or in Washington. The New York office of the SEC was located at 120 Broadway, about a block and a half from J. P. Morgan's offices, right in the heart of the financial district. The room was always overcrowded. The press would cram in. My recollection is that Bill White covered those hearings for the *New York Times.* In those days the newspapers covered trials and hearings in a way they no longer do. Today they get three minutes on television. Then there was much greater interest in trials and in hearings, especially those in which very prominent people appeared, people like the head of the Stock Exchange, Mr. Charles Richard Gay of J. P. Morgan, leading brokers and dealers and partners in J. P. Morgan's.

Dean Acheson and Covington, Burling represented the Stock Exchange, but not J. P. Morgan and Company. I would ride back and forth from New York to Washington. I'd often be on the old Congressional, going back and forth at the same time as Acheson was. After a drink, Dean would start writing poetry, a sort of running poem I've never been able to get hold of, although I've tried to find it. It was a caustic poem spoofing the hearings. I got to know Dean and Ed Burling about the time Dean went to State in 1940. Old Harry Covington, who was then head of Covington, Burling, remarked that he didn't know whether he wanted this New Dealer coming over. By then I had written some books and done other things that left no doubt I was a New Dealer. So Judge Covington went up to talk to George Whitney, Richard Whitney's brother, to see how he felt about me. George Whitney was a man of great influence with many of our clients. He was on the board of General Motors and of many other corporations. Judge Covington told Whitney he was thinking of taking this fellow Gesell into the firm and what did he think about it? Whitney replied, "That's a good idea. He's a fine young lawyer and he did a good job. I have no complaint." Then he added, "But you'd better get rid of this fellow Acheson. He's no good." I doubt that anyone, before or since, has made such a comment about the much-admired Secretary of State.

George Whitney was extremely respected and deservedly so. He always stood by his brother. There were newspaper pictures of George going up to Sing Sing and taking Richard Whitney a baseball bat or a glove because Whitney was on the Sing Sing baseball team.

Richard Whitney epitomized the position against regulations, against the New Deal, against the intrusion of government into private finance. When he toppled, he toppled all kinds of practices with him. He was really a traitor to his class; the wounds were very deep and remained so for a long time.

Many people wondered what motivated him. I have never found any reason except self-gratification. Perhaps he had some need to prove his ability to make speculative choices that would pay off. His wife knew nothing; he sold all her securities and everything else she owned. I never heard of a greedy mistress or of someone who was draining it all. Of course we did not go into all his motivations; they were irrelevant. That he was appropriating was clear. The Richard Whitney firm failed on March 8, 1938. I never heard anything about Richard Whitney after he was paroled. Apparently he ceased to be involved in any public activity.

At the trial, there were masses of lawyers trying to keep the reality of the case from becoming too clear. I don't think any one of the members of the Stock Exchange supported Whitney. Everyone was embarrassed by him. Douglas, because he saw the case as an opportunity to reform the Stock Exchange, became tense about me, although he hadn't had anything to do with my assignment to the trial. He had been one of my teachers at Yale, but at the SEC I'd been assigned to the general counsel's office. Douglas was constantly curious as to whether I was doing a good job or not. I got telephone calls from him at three o'clock in the morning. He would ask incisive questions in that clipped voice of his and then hang up. One day he called me into his office. He had a couple of newspapermen there; I don't know who they were. He suddenly said, "The press tells me that you're being soft on George Whitney." I said, "Bill, that's beneath you. I've been bringing out the facts, but I'm not going to rub George Whitney's face in the dirt simply because he helped his brother. And I'm not being soft on him." As I left I said, "I'm not going to change my tactics."

Bill remained very interested in the reports. A fellow named Sam Clark, who had heard all the testimony, wrote a report based on all the facts. While he was writing it, Bill called constantly. "Well, does the record hold together? Is it complete? Have we got what we want?" Even before it was out, Bill was calling in people from the business community and discussing the regulations that he wanted and the new legislation that he felt we needed.

I don't think anyone could convey the drama of the case, but it was a very disturbing event, especially for me, and it was a matter of great public interest. The legislation that developed included a rather comprehensive system of reporting and greater inspection, greater auditing of brokerage and investment banking. There is a report containing the official government recommendations of the commission. Some of them became law and some did not. There is no doubt that the Stock Exchange itself changed. Their officers realized this could not happen again. Since then they have certainly developed energetically and successfully. Bill Martin was brought in as president of the Exchange. Later he became head of the Federal Reserve Board. He's a straight arrow.

The members developed a very conscientious and definitive regulatory system. They began to do the job they should have been doing, and the private club atmosphere disappeared. The Securities and Exchange Commission did more auditing and the Stock Exchange mended its ways.

The Whitney trial was not my only association with Douglas. I'd known him at Yale Law School, where he taught business courses. I took every course Douglas gave. I found him a fascinating professor; in those days he was full of energy and enthusiasm. We might go out to dinner with him and play poker half the night, and then go back and sit in his class in the morning. I got to know him and Thurman Arnold, who was also teaching at that time, as more than just professors. I also saw a good deal of him in Washington, not only because of the Whitney matter, but also because Douglas was a great friend of Jerome Frank's, and for a while I was assistant to Frank. I'd be at his house and Douglas would come by, and so I got to know Douglas in different ways. I was with him when the President called and told him he had appointed him to the Supreme Court. I can't say he was pleased. He said, "Dammit, I don't want this job right now." I asked him why he was taking it. He said, "I need the money." I think he was putting me on. My impression was that he wanted the job for lots of reasons. But he didn't like the timing; it cut him off right in the middle of his work. He was a restless man, always picking his nose and scratching his head and moving around. At hearings he would get restless as soon as he saw the point. Then he wanted to move on to something else. He grew impatient when the record was developed. He was very incisive, very abrupt. He always asked you a question that went right to the root of the matter.

A typical Douglas episode, an illustration of how he operated, occurred as follows: I was sitting in my office one day and I got a message, "Come through to the back door of the chairman's office right away." I went up to the chairman's office, and Bill pointed his finger at me and he said, "You just agreed to become special counsel to the Temporary National Economic Committee."[1] "What's the Temporary National Economic Committee?" "I don't want you to go into it—but you've agreed, haven't you?" "Yes." "Show Mr. Corcoran in."

1. Established by Congress in April 1938 to thoroughly scrutinize the performance of the economy and the role of monopolies in it.

Outside was Tom Corcoran, and he had with him Bill Youngman, a young protégé. He wanted Bill to appoint Youngman special counsel to the Temporary National Economic Committee. So in walked Tommy, whom I knew, and Youngman, whom I did not know. Bill said to Tom, "You know Gary Gesell, Tom. He just agreed to be special counsel to the Temporary National Economic Committee." And that's the way I committed myself to two years of the hardest work you could imagine. This episode shows you how Bill operated. I had no reason to question him, nor any sense of what I was getting into. He knew why Tom had come, and he was determined to block him. He wanted me because I was a known entity; I had done the Whitney case. He did not want to deal with an unknown. Later he got to know Youngman and liked him.

The Temporary National Economic Committee was concerned with a broad range of economic power and various agencies were involved. I was responsible for investigating the concentration of economic power in the life insurance industry. We conducted extensive investigations, and all the work of the TNEC was just coming to legislative fruition when the war came, and that was the end of the investigation. Joe O'Mahoney, the senator from Wyoming, was chairman of the committee.

Douglas and Leon Henderson, later of Office of Price Administration fame, were members of the TNEC. Those were very busy days. You would go to work, not knowing from one day to another what you were going to do, and everybody had more work to do than they were really competent to handle. We were all stretched to the limit. As a result we all did better work than we would have done if we had had more time.

At the beginning I worked with Gerard Swope and John Burns and those people at the SEC. One day I decided I had to dictate and called for somebody from the pool. I had no secretary; I was just starting off. I began by dictating a letter that I had written out. The girl's eyes described her fear. She fainted away. Later I found out it was the first time she'd ever taken dictation. It was all a case of the blind leading the blind. That's the way we functioned.

There was just so much to do and everybody was eager to do it. Nobody thought of going home at five o'clock. It was just understood that you'd stay and work, often till midnight. Nobody ever thought of not being at work on Saturday. No one forced you to work Saturday, but we all showed up. We were just busy, busy. I remember the time they sent me out to help an experienced lawyer. I, who had just started out, went to Detroit and we worked on his case for a while. One morning I found a note under my door saying, "My father is very sick and

I've had to go home. Please draw up the complaint. Sign it and file it before the close of business today." I didn't know then what the hell a complaint was! You were forced into doing work when you were young; it gave you a chance to learn and perform. It was exciting. The difference between the New Deal and other Administrations we've lived through was the magnetism, the excitement. First of all it was new, it was peculiarly nonbureaucratic; and we were all zealous: Everybody thought he had a mission. There was a lot of inequity in our society that had to be corrected. Then there was a common goal. There were many talented people around. For instance, the legal office of the SEC was as good a law office as I ever saw. When I turned to private practice, I joined one of the best firms in the country, but I found that the SEC matched it in ability and skill.

In the SEC there were about twenty young lawyers, but John Burns was the first general counsel. He was an extremely brilliant fellow from Boston who had been a judge at the age of thirty. He was appointed by Joe Kennedy. Gerard Swope, Alex Hawes, Ganson Purcell, and Abe Fortas were among the others I recall. They were all able and hard-working and enthusiastic. I was making $2,000 a year, and on $2,000 a year my wife and I could afford a maid and a car that I bought for about $450. We rented an apartment off Connecticut Avenue at California Street with a balcony, a bedroom, a kitchen, and a living room for $60 a month. I didn't stay at $2,000 for very long, but you were able to live comfortably on $2,600; without children $2,000 a year was ample.

One day I got a telephone call. Felix Frankfurter wanted to talk to me. I had no idea who Felix Frankfurter was because I hadn't gone to Harvard Law School. He wanted to have lunch, so we made a date. We went over to the old Powhatan Hotel. Felix said he wanted to get to know me; he had been very impressed with the Whitney transcript. He'd been using the transcript in his law classes, and he wanted to know how I had learned to ask such pointed questions. Then he said he thought that Brandeis would like to meet me and later introduced me. I met Joe Rauh and Adrian Fisher and all the Brandeis clerks. I used to go to the Brandeis teas. When Frankfurter became a Justice, the Justices still had their days "at home." The public could go by and have tea with the Justice one afternoon a week. Frankfurter's teas were held on Tuesday afternoon. Peg, my wife, used to pour. In a very informal atmosphere, he encouraged lively conversation. One always met celebrities like Henry Wallace, the Vice-President, and all kinds of people active in the New Deal. A youngster like myself would never have had occasion to meet these people had it not been for the teas.

At that time Washington was a sleepy southern community. When you walked down the streets in 1935, blacks would tip their hats. There weren't a lot of lawyers, there weren't masses of businessmen flying into town every minute. There wasn't any TV and all the intrusion TV involves. Above all, there was a greater camaraderie. Roosevelt used to have receptions. Even if you were a young $2,600-a-year lawyer, you would be invited to the White House to meet President and Mrs. Roosevelt. She'd gently push you down the line, but you were at a White House reception. The receptions were not just for people in high positions. They were also for people of modest importance, which made you feel you were part of it.

I remember the time that Congress passed a bill involving the regulation of investment trusts. A fellow named Schenker had written the legislation. Jim Rowe was working in the White House. He called me and said, "FDR wants to issue a statement about the bill. Write me up something." I wrote a page and sent it over to him. The next day Roosevelt took my statement and read it verbatim. I was very impressed. Today a statement like that would go through nine public relations men and sixteen special assistants and be rewritten into a long draft, a short draft, and an alternative draft. The political implications would be weighed and because it was from the President, several persons would check with the leadership in Congress. But in our day it was simple, and it accomplished its purpose. There was no bureaucracy, none at all. That piece of legislation was not an important matter, but the event is illustrative of what could be done by people who were really inconsequential cogs in the machine. We were all people who knew one another. When there was a job vacancy, every one of us would hear about it. Often you'd have to decide, would you move to this agency or wouldn't you? Everything seemed to be in the open—and informal.

There were a lot fewer people. That had an awful lot to do with it. I can remember when the Pentagon was built. That seemed like a monstrosity to all of us. Now we accept huge buildings. The SEC was in a little office building opposite the Powhatan. The entire commission was housed in that place.

The FBI didn't have a building, Congress didn't have all the office buildings that they now have. Everything was simpler. Since the government has become more important, we have passed a lot of laws and launched a lot of regulations and these involved a lot of people to run them. I'm certain the New Deal increased the number of lawyers. We certainly helped spawn lawyers.

CHAPTER 9

The Securities and Exchange Commission

From its inception, the New Deal got into the business of regulating the stock and securities markets. The Securities Act of 1933, passed during the First Hundred Days, required anyone marketing new corporate securities to the public—through the mails or across state lines—to publicize the financial condition of the company. It also required new issues of securities to be registered with the Federal Trade Commission. The 1933 act, however, did not regulate the stock exchanges themselves or existing securities. To eliminate this loophole, FDR pushed through the Securities Exchange Act of 1934. This law provided for federal regulation of stock markets and the reform of unfair market practices. To enforce the regulations, it also established the Securities and Exchange Commission and transferred to it the stock registration functions of the Federal Trade Commission. The act empowered the SEC to license stock exchanges, to issue regulations governing market operations, and to prohibit price manipulation.

In 1935, the Public Utility Holding Company Act (Wheeler-Rayburn Act) gave the SEC authority over the financial practices of public utility holding companies. The law was designed to end the monopolistic public utility holding company device for controlling gas and electric companies and restricted holding companies to operations as unified and compact systems within a limited geographical area. It required the simplification of utility corporate structures to prevent "pyramiding." The so-called "death sentence" provision, which would have authorized the SEC to dissolve any utility holding company that could not justify its existence after 1 January 1940, was defeated, but a compromise version passed that won the substance of what FDR sought.

When I was a student at Columbia Law School, Congress passed the Securities Act of 1933. A friend and I wrote an article on it in the *Columbia Law Review* that came to Jim Landis's attention. He offered me a job at the Federal Trade Commission, so I went to Washington to work for Baldwin B. Bane, director of the Division of Securities Regulation. Two weeks later I told him writing opinion letters did not keep me busy and I was going back to New York. I don't know why I said it; there was no job in New York.

Baldwin said, "Now don't get excited. John Burns, the new general counsel of the Securities and Exchange Commission, arrived on Monday. You will work for him." This was in July 1934. The Securities and Exchange Commission, which had not yet taken responsibility for the Securities Act of 1933, moved to its own building on September 1st, and Joe Kennedy became chairman. Jim Landis, Judge Robert Healy, and George Mathews came over, and the man whose Senate investigation created the Securities Exchange Act of 1934, Ferdinand Pecora, was appointed as well. John Burns, a classmate of Tommy Corcoran's and a Boston judge, had a lifetime job at $12,000 a year which he gave up to take a temporary job at $9,000. Burns was an unusual fellow. His father was a motorman, but he went to Harvard Law School. His brilliant career caused him to be appointed to the faculty. Thus he had the irresistible combination of being a Harvard professor and a Boston Irishman. He was appointed to the bench. As a matter of fact, the general counsel's office soon became the roosting place of the Class of 1925 of Harvard Law School.

I remember the first letter I wrote for John. He had received a twelve-page letter in green ink all blotted up complaining that Congress was destroying the American people by having a bunch of foreigners like Pecora telling them whether they could buy or sell stocks. I got off a reply: "Dear Mr. So-and-So: This will acknowledge receipt of your letter of such-and-such a date. Very truly yours, John J. Burns, General Counsel." He said, "Good letter!"

Burns was quick, lively, and humorous. Kennedy was very businesslike and polished; the rest of us New Dealers were pretty sloppy in our ways. I remember Kennedy's sending out a memorandum saying, "The Securities and Exchange Commission is a government organization. Businessmen and the public have to deal with it, and they have a right to have everybody here during office hours, which are 9:00 to 5:30." He added that at 9:00 he had called up a number of people who had not answered. He went on, "From now on everybody must be at his desk at 9:00 unless he received my personal permission to the contrary. Joseph P. Kennedy, Chairman."

We had a young fellow named Frank Walker. About 3:00 one morning the phone rang out in Chevy Chase, where Joe Kennedy lived. Frank Walker said, "I have got to speak to Mr. Kennedy personally." "He's sleeping." "I've got to speak to him personally." So Joe got up, and Frank said, "Mr. Kennedy, I'm down in the library at the office. I've just finished up a memorandum that the general counsel wants the first thing in the morning. It's 3:00, I'm awful tired, and I'm wondering whether, pursuant to the memorandum, I could have your personal permission to come in at 9:30 tomorrow."

Everybody was working very hard. We were remaking the world. I remember being in the hall talking to Burns when Kennedy said, "After Frank Shea, no more Irish. The place is beginning to look like the Irish Free State Embassy."

Bill Douglas was brought in to be head of the Protective Committee Study. In the depression companies got into trouble and had to be reorganized. All kinds of shenanigans were going on. Bill Douglas brought Abe Fortas in as his associate director. They had a staff of fine lawyers and accountants; their studies resulted in the creation of Chapter 10 of the Bankruptcy Act of 1938, plus other revisions in bankruptcy laws and the Trust Indenture Act of 1939, which required substantial restructuring when companies got into trouble.[1]

The Securities Act of 1933 was regarded as so drastic that people were afraid to register securities for fear of any liabilities that could be imposed. Subsequently there were very substantial amendments to the Securities Act that made penalties less onerous and provided procedural protections. But people were frightened; they wouldn't register. Kennedy and Burns went on tour to various companies to reassure them. They succeeded in persuading Bethlehem Steel to file a registration for a special offering. A special regulation was made, yet when filed it didn't fit. Someone called Landis: "The rule doesn't fit the Bethlehem Steel case." So of course they fixed it. We were all young, with very little experience, so we struggled along and frequently we listened.

One day Bill Douglas said to me, "By tomorrow morning I want a draft of a law for federal incorporation. All corporations have to be fed-

1. Authorized by the Securities Act of 1933, the Protective Study Committee was formed in 1934 to investigate corporate protective and reorganization committees that were creating scandals in their handling of bankruptcies and receiverships. Its work resulted in the passage of Chapter 10 of the Bankruptcy Act of 1938, which made the SEC the financial adviser of the federal courts in charge of reorganizing bankrupt corporations, and the Trust Indenture Act of 1939, which increased the fiduciary responsibilities of corporate agencies in charge of reorganizations.

erally incorporated. It mustn't be more than two pages, and it mustn't stop payroll." We were trying to get people jobs, so whatever reforms we were to institute in the way corporate America operated, they were not to eliminate jobs.

We were always ready to learn. One of the things that was sensible and remarkable is that none of us resented the people on Wall Street. We'd send a form saying, "Tell us what's wrong." We listened to their arguments.

It was a remarkable place. I was in charge of operations and I required that every letter we received be answered within three days. We got a lot of compliments: "We're sorry you said we couldn't do it, but we're glad to have a government agency that gives a prompt answer."

There were very strong feelings on Wall Street hostile to the commission. When Bill Douglas made a speech to the Investment Bankers' Association, at the end no two hands met in applause. He told them they were collecting too much money for inadequate services, and they didn't like that. There was a very strong movement at one point to repeal certain sections of the Securities Exchange Act, particularly the section relating to insider trading.[2] Douglas always stood his ground. This was undoubtedly one of the reasons FDR appointed him to the Court.

Section 16b of the Securities Exchange Act says if you're an officer or a director or major shareholder of a company and you buy and sell its stock within a six-month period you have to turn profits over to the company. Wall Street didn't like that. They had strong proposals to amend it. A group from the SEC met with industry people to discuss revisions. Bill Douglas caught the old Wall Streeters trying to undermine the securities laws. When he was appointed to the Court, some of us went in to say good-bye. He said, "I shot those fellows down, but there's going to be a war. You guys hold the fort." We did pretty well, but I got called all kinds of names in the process. There had been special privileges for insiders who would know when to buy and to sell. Some of them felt that was something they ought to be allowed to do. Nowadays, nobody questions it.

Joe Kennedy was a lively fellow. In a speech he quoted Mark Twain in reference to gold-mining promotions in the West. "A gold mine is a hole in the ground owned by a liar." He was funny and quick. He would walk in absolutely polished, with Eddie Moore, his sidekick, carrying his briefcase. Eddie Moore was his factotum. Later he went off to the Maritime Commission as chairman and took John Burns with him.

Commissioners Mathews and Healy were very able Republicans. They were very good commissioners. Mathews came from Wisconsin.

2. Trading by any corporate officials, brokers, or others who have special information about a particular stock transaction that gives them advantages over the general public.

He was not a lawyer but he could add and subtract. He did a great thing when he got his nephew, Gary Gesell, to come and work. Gary ran the investigation of Richard Whitney, the president of the New York Stock Exchange, the man who embezzled everyone's money. J. P. Morgan himself testified, and Gary asked, "Do you know Richard Whitney?" Morgan said, "I knew him," thereby reading him out of society.

Commissioner Sumner Pike, a Republican, a bachelor, was a wonderful fellow. He was somebody who had been successful in the investment community, and he made a lot of sense. He was very receptive to the improvements that the staff wanted to make. He was also in a position to say, "That's nonsense, because you never owned any securities."

You felt you were making a difference, correcting evils, fixing up the country, and getting things moving. We felt that you didn't have to accept a society in which there weren't any jobs. We didn't care about anything. We got to one point, for example, when the SEC library subscribed to Communist magazines.

We had people like Louis Gilbert. He was a young man whose uncle left him shares in several companies, a lot of money in those days. He got himself a Fifth Avenue apartment. One day he got a notice that the Consolidated Gas Company was having a meeting to which, as a shareholder, he was invited. They put the deep freeze on him, so he said, "I wonder if this is happening all over." He started going to all of these meetings and got the same treatment, so he complained to the SEC. We adopted a regulation whereby if a shareholder said, "I'm going to come to the meeting and make a proposal," the company would have to put it in the company's letter to its shareholders. That caused a flap. Now it is accepted, but there was a terrific revolt. He owned maybe fifty shares of General Motors and forty shares of something else, and he would get up at these meetings, and he's still doing it.

One rule we adopted said, "Before you solicit shareholders to give you a proxy in favor of your slate of directors, you have to send out the annual report to them so they can know whether they are voting for a management that made or lost money."

After Pearl Harbor, the SEC was ordered out of Washington because it was not an essential war agency. We operated out of Philadelphia beginning in about March 1942. Shortly after we got there, the Air Force approached Thurman Arnold, the head of the antitrust division, for assistance in getting information from American businesses about dealings with foreign companies. Arnold explained he didn't have facilities but that we had regional offices all over the country, so he arranged to send SEC people to Washington. There the SEC fellows could explain how munitions factories might be created out of shoe machinery factories. Somebody from the Boston office of the SEC would go to the

United Shoe Machinery Company and get maps they had made of installations of plants in Rumania indicating exact locations so that the bombs would hit in the right place. For instance, the Stock Exchange, in connection with a bond issue of the Tokyo Street Railway, had a map of the entire street railway system there. A great deal of such information was provided; little is known about these SEC services. The Air Force was most grateful for the contribution this nonessential agency made.

FRANCIS THORNTON GREENE

The friendship between my father, Colonel Frederick Greene, and Tommy Corcoran led to tentative discussions about my joining the Securities and Exchange Commission. On several occasions I was told to meet Tommy at Pennsylvania Station, where he was changing trains between two and four o'clock in the morning. By September 1934 it all came to pass, and my income rose from a law firm's $1,500 to the $3,200 per year the New Deal was willing to pay me. My wife and I lived in Warrenton, Virginia, and now I could go fox hunting at least one day a week, which was just as important as making a living.

In a Model A Ford I became the first commuter by automobile. I believe I broke all records for speed. My first job was with a rather dour man who had been chosen because they thought he had connections with Carter Glass, the senior senator from Virginia, who as chairman of the Senate Finance Committee was responsible for the SEC legislation. My first task was to prepare a memorandum of law on the meaning of "public offering." I finally came up with a definition which is still in effect: the rule of thumb is that an offering to more than twenty-five people is a public offering.

One of the major jobs for the general counsel's office in those early days was to answer perfectly legitimate inquiries from lawyers and others in the securities business. Inasmuch as I was by no means an intellectual or a dedicated New Dealer, I figured that the only way I could get ahead was if I wrote more of what we called opinion letters. I ground out a great many, but none ever passed Allen Throop's scrutiny until he marked it up like a Chinese puzzle. But he did teach me legal drafting. Ultimately all of those opinion letters accumulated to thousands. They were put into a book nicknamed "The Bible."

The trial examiners at that time were mostly political hacks needing jobs. Nonetheless, they compiled records of thousands of pages of testimony and would render a recommended decision. The commission would then make the final decision. My job at that time was to prepare the informal written opinion for the commission based on how I appraised the record and the evidence.

After the disclosures of Whitney's bankruptcy and the theft of securities, Ganson Purcell, the chairman of the New York Trading and Exchange Division, and I worked as a team with a committee of New York bankers which included Henry Rosenfeld of Salomon Brothers, Lee Limbert of Blythe, Ben Buttenwieser of Kuhn Loeb, Arthur Dean of Sullivan and Cromwell, and Alex Henderson of Cravath, Degendoff, Henderson, Swain, and Wood—"the Cravath firm," as it was then known. They were interesting and brilliant people to work with. They did all they could to assist us in achieving a reasonable result without lousing up the delicate machinery that supported and made possible the securities industry as it then existed—and as it exists now, except for the introduction of computers.

My downfall at the SEC started at a meeting in Ben Cohen's office. I was to start work on a brief in support of the constitutionality of the Public Utility Holding Company Act of 1935. The old team was there: Jim Landis, Tom Corcoran, Ben Cohen, and others. We started to work about 9:30 P.M. There were general discussions; time ran on to eleven, twelve, one, two, and three, yet no words had been put to paper. There were long discussions about the plight of the poor and how we could achieve a greater distribution of wealth. About three A.M. I said, "Gentlemen, I've got a wife miles away, and I'm going back to her tonight. I came to work on a brief, not to discuss social philosophy. I'm going home."

Bill Douglas became SEC's chairman. Bill was always a bit radical. He had become friends with Paul Shields, whose glasses were almost opaque, so nobody ever knew what he thought, and A. E. Pierce, of the huge wire firm A. E. Pierce & Company. We were anxious to have customers' money that had been left with their brokers treated as trust funds rather than as simple debtor-creditor funds. If they were trust funds, no other creditors could reach them. The member firms of the New York Stock Exchange and all other broker-dealers had always financed themselves to a considerable extent on the customers' balances, even on customers' margin securities which they repledged with banks for brokers' loans.[3] Paul Shields, Bill Martin, then president of the New York Stock Exchange, as well as Pierce, thought that what we ought to

3. A margin security is purchased with a fraction of the face value of the stock; the margin is the percentage of the stock's value deposited by an investor with his stockbroker to insure the broker against losses in a stock transaction. A brokers' loan is made by the stockbroker to his customers to cover the difference between the customers' margin payments and the actual price of the stock.

have was a so-called "brokers' bank," modeled on the German Kassen-verein of Berlin. For many years all German brokers had handled all customers' securities funds and brokerage funds through one central brokers' bank. They simply recorded transactions as a bookkeeping matter. The German broker never had in his possession customers' funds or securities. This sounds fine, but you don't build Rome in two weeks or two years or anything less than several hundred years, the time it had taken in Berlin. But Bill Douglas bit on this hook, line, and sinker. He made several speeches in favor of what was known as the brokers' bank. He seemed to forget about the simple device of having all customers' funds, free-credit balances, held as trust funds and thus made safe from the creditors of any bank͏ upt brokerage firms.

We worked month after month and got nowhere. The complexity of creating such an institution would have been incredible. I was called in by Bill to tell him how we were getting along. What was the reaction on Wall Street? In my usual rash way, I warned him he had become a laughingstock because everyone knew this brokers' bank could never be brought to pass within our lifetime. The simple thing was to have cus-tomers' funds held as trust funds; that way we could get the safety we needed. A look of dismay and irritation came over Bill Douglas's face. I still can't forget it. That was the end of me with Bill.

One summer evening several of my contemporaries were sitting out on our lawn. One of my close friends complained bitterly, "Francis, you know what's wrong with you? You have no social conscience at all." That's what finished me with the SEC, and what drove me into the Navy.

CHARLES R. KAUFMAN

In August 1934 I stopped in Washington to see a number of law school friends, including Jim Landis and John Burns. They offered me a post as the sixth or seventh lawyer on the general counsel's staff, which I promptly accepted. I well remember my first Securities Act interpreta-tion. I received a telegram asking whether an assistant treasurer was an "officer" within the meaning of Section 16b, which was to be effective Labor Day. I had enough sense to send my draft reply in the affirmative for clearance. After Labor Day my initial opinion came back with the one word "not" inserted. Clearly an indication of my distinguished career!

In contrast to the rest of our country, Washington was alive and able to attract excellence. We believed that what we were doing was important, if not essential for a return to reasonable prosperity. Our girlfriends or wives were expected to assist. I well recall two weeks when my wife acted as my secretary every night, typing memoranda and draft briefs. If additional help were needed—whether for Justice, the Reconstruction Finance Corporation, Labor, or drafting legislation—we were borrowed informally after hours. We were put to work where the greatest urgency existed. Staffs were small and there were great amounts of work to be done.

The variety of work available on the general counsel's staff is unbelievable in contrast to the structured setup of today. My SEC assignments included trial litigation, drafting for the corporation finance division, investigating for the trading and exchange division, and the conduct of hearings as a presiding officer or as counsel. At my first conference with the full commission, I thought I was fully prepped. Commissioner Mathews, who had been with the Wisconsin Public Service Commission, asked the name of a utility holding company, a subsidiary that had nothing to do with the issue. I learned to say, "I don't know."

The trading and exchange division borrowed me for assistance in drafting regulations concerning the over-the-counter securities market. There was only a short section in the Securities Exchange Act to support broad regulations and virtually nothing in reports of committee hearings. I went to Ben Cohen, the draftsman of the statute, and asked him what was intended concerning the OTC market. His reply was interesting but not helpful. In essence, it turned out that none of those drafting knew very much about the OTC market except that it existed. Later the very limited initial regulations were expanded. I recall abortive late night sessions, and having to get up by 6:30 because I was certain the early morning revisions were nonsense—and finding, unfortunately, that I was right.

We had our disappointments. The first case involving the SEC to reach the Supreme Court was *Jones v. SEC* (1936). A sweeping subpoena had been issued to J. Edward Jones, a Wall Street promoter, whose record was execrable. Frank Currie and Alger Hiss and I worked on the brief and were satisfied with it. But the argument was a shambles. In the first few minutes the "nine old men" were thinking of Senator Black's seizure[4] rather than the case. We fully expected the reversal.

4. Senator Hugo L. Black, who was leading the fight for the Public Utility Holding Company Act, had launched an investigation into the highly dubious activities of public utility lobbyists against the measure. The lobbyists were using every possible device, including inundating Congress with telegrams to which they had forged the signatures of unknowing persons obtained from telephone directories. Black issued dragnet subpoenas to seize the telegrams, and for this invasion of privacy, Congress eventually censured Black and a Court of Appeals ruled the subpoenas illegal.

At the SEC everyone below commissioner was on a first name basis. We all ate at the "quick and dirty" beanery next door. Chairman Kennedy said that on a damp day it still smelled of horse cars. Chairman Kennedy and John Burns lived bachelor lives in Washington. Sometime after midnight, one of us would suggest going home. "Don't let's be stampeded," came the cry.

Dr. Francis Townsend headed an organization of the elderly asking for government support. The SEC was involved only because the Townsend Old-Age Revolving Pension Plan burgeoned, with facilities springing up in cities and offices that issued notes to raise funds. Many of these funds disappeared into local pockets. I was assigned to explain to Dr. Townsend that this violated the Securities Act and should stop. He wondered why I was selected rather than some senior citizen. Dr. Townsend was a friendly gentleman. He promptly tried to stop the issuance of these notes, although we continued to have difficulty with some of the local officers.

We were constantly dealing with SEC authority, with lawyers more mature and generally wiser than we were. We were supervising them from positions of authority as a result of being early on at the SEC. There's also something very heady or sanctimonious about representing the government. The result may be a tendency to excess, a feeling that the end justifies the means. This was my major concern about Bill Douglas, both as SEC commissioner and as Justice of the Supreme Court, notwithstanding my admiration for his ability.

My wife thought it was high time that I left government service before I caught Potomac Fever. My relatively early departure caused Professor Frankfurter, who had appointed me, to call me a black sheep.

CHAPTER 10

The Advent
of Social Security

On 17 January 1935, FDR asked Congress for social security legislation. Despite widespread public approval, the request faced strong opposition from many points of the political compass. Dr. Francis E. Townsend, the retired dentist who was the leader of the Townsend Old-Age Revolving Pension Plan movement, Senator Huey "Kingfish" Long, the leader of the Share Our Wealth movement, the American Federation of Labor, and the National Association of Manufacturers as well as the Communist party all opposed the Administration's plan. In Congress it faced opposition from liberals, who thought it did not go far enough, and conservatives, who thought it went too far. Congressman Ernest Lundeen of Minnesota nearly won approval of a far more radical proposal by which elected committees of workers would distribute unemployment benefits from funds raised by the federal income tax. Of course, it faced nearly unanimous Republican opposition. Despite these hurdles, the Social Security Act passed both houses of Congress and FDR signed it into law on 14 August 1935. Within the context of the times, the Administration measure was both the most liberal and the least radical possible.

The 1935 act provided for several programs. It established a cooperative, federal-state system of unemployment compensation programs by which the federal government taxed equally both employers and employees and rebated most of the money to those states that agreed to set up their own systems. It also provided an entirely federal system of old-age and survivors' insurance, financed by a federal tax—again paid equally by employers and employees. Workers reaching the age of sixty-five were eligible for retirement benefits depending on how much they had contributed in taxes over their lifetimes. Finally, the act authorized federal matching grants to the states for a wide variety of social services.

The Social Security Act of 1935 was a landmark in American history. It may be the New Deal's most important legacy. While it was surprisingly conservative—it was financed by regressive, or flat rate, taxes, it had no health insurance provision, it excluded many classes of workers, and it may have prolonged the depression by withdrawing large sums of money from the economy to build up reserve funds—it established for the first time that the federal government had a social responsibility for the welfare of its citizens. Once, when criticized about the regressive nature of the taxes, for no other welfare system in the industrial world required workers to contribute part of their wages to pay for their own old-age pensions, FDR conceded as much, but he added: "I guess you're right on the economics, but those taxes were never a problem of economics. They are politics all the way through. We put those payroll contributions there so as to give the contributors a legal, moral, and political right to collect their pensions and their unemployment benefits. With those taxes in there, no damn politician can ever scrap my social security program."

WILBUR J. COHEN

I was a student at the University of Wisconsin from 1930 to June 1934 in economics, and when I returned to Madison early in July I was told to go immediately to see Professor Edwin Witte's wife, Florence. He had gone to Washington to become the executive director of the President's Cabinet Committee on Economic Security,[1] Mrs. Witte said, and he had been looking for me to be his assistant in Washington. That was thrilling news. I was twenty-one years old and I didn't quite know what to do. Money was a scarce item. I went to see Professor Witte, who was in Harry Hopkins's office. The following Monday I went to work.

My primary responsibility was research; I did the summaries of all the foreign systems of old-age assistance, old-age pensions, and unemployment insurance. There was then no widespread system of social security in the United States. There were few pension plans. Some unions had unemployment assistance for their members, and some of the states had old-age pension plans. I learned about all the foreign systems, and

1. Established in June 1934 and chaired by Secretary of Labor Frances Perkins.

the summaries I prepared were published in the report of the Committee on Economic Security in 1935.

Professor Witte was a man of encyclopedic knowledge. As the executive director from July 1934 to January 1935, he put together reports to the President that covered the whole field of social insurance, including old-age, survivors, disability, unemployment, mothers' pensions, vocational rehabilitation, aid to the blind, aid to the disabled, and maternal and child health. In a period of six or seven months he drafted the essential plans. Today it would take someone six years. Then nobody knew much about the subject, neither the problems nor the solutions. There was a lot of controversy about the old-age part of the plan, and the constitutionality of it was in question.

Professor Witte, Arthur J. Altmeyer, John Winant, Frank Graham, Molly Dewson, Tom Eliot, and others deserve credit for seeing it through Congress. It was Tom Eliot's genius in putting together the actual draft of the Economic Security bill, the bill the President originally okayed, that made it possible to create Title I, Grants to the States for Old-Age Assistance. When the bill went to Congress everybody concentrated on Chapter 1 and the other ten chapters became less a matter of controversy. Tom had help from Charlie Wyzanski, who was then a solicitor of the Labor Department. The Economic Security bill was redrafted in Congress by Middleton Beamon, who was the legislative counsel of the House of Representatives, and became the Social Security bill. "Social Security" has now become a household term that has worldwide significance. It superseded the earlier terms: old-age pensions, social insurance, social assistance, social welfare.

It is phenomenal that Congress passed this major piece of legislation in about eight months. The men who were most significant were Representative Robert L. Doughton of North Carolina and Senator Pat Harrison of Mississippi, chairmen of the House and Senate Finance Committees, respectively. But the two men whose names were catapulted to public attention were Senator Robert Wagner of New York and Representative Davey Lewis of Maryland, who had been the sponsors of similar legislation before Doughton and Harrison came on the scene. The Wagner–Lewis bill of 1934 was really the precursor, but Roosevelt knew that the chairmen of the two committees should be given the major credit. It took the genius of Franklin D. Roosevelt to get these conservative southerners to back this radical financial instrument. People like Robert Wagner and Davey Lewis had been in favor of it a long time; the problem was how to get others to go along. I've pondered that for some years—how he was able to persuade these very conservative southerners to be his lieutenants in the legislative development of

Workers at Greenbelt, Maryland, 1936, a model community
planned by the Resettlement Administration

FDR signing the Social Security Act, August 14, 1935,
with Edwin E. Witte, Robert L. Doughton, Alben W. Barkley,
Robert F. Wagner, unidentified man, Frances Perkins,
Byron Patton Harrison, and David J. Lewis

this act. It was not because they were believers in the redistribution of income in the United States, but they had seen the South devastated by the depression, and the fact that there was going to be *some* kind of income for the old and the unemployed seemed to them a way of preserving the southern way of life. The South was on the verge of bankruptcy because of low farm prices and the impact of the world depression. Pat Harrison waited until he had the extra vote he needed to get the bill out of the Finance Committee, which in turn made it possible to get it endorsed on the floor. On all other items he was a pretty conservative Mississippi senator.

On 15 January 1935, the Committee on Economic Security made its report. By that time many of the staff had returned to their original assignments. Mr. Witte went back to his professorial duties. Mr. Altmeyer and Frances Perkins had their jobs in the Labor Department. By a stroke of good fortune, Mr. Witte suggested that I monitor the legislative development of Social Security as it passed through Congress. Some years later I was doing that on a rather gigantic scale for Presidents Truman, Kennedy, and Johnson.

In those days I had no authority to do anything, but I monitored the program. I went up to the Hill and listened to the hearings, and I became acquainted with the legislative process. After the Social Security Act was passed I went to work for the Social Security Board. Over the years I was able to make significant contributions to legislation because I got to know the process and the people. Senator Harry Byrd, Sr., when he retired, remembered: "Over the years I've disagreed almost 95 percent with Wilbur Cohen, but whenever we asked him a question, he always gave us an honest answer and we always relied on him."

A lot of changes were made as the legislation went through. For instance, Senator Robert M. La Follette changed the unemployment insurance provisions. I was particularly interested in that because the first state to pass unemployment insurance was Wisconsin.

Soon after the act was passed, President Roosevelt appointed Mr. Altmeyer, who was then the Assistant Secretary of Labor, to the Social Security Board. The legislation provided that there would be an independent Social Security Board. Once again, Franklin Roosevelt did something of great importance. He appointed a Republican, John Winant, to be the chairman of the Board. Vincent Miles from Arkansas became the third member. The very fact that Mr. Winant, a liberal and independent Republican, was the chairman of the Board made it nonpartisan, which I thought was important in the handling of the legislation for many years afterward. The Board was nonpolitical, nonpartisan to the extent that that was feasible in our society. When Mr. Altmeyer was appointed, I got a call: "Mr. Altmeyer says for you to come over to the Labor Department immediately and bring all your things with you."

Well, on that particular day, there were only two women in the office with me. I called a cab. I took a typewriter and told the two ladies to take a couple of files. On August 23, 1935, the three of us plus that typewriter and the files went over to the Labor Department and started the Social Security Board. Miss Perkins gave us space on the third floor. The request for the appropriation for Social Security died in the Congress because Huey Long filibustered the legislation to death. Mr. Altmeyer persuaded Harry Hopkins to let us have WPA funds to get the Board started.

The person who played the biggest role first was Frances Perkins, then Mr. Altmeyer, as the second assistant secretary. Henry Wallace played a very significant part because of farm labor. The final product, in my opinion, was the joint undertaking of somewhere between twenty-five and forty people. One cannot assume that legislation of such significance could have been created by one person or even two or five or ten. We were idealistic, highly motivated, hard-working people with a sense of mission and a sense of history. We seized the historical opportunity to do something on a large scale, which, in my opinion, only occurs once or twice in a century. Knowing that we had the backing of Miss Perkins and Franklin D. Roosevelt and the sympathetic concern of the people of the United States, we were able to do in a short time, and under great pressure, something monumental. We worked long and hard and enthusiastically, spurred on by the idea that unless our mission was accomplished, our social fabric was going to decay. I have on my wall at home an excerpt from the testimony for the first appropriation. Mr. Altmeyer and I went up to the Hill to testify. So in addition to being the first employee, I'm the only remaining person alive who testified in 1935 for the first appropriation.

Mr. Altmeyer and Mr. Winant personally selected every single initial employee of the Social Security Board. I once happened to be in the office on a Saturday. When I opened the door to Mr. Winant's office I found both of them on the floor with little three-by-five personnel cards that they were sorting to decide who would be the final two or three candidates for each office throughout the United States. The fact was that in 1935 you could get the cream of the crop. There were hundreds of people who had lost their jobs during the depression or for whom a job in Social Security was a wonderful opportunity, people of ability who had worked for insurance companies or state governments, or had had businesses or been in banking.

Representative Fred Vinson saw Social Security as having a potential for political patronage. Mr. Altmeyer and Mr. Winant were opposed
to that. Confrontations between Fred Vinson and Mr. Altmeyer were
frequent. Mr. Miles, the third member of the Board, had been a political
appointee, but Altmeyer and Winant would customarily outvote him on
the political appointees. President Roosevelt never interfered with the
decision to make appointments based, as far as humanly possible, on
merit rather than politics. We always ran our program wisely, effi-
ciently, and at low cost.

One of the first big issues to be decided was how to enroll all these
people in Social Security. The original estimate for coverage by old-age
pensions was 26 million people. Nothing that big had ever happened,
even in connection with the World War I draft. Who were they, what
were their names, how many Smiths, where would you find them, and
what do you do? Do you give them a number? We brought several experts over from Europe, and I spent a lot of time talking to them. Their
conclusion was that it couldn't be done. The United States was too big a
country. You'd have to break it up in some way. Altmeyer and Winant
debated that question for weeks. Finally, taking all the risks into account, they decided the best way was to ask the Post Office to enroll
these people.

To enroll people meant you had to give them a number. The Social
Security numbering system is now used on income tax forms, in some
states on driver's licenses, even in order to get a check cashed. We
wanted to know the age of the person. It was decided that the fourth and
fifth number would indicate the year of birth. The opposition to this
idea was unaminous. During the depression a lot of people had fudged
their age in order to keep their jobs. We also discovered that there was a
natural reluctance on the part of women to disclose their age. The enu-
meration went off successfully. Everyone had wondered what would
happen. Would people object? I can now disclose the fact that President
Hoover would not take a number. Hoover said he was constitutionally
opposed to being "numberified," so we gave him a number; he didn't
apply for it. We kept a little file of conscientious objectors, but it wasn't
very big. I never did check whether Hoover ever applied for Social Security benefits or not. Probably he didn't.

We sent out a little pamphlet of four pages to tell people what Social Security was all about. An older woman employee by the name of
Ethel Smith wrote it. The *New Yorker* magazine called it one of the best
things ever written by any government agency. She wrote it in a way
that anyone with an eighth grade education could understand. At that
time we were not giving any benefits to anyone. All we were doing was

getting people enrolled to pay their taxes by giving them a number. That was not exactly what one would call the greatest lure in history. Yet it went off successfully. A great deal of credit is due Ethel Smith's little pamphlet.

Everybody was worried about the impact of the 1936 campaign on Social Security. In the spring, Alf Landon, who was the Republican presidential candidate, went to Milwaukee to make a speech on Social Security. Landon wanted to finance Social Security out of the general revenues of the government, out of the income tax. Instead of having benefits related to wages, everybody would get the same amount. It was a reasonable counterproposal; he wanted to have a Republican alternative. I happen to think it's a very un-Republican proposal to pay it out of the income tax. Landon's Madison Avenue public relations people added a couple of sentences to the speech to jazz it up: "Social Security is a cruel hoax, Social Security is a fraud." Landon made a mistake; nobody even remembered what his alternative was. John Winant resigned. He said, "I cannot any longer be the chairman of the Social Security Board when the leader of my party has said Social Security is a cruel hoax."

As a result, Social Security became a big issue in the 1936 campaign, and I needn't tell you who won that election. Landon took only two states. The voters indicated their approval of FDR's Social Security program. The Republican National Committee decided they had to back Landon's proposal. They made a fatal mistake. When workers, particularly in the automobile industry, got their next weekly pay they found a stuffer, a payroll insert, which read, "On January 1st next year your pay is going to be cut 1 percent by virtue of an order from President Franklin D. Roosevelt." The worker was going to pay a 1 percent tax under Social Security. The Republicans and the companies who cooperated with them thought the workers would rebel and vote Republican. The reaction was just the reverse: "If the automobile companies think I'm doing badly by paying 1 percent into Social Security, there must be something good about it. The employer couldn't be looking out for me." Unionization was not widespread, and antiemployer attitudes were strong. Franklin D. Roosevelt won so overwhelmingly at the polls that Social Security became an accepted institution politically, despite Landon's sincere effort to be constructive.

In 1937 FDR wanted to "pack" the Supreme Court by increasing the number of Justices. He lost the battle but won the war. Up until then almost every piece of New Deal legislation had been declared unconstitutional, including the NRA, the AAA, and the Railroad Retirement Act. But on May 24, in *Charles C. Steward Machine Co. v. Davis,* the

Supreme Court, by a vote of five to four, held unemployment insurance to be constitutional. The vote on old-age pensions in *Helvering v. Davis* was seven to two. Roosevelt won the war. He didn't succeed in "packing" the court, but the effort caused some Justices to modify their views.

I went to the Supreme Court that day to hear Mr. Justice Cardozo deliver the decisions. In my opinion, they could be printed as poetry. Cardozo wrote his decisions as if he were carving them into stone. They're beautiful, alliterative, asymmetrical. I had also been to the Supreme Court to hear Charles Wyzanski give the oral argument in the case. He made his oral presentation practically without a note. He was so articulate, so persuasive; it was an absolutely first-class performance.

After the Supreme Court upheld the Social Security Act, a problem remained: how to get it accepted by people who had been opposed to it. Conservatives, Republicans, the financial, banking, and business communities had gone along with it, but simply because they knew that *something* had to be done. They weren't sure that it was the *right* something. The reserves that financed the system could eventually be so big that they would inundate the federal government. The government would spend more money to keep the debt than it would get by using the money from Social Security as an investment. That never came to pass, but in 1938 it was an acceptable argument. If the Social Security tax rate kept increasing so that much more was collected than was paid out, the reserves would be so big that the debt to the United States would not be sufficient to handle them and the government would have to invest in private property or spend the money and bankrupt the financial system of the United States. That argument had been made in part by people like Landon. In Congress Senator Arthur Vandenberg of Michigan took this view.

Senator Vandenberg was an extremely responsible, intelligent, able conservative, as we later discovered when he changed his mind and became an internationalist and worked in such a cooperative fashion with Roosevelt. Vandenberg was willing to listen to Mr. Altmeyer, who went to him and said, "If you think that is a problem, why don't we jointly appoint a distinguished commission to look into the matter and see if we can't resolve the question."

Vandenberg agreed. They appointed an Advisory Council on Social Security in Feburary 1937. J. Douglas Brown of Princeton was chairman; included were Paul Douglas, then a professor at Chicago, Edwin Witte, my old professor, Lee Pressman, and others. They met throughout 1937 and 1938, and I worked very hard for them as a staff assistant. They decided that the system ought to be put more or less on a pay-as-you-go basis. They also proposed to add benefits to widows and orphans. In 1939, we were able to put through the first changes in the Social Security Act, which transformed it from just an old-age insurance program to an old-age and survivors' insurance program.[2] The final step occurred in 1950, after the war, when the program truly went on a pay-as-you-go basis.

Looking back, that change bred some of the problems we face today. Because of inflation and high unemployment, not enough money is coming in. But I still consider the enactment of the 1939 amendments a great triumph. Legislation which had been enacted under the stress and strain of the depression was converted into something the Republicans could support. The 1939 amendments went through Congress with hardly a murmur. There was some dissent, but it was bipartisan in nature.

Roosevelt's genius showed in his handling of the Social Security Act, which, after fifty years, remains the centerpiece of his accomplishments. When he entered the White House, he had not been heralded as a radical, nor had he had a very promising platform. But he didn't need one. All he had to do was run against Herbert Hoover. As a matter of fact, his statements about balancing the budget were quite conservative. But when he said "All we have to fear is fear itself" he showed that his government was not afraid to undertake bold, innovative programs. I think that gave the American people hope after a period of despair and frustration. The dramatic closing of the banks and the First Hundred Days of legislation gave people a sense that he was going to do something. He showed compassion for people by going out and shaking their hands, talking to them. He changed the attitude of people toward their government. He was a man who wanted to try, wanted to experiment, wanted to innovate; and many wanted to be a part of that mission. Young and not so young people flocked to Washington in 1933. The people who hated Roosevelt understood the powerful impact he had upon millions who trusted him implicitly.

Roosevelt was a master politician in the best sense of the term. Senator Claude Pepper likes to recount the time he went to see Roosevelt about a matter which Roosevelt didn't want to talk about. Their meeting was of some duration. Roosevelt talked the whole time about a man named Livingston. Pepper came back an hour later and reported that he hadn't had a chance to bring up what he had in mind, but he was now the second-best informed man in the world on the subject of Mr. Livingston.

2. These amendments advanced the starting date for old-age benefit payments to 1940, provided old-age benefits to the wives of covered workers, changed the basis of benefit computation from total wages to average wages, extended coverage to new classes of workers, raised social security taxes, and increased both disability and dependents' benefits.

Now many people in political science and government are critical of Roosevelt because instead of firing people when he found they weren't doing what he intended them to do, he promoted them upstairs. He was not what I would call a straight-line, hierarchical administrator. He had a sense of the human aspect in everything he did. He was compassionate, and he understood both the strengths and the weaknesses of the human being.

The genius of Roosevelt included his ability to attract innovative, intelligent, and outstanding people. He took ideas that other people had and adapted them to the economic and political system of the time. Today he is accused of sponsoring big government. That was hardly the issue in 1933, 1934, 1935. Private business was paralyzed, the banks were closed, the economic system was paralyzed. Government had to take a role; it had to do something in the interest of the people of the United States.

THOMAS H. ELIOT

I got into the New Deal almost at the beginning, but not quite. In the fall of 1932, I was practicing as a fledgling lawyer in Buffalo. Under the aegis of the Democratic Committee, I went out and spoke for the ticket, for Roosevelt primarily, because I thought this might stand me in good stead later, and it did. After the Inauguration a lot of people I knew began to go to Washington and get interesting jobs there. One of them was Charles Wyzanski, whom I had known well in college and later at Harvard Law School, although he was a year or two ahead of me. I wrote a letter to a mutual friend, in the course of which I mentioned Charlie's appointment as solicitor of the Department of Labor. I said casually, "Boy, how I would like to be down there as one of his staff," and it worked. The mutual friend relayed this information, and I was invited to come down and talk with him and with Frances Perkins, the Secretary of Labor. By early July 1933 I was there as assistant solicitor of the Department of Labor, doing a variety of jobs.

Miss Perkins was a perfectly wonderful boss for the young men she employed. Charlie was twenty-eight and I was twenty-six. Later Gerard Reilly and other young men about the same age came in. Miss Perkins had a lot of confidence in the integrity and the brains of these kids. Certainly in the case of Wyzanski her confidence was not misplaced. He was terribly good, and she recognized that right from the start.

Miss Perkins had a Cerberus in her outer office, an absolutely loyal, very abrasive woman called Miss Jay. Her name was Frances Jerkowitz but she was always Miss Jay. Her method of dealing with people, from powerful senators to labor leaders to men on the street, was to say, "Miss Perkins is not in, I don't know when she'll be back, I really can't say, I really can't say," no matter where Miss Perkins was. She was infuriating, just infuriating! She made enemies for Miss Perkins among the politicians and the labor people, but chiefly the politicians, the senators. I'm sure Miss Perkins wanted her to be warm and gracious. She was quite incapable of being warm and gracious, but she was so hardworking and so utterly loyal that Miss Perkins reciprocated that loyalty. I think it's fair to say that of all the virtues, Miss Perkins put loyalty first. She was an intensely loyal person herself.

Miss Perkins told me about one of her visits to California to meet with union people. She left her hotel room, but she forgot something and went back. As she went down the corridor toward her room, she met a workman coming out. "What are you doing here?" she said. "You're Miss Perkins, aren't you? You're Secretary of Labor?" "Yes." "Well, I think I'd better tell you what I've been doing. I've been putting a bug in your room." Presumably the shipping owners wanted to find out exactly what was going on and they had hired this guy to install a bug. She was perfectly delighted by all this because she could operate knowing that everything was being transcribed and even tell the labor people that this had happened. What a break!

I did a number of different jobs until the early winter of 1934. During the Christmas holidays, the Paul Raushenbushes came to Washington for Christmas. Mrs. Raushenbush was Elizabeth Brandeis, daughter of the Justice, and they stayed at the Brandeis's apartment. Paul Raushenbush had been appointed administrator of Wisconsin's Industrial Commission, which had been established the previous year by the State Unemployment Insurance Act of 1932. But he had no job because the depression caused the Wisconsin authorities to postpone the effective date of the law. Business just wouldn't be able to stand it, they thought, and certainly not on a competitive basis. Paul discussed the problem with Justice Brandeis. He said, "Look, it is terribly hard for a single state to pass an unemployment compensation law because that adds to the cost of doing business in that state. It will drive business out of the state. People won't be able to compete because they have these extra costs; you've got to have some kind of equalizing national legislation."

Mr. Justice Brandeis said, "Have you ever read the case of *Florida v. Mellon?* That's Andrew W. Mellon, who had been Secretary of the Treasury at the time. The state of Florida, in the boom period of the twenties, advertised for rich people to come to Florida to die because then they could avoid state inheritance taxes. The states in the North, where the rich people were, had inheritance taxes. If only these people would come to Florida, they would not have to pay huge state inheritance taxes and their heirs would get more money. To remedy this, the Congress passed a new federal inheritance tax law, but then forgave the federal tax if tax was owed to a state. The result was that people paid their state inheritance tax and only a token amount of federal tax because they could offset one against the other. People didn't have to pay any inheritance tax to Florida because there wasn't any, but they had to pay the national government. So the Florida advantage was lost and the disadvantage to the other states no longer existed. The Justice was giving his son-in-law a hint that this was the way to go for unemployment insurance.

Miss Perkins assigned me to help Paul Raushenbush draft a national unemployment insurance law in the early winter of 1934. The law would impose a national payroll tax but then forgive it, or most of it, if the state would pass an unemployment insurance law and collect the same amount of money. Then the employer would only have to pay the state and not the national government, so all states would be even. The employers in all states would have to pay one tax or the other. We thought that the states would rather keep the money at home by passing their own unemployment insurance laws, and that's what actually happened later.

That's how I got involved in Social Security. I had great fun because I was put in charge of arranging the affirmative side for the hearings that were held before a subcommittee in the House Ways and Means Committee. The bill was introduced by a marvelous little congressman named David J. Lewis from Maryland, a pepperpot of a man, a real idealist and a real scholar. He'd gone into the mines at age seven and he had come out of them, somehow or other. He'd saved a little money and at the age of twenty-one, he began studying law at night. Time went on, and the President said mildly that this was a good bill, but he didn't try to smash it through. Miss Perkins tried to persuade him to do so, but he had other fish to fry and he knew what he was doing.

When Miss Perkins took the job as Secretary of Labor, she did so only on condition that she would be allowed by Roosevelt to battle for things like unemployment insurance and old-age insurance. The President, however, pulled the rug out from under us and also from under various others who were pushing for old-age pension legislation. He said, "I want the whole ball of wax rolled together. I want a Cabinet committee with a staff, to be called the Committee on Economic Security. By January 1935 I want a whole scheme for the economic security of the men, women, and children of America." It was a brilliant political stroke. In the congressional campaign of 1934 he could say, "Among our objectives, we put the security of the men, women, and children of America first."

The committee was headed by Miss Perkins, and she appointed me as counsel, I suppose because of the work I'd already done on the unemployment insurance phase. The committee wanted the law to be comprehensive. I was overconfident and did not get a staff to help me. I should have had other lawyers. The old-age insurance clauses were drafted by very able people, the lawyers in the Treasury Department. But even then it was a rather messy bill when it finally went to the Congress. The bill got perfected by Middleton Beamon and me, working all hours in the basement of the House Office Building. Beamon was the chief legislative draftsman of the House. He was a red-haired, salty, caustic, Vermont Yankee. In a month he taught me more about legislative drafting than I could possibly have learned anywhere. He was a wonderful guy. He disapproved of the bill completely. He was very conservative, but he played it absolutely straight. He was the perfect civil service technician. For years I tried to conspire with Arthur Ballantine, the Under Secretary of the Treasury in the Hoover Administration. I wanted him to get Harvard to give Middleton Beamon an honorary degree. He was just the kind of person I thought ought to be honored, because he was totally unknown, and Ballantine agreed. But Columbia beat us to it.

Beamon completely put aside his own preferences to make this an excellent bill and shore up any constitutional doubts. He may have had one assistant at that time, but I don't think so. Each morning, after the hearings with the Ways and Means Committee were over, we would meet. He would say, "Now please turn to page 8. We are on Article 2, Section 1a. You want me to read it? Is that all right? Do you think that's all right?" I would say, "Well, that's fine." He would answer. "It says that people shall not be paid benefits if their work was done outside of the country. Assume the man was living in Detroit but his job was over in Windsor, Canada. You're not going to give him any unemployment or old-age insurance? Do you mean that, do you mean that?" He was awfully good.

Beamon and I had a bet. Some days the members of the Ways and Means Committee would cover seven pages of the bill and bing, bing, they would come in with their decisions. Other days they would cover less than a page and they'd get into irrelevancies. We would bet on how many pages they would cover. Beamon guessed right each time and then I said, "Okay, I can't afford to lose any more bets to you, Mr. Beamon.

How do you do it?" "Oh, I just watch one member of the committee."
"Fred Vinson." "You guessed right."

Vinson later became Chief Justice of the Supreme Court. He was
not the chairman of the committee but he was the dominating force. He
was very intelligent and very shrewd, but he was also quite tempera-
mental. Beamon would watch him come in, and if he said "Good morning" very pleasantly and then started studying the bill and said "Good
morning" in an abstracted sort of way to the other congressmen who
came in, Beamon bet he'd cover seven or eight pages. If, however, he
just looked at us or paid no attention and then signaled to somebody
and began complaining about the light fixtures or began telling an off-
color story, we weren't going to get anywhere. But he was awfully nice.
He became a very good friend later when I went to the House in 1939.

Just before I actually started to work for the Committee on Economic Security in the summer of 1934, I got involved with the International Longshoremen's Association and International Seamen's Union
strike that tied up San Francisco and then the whole West Coast.[3] That
was Harry Bridges's strike. The National Longshoremen's Board,
headed by the Archbishop in San Francisco, Archbishop Edward
Hanna, included Ed McGrady, who was the Assistant Secretary of
Labor, and a San Francisco lawyer named O. K. Cushing. I regret to say
that Miss Perkins didn't have confidence in McGrady. I think she was
quite wrong, but she felt that he had been forced on her by a combination of union and partisan pressure. The very day the general strike was
ending in San Francisco, I was sent out by plane to help. It was a fascinating two weeks' experience. I was in on the settlement. I was at dinner
with O. K. Cushing, a white-haired, pink-faced gentleman with a moustache. He could have been cast as a minor English lord. He had done a
tremendous job in San Francisco at the time of the fire and earthquake
as the head of the relief committee. Both he and his wife were delightful.
In walked the president of the longshoremen, a fellow named William J.
Lewis, and two of his associates. In the middle of dinner, Mr. Cushing
took them upstairs to a private telephone in the bedroom. Twenty minutes later he came down, pinker than ever, said good-bye to his visitors
and then said, "I think it is time for a stiff drink." He looked terribly
pleased.

We both said, "What happened?" "Well, we got on the telephone
and they're going to end the strike. It's all settled." Mrs. Cushing said, "I
think this is the first major strike that's ever been settled in a lady's bedroom."

3. This strike, which resulted in union recognition, lasted from 9 May to 27 July 1934. The
    San Francisco general strike of 16–20 July turned the tide in labor's favor.

But the settlement included a plan to have elections. The long-shoremen had to vote on whether to go to arbitration or not. I remember going out to Stockton, up the river toward Sacramento, which was a relatively new port. It was basically a farming town, and the longshore-men there were not experienced at all. In Oakland and in San Francisco the longshoremen set up voting machines or ballot boxes. They had everything all designed right, and they did it beautifully. Out in Stock-ton they didn't know how to run an election at all. And they were drinking. I am still amazed at myself and never understood how I man-aged to get through it. I remember thinking, "How am I going to get these people to line up and vote?" There were seventy or eighty of them milling around, and I finally jumped on a table and just plain yelled, using very rough language, and ordered them to get in line and cast their votes, goddamn it, and they did. I don't know why they didn't throw me out because I was still just a kid, and obviously from the effete East, too. But they really were all right.

Then I came back and worked on the Social Security Act and helped to steer it through. It passed the House and then it went to the Senate. It passed the House after a debate, which I missed because I was sick, but I read the transcript. One congressman, a Republican named Harold Knutson from Minnesota, objected to this bill because it had been drafted by someone who was not yet dry behind the ears, meaning me. Congressman Vinson promoted me. He talked about the wonderful work done by the Assistant Secretary of Labor, Tom Eliot. The thing I really was sorry to miss was the speech made by David Lewis, because there was a big attendance at the House and everyone rose and gave him a great standing ovation. That would have been fun.

The original bill made no provision for the survivors of the recipi-ent of old-age benefits. A wage earner, if he had been in the system long enough to be covered, would get benefits when he was sixty-five and had retired. But there was nothing for his widow or minor children. This was pointed out by someone at the time the Ways and Means Committee was considering the bill. I think it was a Thursday. Some quite vehe-ment people on the committee said, "We're going to stop right here. We've got to have something for the widows. We've got to have a survi-vors' clause." "Well, that's going to take some time." "Well, we won't meet then until next Monday and you people," pointing at Beamon and me, "get to work now and bring us in a good survivors' clause."

We were still going through the motions of pretending that the whole scheme was actuarial. I don't think anybody really thought it was but that was the gospel. So we had to consider: "Will this change the number of people who will get benefits? Will this change, therefore, the necessary rates that have to be imposed?" And so on. We got the Treasury in on it, worked all weekend, and came up with a fine addition to the bill.

We came back on Monday with a section for survivors, and we had copies for each member of the committee. They all looked at it and started off. Representative Robert Doughton, the chairman, said, "What's this? What's this?" "That's the new survivors' clause." "Oh, yes, yes." Someone else said, "Well, I don't understand this at all." Fred Vinson said, "This raises a whole new problem that we don't have to deal with now." And somebody said, "I move we table it." In five minutes they tabled it. It was a very odd performance. Survivors' insurance wasn't a part of the act until it was amended four years later.

Then there was the problem of domestic servants. Henry Morgenthau was absolutely insistent that they not be covered, and they weren't in the original act. This whole thing was so colossally new to us that we thought it would just be too much for the poor ignorant housewife to figure out the Social Security coverage. Having seen housewives struggle with their cook's Social Security, I'm not sure he was wrong.

All kinds of new benefits have been added since the original act was passed. There has been a great expansion, far beyond the original intentions.

There was opposition to the Social Security Act from two sources. On the far left there were the Townsend Plan people. In the final vote in the House there were thirty-three negative votes and most of them came from the Townsend Plan districts, where the doctrine of $200 a month for everybody had taken hold. That opposition was not very effective. On the right, the National Association of Manufacturers and the U.S. Chamber of Commerce were specifically opposed to one part of the Social Security Act, namely old-age insurance, what we now call Social Security. The Republicans also opposed old-age insurance. The history books say that the House passed Social Security by an overwhelming bipartisan margin, and that's true. The vote was 371 to 33 and most of the Republicans voted for the final bill. This is just another reminder of how misleading records can be, if you don't know what to look for. The real test of Republican sentiment came when one of them moved to recommit the bill to the Committee on Ways and Means and have them strike out old-age insurance. On that all the Republicans but one voted to recommit. That was the opposition right there.

I often wonder what would have happened in periods of economic downturn if there had not been unemployment compensation. I think unemployment compensation has been dreadfully abused. People who shouldn't get it get it, but the important thing is that many more people get it who should get it. If they hadn't, wouldn't each of the recessions—in the fifties when Eisenhower was President, in 1962 when Kennedy was President, and then in 1975 when Ford was President, and right now when Reagan is President—have accelerated? In a town like Waltham, Massachusetts, if Waltham Watch, a big employer, closes, many people are out of a job. Therefore they can't buy groceries, so pretty soon the grocer can't keep up his rent payments and he's going to go broke. They can't keep their automobiles going, so the gas stations go broke. With unemployment compensation, for at least another six months everybody's able to pay something. They can't buy as much as before, but it certainly cushions the shock and it slows the downward slide. I think this has been an enormously important factor in our economic history.

I am reminded of a nice story about Social Security. A man named Forster, from Philadelphia, had been developing a business selling retirement plans to corporations. He was a parishioner of my father's. Father was a Unitarian minister who filled in once a month at the Unitarian Church in one of the suburbs of Philadelphia, and he got to know Forster quite well. Mr. Forster was convinced that his business would go right down the drain if the Social Security Act were passed with no provision exempting employers who already had a good retirement scheme for their employees. He came down to Washington and he lobbied. He got Senator Bennett Clark of Missouri interested, because Socony Vacuum, who must have had a big plant in Missouri, had a good retirement scheme that Forster had put in. He produced a thing called the Clark Amendment, which exempted from the taxes under the Social Security Act employers and their employees who had a proper old-age retirement system in effect. This threw everybody into a conniption fit, because what was a proper system? There were too darned many systems—not Mr. Forster's—where employees had to suffer pay deductions for thirty years, and then when they were sixty-four years old they were fired so that they wouldn't get a pension at sixty-five. There were plenty of examples of that. How were you going to set up Social Security if many big employers might be exempt? How could you predict what the rates should be? So the Administration was vehemently against the Clark Amendment. But Mr. Forster spent $50,000, which was some money in those days, entertaining and distributing printed materials to congressmen. Miss Perkins must have talked with the President about it, because the Administration put three lobbyists in to fight the Clark Amendment, and each was assigned four senators who were doubtful. I was one of the lobbyists. The others were Charlie West, a former congressman who had been defeated but was then in the White House as Roosevelt's legislative liaison, and one Thomas G. Corcoran. I think this was his only involvement with the Social Security bill. Each of us had four senators and I think it was pretty much chance which four we got, so it was an excellent test of our skill as legislative lobbyists. I got two of my four to vote against the Clark Amendment. Charles West got none at all. Tom got all four of his. One of the ones I lost was Marcus Coolidge of Massachusetts. Marcus Coolidge was a senator whose handlers desperately tried to keep off the air and off the stump in the fear that he might say something foolish. They missed him on election day itself, and he was commandeered early in the morning by a reporter from a radio station out in his home town of Fitchburg. He was on the air just long enough to say, "I have a message for all good Democrats in the state. Vote early and often." I worked on Marcus, and he was very polite and gentlemanly but noncommittal. I went to my friend David I. Walsh, the senior senator from Massachusetts, and he said, "I'll talk to him." Walsh came back and said everything was okay. "You've convinced him and I've convinced him and everything's okay." Then the vote came and Coolidge voted for the Clark Amendment. David I. Walsh saw me coming and he grabbed me and said, "Tom, the junior senator from Massachusetts, he's a very strange man."

So they adopted the amendment, the bill went to conference, and in desperation the conference committee stopped because the House wasn't going to give in on this at all and the Senate wasn't going to give in on it because they'd just passed it. So they appointed a committee to see if they could work out a revised version of the Clark Amendment that wouldn't do all the terrible things that we all said it might. The committee was composed of me; Leonard Calhoon, who was Senator Pat Harrison's legislative assistant, a lawyer and a good one; and a man named Clark Woodward, who was Senator Clark's nominee, the counsel for Socony Vacuum. We worked like dogs trying to get a decent amendment. Even Clark Woodward thought we couldn't do it in the amount of time allotted. We finally reported that it couldn't be done, and we suggested that they put the whole thing aside, with the promise that we come up with a viable Clark Amendment by the following winter. The actual tax and the benefits were not going into effect for a year and a half anyway, so there was still time to exempt these plans. The senators rather reluctantly bought this, and the bill went through without the Clark Amendment. It was finally signed in August 1935. Then I became general counsel of the Social Security Board, which was established to administer the whole program. Leonard Calhoon became one of my assistants. The months went by and I suddenly said to Leonard, "Hey, you know, we forgot all about that damned Clark Amendment, and we ought to do something about it. We promised we would."

"Well," he said, "Senator Harrison's not here. He's back in Mississippi. Otherwise I'd go over and see him." "Well, I'll go and see the ranking member of the committee, Senator William H. King of Utah. I know him. I'll go up and see him." So I trotted up to the Hill and said to Senator King, "We're ready to get into business now. If I can get hold of Woodward, we'll work on this. When do you want the Clark Amendment?" "Clark Amendment?" "Yes, the Clark Amendment that you were all so eager for last August. We promised you a new one. I can't give it to you right now, but maybe we can get hold of these other people and get it for you in two or three weeks." He laughed. "I remember. Oh, no, don't do that. Mr. Forster was in here the other day. Since the Social Security Act was passed, his business is booming. He doesn't want any Clark Amendment." That was the end of that.

The Social Security Board was headed by John Winant. He was a lovely, fascinating man, one of the real figures in my life. Later, I was in Washington when he was ambassador to England. I was with Jack Tate one day, and I picked up the newspaper. Jack said, "There's a picture on page four. I've got a confession to make." I opened to the page, it was a picture of Winant, and I said, "Your confession is the same as mine? Shivers went right down my back as I opened the paper and saw the picture." Jack said, "Yes, that's right." Winant had this extraordinary quality. He was an impossible man in many ways, but he had an internal fire of idealism that looked out, and it had an enormous impact on people. Miss Perkins wanted him to appoint me as general counsel to the Board, and he did, but before he did he had lunch with me. He asked me what the most important thing for a public servant in a fairly important position was. I don't recall what I said, honesty, intelligence, or something, and he didn't seem very impressed. I said, "What do you say it is, Governor?" He said, "kindness."

I was general counsel from the fall of 1935 until the early summer of 1938. I had ninety employees. We had the whole question of constitutionality facing us; Charles Wyzanski and I did those cases. The staff worked on rules and regulations with respect to old-age insurance before it went into effect. The stars of the staff worked with the states in drafting unemployment compensation laws, which we had encouraged by our statute. The original bill that I wrote with Paul Raushenbush appears all over again in the Social Security Act as the unemployment compensation part.

Then we won our cases in May 1937 when the act was held constitutional by the Supreme Court. After that I was asked to teach at Harvard, and I announced for Congress in the spring of 1938.

CHAPTER 11

Madame Secretary

Frances Perkins was a most unusual Cabinet appointment. Not only was she the first female Cabinet officer in American history, she also was the first nonunion member to be appointed Secretary of Labor. Union leaders traveled from around the nation to speak against her at her Senate confirmation hearings. It was a great tribute to her abilities that within a few years those same union leaders granted her their nearly unanimous support. Born in Boston in 1880, there was nothing in her middle-class upbringing to suggest her singular future. She first became interested in economic history and social conditions in college, where she came under the influence of Florence Kelley, the general secretary of the National Consumers' League.

Diverted from an early career in teaching by her volunteer work at Chicago settlement houses, she became secretary of the New York Consumers' League in 1910. Two years later, she witnessed the Triangle Shirtwaist Company fire in New York city in which 146 workers— mainly women and children—died. She was left with searing memories of the workers poised on the window ledges in prayer before they jumped to their deaths and with a determination to do something to improve conditions. As a member of the Factory Investigating Commission that proposed remedial legislation she came to the attention of Al Smith, who appointed her to the New York State Industrial Commission in 1918. When FDR became governor, he made her chairman.

As Secretary of Labor from 1933 to 1945, Miss Perkins was totally dedicated to her boss, FDR. She helped him draft all his speeches to labor leaders and formulate many of the major New Deal measures. She purged the Bureau of Immigration and Naturalization of racketeers, she greatly expanded the Bureau of Labor Statistics, she established the Bureau of Labor Standards, she won labor's confidence for the Federal Mediation and Conciliation Service, and she maintained the high standards of the Women's and Children's bureaus.

After FDR's death, Miss Perkins served briefly under President Truman. She resigned on 1 July 1945, but within a few months, returned to office as a member of the U.S. Civil Service Commission, where she remained until 1953. In 1957, at the age of seventy-seven, she became a professor at Cornell University's School of Industrial and Labor Relations and taught until her death in 1965.

GERARD D. REILLY

I first met Miss Perkins when I was asked by the solicitor, Charles Wyzanski, to join his staff in the Department of Labor. I had known of her for some years. In 1928, when I was a political correspondent for the Providence *Journal,* the reporters on the Al Smith campaign train relaxed by figuring out who would be in Al Smith's Cabinet. During the Hoover Administration there had been favorable reaction to his holding a White House conference in honor of Grace Abbott, the head of the Children's Bureau, and since Miss Perkins was Industrial Commissioner of New York state, the reporters assumed that Al Smith would break precedent by having a woman Cabinet officer and make her Secretary of Labor.

When I met her she'd been in office for approximately a year and a half, and the Labor Department then was small. It was in rented space in an old-fashioned office building, which has since been torn down, on G Street just off 17th. Shortly after I was sworn in, Charlie Wyzanski took me down to meet her. I was quite impressed with her cordial manner and the way she was dressed, with her tricorn hat. She talked freely about some of the problems she was confronted with in Congress and in other agencies.

The National Industrial Recovery Act had not yet been declared unconstitutional, so in a sense Miss Perkins wore two hats. She directed the labor advisory committee to the different codes under the NIRA and kept in touch with the temporary labor board that had been set up with Senator Robert Wagner as chairman. The board was supposed to decide cases involving union discrimination under Section 7a of the Recovery Act. She also chaired a Cabinet committee, the Committee on

Economic Security, which was drawing up plans for the Social Security Act. There were, in addition to the solicitor, Tom Eliot, who had come from a Buffalo law firm and whose primary duty was to handle the preliminary draft of what later became the Social Security Act, and the three older men who were concerned with reviewing decisions made by the Commissioner of the Immigration and Naturalization Bureau. These decisions dealt with the exclusion and deportation of aliens; an arrest warrant, let alone a deportation warrant, couldn't be issued without the approval of the Secretary of Labor.

I'd been a state house reporter before I went to law school. I'd been at the bar for about two years, having worked in the Boston law firm Goodwin, Procter, and Hoar. At the Labor Department I was assigned to write opinions on some of the controversial immigration cases, to lay down policy. If Charles Wyzanski agreed, he would sign them and present them to Miss Perkins.

When the NIRA was declared unconstitutional the next year, I was asked to draw up some amendments to the Davis-Bacon Act concerning the prevailing wage law on federal construction projects.[1] Another act—the Walsh-Healey Act—ran into some flak almost immediately; its purpose was to preserve the minimum wage and maximum hour standards of the labor codes under the Recovery Act, which roughly provided for a minimum wage of forty cents, a work week of forty hours, and nonemployment of children under the age of sixteen.[2] A Massachusetts Senator, David I. Walsh, elected in the Woodrow Wilson Administration, was chairman of the Senate Labor Committee. He was on rather friendly terms with Miss Perkins. This was before there were any big legislative staffs on Capitol Hill, so Miss Perkins relied on me to handle the drafts of these bills.

Shortly after the National Labor Relations Act was passed, the Social Security Act passed in 1935, but the Walsh-Healey Act got stuck in the House and didn't pass until 1936, and the amended Davis-Bacon Act passed just shortly before that. Wyzanski went over to the Solicitor General's office because the Solicitor General, Stanley Reed, had had a collapse and he wanted Wyzanski to argue most of his cases. Meanwhile, Tom Eliot had left to become general counsel of the Social Security Board, so I became the associate solicitor and got Donald Hiss and Jim Rowe to come over and fill some of the vacancies in the office. We

1. The Maximum Wage Act of 1931 (Davis-Bacon Act) provided that on any federal contract over $5,000 the government would pay the highest wage scale prevailing for laborers and mechanics and, in practice, no longer undercut local union contracts.
2. The Public Contracts Act of 1936 (Walsh-Healey Act) required that all contractors doing business with the federal government pay no less than the prevailing minimum wages in their geographical area, set maximum hours of work, and banned child labor.

had to expand because of the Davis-Bacon Act and the Walsh-Healey Act.

In the spring of 1937, on Miss Perkins's recommendation, I was nominated and then appointed solicitor. I'd already been engaged in the previous session of Congress, primarily in following through on the Fair Labor Standards Act of 1938. Most of the drafting had been done originally by Ben Cohen and Tom Corcoran. They'd created a board which had unlimited authority to set the minimum at whatever the board deemed appropriate and also to set different standards on the work week. The bill ran into difficulties in the Senate because of the broad discretion given this board. Senator Hugo Black of Alabama had succeeded David Walsh as chairman of the Senate Education and Labor Committee, and the bill ran into a lot of opposition from southern Democrats. The only southern Democrat on the committee who went along was the newly elected Senator Claude Pepper of Florida. The House of Representatives adjourned without taking any action on the bill. The chairman of the House Labor Committee, a Massachusetts congressman, died and was succeeded by Mrs. Mary Norton, chairman of the District of Columbia Affairs. The press referred to her as Mayor of Washington. She had been deeply involved in the District of Columbia's affairs.

In 1937, after the atmosphere had been cleared as a result of the defeat of the Court-packing plan, Roosevelt called a special session of Congress. Miss Perkins had me draft a substitute wage and hour bill based on the British Board of Trade Act. The American Federation of Labor and most of the Congress of Industrial Organizations gave the bill lukewarm support. The AF of L insisted on some amendments that would take unionized industries out of the act entirely. Miss Perkins told Mrs. Norton that it was better to go along with these AF of L amendments than to incite active labor opposition on the floor.

The bill also ran into some other difficulties concerning the imports of foreign goods not complying with the same labor standards. Secretary of State Cordell Hull was also indignant because of his devotion to reciprocal trade agreements. A member of the Ways and Means Committee knocked the bill out on a point of order. Finally after many complicated parliamentary struggles, the bill, omitting the tariff provisions, was pronounced in order. But the debate went on far into the night. Finally, late in December the bill was recommitted, which was a setback for the Administration as well as for Miss Perkins.

In the spring of 1938, much to Miss Perkins's delight, a revised version of the wage and hour act was passed by the House, but there was great divergence between it and the bill the Senate had passed. The final draft was the result of a conference in which Ben Cohen and I were the principal legal advisers, as neither the House nor Senate Labor Committees had any legal staff. The reason the House changed its mind was that Senator Pepper, in a special election, had won a surprise victory in the Democratic primary. The House Rules Committee, even though the Labor Committee had reported out the new bill, had refused to give it a rule. A discharge petition to get the bill out of Rules had been filed, but only about 120 members had signed. On the day after Pepper's election, however, lots of Democrats felt they had guessed wrong; the aisle was filled with persons wanting to sign up. So the wage and hour act went into effect in the late summer of 1938.

During the course of its revisions, the President told Miss Perkins he thought that, since the bill dealt with such simple issues, they didn't need the long draft passed by the Senate or the other draft that the House rejected. He suggested that she attempt to bring out a bill he could back that might take up only two or three pages. I was assigned to do that. It was impossible to get it all into two or three pages, but I finally got down to about eight pages. Miss Perkins wanted the President to see it, so one Saturday afternoon we went over to see him at the Oval Office. He turned out to be more of a schoolmaster than I thought. He read every word, made some suggestions for revision. He would say, "I don't understand. Explain it." Not that he was brusque, but he was not as relaxed or genial as he seemed at his public appearances or White House receptions. The draft, however, was eventually passed.

Miss Perkins always felt unhappy that, after passing the Wagner Act Congress accepted a Senate amendment which made the National Labor Relations Board an independent agency. She felt that the staff was infiltrated by radicals. She was quite pleased when the Supreme Court upheld the constitutionality of the act. In fact, she was so surprised that she walked from her own office and burst into mine rather than the other way around. She even suggested that we have some sherry together and celebrate. After the constitutionality had been upheld, the Board started taking a meat ax to employers who were accused of even the flimsiest unfair labor practices. Also it rigged elections so they generally favored CIO unions rather than AF of L unions.

She then became insistent that the Wage and Hour Division become part of the Labor Department. She had enemies on the Hill who didn't like that idea. The bill finally stood, and the Wage and Hour Division passed under the aegis of the Labor Department.

In the 1938 mid-term elections, the Republicans picked up about ninety seats in the House. Among these was a Republican, J. Parnell Thomas of New Jersey, who became overenthusiastic for violent confrontation with the Administration. He introduced a resolution on 24 January 1939 that called for the impeachment of Miss Perkins, the Commissioner of Immigration, and myself, because we had deferred hearings on the Bridges case.[3] He later became chairman of the House committee to investigate un-American activities that conducted the Alger Hiss hearings. He had a downfall too. He was accused by some of his staff of taking kickbacks and he resigned from Congress, was indicted, and served a prison term. The only time I can remember Miss Perkins being depressed was during the impeachment proceedings. She took it seriously. From reading her diaries in later years, I discovered that on the morning she appeared before the committee, she felt like Joan of Arc being called before the Inquisition, leaning on the arm of a priest whom she trusted and confided in, I being the priest. I was rather deeply touched to discover that after her death, because I never knew about her confidence in me while she was alive. She never indicated that she was so very nervous.

After the Civil War broke out in Spain in 1936, Miss Perkins, on several occasions, became concerned. There was one Communist faction that tried to recruit volunteers to go into the war, and one of their undertakings was to collect munitions and send them to the loyalists. Miss Perkins warned Mr. Roosevelt of this activity. Much to her dismay, when the ship was leaving New York harbor, Mrs. Roosevelt appeared as the cosponsor of the drive.

All this happened long before the Voting Rights Act of 1965 was passed. Southern senators, whether conservative or liberal, were always opposed to any legislation that favored blacks. During World War II, Mrs. Roosevelt supported the Fair Employment Practices Commission, which would force employers to have black employees.[4] If employers did not conform, they would be cut off from government contracts. Miss Perkins knew the President was very much embarrassed by this because it put him on the spot. Virtually all the southern senators were opposed. Miss Perkins mentioned some similar incident that had happened in

3. Miss Perkins postponed the deportation hearings of International Longshoremen's and Warehousemen's Union President Harry Bridges in April 1938, following several lower court decisions that undermined the Administration's legal position in his case. The Commissioner of Immigration referred to in the impeachment resolution was James L. Houghteling. On 4 March 1939, the House Judiciary Committee unanimously decided that they did not have enough evidence to impeach any of those named in the resolution and dropped the issue.

4. FDR established the Fair Employment Practices Commission to curb racial discrimination in war contracts and government employment in June 1941 at the urging of Eleanor Roosevelt and black civil rights leaders, who had threatened to march on Washington to protest discrimination in war industries and the armed services. It was the model for much of the civil rights legislation in force today.

"Ring around a Roosevelt, pockets full of dough."
Pen and ink cartoon by Clifford Berryman, *Washington Evening Star*,
May 26, 1938

Harry Hopkins

we took care of them. Hopkins had put out an order that we were not to take care of any migratory workers. I'm not sure what his theory was, but I think he felt that we would be supporting these people in behalf of the farm owners. But in practice we could not exclude them, so they became our responsibility too. At the peak of the program we were taking care of about 500,000 people and a substantial number were in family groups. Many traveled almost continuously. For our own convenience, we made up a list of all the camps and shelters, and copies of it became very much sought after by the people who were traveling. It was like a travel directory. "Well, there's a shelter in Tucson and maybe we can get to Tucson." It wasn't an ideal system because apart from agricultural work there simply was no work. The optimistic social workers who ran the program in the beginning called these places "treatment centers." A lot of social work terminology was used. I objected violently to that because for what were these people being treated? There was nothing wrong with them except joblessness.

Some of these people were traditional hoboes and some were alcoholics—a terrible problem. Mixed in with them were the plain unemployed workers. We had a large number of wandering young people, and we tried very hard to get them back home. As the program expanded, we set up special camps for transient young people that were comparable to the National Youth Administration and CCC programs. The NYA later had some residential programs.

At that time the military program was at a low ebb, so there were a great many old Army camps that were not being used. One of the first jobs I was given as the young assistant was to go over to the Munitions Building to see how we could get not only the camps but also their surplus property. Well, the major who received me was somewhat dumbfounded by this young lady asking for Army camps and equipment, but we worked out a system whereby we could borrow them. I recall one instance of Harry Hopkins's reaction.

Among the abandoned camps that we managed to acquire was Fort Eustis, a huge camp near Norfolk, Virginia. To run it we brought in a very aggressive man from Arizona named Paul Murphy, and he began to invite all the neighboring transient shelter officials to send their people to Fort Eustis. We just kept adding and adding and adding, and it became a remarkable place. One day Hopkins called me in and said, "I hear you're running a camp at Fort Eustis. How many people have you get there?" When I told him 3,600, he was absolutely appalled that we had so many transient men in one place. So we had to reduce the population.

Paul Murphy was a great one for gathering up anything he could get. One day he was over at Langley Field having lunch with the commanding officer, who didn't have much to do because things were very slow. Murphy said, "That's a nice hangar you have over there. You don't seem to be using it." "No, we haven't got enough planes." And Murphy said, "Well, we could use it over at Fort Eustis as a mess hall. How about our moving it over there? We've got plenty of labor." So this guy said, "All right," and they made some kind of very casual arrangement. The transients came over in trucks and started moving and reassembling the hangar. They had it about halfway assembled when the rearmament program began. If you recall, there was a time when we did an about-face on the size of our armed forces, particularly the Air Force. Word had gone out to Langley Field that they were to receive so many hundred more planes and this fellow was frantic. He called up Paul Murphy, who called me to ask what to do. I told him I'd go over to the Munitions Building and talk to my friends over there. The military was more relaxed in those days, and my friend said, "Well, I think we better do a Solomon's baby. You keep your half and we'll keep our half." And that's how this great crisis was resolved.

Hopkins was a remarkable character, in ill health most of the time. We had the feeling that in the FERA our one compelling, urgent job was to get that money out fast but honestly, and we did. By the time I got there in September 1933 every state had developed an Emergency Relief Administration to receive funds and most of the basic rules had been set up.

In 1935 the FERA was phased out in favor of the Works Progress Administration and the Social Security program. I moved out of the transient program and became a general assistant to Aubrey Williams, who was a general assistant to Hopkins. During the election campaign of 1936 there was criticism that the WPA was used for political reasons. Hopkins was very distressed because our record had been extremely good. Aubrey Williams asked me to take charge of reviewing every complaint of political activity or dishonesty that came to our attention. We had investigators who went out to check complaints. Because Hopkins hated lawyers, we never had a decent legal division, and many of the things that would normally be done by a lawyer I did. I reviewed every investigative report and then recommended whether or not to refer a complaint to the Justice Department. I saw every one of them, and there were very, very few, considering the fact that the WPA was a huge program employing 3 to 3.5 million workers. There were naturally a few cases of kickbacks or cheating or payroll padding, but we never had a really major scandal.

In 1938 we had another political problem. I was in the hospital having a baby and word came to me that Hopkins wanted something drafted. I was considered to be very good and wrote a lot of things for Roosevelt. Every time there was an appeal for the Community Chest or the Boy Scouts or any of those things, I was called. Aubrey asked me to write a communication to go in every pay check making it absolutely crystal clear that people may vote as they choose without being influenced by their superiors. I wrote a simple, straightforward letter, and whether it was having a baby or whether it was the times, I made a terrible mistake of omission. I wrote, "As a WPA worker you are entitled to vote for whomever you wish. Do not let anybody try to tell you who you have to vote for." Pretty soon we began getting a lot of letters along the lines of: "Dear Mr. Hopkins, I am a colored and I got your letter, and I thought, 'Great Day has arrived. Now I can vote.' And I took your letter to the courthouse and they said, 'You know we don't allow no coloreds to vote.'" In some places there were practically riots. Our lives were full of these extraordinary events.

Among my other duties, I supervised the mail room. We received 3,000 letters a day. Many of these were addressed to President Roosevelt or Mrs. Roosevelt. The custom in Washington had been that letters addressed to the President went to the State Department. During the first few months of the FERA, communications would come over: "The Secretary of State presents his compliments to the Administrator of the Federal Emergency Relief Administration and wishes to transmit the following letter." They quickly gave that up. During the campaign of 1936, a man whom we had fired as chief of the mail room because he was trying to get kickbacks from the workers under him went to the Republican National Committee and said, "I've got a hot piece of ammunition for you. Did you realize that President Roosevelt and Mrs. Roosevelt not only don't answer all the mail that comes to them, but they don't see it? It goes over to the FERA, where it's handled by a secretary of Aubrey Williams." Needless to say, this didn't make a big dent in the political campaign of 1936, but my husband was furious because I was called a secretary. Aubrey Williams was furious because he felt that it implied some favoritism on his part, but in fact this was just one of many, many things I did.

I used to ask the woman who actually ran the mail room, Betty Reasoner, to select a certain number of letters that were particularly interesting. Each week we sent these samples to Aubrey, to Hopkins, and to Mrs. Roosevelt to give them a feeling for the kind of mail that was coming in. Most of it, of course, was, "Dear Mr. President, I have four children and all I have in the pantry is such and such. Please send me help right away."

What is now the Food Stamp Program got started at that time.[1] Someone said, "Here we're gathering all this surplus food under the Price Support Program of the Agriculture Department, and we have all these hungry people. We should do something about it." Tex went to Rex Tugwell, whom he knew from his Columbia University days, and they worked out what was first the Surplus Food Distribution Program, which later became the Food Stamp Program.

FERA was the breeding ground for all kinds of programs. The Social Security Act is another example. Whenever anyone wants to attack the Aid to Families with Dependent Children program, they quote Roosevelt as having said, "We must get the federal government out of this business of relief." What Roosevelt really meant was, we must get out of this business of emergency relief and create more secure, more dignified programs. The biggest of those was, of course, Social Security. Hopkins, with Frances Perkins and others, constituted what was called the Committee on Economic Security, the planning group for the Social Security Act. The money to staff it came from the FERA.

I have since worked closely with Wilbur Cohen. He then worked for Ed Witte, who was the executive director of the planning committee staff. At that time we worked in a room across from the old Interior auditorium. (I think the other thing they did there was have dance marathons.) This vast space was divided by file cabinets. I sat on one side of a row of file cabinets, frantically looking after my troublesome family of transients. On the other side sat Wilbur Cohen, planning the Social Security Act. People think I had something to do with the creation of Social Security. Actually I did not, because I was so busy with the people I had on my hands right then and there.

The Resettlement Administration, which Tugwell ran to help poor farmers get reestablished, came out of a FERA program called Rural Rehabilitation. There was great unease between the old departments of government and the new emergency agencies. Rural Resettlement and later the Farm Security Administration were part of the new crowd and lived uneasily with the Department of Agriculture, though Farm Security eventually was brought into the department.[2]

1. The Food Stamp Program distributed surplus foods to schools for lunches and, through stamps redeemable at grocery stores, to families on relief. A small-scale, experimental project, it was administered by the Agriculture Department's Surplus Marketing Administration from 1938 to 1939.
2. The Resettlement Administration, set up in April 1935 to take over the rural rehabilitation and land programs formerly run by the FERA, eventually resettled 4,441 farm families. It was replaced by the Farm Security Administration, set up under provisions of the Farm Tenancy Act of 1937 (Bankhead-Jones Act). The FSA extended loans to farmers to rehabilitate their land and to tenants to purchase land and provided funds to establish and improve migratory labor camps.

Aubrey Williams was a populist of the old order. He came from Alabama and was a very poor boy. I think his father was a tenant farmer. The Baptist church to which they belonged put up the money to send Aubrey to Maryville College, a small school in Tennessee, with the intention of having him become a minister. This came out later when he was nominated to be Rural Electrification administrator.[3] He was turned down by the Senate because the people who had put up the money to send him to Maryville College said he had let them down by not becoming a minister. The Senate also thought he was too radical. After World War I he had decided that his faith was shaken; in any event he didn't want to be a Baptist minister and became a social worker. I don't believe he ever went to a school of social work, but in Wisconsin he ran a statewide program in the area of social planning.

I don't know how he came to Hopkins's attention because he was there by the time I arrived. Aubrey was absolutely dedicated to Hopkins, and Hopkins was absolutely dedicated to Roosevelt. And I suppose I was dedicated to Aubrey. At least I worked for him beyond imagining. I did everything for him, protected him, drafted things for him, assisted him.

I would say that this huge, controversial WPA program worked on a bond of loyalty, that Roosevelt trusted Hopkins, as was demonstrated later in the war years when Hopkins became his primary confidant and helper. Hopkins trusted Aubrey Williams to be totally loyal and honest. Aubrey trusted me. Hopkins was ill a good deal of the time, but we in the WPA did not want that fact to become too apparent. So Aubrey issued all orders in Hopkins's name. I remember one occasion when Aubrey himself was sick in bed, and in order to maintain this fiction I went out to Aubrey's house, he told me what he wanted Hopkins to say in a particular circumstance, and I went back and wrote out the order in Hopkins's name.

We never had money for more than three months at a time, and my husband likes to boast that all our children were born between the regular and the deficiency appropriations, because I was constantly on the Hill trying to plead for these 3 million families.

One time I was before Senator McKellar with Aubrey Williams. The Senator said, "I assume that everyone who receives an NYA check is expected to sign an affidavit that he has not advocated the overthrow of the government by force of arms." I said, "Why Senator McKellar,

---

3. The Rural Electrification Administration was created by FDR in May 1935 to bring electricity to rural areas where private power companies could not operate profitably. It sponsored regional power cooperatives through low-cost loans.

you know how suggestible young people are. We would never dream of asking high school students to sign an affidavit that they had not advocated the overthrow of the government by force of arms." Well, Senator McKellar had one of his renowned temper tantrums and really took me apart.

The NYA started a National Youth Orchestra, and contests were held around the country to select the musicians for this orchestra. Leopold Stokowski agreed to be the conductor. This came to the attention of the Appropriations Committee of the House. A Republican congressman from Wisconsin expressed outrage that we should have this man Stokowski conducting an orchestra made up of young people. He sent for Aubrey and Aubrey took me along. "We have heard some very scandalous stories about Mr. Stokowski and Greta Garbo, and we think this is something that should be investigated. We even hear that he and Greta Garbo were known to be together in a villa. Should we subpoena Mr. Stokowski to come before this committee and explain his behavior?" Aubrey immediately said, "Oh no, don't do that. I will undertake to investigate." He went up to Philadelphia to see Stokowski and came home beaming. We went back to the committee. Aubrey explained that he had put this issue before Stokowski and Stokowski provided a letter that went something like this: "The reality, the truth of the matter is that in the spring of 1937 I found myself in Rome, and I went to the Vatican. I was in the Sistine Chapel studying the paintings on the ceiling, and I said to myself, 'This is so beautiful that my great good friend, Greta Garbo, should be here to see it with me,' and I cabled her and said, 'Please come; I want to show you the Sistine Chapel.' I wish to assure you gentlemen of the committee that our relationship was always on the highest plane." This was read into the committee record and a vote was taken as to whether they were prepared to accept Mr. Stokowski's explanation. They voted yes. So that was the end of that particular scandal.

Aubrey was a highly dedicated man. He looked very much like Lincoln, with a seamed face and a country boy manner. He was not a very good administrator and often made public utterances that got him into trouble, but he was enormously charismatic. He could arouse a group of people by the depth of his sincerity and dedication. His strength really lay in the leadership that he was able to give to people who worked for him, particularly in the NYA.

When I knew Lyndon Johnson first he was the NYA director in Texas. That was in 1935. He was a very good administrator and devoted to Aubrey. So when he came to Congress, he became our primary connection, helping us with the terrible battle of appropriations. All I've learned about dealing with Congress I learned from Lyndon Johnson.

We would prepare three-minute speeches when we had an appropriation coming up. We would tailor these for specific targets, and Lyndon
would then pass them out to various people who put them in the record.
We had continuous advice from him on how to proceed.

I find it astonishing how much work we were able to do with such a
minuscule staff. The transient program, which involved feeding millions
of people, had, I think, six professional workers; that's all. We had a
brilliant accountant-statistician, who developed a system for us whereby
we could figure out exactly what was being spent in each state for food,
clothing, and shelter and then make comparisons. If anything seemed to
be out of line, we pursued it further. We had an engineer who did the
work program, and a couple of clerks. It's impossible to say how many
million people were kept alive this way. We made one major change in
1935, when we shifted from direct relief to work relief. Hopkins and
Roosevelt had very strong convictions that it was better for people to
have jobs than to take handouts. It was also more acceptable to Congress and to the people, and the evidence is that the average payment
doubled when we went from direct relief to work relief. Under the
FERA we were giving an average grant of $25 a month. The average
wage went to $50 a month overnight. People literally lived on this pro-
gram. In 1938, it was decided that the WPA needed a tighter administration—it had a very relaxed kind of administration—and that the
Corps of Engineers would be better able to do the job—a crazy decision
in my opinion. It gave certain officers marvelous training. Many of the
major officers in World War II came from the WPA. Colonel Francis
Harrington became the administrator, and a series of other officers ran
the WPA. At that time Hopkins went to Commerce as Secretary, Aubrey was limited to the NYA and was no longer deputy for WPA, and I
went to the NYA along with Aubrey. After he was rejected by the Senate as administrator for the Rural Electrification Administration, Aubrey worked for the Farmers' Union.[4] Then he bought a newspaper in
Alabama, a rural populist-type paper.

Tex moved out of the relief area, but I never did. I stayed on until
1940 or 1941, and our work was so enormously absorbing that I didn't
have many contacts outside the department. But there was one. We ran
this enormous operation without a proper legal staff. We had somebody
called chief counsel but all he was allowed to do was handle claims
cases. I did practically everything else that a lawyer would normally do.
Needless to say, I needed a little advice from time to time, and I used to
get it from Abe Fortas. Abe was sort of a sub rosa lawyer for the WPA,

4. Founded in Texas in 1902 as a populist-progressive reform movement, it attempted, with
   some success, to establish farm cooperatives and to maintain prices through crop reduc-
   tions.

because I would get Abe to tell me what he thought of a particular situation.

When the Federal Security Agency[5] was created and the NYA was put into the Federal Security Agency, Fowler Harper was general counsel. He was one of Wayne Coy's associates, and I worked for Wayne Coy, too. Fowler called NYA and they said, "We don't have a general counsel. Miss Wickenden does anything for us that we need of that kind." I went over to talk to him, and he said, "You know, you really belong in jail for illegal practice of the law."

We had every kind of crisis you can imagine. We had a big fire in Lynchburg. We had a flood in the Florida Keys. We had a meningitis epidemic with people carrying the illness from one camp to another. But the funniest one was a telegram that came to my desk one day from the administrator in Vermont: "The circus is stranded in some town in Vermont. This includes ten people, one elephant, many horses. Please advise." We gave the people relief, but I can't remember what we did with the elephant.

Roosevelt felt very cut off from life because of his inability to travel. So he used Mrs. Roosevelt as an ear to the ground, and he also got Lorena Hickok, who was a newspaperwoman, to go around the country. In due course he had Lorena recruit other writers. One of those she recruited was Martha Gellhorn. Martha had been in France, where she was married to Count de Juvenal, and had supposedly separated from him. In any event, she came back to the United States and became one of Lorena's reporters, and Roosevelt took a great fancy to her. She was a very glamorous young woman.

Roosevelt sent her to Hopkins. Hopkins was a little dumbfounded by her and sent her to Jake Baker, who was also dumbfounded. He sent her to Aubrey Williams, and Aubrey sent her out to the field. She was to interview the unemployed and see how the relief work was going, where it was good, where it was bad, and generally make narrative reports. Well, this went along fine until she reached Idaho. One day we received a telegram from the Idaho relief administrator that went something like this: "There has recently arrived in Boise a young woman who claims to work for you who calls herself Martha Gellhorn. She has been meeting with the Unemployed Councils"—a Communist organization at that time—"and other radicals and seems to be stirring up trouble. She has been recently joined by someone who calls himself the Count de Juvenal, and the two of them have been sending constant cables in code to France. I feel that this is a very disruptive influence. Please advise."

5. Established by Executive Order under the Administrative Reorganization Act of 1939, it included many former relief and welfare agencies, including the National Youth Administration.

Well, of course, what happened was that the count was a newspaperman and he had been sending his reports in French, which alarmed the Idaho relief administrator. Aubrey didn't really know what to do. Marty was not the kind of person you could control, even if he'd wanted to. So he summoned her back, and she wrote *The Trouble I've Seen,* an excellent book on relief families.[6]

ARTHUR GOLDSCHMIDT

My connection with Harry Hopkins started late in the summer of 1933. I was brought into the Federal Emergency Relief Administration by Jacob Baker, with whom I had worked in New York. I had to write a job description, and at that point Jake introduced me to Hopkins. Hopkins's entire organization was on two floors of the old Walker Johnson Building. Jake Baker was in charge of work relief, and he had one assistant. I was the third person hired. It was a very small organization, but so many things happened quickly that we soon took over the whole building and several other buildings in Washington. The Civil Works Administration was created, and our goal was to put 4 million people to work in a four-week period. We failed by half a week!

All the work relief programs were scoffed at as "leaf-raking," but this one was particularly vulnerable because it cost so much money. We spent about $900 million between the first of October 1933 and February 1934, as we put 4 million people to work at regular wages and on regular work. It was probably the most important crash program that the New Deal had at that time. In that winter of 1933–34, we managed to survive long working hours and the fact that we had to rush around the country getting things going. Anyone who was over thirty was likely to have a heart attack, but we young people were able to stand the pressure.

Our lives were spent on the job, and when we weren't on the job we were talking about it. We would go to the roof of the Powhatan Hotel. Our wives thought we went there to dance, but we didn't. We just went there to talk. Fortunately, my wife didn't care about dancing any more than I did, but she enjoyed talking, so she entered into those discussions that went on all night on the roof of the Powhatan.

I provided the means by which the program was financed quite incidentally. Our big problem in work relief was to avoid criticism and

6. Martha Gellhorn, *The Trouble I've Seen* (New York: W. Morrow, 1936) focused on rural rehabilitation projects.

create the kinds of jobs the public would accept. My first task was to check the needs of the other federal agencies. I went to Commerce, Agriculture, and a number of other departments and discovered that they all had very important jobs to be done. The Coast and Geodetic Survey, for instance, wanted to coordinate the various mapping work being done in the United States. The railroads had one set of maps, the highway departments had another, states and cities had others. Unemployed surveyors and engineers could tie these different mapping systems together. This was a very labor-intensive program. It didn't cost much in materials, and that was the sort of relief we were always seeking. But the Commerce Department and the Coast and Geodetic Survey didn't have even the small amount of material that was needed. I found this was true in all the departments I went to.

Among the very important projects was the famous privy project. We helped build sanitary privies in the rural areas by putting the unemployed to work and letting the rich people in the community provide the materials. That cut the incidence of typhoid and hookworm.

I came back to Jake and said, "Look, we've got real trouble because we can't afford people to supervise these wonderful programs, and we don't have the money we need for materials." Then I went to Rex Tugwell, whom I knew on a first-name basis. He was then Assistant Secretary of Agriculture, but his title wasn't important, as he was very close to Roosevelt. I went to see him one afternoon and said I had an idea and I wanted his help because he was the vice-chairman, under Ickes, of Public Works. Public Works financed local, state, and federal projects. I told Rex I had wonderful projects that could use relief labor if we could get the money to provide materials and supervision. I thought that the Public Works fund could be used for that purpose. I wasn't a lawyer, and I didn't pretend to be, but it seemed to me that this would be legal. The board of Public Works could give us the amount we needed. He asked me how much I thought was needed, and I said $400,000. Rex said, "Gee, that's a great idea," and he was very positive about it. When I reported to Jake, he yelled, "Why the hell did you go and talk to Rex Tugwell without telling us you were doing it? It's very improper."

I said, "Well, I didn't want to take it up with Hopkins because it may be a cockamamy idea. But Rex is an old friend of mine, and I was willing to try it out on him." (At that time Rex was a high priest, but Hopkins was not yet close to Roosevelt at all.) Fortunately Hopkins met Tugwell at some White House meeting and Tugwell said, "You people over there had a bright idea that Tex told me about." So from being somewhat in the doghouse I became a hero because we got the money.

There were big jobs that needed a lot of engineering in advance, things like the Bonneville Dam. We got the money, $400 million, from Public Works and used some of it as FERA money. It was through these measures that CWA, the Civil Works Administration, was set up, covering people who were unemployed. They were put to work at the regular wage rates, with a minimum of 25 cents an hour. CWA was set up in every state, and it was done as a crash program. Roosevelt agreed to do it sometime in September, and it was supposed to start October 15th. Everything had to be done. In the first place, everyone who was employed had to be paid by a federal check. In the earlier relief programs, the money was given to the states and the states allocated the funds to individuals. But these people were put on as federal employees, and state administrators were made federal administrators for the purposes of this program. Suddenly we had to issue as many as 4 million checks a week. William Woodin, who was Secretary of the Treasury, called his top people together and asked whether this was possible. Everybody told him it was not possible except one young man whose name, unfortunately, I don't remember. He said, "Well, Mr. Secretary, I'd like until this afternoon to let you know whether it's possible or not." He came back to Woodin in the afternoon and said, "We can do it." "What have you done since this morning that makes you think we can do it?" Woodin replied. "Well, I've taken a lease on a building and I've ordered checkwriting machines." They ran out of ink for writing the checks and they ran out of the paper from which the checks were made, but they still managed to do it.

It was an extraordinary program and it worked very well. Civil Works managed to put these people to work and do good work, despite the fact that the weather in the winter of 1933–34 was about the worst in history. The program worked better in those communities that had some kind of advance planning. For instance, in Cincinnati there had been a committee on city planning. They just stepped up work on all the things they were planning to do. They did ten years' work in one year, and they did good work. In places where there wasn't much of a plan, it faltered. There was some leaf-raking and projects that were of lesser importance. But it was a very exciting period, and whenever you get New Dealers who worked on that program together there's a kind of camaraderie that you only find with people who have been in the same campaign. It was a very real battle because there was an awful lot of criticism.

I was also put in charge of the work involving professional and white-collar people. We had one important program, the Historic American Buildings Survey, where we put unemployed draftsmen, engineers, and architects to work on buildings of·historic interest. We started all kinds of things. One was the Watergate concerts, and I'm very unhappy that Watergate has gotten the name it has, because for me Watergate was for concerts. The Watergate was built as part of the bridge from the Lincoln Memorial across to Arlington. When the engineers planned it, they provided for a massive flight of steps to the spot where the President could meet important visitors to Washington. It was supposed to be a place to welcome returning heroes. We got an old Navy barge and a local unemployed orchestra and put them together at that place, and they were an instant success. Out of that came similar programs in New York and throughout the country. There was music, there was art, there was theater in places where they had never been before.

I think the real problem with the Hopkins story is that Hopkins was many different persons throughout his life. During this period he was a great doer in getting people going and inspiring them. Without being flamboyant, he was kind of cocky. At the same time he was absolutely dedicated to the cause of the unemployed, and he was prepared to try anything that could be done to help poor people. He was an enormously good experimenter, and he was also good at getting people to work way beyond their capacity. When the drought of 1934 came, Hopkins took a whole group of his top people off what they were doing and said, "Go out there and look at the situation and come back a week from now with a plan." We all fanned out through the drought area. I went to South Dakota. We organized teams and went and talked to people, all kinds of people. Then we all got on a train in Chicago and spent all night arguing what our report was going to be. We produced a report that recommended a whole series of things, including the famous Shelter Belts,[7] more water projects, and buying surplus cattle to get them off the plains and canning the meat for distribution to the unemployed.

Isador Lubin said to me once, "You know, I was at a meeting with you in Hopkins's office and I was just shocked because I thought you were drunk. I thought, how terrible for a young man to be in this important group drunk. Suddenly I realized that you weren't drunk, you were just exhausted. You were just weaving from exhaustion because you'd been up for several nights in a row." It was true; I don't drink very much. This was a meeting about a labor problem in Pennsylvania. Hopkins said, "Two of you guys will have to get to Harrisburg by eight o'clock tomorrow morning." I was one of them. I went home and took a shower, and we got into the car and drove up to Harrisburg to settle the labor problem for Eric Biddle.

I knew Hopkins better than most people alive today, but I wasn't

7. The Shelter Belt programs, authorized under the Soil Conservation and Domestic Allotment Act of 1936, were large reforestation schemes for the plains states which helped reduce the wind erosion that had caused the Dust Bowls.

one of his close associates. I thought he was a marvelous person, a great no-nonsense guy. He called a spade a spade and worked very long hours. I liked his style very much. Hopkins was a man with a mission. He had a great capacity for hard work. I never knew him to get involved with cant or crusade. He was just concerned about the job. He didn't believe in what he termed "bullshit." He was a rather soft-spoken person and I don't think he ever shouted at anyone. He had a very good sense of humor.

I remember when CWA was running into trouble on the minimum wage. There was a very real problem because having Negroes getting wages of that kind was tantamount to revolution, and there were a lot of people who objected to it because most of the workers were unskilled. Roosevelt decided he had to drop the minimum wage requirement. Hopkins told Jake and Jake told me and I was disappointed. This was about January or February of 1934. I said,"Jake, this is just shocking. Here we've fought this thing, and we've won. We've done it for three months, and now we've gone into a back-up program. I just feel very angry." For the first time ever, Jake said, "You have no right to talk to me like that. You're just an employee." So I decided to get out. I slammed the door and went back to my office and began drafting all kinds of resignation letters. Jake came in later and said, "I've got something really funny to tell you." And I said, "I'm not in the mood for funny stories." He said, "After you bawled me out this morning, I went up to Hopkins and said exactly what you had said, as my own view. Hopkins had the same reaction and bawled the hell out of me. He told me I had no right to speak to him that way. So I began laughing, and I told him that you had come in to see me with the same thing." Obviously Hopkins had made the same points to Roosevelt. I was the last man on the totem pole.

But Hopkins had his lighter moments. He liked to drink, he liked to go to horse races, he liked the good life. He had a curious poor boy's interest in social life. He was impressed with people. This seemed completely out of character to me, but I realize that he was interested in connections with what would now be called the "right people." As a matter of fact, his third wife, whom he married when he was in the White House, was a Macy.[8]

Hopkins was a minor character, but to many people he was the embodiment of the New Deal. His name was widely known throughout the country. When I first knew him, he was completely nonpolitical except

8. Hopkins married Louise Macy in 1942. His first wife, Ethel Gross Hopkins, divorced him in 1930; his second wife, Barbara Duncan Hopkins, whom he married in 1931, died of cancer in 1937.

for a very deep commitment to Roosevelt. He hadn't gotten Potomac Fever. He did get it later.

Hopkins was very well organized when he was thinking through a problem. Once we had Henry Wallace over to discuss the distribution of powdered milk to underfed children. Wallace was very doubtful about it, partly because the taste was so terrible. Hopkins felt that from the nutrition standpoint, this was the sort of thing that was needed. The real problem was packaging it so that it wouldn't spoil.

We had all kinds of distribution programs for the unemployed. Surplus cotton was bought and made into mattresses in the workshops. All through the country, people got mattresses for the first time.

Hopkins always wanted to get to the bottom of the problem. He was a very fact-oriented person. He was certainly not interested in anything theoretical. I once had one problem with him. Someone convinced him that the unemployed should all have market gardens to help them raise their own food. As a youngster right out of college, I had been involved in a self-help program for the unemployed and had actually managed a garden development in New Rochelle. We took over a golf range and made gardens for the unemployed out of it. In New Rochelle there were a lot of unemployed gardeners, mostly Italians, and they were damned good at it. But by the time their food was produced, the surplus food from the rest of Westchester County just inundated New Rochelle, and there it was, rotting in the streets. So the cost benefit was just nonsense. I talked Hopkins out of it. I said, "I don't think there's anything wrong with giving the unemployed a chance to have gardens, but to make it a requirement is absolutely absurd. This is not a solution to the problems of the unemployed." That is the kind of thing he understood very quickly.

One day I got a call directly from Hopkins, which was very rare. The *New York Times* had a piece on the front page about boondoggling. He wanted to know where the hell the word "boondoggle" came from. Well, I happened to know. In one of our programs for the unemployed, we had set up training workshops to teach women how to sew and there was a guy, some ex-Boy Scout up in Milwaukee, who set up training for young people in what he called "boondoggling." Boondoggling was a Boy Scout word meaning "to make things, little artifacts, to make useful things." Boondoggling in the old sense, the word that came out of the West, meant "fixing the harness" for a team of horses. It was the fixing of things that were in hand. Well, unfortunately, the Republicans got hold of the word "boondoggling," and boondoggling became the buzz word for any nonsense in the relief programs. I still remember Hopkins's dismay when he saw the headline. I told him it was a perfectly respectable old American word. But it no longer is. Now it means goofing off, doing something useless. He was absolutely furious. He said, "Well, they haven't heard the last of that," and he was perfectly right.

We had Hopkins and his second wife, Barbara, to our house for dinner before taking them to see *The Taming of the Shrew,* a performance put on by unemployed actors for the CCC. These actors from New York toured all over the eastern United States. We booked them into the Press Club Auditorium and brought in their costumes and scenery to show the officials in Washington how this program worked. I was responsible for getting the performance organized. Hopkins was enormously impressed by these unemployed actors. After the show we had a little party, and they all were very impressed at meeting Hopkins. They were so pleased to be given an opportunity to bring culture to poor people who had never had an opportunity to see Shakespeare before, who never had any feeling that they were being helped through relief. One actress said she felt like Lady Bountiful, giving her talent to entertain those poor kids. Actually, she was down on her uppers, and so were most of her colleagues.

In those days they didn't charge for admission, so later on Hallie Flanagan took over the Federal Theatre Project as part of the Works Progress Administration, and they did charge. But at that time they had no way of getting materials. I had a call from New York, one of the great centers of the theater program because there were so many unemployed actors there, requesting materials for costumes. I pointed out that we had a big mattress program going, and there was a workshop in New York. Why didn't they just go and borrow some mattress ticking. They did, and they made costumes and drapes and curtains and backgrounds out of mattress ticking, dyeing it when necessary. But the stripes in the ticking always showed through. I remember meeting one critic who said they had managed to get a kind of a unity between the costumes and the scenery by using the same material. So a virtue was made out of necessity.

I think Hopkins was very touched and impressed by the work the actors were doing. Hopkins was the real spokesman for the lowest of the low, the really depressed people. He was a great believer in work relief, because he saw, as this visit to the theater showed, that people got a sense of respectability by working instead of getting relief. I suppose it was part of the Protestant work ethic. He came out of Iowa, Middle America.

Hopkins's friendship with FDR was a long time in coming, and I think it probably came through Mrs. Roosevelt originally. She was tremendously interested in what we were doing and was very much in-

volved in it. In the early periods of the work-relief program, we had theater, music, and writing projects, but local people didn't like to finance
them. Under WPA, the communities had to put up money for supervision and materials. We realized that under WPA we would have very serious problems in employing professionals. So we set up projects that
were totally financed with federal funds. We planned the four arts projects. I had very little to do with the administration of them because I left
Mr. Hopkins shortly after they got going. But I had a lot to do with the
planning and a lot to do with finding the people who could supervise
them.

We had a problem finding someone in the theater who was prepared to set up a project for unemployed actors. Jake Baker and I went
to New York and talked to the Theatre Authority Actors' Equity people.
They said, "Well, to help the theater the best thing is to provide money
to the theatrical producers and they will produce plays. And unemployed actors, the good actors, will get jobs." We were very resistant to
that. We said, "No, this has to be a program that employs actors, not
just producers. To be sure, the industry likes to do both. But we have to
have an entirely employee-oriented program." We got into a lot of trouble with the producers, although I managed to get the best seats at
"Anything Goes," one of the great musicals of the period.

CHAPTER 13

The Minimum Wage and the Wagner Act

Robert F. Wagner, Democratic senator from New York from 1929 to 1947, was not a colorful politician in the style of Huey Long or Fiorello La Guardia. For the present generation, however, he may have been one of the most significant figures in the Congresses of the New Deal.

Born in Germany, Wagner grew up in New York city, an urbanite who became uneasy when away from the rumble of the el train. Together with Al Smith, he began his political career in the Tammany Hall political organization. At first, he was indistinguishable from any other Tammany politician and served in the New York State Assembly (1905 to 1908) and Senate (1909 to 1914). It was not until he was chairman of the commission appointed in 1911 to investigate the Triangle Shirtwaist Company fire that he became convinced of the need for effective social legislation. As he said: "Of what use are material resources and scientific resourcefulness, all our equipment, our enterprise, and our efficiency if the sum total of human happiness enjoyed by our people—*all* our people—be not increased thereby? I firmly believe that human welfare and social security will play a far greater role in the world of the future than any mere political combination or military alignment."

As lieutenant governor of New York (1914 to 1919), Justice of the New York Supreme Court for the First District (1919 to 1925), and Appellate Justice for the First District (1925 to 1927), Wagner never forgot those sentiments. As U.S. senator from New York, Wagner introduced into Congress the National Industrial Recovery Act of 1933, the Social Security Act of 1935, the National Labor Relations Act of 1935, the U.S. Housing Acts of 1937 and 1949, and many other social and economic measures which together formed the core of the New Deal.

I went to Washington in March 1933 with Rex Tugwell, who was slated to be Assistant Secretary of Agriculture, and he said, "You know, you could get better pay if you went into the legal division. You'll help Wallace and me, but you go into the legal division. Go over and see Jerome Frank." The Agricultural Adjustment Act hadn't been passed yet, so they couldn't pay anybody, but I went to see Jerome Frank. Frank said, "Tell me what you know." I replied, "I know Cotton Ed Smith." Smith was the chairman of the Senate Agricultural Committee who had sworn that the Triple-A would never become law and that even if it did, that blankety-blank Jerome Frank would never be confirmed. So Frank said, "You know Cotton Ed Smith? Let's go." We jumped into a taxi and went up to the Hill, and in ten minutes Smith put his arms around Frank and said, "My boy, you're gonna get your law and you're gonna be confirmed too." The reason was that Cotton Ed Smith was a lifelong friend of my father's. The farms and organizations headed by my father were very big cotton ginners and dealers and the biggest truck growers and shippers in either of the Carolinas.

We started back for the Department of Agriculture in a cab and Frank said, "We haven't talked about your pay. What about $4,000 a year?" As an instructor at Columbia I had been getting $100 a month plus what I got from a couple of other little jobs. I gazed out over the Washington Monument and said, "I think that would be all right as a starter, but in the meantime please lend me $20 to go back to New York to get my clothes." So I joined the legal staff, but I was there for only two weeks.

One day I went with some important New Dealers to see Senator Robert Wagner of New York. They talked for two hours about how we could get the country out of its difficulties by playing around with gold and exchange rates and everything except anything that mattered. I didn't say a word until the two hours were over. Senator Wagner rubbed his face and said he was tired, but he asked me if I had anything to say. So, being a newcomer to Washington, I commented, "I don't want you to think that we're all in agreement. I'm not in agreement with anything that's been said. If the National Industrial Recovery Act is going to be effective, it's got to have something in there that enables people to have the purchasing power to buy products. The whole trouble now is that they haven't got enough money to buy anything, and so the factories aren't running." I suggested that they should throw into the NIRA the $3.3 billion public works program that had been drafted over the years since 1930 for Senator Wagner and Senators Robert La Follette of Wisconsin and Edward Costigan of Colorado, and he agreed. Then I added, "You've got to have something about wages and working conditions and collective bargaining." At the end of this talk Senator Wagner asked me to be his legislative assistant.

Thus I became involved in the drafting of the NIRA. I wrote into the NIRA the famous Section 7a guaranteeing the right to bargain collectively which later on became the basis of the National Labor Relations Act of 1935, the Wagner Act. I wrote in the provisions on wages and working conditions which abolished the sweat shop and child labor and were the forerunners of the Fair Labor Standards Act of 1938, the minimum wage law. These provisions have been of lasting significance even though the act was later declared unconstitutional. I wrote in the $3.3 billion for public works, so the NIRA was also the origin of Harold Ickes's public works program, which led to some of Harry Hopkins's work programs, as well as the national concern with wages and working conditions.

Housing was another great problem of the period. Homes were all owned, in effect, by the banks, and the banks couldn't collect on their mortgages because so many people were broke. There in the senator's office we helped to write the Home Owners' Loan Corporation Act—I was one of the draftsmen—which rescued the banks by taking mortgages over and setting a low interest rate and then returning them to the banks when they became profitable.[1] The National Housing Act of 1934, which I helped draft, established the Federal Housing Administration for mortgage insurance, probably the best known of all the housing agencies.

Although Wagner was instrumental in so much of this legislation, most of which was drafted in his office, and although he was the chairman of the Banking and Currency Committee, I was the only professional person he had on his staff. The senator was getting 8,000 letters a day and making speeches and radio addresses and speaking in many political campaigns. That shows how different the burden of work was and how different the whole system was from what it is now. Now any senator who amounts to anything has many employees, paying them each $40,000 or $50,000 a year. I got $3,900, reduced to $3,150 when the large reduction in government expenditures was put into effect.

We went on to other aspects of the housing problem, and I wrote the United States Housing Act of 1937, which set up the first nationwide

1. The Home Owners' Loan Act passed in June 1933 allowed creditors to exchange mortgages they were owed for government bonds instead of foreclosing.

program of low-rent housing and slum clearance.[2] It did not get much support from the Administration. I remember a very interesting episode in my early experience when I had my first substantial visit with Roosevelt. When the housing bill was under consideration, Senator Wagner said to me, "I've called Frank"—he called him by this name because he had been the leader of the New York state Senate from 1910 to 1913 when Roosevelt was a young member. "I'm going up there to talk to him about this housing bill and get it straightened out." All the agencies were opposing the bill.

So for two weeks I couldn't sleep thinking of all the questions that we'd ask the Great White Father and how we would get it solved. Henry Morgenthau, Secretary of the Treasury, was there, as well as Daniel Bell, Director of the Budget, Harold Ickes, Interior Secretary, and the heads of other agencies. It was St. Patrick's Day, and Roosevelt had a green flower in his lapel and looked very happy. He'd just been in the swimming pool and looked very strong and ruddy. He said, "You know, this is St. Patrick's Day, and it's also my wedding anniversary. I'm not going with you; I'm going to lock you all up in the Cabinet room and not let you out until you decide it." So we went into the Cabinet room and we fought like cats and dogs for two hours. When we came out Roosevelt told us good-bye. Then he said to Wagner, "Wait a minute. I want to ask a question." The President turned to me and said, "I just want to ask you one question about the housing bill. Have you got anything in there to keep the sand and gravel men out of it?" I said I didn't quite understand. He said, "You know, to keep out the people who sell the government materials for mixing sand with cement." "Yes, Mr. President, we've got something in there to keep the sand and gravel men out of it." "That's all. Good-bye. Good-bye." I went back to the Capitol a sadder and a wiser man.

Let me say that despite these peculiarities of administration, I think Roosevelt was by far the greatest President of the twentieth century. His parting remarks must have come from his experience as Assistant Secretary of the Navy during World War I, when he had had to do a great deal of procurement.

When I went into the administrative side of housing, I became involved with sixteen housing agencies that were warring with each other. Roosevelt asked Sam Rosenman to make an investigation, and he came down and interviewed the two top men in each of the sixteen agencies. Following Rosenman's advice, Roosevelt asked me to draft an Execu-

2. The United States Housing Act of 1937 (Wagner-Steagall Act) created the United States Housing Authority as a public corporation in the Interior Department. The USHA was given an appropriation of $500 million to subsidize low-cost housing loans.

tive Order which in February of 1942 put the sixteen housing agencies into one wartime National Housing Agency, the offshoot of which was ultimately the Department of Housing and Urban Development.[3] I became general counsel of NHA.

My hours were often from nine o'clock in the morning until I walked down those marble corridors at two or three the next morning. In those times, I didn't have any difficulty in getting secretaries to keep those hours.

We got the 1937 U.S. Housing Act through, and later I drafted for Senators Wagner, Allen Ellender, and Robert Taft the Housing Act of 1949.[4] That act declared the right of every family to a decent home in a suitable environment. All subsequent housing legislation has been built on that act. I was consultant not only to Wagner but also to Senator Taft. I had for many years a very close working relationship with Taft. I think he was a great man and would have made a great President, certainly compared to Eisenhower. That was one of my most interesting experiences.

The National Labor Relations Act of 1935, of which I was the main draftsman, was politically speaking a most important asset to the Democrats because it permanently converted the whole labor movement to ardent support of the Democratic party and that support lasted until 1980. I had great experiences working on the Wagner Act. Joe Robinson of Arkansas, the majority leader, and Pat Harrison of Mississippi, chairman of the Finance Committee, took Senator Wagner and me up to see Roosevelt to try to get Roosevelt to persuade Wagner to withdraw the bill. Wagner said, "I don't care whether it passes or not. I just want to vote." Of course when he got a vote, it was six against and ninety for.

In 1943–44 I suggested and helped draft the Employment Act of 1946.[5] During the periods of drafting legislation, I also wrote supportive economic studies, committee reports, and hundreds of speeches and articles. I also participated, though to a lesser degree, in the original Social Security Act of 1935. I continued to help the senator after I left him formally in 1937, until he left the Senate in 1946 owing to illness and resigned in 1949.

Wagner was *the* important figure in the Senate. He introduced the NIRA, he introduced the Social Security Act, he introduced all of the

3. The National Housing Agency was created by FDR by Executive Order in 1942 to determine the housing needs of defense workers. The Department of Housing and Urban Development was established in 1965.
4. The Housing Act of 1949 provided for the establishment of a large-scale public housing program but did not receive sufficient funding or leadership.
5. The Employment Act of 1946 created the Council of Economic Advisors and made the President responsible for the maximum employment program.

housing acts. Roosevelt relied on him because they'd been in the Senate together in Albany. While I was up there, the press took a vote and Wagner was voted the best-dressed man in the Senate, the most popular man in the Senate, the ablest man in the Senate, the most useful man in the Senate, and the one most helpful to the press, all at the same time.

Wagner was very able. On some of the complicated bills, even when he wasn't on the committee, he would be asked to sit with them. He did a great deal of the questioning of the opposition witnesses from the National Association of Manufacturers and the Chamber of Commerce. He was very good at that; he had been a judge. He said he got off the bench because it was like being in a mausoleum. He was a plodder, but he worked hard and he dealt largely with facts. He was a good speaker.

Once I went from New York to Albany with Governor Herbert Lehman, Senator Wagner, Si Rifkind, and one of Wagner's secretaries. We went up in a compartment in the Empire State Express. When we got there, Wagner had gone to a meeting to talk. He never let me go to the meetings where he was talking. He always said, "Stay there and work up an extra." So we were working late at night and the phone rang. A voice said, "This is the police. You shouldn't have those girls in your room." I said, "We haven't got any girls in the room except Wagner's secretary." "Well, yes you have. We don't want to make any trouble. If you will go out and get us some nice ham sandwiches and some beer, we'll forget about it. Bring them up to room so-and-so." So Si and I rushed out and got the ham sandwiches and beer and carried them up to the room and there were Wagner and Herbert Lehman who had called and played this trick on us.

I learned a lot about how senators worked in those days. Take James F. Byrnes: he was a very important man, Roosevelt's primary lieutenant in the Senate, and a strange mixture. Until 1937 all the Democrats were liberal New Dealers because they felt Roosevelt's strength and the emergency was so great. In 1937 a great many of them began to turn around, partly because of the Court-packing plan, but I think it would have happened anyway. Byrnes called me up one day when I was in the housing agency. We were awarding contracts. We didn't have to award them to the lowest bidder if we thought he couldn't do the job. One builder in South Carolina had flopped miserably on his first job; he didn't have the means to do it. The second time around we awarded it to the second lowest bidder. Byrnes called me up and asked me to come to see him. "You've got to help me out. This man is my biggest enemy in Charleston, and if he doesn't get the project, everybody in Charleston will think that I stopped him because I'm his enemy or because he's my enemy. So you have to give him the project." This was a new way of pleading for a project.

When I looked around the Senate as a young man during my first years there, I'd say, "What a remarkable thing it is that our democratic country can send such great men." I didn't agree with them all, but I admired so many of them. I admired the liberals like Wagner and Costigan and La Follette, the conservatives like Walter George of Georgia, Josiah Bailey of North Carolina, and Harry Byrd of Virginia, and on the Republican side men like William Borah of Idaho and Henrik Shipstead of Minnesota, because I knew what they were going to stand for when they spoke.

In my time, the senators that I knew anything about realized that the function of the Senate was to deal with great issues, not to duplicate the work of the executive agencies. Now they think that in order to vote on an agricultural law, they have to have an agricultural expert and they have to have a military expert, they have to have a this-and-that expert. So they have an expert for every function of the government. One agricultural expert can't know as much as the Department of Agriculture. That's not the way that Congress is supposed to get what it needs.

In one respect Congress has been economical. Just think, they had 96 senators and now they've got 100. That's four more senators but only three more senate office buildings.

FDR had a great gift for selecting people. I think Harry Hopkins was a marvelous man for the job. He had administrative ability; he really cared about the people he was helping. I think Frances Perkins had a tremendous amount of ability compared with subsequent secretaries, although she had faults and idiosyncrasies. Henry Morgenthau was underestimated. He was brought in as a personal friend of Roosevelt's, but he was the best administrator the Treasury has had. He had marvelous people helping him, like Randolph Paul, who was the greatest tax expert in the country. Roosevelt had great people helping him, and he was able to inspire them. When he had someone in the Cabinet with whom he didn't agree or who was ineffective, such as Cordell Hull—although Hull was popular on the Hill and in the party—Roosevelt was able to act as if that person didn't exist. He had to operate through other people. He was largely his own Secretary of State, but he also operated substantially through Sumner Welles, the Under Secretary.

I had additional contacts with Roosevelt because Senator Wagner was chairman of the Democratic Platform Committee during the three campaigns when Roosevelt ran for reelection. In those days we didn't have a far-flung committee of hundreds of people all over the country.

Wagner just said to me, "We've got to draft a platform." I drafted three platforms and then he took them to the conventions; the so-called Resolutions Committee changed a few words, and that was the platform.

In 1936 Alf Landon, who was running against Roosevelt, launched his great attack upon the Social Security program, which had been enacted but was not yet in effect. A little slip was put into many pay envelopes—it was called the "pay envelope campaign"—stating that no Social Security benefits would ever be paid. It was part of an effort to get rid of the act, but more important it was a straight-out political attack against the Administration. I was asked to draft for Senator Wagner the nationwide speech answering Landon. I did not just write paragraphs in that speech. I wrote that speech in its entirety.

In 1940 when Wendell Willkie was running against Roosevelt, John L. Lewis bolted the Democratic party and supported Willkie. There had been a labor dispute and Roosevelt said, "A plague on both your houses."[6] That was when John L. Lewis made his famous statement, "It ill behooves those who have supped at labor's table and accepted labor's gifts to condemn with majestic equanimity labor and management when they are locked in mortal combat." I was asked to draft the speech in which John L. Lewis was answered.

When Roosevelt was to make his Madison Square Garden speech at the windup of the 1936 campaign, I was working in Wagner's New York apartment. In that speech Roosevelt said, "In my first term these economic royalists met their match. In my second term they will meet their master." Wagner said, "You don't go to the meeting. You stay here and work on the next one. There's some delicatessen in the icebox." So as soon as he left I left and went down to Madison Square Garden without a ticket. There was a big cordon of police. I went around to the side entrance. I said, "I'm Senator Wagner's secretary. I've got an important telegram for him." The policeman said, "Go on in." I started in, and he said, "Wait a minute. I'll go with you." There were Wagner and Lehman standing under the grandstand. The policeman said, "Here's a man who says he's your secretary and he's got a telegram for you." Wagner looked at me and said, "I never saw that man before in my life."

Only once did Roosevelt change one of the platforms, and that was in 1940. The platform had a sentence in it: "We will not send our men to fight in foreign wars." Roosevelt wrote above it in his own handwriting—I have that piece of paper—"except in case of attack." This was the only thing he ever wrote into any one of those three platforms. When he

6. FDR made his "A plague on both your houses" statement in June 1936 shortly after he rejected Lewis's demand that the Administration support the unions against the managements in the auto, steel, and rubber industry sit-down strikes.

went to Boston later that year he didn't say, "except in case of attack." He said, "I say and shall say it again and again and again: Your boys are not going to be sent into any foreign wars." But this was understandable.

I got to know more about Roosevelt through knowing Mrs. Roosevelt very well in a variety of ways. My wife, Mary, attracted Mrs. Roosevelt's attention when Congressman John Toland chaired the defense migration commitee on the Hill, Mary being its director of research. In consequence Mrs. Roosevelt later made her director of research when she became second in command in the Office of Civilian Defense.[7] So we went up to Hyde Park, or rather to Valkill, a number of times.

As I left to go to the 1944 convention, I said, "Harry Truman is going to be the vice-presidential nominee." The first day of the balloting Henry Wallace was way ahead. He would have been nominated that night, but of course the party leaders didn't want him. Sam Rayburn, who was the chairman of the convention, banged down the gavel and turned it off for the night. The next morning I was standing in the Blackstone Hotel and Bess Truman came by. She said, "Yesterday was Henry Wallace's day; today is Harry Truman's day." Truman was nominated. I happened to be standing right in front of Mrs. Wallace and her daughter, and I remember that scene very well. Four years before, Roosevelt had threatened not to run again if Wallace wasn't the nominee for Vice-President. By 1944 he was terribly busy with the war and he wasn't well. He didn't take any great interest in it; but he refused to tell the convention to nominate Wallace. What he did was typical of Roosevelt. He sent a letter to the convention saying, "If I were a delegate, I would vote for Henry Wallace." But he didn't ask anybody else to vote for Henry Wallace. Then he sent a letter to Bob Hannegan saying that he had three choices: William O. Douglas, Wallace, and Truman. Truman wasn't first on that list of three, but Hannegan put him first of three. And that, among other reasons, is how Truman got nominated.

The New Deal was an electric period, caused in great measure by the terrible national emergency. After all, one man in every three—there weren't many women working—was unemployed. Business was in the red, labor was in despair, banking was in collapse, agriculture was in ruins. That produced a spirit. Much of the real content of the New Deal legislation wasn't generated in the White House, but the reason I say Roosevelt was the greatest twentieth-century President—although I had

7. FDR established the Office of Civilian Defense in January 1942 under Mayor Fiorello La Guardia of New York and, later, James N. Landis. The OCD organized corps of air-raid wardens, fire fighters, auxiliary police, and nurses' aides, encouraged conservation, and helped build civilian morale.

a great admiration for Harry Truman—was that what Roosevelt had Truman didn't have. Truman could make a tremendous decision in an emergency, right or wrong, whether it was the atomic bomb or Korea or MacArthur or anything else, but he didn't have the sustaining power to lead the people and get them to support his programs. Roosevelt had that.

The greatest job Roosevelt did, even beyond the New Deal, was getting the support, or at least not the opposition, of people for the lend-lease deal and the destroyers deal when the country was isolationist.[8] A few weeks before Pearl Harbor the second draft act was passed by one vote.[9] Roosevelt could do that, and that's the most important job a President has. Lyndon Johnson was greater in dealing directly with the Congress and putting pressure on. But Roosevelt could do something more important that Johnson couldn't do: get the people of America to put pressure on the Congress. His general purposes were right in their entirety, according to my tests, and he was unswerving. He was a marvelous politician, and, although he weaved in and out, he never really changed his aims.

8. The Lend-Lease Act of March 1941 authorized the President to transfer, exchange, lend, lease, or sell war equipment and other commodities to any country whose defense he deemed vital to U.S. security. The destroyers-bases deal of September 1940 was an Executive Agreement between FDR and the British government by which the US transferred fifty overage destroyers to Britain in exchange for a number of bases in Newfoundland and the Caribbean.
9. The Selective Service Act of August 1941 extended the period of military service required of draftees under the Selective Service Act of 1940.

CHAPTER 14

The National Labor Relations Board

FDR established the original National Labor Board on 5 August 1933 to enforce the provisions of Section 7a of the National Industrial Recovery Act. At the request of both the labor and industrial advisory boards of the National Recovery Administration, he appointed Senator Robert Wagner of New York as chairman. Soon, however, it became obvious that the NLB lacked the authority to order settlements and employers refused to obey requests. As a result, Wagner began to cast about for ways to strengthen the NLB. On 19 June 1934, he managed to get Congress to adopt Labor Disputes Public Resolution No. 44, which replaced the NLB with a new board, the National Labor Relations Board. The NLRB was empowered to provide for and supervise secret ballot union elections and had some enforcement power. Still, this did not go far enough, so Wagner and his assistant, Leon Keyserling, continued to try to strengthen the labor provisions of the NIRA. At first they did this on their own. When the Supreme Court ruled the NIRA unconstitutional in May 1935, however, FDR threw his weight behind their efforts and their proposals moved swiftly through Congress. The National Labor Relations Act of 1935 (Wagner-Connery Act) created a new, three-man board, also called the National Labor Relations Board, and gave it power to organize appropriate collective bargaining units, to conduct secret ballot union elections, to determine labor's representatives, and to hold hearings on unfair labor practices. The act also defined unfair labor practices and gave the NLRB the power to issue cease-and-desist orders enforceable in the federal courts. Incorporating Section 7a of the NIRA, the Wagner Act was a great victory for the labor movement: it established the rights and privileges of labor and the duties and responsibilities of management.

Following the passage of the Wagner Act, the main issue became its constitutionality. Many employers continued to ignore the act in the belief that the Supreme Court would rule it unconstitutional. Then, of course, came FDR's triumphant reelection in 1936 and the Court-packing plan of 1937, which forced the Supreme Court to reconsider its diehard opposition. In two five-to-four decisions—*NLRB v. Jones and Laughlin Steel Corporation* (1937) and *NLRB v. Friedman–Harry Marks Clothing Co.* (1937)—the Supreme Court upheld the Wagner Act.

Aided by a dramatic shift in public opinion in their favor, unions increased their memberships from 3 million in 1933, to 4.7 million in 1936, to 8.2 million in 1939, to 15.4 million in 1947. As AF of L President William Green said upon passage of the act, "I am confident that it will prove itself the Magna Carta of Labor of the United States."

THOMAS I. EMERSON

When Roosevelt took office in March 1933 and news about the New Deal program started coming out, I began to get itchy to get involved. I asked Walter Pollak at my law firm to call Felix Frankfurter, who was a friend of his, and ask him if he could recommend me to someone in Washington. I had known Frankfurter myself, but I asked Pollak to call because I wanted him to tell Frankfurter how well I had performed during the two years after law school.

Frankfurter sent me to Tom Corcoran, which was the classic way to get a job in the New Deal. Corcoran sent me to Donald Richberg, who was general counsel of the National Recovery Administration, and Richberg sent me to Blackwell Smith, his chief operating officer, and I had an interview with him. I went back to New York and about ten days later I got a call saying that I had a job if I wanted it. I took leave from my law firm for one year, but I stayed in Washington for thirteen years, until 1946.

I reported for work at nine o'clock in the morning and was immediately given a copy of the National Industrial Recovery Act. I was told that I was to be the legal counsel for a hearing taking place at ten o'clock on a cotton textile code. I didn't have much idea of what I was supposed to do at that hearing, but I went. It was held in a room at the Shoreham Hotel. I had taken the night train and hadn't had a chance to find a place to stay, so when the hearing was over, at about four or five o'clock in the afternoon, I just stayed on at the hotel room that had been hired for the hearing. I was so overwhelmed with work and so busy that I didn't get a place to stay for a week. I plunged right in and there was that kind of rush and excitement from the beginning.

There were very few older or more experienced lawyers at the NRA, and we were up against the best of the legal profession in the whole country. The counsel for the Cotton Textile Institute[1] was from one of the leading firms in Boston, and there were others from the big New York and southern firms—all experienced lawyers at the top of their profession. We were confronting them as representatives of the government with hardly any experience at all. It made it very exciting; we had to learn very fast. I don't know how much the government suffered. Probably not too much.

Under the National Industrial Recovery Act, provision was made for each industry to adopt a code of fair competition. The idea originally was that the industry would accept minimum wages and maximum hours and other working conditions as a way of building up wages and increasing purchasing power. In order to persuade industry to accept these minimum wage/maximum hour provisions, the statute as passed also provided for dealing with certain unfair trade practices. Excessive price-cutting and other practices that industry felt unfair would be forbidden by these codes. That was the bait to get the industries to adopt the codes, including the right of labor to organize and bargain collectively, known as Section 7a.

There were hearings in which the members of the industry, labor unions, and citizens with public interest could come and present their views on the proposed draft of the code. After the hearing was over, those views would be considered. The NRA and industry representatives would get together and prepare a draft, which went through the NRA hierarchy for approval. Ultimately the codes were approved by the President.

All the major industries—steel, rubber, banks, insurance companies, retailers, wholesalers—had a code of fair competition which they helped to draft. But the NRA had to take responsibility for seeing that the codes were fit to be signed by the President and promulgated. In the end there were 600 codes, including such minute ones as the hog ring industry and the costume jewelry industry codes.

I was initially assigned to the cotton textile industry and then to all textile industries. Later, my domain covered textiles, garments, retail/wholesale distribution, finance banks, and insurance companies. In the beginning most of our work was in the drafting of codes, then there

1. A national trade association of southern cotton manufacturers established in 1926 to promote efficiency in the industry.

were many questions of interpretation, and finally, we began to get into questions of enforcement.

As a result of the depression, industries were under considerable pressure to reduce prices. In order to avoid that, they devised various price-fixing schemes. In most cases, industries didn't fix prices, but they reported prices to trade associations. Retailers were very interested in preventing practices such as Macy's Department Store had at that time. Macy's had a slogan, "We will never be undersold." They sold at a fixed percent less than any competitor. The competitors, particularly Gimbel's, thought that was an unfair trade practice, and they wanted the code to eliminate that kind of pricing policy.

As it turned out, the larger units of the industries were the ones that drafted the codes because the big operators were likely to dominate the industry or dominate the trade associations. The natural consequence was to produce codes that tended to advance their interests and produce monopoly. That was one of the weaknesses of the NRA. Another weakness was that there was no enforcement machinery. After the first excitement was over, there was no way in which industry could be compelled to comply with the codes. There were a lot of violations, and the NRA was beginning to break down administratively when the act came up before the Supreme Court in *Schechter Poultry Corp. v. U.S.* in 1935. The decision of the Supreme Court in holding the NIRA unconstitutional was a fatal move.

The NRA at the beginning was well-intentioned but essentially a disaster because the Administration didn't appreciate the extent to which industry would take advantage of the codes of fair competition to engage in practices that led to monopoly. It became very difficult for the smaller companies in an industry to exist. The administration of the NRA was inadequate. Everything had to be done in such a hurry and no one had any experience. The result was a real lack of control.

In 1934 I moved to the National Labor Relations Board, in part by accident. I joined one of my colleagues at lunch one day with Lloyd Garrison, the head of the NLRB. Garrison was trying to recruit Larry Knapp as a member of his legal staff; he recruited me as well. I was intrigued by the idea of going to the NLRB. My feeling was that the major progressive force at that time in the New Deal was in the area of labor, and that the guarantee of the right to organize and bargain collectively should be a major goal of the Administration and the country as a whole if any advances were to be made in the political and economic spheres. I felt that it was very important to encourage labor to organize and become a counterforce to industry and a major political force. I was quite anxious to take advantage of this opportunity.

I went to the National Labor Relations Board before the National

Labor Relations Act—the Wagner Act—was passed. But a National Labor Relations Board was operating under Labor Disputes Public Resolution No. 44 of 1934, which didn't give it any powers except to administer the provisions of Section 7a of the NIRA, which guaranteed the right to organize and bargain collectively. Each one of the codes had this provision in it, and the NLRB's job was to administer that part of the code. The only way it could administer was by making interpretations of Section 7a or, in cases of violations of Section 7a, referring the case to the Department of Justice for prosecution. So it had very limited powers. The resolution was passed as an interim measure while Congress was considering the National Labor Relations Act, which became official in 1935.

After that I settled down in Washington. I lived in a house on 34th Street with mostly New Deal attorneys—Leon Keyserling, Abe Fortas, Howard Westwood. At that time Keyserling was legislative assistant to Senator Wagner, and he was in charge of drafting the National Labor Relations Act. I participated with him to some extent in that drafting process, which went on through 1934 and into 1935.

The act was being drafted at the request of labor unions mainly, but it also was a pet project of Senator Wagner's. An independent labor relations board was to guarantee the right to organize and bargain collectively, make provision for holding elections to determine who the representatives of the employees were, and in general set up the ground rules for the right to organize without being discriminated against. The innovative part was that instead of enforcement by criminal penalties, the act was to be enforced by the power of the labor relations board to issue cease-and-desist orders. If there was a complaint of violation of the substantive provisions, the board would hold a hearing before a trial examiner or before the board itself and issue a decision. If it found the employer guilty of violating the unfair labor practices provision, it would issue a cease-and-desist order, and order the reinstatement of employees who had been dismissed. That cease-and-desist order was not in itself enforceable. In order to be enforced, it had to be taken into court. The court would then order the enforcement. It was a whole new process, but it was modeled on the Federal Trade Commission regulations. Under the NRA, if an industry member violated any provisions of the industry code, the only remedy was by criminal prosecution brought by the Department of Justice. Under the final National Labor Relations Act, we had the right to bring our own proceedings.

I stayed with the first NLRB from August 1934 until the Wagner Act was passed in 1935. Then I stayed on that legal staff from 1935 until 1936.

The new National Labor Relations Board was appointed by the

President in August 1935. The chairman was J. Warren Madden, who was appointed for a five-year term. The other two members were appointed for a three-year term and a one-year term, and then they were reappointed. The general counsel was Charles Fahy. The main job for the legal division was to get the statute declared constitutional, to bring some test cases. We knew that until the Supreme Court declared the act constitutional, it was going to be very difficult to obtain any kind of enforcement. We drew up a strategy. Certain test cases would bring before the Court different aspects of the act as it applied to interstate bus companies, a big steel company, a wholesaler, a retailer, and a bank. All of those aspects raised somewhat different constitutional questions. Our strategy was to bring the cases up in the best order possible so that the easiest case would come first. A number of the members of the staff of the legal division were sent out to the regional offices, where the cases would originate, in order to get them started and also to reorganize and expand the regional offices. I was sent to the Atlanta regional office. My job there was, first of all, to fire the existing director, pick a new regional director, and get some cases started. I stayed in Atlanta for about six months.

When I got back to Washington, I was put in charge of the review division. The lawyers in the review division read the records and reported the facts of the cases to the Board. The Board would then make a decision in the case, and the review attorney would prepare the Board's written opinion. Within a short time I had a staff of over one hundred lawyers who were simply reading the records, many of them very long—10,000 and even 20,000 pages. These were cases in which a hearing had been held before a Board trial examiner and a transcript of the record made. Then, on the basis of that record, the Board would issue its decision.

The possibility of getting the Supreme Court to hold the National Labor Relations Act constitutional seemed somewhat remote at that time, because in 1935, in the *Schechter* decision, the Supreme Court had held that the wage and hour provisions of the NRA codes of fair competition were unconstitutional. Our collective bargaining provisions were not that different in legal terms.

The *Schechter* case involved a code covering the slaughtering of chickens. The chickens were shipped from outside the state to the Schechter Poultry Company in New York. They were then slaughtered in New York and sold to retail stores. The code required the company to pay certain minimum wages and recognize certain maximum hours. The Schechter Poultry Company said that this was unconstitutional because interstate commerce wasn't involved. Interstate commerce stopped when the chickens got to New York and stayed there. With no interstate commerce involved, there was no federal power. The *Schechter* case challenged the entire structure of the NRA, because all the other codes for the major industries relied on an interpretation of the Commerce clause that extended beyond interstate transportation. The case came before the Supreme Court, and the Court held that the NIRA was unconstitutional. When the chickens got to New York, they were out of the range of interstate commerce. In the *Schechter* case, the chicken company had violated another code as well, the provision that if you had a crate full of chickens and someone wanted to buy a dozen, he couldn't pick out the ones he wanted—he had to take a random choice.

A year later, in 1936, a case came before the Supreme Court called *Carter v. Carter Coal Co.*, which involved the Bituminous Coal Conservation Act of 1935 (Guffey-Snyder Coal Act). The coal industry was one of the most afflicted industries at that time. It was in a state of depression far beyond that of the rest of the economy. Along with the United Mine Workers, it had persuaded Congress to pass a law very similar to the NIRA, but applicable only to the coal industry. The statute fixed minimum wages and maximum hours, guaranteed collective bargaining, and had some price control provisions in it. The validity of the Guffey Coal Act, named after Senator Joseph Guffey of Pennsylvania, was immediately challenged by part of the coal industry. In 1936, the Supreme Court held that the Guffey Coal Act, like the NIRA, was unconstitutional. They passed not only on the wage and hour provisions but also on the collective bargaining provisions. It looked very much as though the Court would never uphold the National Labor Relations Act.

This was so clear to me that when I had an offer from John Winant at the Social Security Board to join his legal staff, I accepted. I left the NLRB in the summer of 1936 and spent one year at the Social Security Board. I worked with Dr. Isidore Sydney Falk in drafting the first health insurance law. The Social Security Act did not include health insurance on the theory that Congress was not ready to accept a health insurance program. Still, we spent a great deal of time drafting a health insurance law, which Senator Wagner introduced, but it never got anywhere in Congress. The validity of the Social Security Act was being challenged in two cases, one of which involved the old-age benefit provision and the other the unemployment compensation provision. I also worked on that litigation.

Then, in April 1937, in the *Jones and Laughlin* case and four others, the Supreme Court, to everybody's surprise, held that the National Labor Relations Act was constitutional as applied to major industries.

The effect was to hold the whole act constitutional across the board. The NLRB began to take more cases and enforce the provisions of the National Labor Relations Act, so I decided to go back. I stayed there until 1940.

Chairman Madden directed the policies of the Board, and he did an exceedingly good job. He interpreted the act properly, and he held firm against a great many pressures. However, in the course of doing his job, he antagonized the AF of L. The split between the AF of L and the CIO occurred in 1936, and the administration of the act tended to support the position of the CIO because the AF of L was organized mainly along lines of craft unions. Cases came up which compelled a ruling that the whole plant, not just members of half a dozen crafts, should belong to the same union. Inherent in the National Labor Relations Act was a policy to which the AF of L was very hostile. If employers had to choose between the AF of L and the CIO, they would choose the AF of L, believing they would get a better deal. The Board had to say that that was an unfair labor practice because you can't favor one union over the other. There was a lot of opposition to Madden from the AF of L, and he was not reappointed in 1940. At that point I resigned along with Alex Hawes and Nat Witt in protest against the failure of FDR to reappoint Madden.

The National Labor Relations Act was a major triumph of the New Deal in many ways because it established a legal structure for guaranteeing the right of labor to organize and to create sufficient power to secure higher wages, shorter hours, and better working conditions. This seems to me very important, not only from the point of view of the economy, but also from that of the political structure of the country. It provided a counterforce to industry. The concept was entirely in the right direction. In addition, I think that the New Deal lawyers by that time had learned a good deal about administration, and we did not repeat the mistakes of the NRA. We created an enforcement machinery that was workable. It was a major factor in increasing the membership of labor unions. Starting from 3 or 4 million, union membership went up to as high as 14 or 15 million within a relatively few years.

Charles Fahy, who had been general counsel of the NLRB, had moved to the Department of Justice and become Assistant Solicitor General. When I left the NLRB, he offered me a job on his staff. I was with the Department of Justice for about six months, and then I went to the Office of Price Administration.

We can all remember what the situation in the country was when Roosevelt took over in March 1933: a depression that had lasted for years; unemployment at a rate of 25 percent; banks closed down. It was a major crisis, and Roosevelt pulled it together, got it started again without a violent revolution. He wasn't entirely successful. It was a war economy that finally brought back full prosperity. But it was, on the whole, an amazing record.

PAUL M. HERZOG

I came to Washington by a series of coincidences—as so many of us who worked on the early New Deal did—not realizing the experience would have such an impact on my life. In 1933 I took a summer job in the Interior Department because Interior was the only place that hired anyone for two months. They wanted summer people to do various odd jobs. I was paid at the rate of a dollar a year and took the oath of office at a time when President Roosevelt was in one of his rare economy moods. He made everyone in the federal government take a cut in salary of either 10 or 15 percent. My salary check had 15 percent taken off it.

In the beginning, I got a job with one of the great men of our generation, although nobody knew it at that time, Charles Fahy. He became a dear friend, and was later Solicitor General of the United States. He was then acting solicitor of the Interior Department. The department was looking for people to work on problems involving Indian tribes.

By the end of August, the job was over. I was told I could stay on a permanent basis at a decent salary of $2 a year. I didn't want to go back to a third year at Harvard. The law school was in the doldrums in the 1930s, just after the great days of Harvard, and before the current generation took over. Charles Wyzanski, a Harvard classmate, advised me not to stay on because he thought I ought to finish law school. Nevertheless, he suggested I talk to Senator Robert Wagner.

Senator Wagner was a really marvelous person—very relaxed, very easy to talk to. I was much impressed with the senator from my own state; we hit it off well. He asked me: "How much do you want?" My job before I started law was teaching at the University of Wisconsin and at Harvard, and my salaries there were not high, you can be sure. I was working half-time in both universities at $1,000 a year. I was lucky enough to have independent means. I didn't know what to say. "Senator, I think about $3,000 would be all right." Wagner said: "I won't pay you three. I'll pay you four or five. I don't want anybody to work only at three."

So I held a very junior post on Senator Wagner's original National

Labor Board, which was a predecessor of the National Labor Relations Board and was created under the famous National Industrial Recovery Act to handle what looked like serious labor disputes. The National Labor Board was probably the most conspicuous of the New Deal agencies, and yet there were other agencies with a more permanent effect. When the NIRA was declared unconstitutional by the Supreme Court, the National Labor Board survived under a completely new incarnation.

The original Board was a strange institution. There were three members from labor, three from industry, and one—later two—public members. The fiscal public member and chairman was Senator Wagner himself. He did what was probably unconstitutional—taking a position as head of an administrative board. Of course it was voluntary, and these were the crazy first years of the New Deal when everybody was experimenting. The vice-chairman was a very wonderful Catholic priest, Father Francis Haas, who later became Bishop of Grand Rapids. The other six members of the Board were all men of great fame and distinction. Yet all were men who had other things to do and could give it very little time.

They were, as I recall, Gerard Swope, one of the great industrialists, chairman of the board at General Electric; Walter Teagle, president of Standard Oil of New Jersey; and Louis Kirstein of Boston, vice-president of Filene's, who knew a great deal about labor problems and had done a lot to liberalize the attitudes of Boston's employers. The three labor members were John L. Lewis, the powerful head of the mine workers, quiet, famous, vain, and picturesque; William Green, a rather dull and sweet man dominated by Lewis; and George Berry. Afterwards Wagner enlarged the Board. Professor Lew Waldman, who taught labor relations at Columbia, an economist, joined. There was another labor member who was then regarded as a liberal. All this was before the AF of L/CIO split.

The Board was a volunteer one with a staff of half a dozen people, of whom I was a very minor member. I was assistant secretary. Like that of other staff members, my job was to do the dirty work. The Board members met once a week and generally ratified, using their own judgment, our recommendations. Like all bureaucracies, the staff grew. This took place in 1933 and 1934. It was all terribly exciting for a twenty-seven-year-old. So many of us who went to Washington, hoping at some point to go into public service, never dreamed we would have so much influence or so much involvement at such a young age. That is one of the reasons the New Deal was so sharply criticized by conservative elements—young squirts having more power than they should have had. I thought so then, and certainly think so now, looking back from the perspective of forty-odd years. We worked unbelievably hard. There was no air conditioning in Washington then, and those summers of 1933 and 1934 were peculiarly hot.

We dealt largely with cases that came out of the NRA operation involving the probability of strikes. The Board was not like the later National Labor Relations Board—which still exists—a quasi-judicial body deciding cases. It wasn't very long before the mediation functions of this volunteer body ran out because mediation didn't always work. The question was: Would this agency need enforcement powers; would it need authority? It became a very hotly fought battle, and employers by and large were still on the defensive and very much opposed to giving the Board authority because they realized that most of the decisions would probably go against them. They suspected that the Board was itself too liberal. They were quite suspicious of staff members like me. Gradually, statutory authority and court actions were required.

I concentrated entirely on Section 7a of the National Industrial Recovery Act, which was the origin of the Board and ultimately the Wagner Act and protected the right of labor to organize and bargain collectively with the employers. The Board had a huge job. Who would they bargain with? What do you use to bargain with? The employer bargains with whomever represents the majority of his employees. Who finds that out? The Board invented the election for this purpose, and ran the elections. A very important part of today's statute, the 1947 Taft-Hartley Act, is the conduct of elections to find out who represents the majority. The NLRB, very early in its history in probably its most controversial early decision, resolved that the employer must bargain collectively with the representatives of the majority of the employees. That was fought for a long while. Many conservative elements wanted proportional representation. This was the most important early philosophic decision of the Board, made by the Board members themselves after a very, very long discussion.

Then, of course, the running of an election to determine the majority was all-important. That side of the Board's work became increasingly affirmative, and the handling of unfair labor practices, which was the other side of the Board's work and very unpopular with employers, became less important. I cannot pretend to have played an important role in making those decisions; I was much too junior.

At the end of about a year, in 1934 before the NIRA was declared unconstitutional by the Supreme Court, something more was needed to keep the labor relations function alive. Strikes were increasing. The lawyers were not complying very well with decisions. Labor Disputes Public Resolution No. 44 was passed by Congress pending the passage of a permanent statute. The permanent statute was to become the Wagner Act a year later. For a year they ran on a voluntary basis, kept the staff which included me, and waited until the statute could be passed in 1935. The Wagner Act was not found constitutional by the Supreme Court— and therefore not enforced—until 1937 and by then I had left.

The 1933 to 1935 years were very informal, therefore all the more exciting. We worked in terribly crowded conditions; the summer heat was the half of it. It was sheer hell, and yet tremendous fun. My job, and that of others, was to read a lot of material and prepare recommendations for the Board members which they could either ratify or not. The problem, of course, was whether the public members, Senator Wagner and Father Haas, would agree.

The first year or so, the labor members voted labor and the employer members voted for employers. The employers were more objective than labor because they didn't have as much at stake. Delegation of power to the staff was a simple matter because Board members were too busy with other things. John L. Lewis had his union to run. Gerard Swope had his General Electric Company to run. As members, they probably worked on the Board one or two days a week. They left it to the staff to carry things out.

We were moved around. Our first location was the most exciting: the Department of Commerce. The Commerce Department then had very little to do. We worked in the "four hundredth" corridor of the Commerce Building, where the NRA and the Board had a few rooms. In the thirties, the Commerce Department was a very moribund place. The Secretary did not have Roosevelt's confidence. The NRA was the big thing, with all the big shots in America walking up and down the four hundredth corridor. The NRA was where the action was as far as the press was concerned. The press were all over the place, and they would try to get stories out of us. Some of us, like myself, were easily picked up by flattery. I'm sure we leaked information we never should have.

Someone finally decided we really weren't that important. We were on the main street of the NRA, and they had to put us elsewhere. They moved us to another building within half a mile from there. Although we had our own quarters, life was a little less exciting because we were no longer in the mainstream of the National Recovery Administration. We did, however, get more work done, and it was more peaceful. They moved us three or four times.

What building you were in and whose office you were next to was ridiculously, terribly important. Senator Wagner saw through that. He was mainly in his office on Capitol Hill. When he was handling Board business, he came to the Commerce Building, or some staff member took things down to him in the Senate. The part-time Board members, like Swope, Green, and Lewis, each had an office. Many complaints were heard about the wasted space, giving a whole room to one person who occupied it only one or two days a week.

I don't remember all we did. I know we worked awfully hard and did a great deal of drafting, even though we were not yet technically lawyers. We very often had to present information to the Board. It was terrifying suddenly to appear before these men whom we had been reading about. We were brought into matters in which we were not experts and I doubt that the employers or the union had much confidence in us. But the real problem was to hold the confidence of the members of the Board, who had to follow our rather sparse information and act on our recommendations.

The needs of 1933–34 were met emphatically by the NRA. President Roosevelt was spared a worse disaster by the action of the Supreme Court in declaring the NIRA unconstitutional. A lot of people thought the NRA would itself have been a mess within ten years, and Roosevelt would have had this mess on his hands. The Supreme Court, by declaring the NIRA unconstitutional, did him a favor. FDR had wished the country no harm, and yet he didn't have to suffer the disadvantage of having this attempt fizzle out.

The problems of the NRA became obvious to economists and the people who lived with it within a year or so. For one thing, the NRA assumed a greater willingness to make voluntary sacrifices than is possible except in times of terrific emergency. In the great emergency of the depression, in 1932, 1933, and 1934, people pulled together because the alternative was to drown together. As the country got a little stronger, as the Roosevelt medicine began to work, and as willingness to make voluntary sacrifices diminished, the NRA lost its force. The monopolistic potential of the NRA was very great, and that was what a lot of people feared. Justice Brandeis, who was known as a liberal, did not like the NRA because he thought that in the long run it would lead to too many monopolistic practices—that it would encourage rather than discourage such practices.

It was a very, very wonderful experience for a young man. I lived in a Georgetown house. Georgetown was considered by conservatives to be the source of all sin. That's where all of the liberal New Dealers lived. One of the men I lived with—James Rowe—was the last secretary to Mr. Justice Holmes. As a result of our friendship, I have the last letter that Justice Holmes ever wrote, given to me in 1935, two weeks before he died, because it refers to an aunt of mine whom he had adored. Another person I lived with, Thomas Eliot, was a lawyer in the Labor Department working with Miss Perkins. Later he helped draft the Social Security Act and was a congressman from Massachusetts. A third resident of the Georgetown house, Edward Rhetts, was a delightful man who was very active in a number of New Deal agencies. We lived a bachelor existence. We entertained as many of the greats as we could lure to our table, and it is all unforgettable.

In 1935, I left all this to return to my third year of law school.

CHAPTER 15

The Douglas-Fortas Odyssey

William Orville Douglas was born in 1898 in Maine, Minnesota, into an impoverished family and raised in Yakima, Washington. He worked his way through Whitman College and Columbia Law School, graduating in 1925, and became a leading expert in corporate and financial law as a professor at Columbia Law School and at Yale Law School from 1927 to 1936.

FDR appointed Douglas to the Securities and Exchange Commission in 1936, and raised him to chairman the following year. Douglas promptly turned his attention to bringing about self-regulation and greater public accountability by investment bankers. He encouraged the New York Stock Exchange to reform itself by launching investigations into past abuses, using provisions of the newly passed Public Utility Holding Company Act. In a fighting speech on 23 November 1937 he warned: "The time is past when the country's exchanges can be operated as private clubs ... There would be greater public confidence in exchanges (and the prices made thereon) which recognized that their management should not be in the hands of professional traders but in fact, as well as nominally, in charge of those who have a clearer public responsibility." It was in the midst of this campaign that the Richard Whitney scandal broke. In its aftermath, a new reform-minded Board of Governors took over the Exchange and adopted a program to safeguard investors' securities.

While on the SEC, Douglas was best known for his unwavering support for the underdog and for the general public interest rather than as a champion of civil liberties. But his judicial idol was Justice Brandeis and it should have come as no surprise that after he was appointed to the Supreme Court in March 1939, he became a leader of its liberal bloc. In his long career on the Court, Douglas strongly defended individual rights and called for strict enforcement of the guarantees in the Bill of Rights. Eventually, he moved toward an absolutist position on freedom of speech, the press, and religion. Although the Court never adopted Douglas's view of the First Amendment, it did accept many of his views regarding the rights of defendants, reapportionment, and citizenship. Douglas left the Court in 1975, after a stroke made him unable to participate fully in its work. He died in 1980.

ABE FORTAS

In the summer of 1933, I had just received my degree from Yale University Law School and had been elected to the faculty. One of the professors on the faculty was Wesley Sturges, who was called to Washington to the Department of Agriculture. He asked if I would join him. I told him I would speak to the dean, and apparently Sturges also spoke to the dean, for I was encouraged to go down for the summer. I went and stayed until January or February of the following year because Sturges, or Jerome Frank, who was then the general counsel for the Agricultural Adjustment Administration, telephoned the dean and asked that I be permitted to stay on. I continued to teach at Yale part-time.

In 1933 there were very few lawyers at the Department of Agriculture or at the Agricultural Adjustment Administration. I have two recollections which may illustrate the format there that was so exciting to lawyers and law teachers. The first is of the brief period that I sat with Professor Sturges and others on a committee trying to decide what to do about the repeal of Prohibition—whether there should be government monopolies or a licensing system or some other plan. The other is of immediately being put to work on the drafting of marketing agreements and licenses for certain units of the agricultural industry. I remember people sitting in the anteroom waiting for one of the young lawyers to give them some time. These people were executives of large agricultural businesses who wanted the help that they thought they could get from the marketing agreements.

On my arrival in Washington, I did not unpack my suitcase or get to bed for three days and three nights. The same thing was true for the other lawyers who were called down at that time. There was great fer-

William O. Douglas

Eleanor Roosevelt and Mary McLeod Bethune addressing the
second national conference on Negro youth,
Washington, D.C., January 12, 1939

ment, great excitement, and great dedication on the part of the few who constituted the staff trying to work out this marketing system for agricultural companies.

As a young lawyer who had never tried a case, I was sent to California with Thurman Arnold to try the first case that arose under the Agricultural Adjustment Act. We went out on a Ford trimotor plane. I have a visual recollection of Thurman Arnold getting out at some way station, wanting to stretch his legs and get some coffee in the middle of the night. It was a horrible journey.

Before we went out, a group of lawyers from the Department of Justice were sitting in the library trying to find a case that covered a point of law that was involved. The case to which we were assigned had to do with canned cling peaches in the state of California, and we were trying to find a case supporting our plea for an injunction for violation of the marketing agreement and license. The young lawyers were unable to find a case on the point. When Thurman Arnold and I came back from dinner, Thurman asked, "How are you getting along?" The lawyers said they couldn't find a case in point and Thurman replied, "That's nonsense. There's a case on every point." He went to the shelves and came back with a case that was precisely the point. Thurman was a genius of the law, a real genius. I said, "How in the world did you find this, Thurman?" and he responded, "It was very simple. This involved canned peaches. Can, can, can reminded me of sardines. I looked under sardines in Words and Phrases and I found the case." Now that is a genius. Thurman frequently had the answer to the impossible question.

I went to the Securities and Exchange Commission in 1934 at the request of William O. Douglas, who was then a colleague of mine on the Yale faculty. I participated with him in teaching courses in various phases of corporate law. I would be in Washington, and he would be in New Haven and vice versa. We were doing the well-known Protective Committee Study, which dealt with the reorganization of corporations that had failed during the depression.

I went to the SEC with Douglas after it was pretty well established. It had taken over the job from the Federal Trade Commission. The SEC was organized by Joe Kennedy, its first chairman, and Kennedy was a superb administrator. He also had a talent for spotting able men. That's how he got Bill Douglas to come down and do this particular study.

Bill was a fine organizer and a fine inspirer of people, and he didn't spare himself or anybody else. We had many adventures on that job. I remember an amusing one. We had brought Thurman Arnold in to be the presiding officer at some of our hearings. The SEC Building was then at 18th and Pennsylvania, across the street from the old Powhatan

Hotel. When we broke for dinner, usually around ten o'clock at night, we frequently went up on the roof of the Powhatan to eat. One night at dinner, Bill said, "We ought to get Wes Sturges down here." Professor Sturges had gone back to Yale by then. We decided that the thing to do would be for Thurman, as presiding judge in the hearings, to issue a subpoena for Sturges. The subpoena was issued and duly served at Yale by a United States marshal, commanding Professor Sturges to appear and testify when called at the hearings. So Wes, being a law-abiding citizen, came down, and we kept him around and had him join us for dinner and lunch. He wanted to know what he was supposed to testify about. We told him all that would become clear, but he had to stay around, he was under subpoena. We kept him around and enjoyed his company for about a week and then told him he was excused. Bill was a great practical joker.

The story of Bill Douglas's accomplishments at the SEC has not been told, certainly not adequately. It was a great achievement, which in some respects rivals those of his subsequent career. At that time, Wall Street was in disarray and disrepair. I think there was a real question as to its viability in the minds of many people. It was regarded popularly as a private club, and Wall Street wanted to keep it that way. Then came the great Richard Whitney scandal, and Douglas made his famous New York Bond Club speech in which he, in effect, said to Wall Street that it would have to shape up. Having administered that shock treatment, he then did a highly constructive job of formulating regulatory measures with which Wall Street finally learned to live.

There was much opposition on Wall Street and on the Exchange, but there were also some people who realized that this call for reform and for public accountability was an appropriate one, and one that was necessary for their own survival. Douglas, in that process, acquired enemies as well as friends. Some people on Wall Street regarded themselves as victims of Douglas's dictatorial commands, and the liberals regarded Douglas as someone who catered to Wall Street. The truth was right in between, which in my opinion was an indication of his genius. He did a very constructive job.

I've said "genius" about Thurman Arnold and Bill Douglas. I don't use that word freely, but I would apply it to both those two men, although they were very different—Bill was a practical joker; Thurman Arnold was a wit.

Bill was quite ambivalent about whether he did or did not want to run for President or Vice-President. Each time it came up, he decided against it. In 1948, he didn't want to be on the ticket. I remember the telephone calls and people coming to my house and asking me if I knew how to reach him. He'd been avoiding calls. I thought it was appropriate for me to contact him, but I did not try to persuade him to run. He had obviously done a lot of thinking about it and had decided that he would rather stay on the Court.

I continued to commute to Yale and to try to do both jobs until the beginning of 1938. I tell people that the reason I finally quit Yale was that it just got too burdensome with two dachshunds, one of whom got carsick. I had to drive from Washington to New Haven on U.S. 1 with the Sunday *Times* piled in the back of the car. The dog would get sick; I'd get out, take away a couple of layers of the *Times,* and leave the dog on the other layers. Pretty soon that got boring, so I decided I had to quit. But the immediate reason was that by then Bill Douglas was chairman of the SEC and had a very difficult problem in connection with the administration of the Public Utility Holding Company Act. The director of that division was a man with whom Bill was not in accord, but who had the support of two or three of the five-man commission. Bill asked me to come down and take on the job of general counsel of the public utilities division. He made it quite clear that he would look to me to control the job and help him administer the law as he rightly viewed it. It was a mighty uncomfortable job, and I guess I would not have done it for anybody except Bill Douglas. It was very strenuous and many things happened.

The Public Utility Holding Company Act was passed in 1935. Those were the days of Sam Insull and Harley Clarke, who were the heads of great utility combines possessed of enormous political and economic power. The act was designed to break up these vast combines. The administration of the act has never been literally carried out to the extent that Congress prescribed, but its administration was sufficiently vigorous, so it had a very beneficial effect.

We made a lot of progress, but in 1939, when Bill was nominated to the Court, I was still in this anomalous position. Bill thought, and I thought, that I should not stay on after he left. I think he talked with Harold Ickes at the time. Ickes asked me to come over as general counsel of the Public Works Administration, which I did for a short time during the liquidation phase of the PWA. Then Ickes asked me to come to the Office of the Secretary as director of the division of power. That was in Interior. My assistant director was Tex Goldschmidt. Ben Cohen had some floating connection with that operation. I stayed there until 1942, when I was nominated as Under Secretary of the Interior.

When I first went to Washington in 1933, the dedication, the team spirit, to use a hackneyed phrase, were fantastic. Everybody worked ceaselessly in the belief that we were contributing to the salvation of the nation and the people. I think the first crack in morale—and it was a big one—came with the famous conflict in which Jerome Frank was a central figure. In 1935 he was general counsel of the Agricultural Adjustment Administration, an extraordinary man. The conflict between him and Chester Davis was most disruptive. Henry Wallace, then Secretary of Agriculture, decided to take a remote position in this conflict. The conflict was pretty complex, but basically there were differences on a fundamental point of policy having to do with the relative treatment given to farmers on the one hand and people who engaged in agricultural business on the other hand. Frank supported the small farmer. I'm sure that the opponents of Frank and Roosevelt and the younger liberals in the department would never agree to the statement that they were in favor of the big fellas instead of the little fellas. Everybody says he's in favor of the little fella, and sometimes people think they are, even though their policies seem to be weighted the other way.

It was publicly charged many years later that in this apparently extraordinarily homogeneous, hard-working, dedicated group of lawyers at the AAA there were some people who had Communist affiliations. Once in a while, it's occurred to me to wonder why I was never aware of it, why there was never any attempt to recruit me, either directly or indirectly. If there was, I wasn't aware of it. Maybe it was because I was a southerner or too conservative. I hope it wasn't because I was regarded as a reactionary.

The Tennessee Valley Authority was part of a whole movement to try to give a profound sense of public accountability and responsibility to the function of supplying electric power to the people. The TVA was a very special aspect with broader objectives. It was somewhat akin to what we were doing at the Department of Interior with the Bonneville Dam. We were launching great hydroelectric projects at Bonneville and at Grand Coulee,[1] and I was deeply involved in them. The basic fight there came from the privately owned utilities, which liked the idea of the government building vast hydroelectric facilities, as long as the government built them, generated the power, and then turned the power over to them. Some of us wanted some reasonable assurance that the power would be distributed at low rates to aid the economic development of the area. It was a long and bitter fight, and it was somewhat successful.

1. The Bonneville Power Act of 1937 established the Bonneville Power Administration to manage the various dams built by the Corps of Engineers and others on the Columbia River from 1935 to 1937. Grand Coulee Dam, built by the Bureau of Reclamation on the Columbia River and financed by the PWA, was under construction from 1933 to 1941. After 1937, it came under the jurisdiction of the BPA.

Fortunately, the Bonneville and Grand Coulee power installations, which were built in the face of great opposition, were in place when World War II came. The power was available for the manufacture of aluminum and for an installation at which nuclear components were made.[2]

In 1939 the New Deal was in bad shape. It was a low point for Roosevelt. One day Tex Goldschmidt and I were in Ben's office, and we were talking to Ben about how the New Deal might recover. He walked over to a globe at the end of his long office and he twirled it around slowly and said in his quavering voice, "I don't think we're going to have much to worry about in this respect because I think that in a few years we'll be at war." Ben was tremendous. A wonderful man with a remarkable character and mind. I remember somebody saying, "Ben Cohen is the greatest Christian in the world." The person who made that remark was a Christian.

The New Deal was in trouble in terms of general public opinion. It was quite natural that it should be because the reforms that the New Deal instituted and the measures that it enacted represented such a drastic change. The difference in the approach to government from laissez-faire to government participation in economic and social problems was so drastic that it was bound to create a reaction.

It was an exciting and inspiring time. Of course there was friction. There always is friction where extraordinary men work at an extraordinary pitch of intensity. There was friction between Ickes and Jesse Jones, who was in the Reconstruction Finance Corporation. There was friction between Ickes and Roosevelt, between Harry Hopkins and Ickes. Roosevelt was a master at controlling friction and making it constructive. He was a real Toscanini. He knew how to conduct an orchestra and when to favor the first fiddles and when to favor the trombones. He knew how to employ and manipulate people. As you go through life you see giants become men, but in the New Deal days men became giants.

The beginning of the New Deal was a time of despair, a time of hopelessness, and the country was turned around in a remarkable way. The interesting thing is that the New Deal program was not radical in the sense that the New Deal was an effort, and a successful effort, to salvage the existing way of life, using objectives, procedures, and methods that were in existence. It was an American idea that people ought not to starve. The New Deal was dedicated to such an idea and the idea that government had responsibility. It is an idea that went back, in the social

---

2. Much of the work on the atomic bomb was done at the Hanford Engineer Works in Washington state.

welfare field, to the birth of the Doctrine of Entitlement under the first Queen Elizabeth of England.[3] The invention of new methodology to continue the capitalist system and to continue the efforts to move the entire population along was very constructive.

3. The Doctrine of Entitlement in the Elizabethan Poor Law of 1601 required local parishes to provide for the needy within their jurisdictions.

CHAPTER 16

The Tennessee Valley Authority

During World War I, the federal government had built, at a cost of $145 million, a large hydroelectric plant and two munitions plants at Muscle Shoals on the Tennessee River in Alabama. In the 1920s, various Republican Administrations tried to sell the plants to private power interests, but Republican Senator George Norris of Nebraska succeeded in preventing the sales. On two occasions, in 1928 and 1931, he pushed bills through Congress providing for continued government operation of the plants. Coolidge vetoed the first bill and Hoover the second.

As governor of New York FDR had sponsored and executed a statewide planning movement and helped establish a state power authority. As a presidential candidate, he promised to establish regional power developments combining power production, flood control, land reclamation, reforestation, soil conservation, industrial diversification, and the general improvement of the social and economic welfare of the people. The Tennessee Valley Authority Act of May 1933 embodied the aims of both FDR and Senator Norris. The act created an independent public corporation, the Tennessee Valley Authority, with a three-man board of directors that was empowered to construct dams and power plants, to produce, distribute, and sell electric power and nitrogen fertilizer to the people and industries of the region, to sell explosives to the federal government, and to develop the economic and social well-being of the seven-state Tennessee Valley area.

For six years the private utility interests fought the TVA every step of the way. The TVA, led by its brilliant young director David E. Lilienthal, fought back and won. In the end, the private utilities found, as FDR had predicted in November 1934, that "if the utilities want to get into real trouble with the Congress and the public they will start a fight—and such a fight can only hurt them and their stockholders. As an actual practical fact it cannot succeed." Between 1933 and 1944, the TVA built nine main river dams and many others on tributary streams. During World War II, TVA supplied the power for the manufacture of explosives, the production of aluminum, and the construction of the atomic bomb.

HENRY HAMILL FOWLER

In the summer of 1933 I was on my way from Roanoke to New York to go into law practice. I had graduated from Yale Law School in June. I stopped in Washington to spend the weekend with an old friend from law school and that evening we went to a dinner dance at the Chevy Chase Club. The distinguished looking gentleman ahead of me in the hat-check line introduced himself as Stanley Reed, the general counsel of the Reconstruction Finance Corporation. He asked me what I was doing. When I said I was on my way to New York to begin the practice of law, he said, "Well, you're making a mistake. You ought to stay in Washington. Lots of very interesting things are happening here now. There's a great deal of legal work ahead." I was impressed and decided to stay over a day or two.

One of the gentlemen at the party was Quinn Shaughnessy, a friend and protege of Tommy Corcoran, as were many of the young lawyers in Washington, and he arranged for me to see Mr. Corcoran. I told Mr. Corcoran that rather than do the usual thing and jump into one or another of the New Deal agencies being organized at that time, I thought I would much prefer to go with a private firm for a year, look the scene over, and then perhaps go with some particular agency or operation that appealed to me.

Well, Tommy was very kind and generous with his time and consideration, as he always has been. He mentioned two or three people, Jerome Frank in the Agricultural Adjustment Administration and another gentleman in the National Recovery Administration. I saw these people but came back and said, "My intentions are still the same. I'd like a private law assignment." "Well," Corcoran said, "I think I know just the place, but I can't handle it right now. You go back home to Roanoke and wait there for a week and you'll hear from me." Sure enough, on the following Saturday night he called me and said, "You have an appointment to see Mr. Edward Burling, one of the two senior partners of the firm of Covington, Burling, and Rublee." I went up the following week and had an interview with Mr. Burling, one of the most fascinating and interesting men of that time or any other time. Covington, Burling was then the largest law firm in Washington, and certainly one of the finest in the country. There were only about seventeen lawyers. I became number eighteen and stayed with the firm for a year.

In the process of locating in Washington, I again saw Mr. Shaughnessy and became part of a bachelor establishment of four or five, mostly young lawyers just out of school. We had a small house in Georgetown and later moved over to Euclid Street and joined with several other native Washingtonians. In the summer, having exhausted ourselves with work and play—the debutante season that year was a very heavy one—we accepted an invitation from our friends Smith and DeLong Bowman to live at the Fairfax Hunt Club on their family property in what is now the site of Reston. We had a great bachelor's establishment far out in the country, with a swimming pool and, through the good offices of a Canadian diplomat, the best wines and whiskeys available at that time. It was a great summer, but we didn't get much rest for the traffic from Washington was very heavy most nights.

Washington was a very exciting city in 1933. On March 4th, Franklin Roosevelt came to town. The First Hundred Days saw many new laws, many new agencies, and many new types of activities by the federal government, some regulatory in nature but all more or less designed to bring the country out of the despondency and depression of the years 1929 to 1933. There was an air of great vitality, great movement.

I had very close and extensive working relationships with Judge Harry Covington, who was senior partner with Mr. Burling, and a younger partner, Mr. Thomas Austern. Dean Acheson had been a partner of the firm but was Under Secretary of the Treasury when I arrived. He had a bit of a dispute with President Roosevelt and whether he resigned or was fired has never been accurately determined. He came back to the firm as a partner and I worked for him on many occasions.

We worked on Saturdays in those days and, as the low man on the totem pole, I would end up on Saturday morning with a number of assignments I hadn't had on Friday night. That was very disruptive of weekends. One Saturday morning in the late summer of 1933, Judge Covington called me. He said, "There's been a mixup and there's a hearing before the Senate Finance Committee involving amendments to the Agricultural Adjustment Act." He outlined an amendment in which one of our corporate clients was greatly interested. He said, "Would you go up and present this statement and try to understand it before you go. Be prepared to answer any questions." So I went to the hearing in the Senate Office Building. The room was packed with people, and many witnesses were waiting to be heard. I went up and gave my name and identification and asked to be heard.

As one after another of the witnesses made their presentations, it became very clear that we were not going to finish that day. The presiding officer was the chairman of the Senate Finance Committee, one of the outstanding characters in Washington at that time, Senator Pat Harrison of Mississippi. Finally the clerk said, "We're not going to finish this hearing today. Anybody who insists on being heard today can have two mintues." So I went up and gave my name because my statement required no more than two minutes.

Eventually, I started to deliver my statement. Chairman Harrison resumed a periodic conversation with another senator that had gone on most of the morning. Since my pearls of wisdom were not getting any attention at all, and being young and feisty in those days, I just stopped in the middle of a sentence and Harrison noted the absence of the drone of my voice. He looked up, saw me looking him squarely in the eye, and said, "I believe the speaker is annoyed by our conversation." I said, "No, Mr. Chairman, I'm not annoyed, but I only have two minutes now and if I could have your undivided attention, I think I could make my presentation adequately." Well, he got red in the face and I could see this had been a disaster. "Well, young man, have you been to the Department of Agriculture with this proposed amendment?" "Yes, sir, and they heartily approve of it and I think you will find that they would endorse it as being corrective of the existing legislation and the inequity in it." "Well, then, proceed." And I proceeded with their full and undivided and hostile attention.

I went back to the office and said, "Judge, I've really goofed it for our client. I've really ruined this one." I described what happened and he threw back his head and laughed. He picked up the phone and asked for Senator Harrison. "Well, I hear you had a witness down there from my office today." I could hear the explosion on the other end of the phone. He said, "Oh, well, calm down, Pat. I'll see you out at the Burning Tree (Golf Club) at 3:30 and tell you all about it." Washington was a small town in those days, and a senior partner of Covington, Burling who had served in the Congress could have that kind of informal and personal relationship with a senator.

Judge Covington was an outstanding figure and I attended many hearings before the New Deal agencies with him, carrying his bag, so to speak. He would have the rapt attention of the hearing officer and of those in attendance. He would invariably end up with a marvelous dissertation on what we would call "procedural due process of law," which at that time was a somewhat underdeveloped aspect of administrative law.

Most of my young lawyer friends were on the other side of the table, having been recruited by Mr. Corcoran and Professor Felix Frankfurter and others to come down and help manage the legal ramparts of the New Deal agencies. So play and work were both very much concerned with what was going on in the public field.

Our clients were by and large blue-chip corporations—for example, Du Pont Corporation, American Smelting and Refining, various textile firms. It was our job to see that the various arrangements set up under the New Deal laws were constructive, embodied the elements of fair play and due process, and brought a practical application of good sense and good judgment as well as the legal requirements of the Constitution to what lawyers would call today "administrative law."

At the end of that year, I went to Mr. Burling and said, "I hope you understand that I've enjoyed it here. I've gotten a tremendous amount out of it. But now, in line with our initial conversation, I'd like to go with one or another of the New Deal agencies to see it from the other side of the street."

When I left the firm, I went to see Judge Covington, Mr. Burling, and Dean Acheson to thank them for their patience and their training. Judge Covington was a very colorful person. He was from Maryland and had been a leading member of Congress in the Administration of Woodrow Wilson. To talk of him in this day and age is to talk of another completely different era. He joined with Mr. Burling at the end of World War I to establish what became a great law firm and legal institution. The judge had a good deal of the South in him. He was a very pleasant, affable, and likeable person, yet the thing I remember most about him was his veneration for the principles of the Constitution involving due process of law.

My dealings with Dean Acheson involved antitrust cases or Federal Trade Commission cases. I would typically come up with four points on which our clients should prevail, and he would say, "Let's see if we can't reduce it to one or two points." I would say, "Oh, Mr. Acheson, don't drop point four." There was therefore a certain amount of tension between us. We would, of course, always end up doing it his way. "Joe," he said, "you have a very active mind. You think of a lot of different aspects in any problem. In a way it's too active; you soar a lot better than you pounce." That was probably as valuable advice as an older lawyer could have given to a younger lawyer.

I went again to my friend Mr. Corcoran and spent about a month or six weeks with the Reconstruction Finance Corporation. Then the constitutionality of the Tennessee Valley Authority was challenged in what became known as the *Ashwander* case. Six or seven young lawyers were recruited to carry on that litigation. Mr. Corcoran introduced me to the general counsel of the TVA, James Lawrence Fly. Mr. Fly made me an offer and I accepted it. I left Washington in early September 1934 to go to Knoxville, Tennessee, to work with the TVA in the preparation and conduct of the *Ashwander* case. I was on that assignment steadily for a year and a half.

The *Ashwander* case was brought by a group of preferred stockholders in the Alabama Power Company. They sought to enjoin a contract by the company to sell certain transmission lines surrounding and leading out from the Muscle Shoals dam. These lines serviced a number of small towns and rural areas in northern Alabama. The ground of the suit was that the TVA had no constitutional authority to sell or transmit electric energy other than to the power companies.

Among the basic purposes of the TVA was to build dams on the Tennessee River and its tributaries, thereby improving navigation and flood control, and to dispose of the resulting hydroelectric power in the public interest. In order to avoid a monopoly, or being limited to sales at the so-called bus bar[1] to whatever was the adjacent power company, the TVA claimed the authority to enter into contracts to sell electricity to municipalities, rural cooperatives, industrial plants, and others in the vicinity. The suit claimed that the TVA did not have this power.

The TVA was created by the Tennessee Valley Authority Act of 1933, which was one of the inspirations of President Roosevelt. Senator George Norris of Nebraska had long waged a fight in the Congress to keep the Muscle Shoals properties built during World War I—a dam and some fertilizer plants—in the hands of the government rather than selling them to private interests. He wanted Muscle Shoals to be the nucleus for a channel from the origin of the Tennessee River in Knoxville to its mouth in the Ohio River which would bring cheap navigation to the entire Tennessee Valley. These dams and others in the tributaries of the Tennessee River would control flood problems that were afflicting the area and contributing to the floods along the Mississippi system. The act was very broad-gauged because it also contemplated the use of this

1. The bus bar rate, one of a number of competing rate formulas proposed for public power developments, would have required the sale of power according to distance from the dam site. Private power interests, the Corps of Engineers, and nearby residents and industries favored the bus bar, since they would get the cheapest rates. Other public power advocates favored rates that equalized the cost of power over the TVA's entire jurisdiction.

power to develop fertilizers to restore the eroded lands of the Tennessee Valley and to carry on what one would term today exercises in soil conservation, regional planning, and agricultural and industrial development.

The case was tried in Birmingham, Alabama, and the trial was a fairly exciting and widely publicized event. It was one of the major legal challenges to the New Deal. The NIRA was challenged and later declared by the Supreme Court to be unconstitutional. The Agricultural Adjustment Act was challenged and declared to be unconstitutional. So when our case finally reached the Supreme Court and, to the surprise of a great many people, the Court decided eight to one in favor of the government, President Roosevelt was highly elated. It represented his first major judicial victory.

The TVA case was very close to all of the people of the Tennessee Valley, which was a relatively underdeveloped part of the United States at that time. They hoped that the TVA might be the opening wedge by which the poor and less developed parts of the South might come into their own. That territory today bears no resemblance whatsoever to what one found there in 1933 and 1934.

I was the young fellow in the background who was charged with the responsibility of preparing for trial the facts bearing on the issues in the case. A trial of constitutional issues was a rather unusual event at that time. The basic question involved in the constitutionality was whether or not the building of the dams for navigation and flood control and the building of the Muscle Shoals dam in World War I for national defense gave extended authority to the government to reduce the kinetic energy of the falling water to electric energy by the generation process, and then to sell and transmit that energy on the widespread scale contemplated by the act.

A great deal of technical testimony from hydraulic engineers, from various kinds of technicians, was required. The Army and the Navy sent many witnesses to explain how the availability of this pool of electric energy would make it possible to produce not only ammunition but also many of the other elements that would go into the national defense in the event of a war.

The key to the case, which was a technical one, was a clause in the Constitution that goes something like this: "Congress shall have the power to dispose of public property and make needful rules and regulations concerning this disposal." Well, the basic case was to prove that the energy created by a dam built to improve navigation became the property of the agency that had the authority to build the dam, that is, the federal government, and that under the mandate of making needful rules and regulations to dispose of, to sell, this property, the government had the right either to build or to buy transmission lines and the necessary equipment to avoid a monopoly of the benefits of the public property and to assure a widespread disposal of those benefits.

It was a long drawn-out trial. It took about four or five weeks, and I must say I averaged about one hour's sleep a night. The trial lasted all day and then I sat down with the general counsel, James Lawrence Fly, and with several other colleagues who were specialists in one or another area of the law to go over the ground with the witnesses for the next day and see that the necessary exhibits were all prepared. It was a very demanding performance, but we were blessed with the leadership of Larry Fly, who had had long and extensive experience as a trial lawyer with the antitrust division of the Department of Justice. He was very ably assisted by the assistant general counsel, William Pitts, who was a very experienced trial lawyer from Alabama. So it was an exciting experience.

We lost the case in the lower court. Judge Grubb, who was with the Federal District Court, declared the act unconstitutional. We appealed it to the Fifth Circuit and prevailed by a two-to-one vote.[2] In October 1935 the case was argued before the Supreme Court by a special counsel who had been retained by Mr. Fly, Mr. John Lord O'Brian, a very famous lawyer of that day and Mr. Fly's former boss. He shared the argument with the Solicitor General, who by that time was Mr. Stanley Reed. Perhaps the most exciting moment was during the question period in the argument before the Supreme Court, when it became clear that the one point on which our whole case depended was sinking through to several of the leading Justices.

In the meantime there'd been another burst of constitutional litigation in which a number of electric holding companies in the United States challenged the Public Utility Holding Company Act. Being the greatly experienced trial lawyer in TVA who had all of one case under his belt, I was recruited by Mr. Benjamin Cohen of the famous Corcoran and Cohen group to be part of the team that would go to New York to carry on the test case that the government brought—*Electric Bond and Share Co. v. SEC.* (1938). I stayed there for four or five months working on that case, which did not go to trial because we were able to stipulate the facts. After I completed the factual stipulation and

2. In the U.S. District Court for the Northern District of Alabama, Judge William I. Grubb, on 26 February 1935, rejected the TVA's claim that the complainants lacked standing to sue and ruled in favor of the stockholders. The TVA appealed the Grubb decision to the U.S. Circuit Court of Appeals for the Fifth Circuit on 1 April 1935. The Appeals Court reversed Judge Grubb's decision on 17 July 1935, reasoning that Congress might dispose of the power produced at Muscle Shoals as freely as any other kind of property.

the briefs, I was called back to the TVA because a second case, the so-called Eighteen Power Companies case, had been filed and the second round of the litigation involving the TVA was under way.[3] Its successful conclusion for TVA established with finality the constitutional basis for the TVA program. I stayed with it to the end in 1938.

Mr. Corcoran called me again in September 1939 and sent me to Senator Robert La Follette, chairman of what was then called the Senate Civil Liberties Committee, although it was a subcommittee of the Education and Labor Committee. Senator La Follette needed someone to run the staff and complete the investigation that was under way on the west coast involving the rights of agricultural labor and the situation of the migratory workers.

I finished the assignment with Senator La Follette in late 1940 and undertook a new one as special counsel for the Federal Power Commission: to negotiate an agreement between Canada and the state of New York that would lay the basis for what some years later became the St. Lawrence Seaway Project. President Roosevelt decided in the summer of 1941 that the seaway could not be completed in timely fashion with all the threatening pressures overseas. So it was arrested for final congressional authorization.

In September 1941, I joined with my old mentor, Mr. John Lord O'Brian, as an assistant general counsel in the Office of Production Management, which later became the War Production Board. Although a leading Republican, he had been drafted along with Messrs. Stimson and Knox to meet the coming crises. His assignment was to serve as General Counsel to the agency set up to organize the U.S. economy for defense production. I considered it an honor to be selected by him for that purpose. That assignment brings me to the end of my New Deal experience.

3. In *Tennessee Electric Power Co. et al. v. TVA* (1939), the Eighteen Power Companies case, the Supreme Court ruled that the power companies operating in the TVA's territory had no standing in court to question the validity of the TVA's power program or the constitutionality of the TVA Act.

CHAPTER 17

The Agricultural Adjustment Administration

During World War I, the federal government had encouraged the expansion of farm output in order to supply our allies. After the war, however, foreign demand for farm products fell and a severe agricultural depression ensued that lasted long after the rest of the economy recovered. During the 1920s farm representatives proposed several relief measures. One of the more successful was the Agricultural Marketing Act of 1929, which established the Federal Farm Board to stabilize farm prices by purchasing and storing surplus agricultural products. It failed because it could not control production, it ran out of money, and the depression caused a further catastrophic decline in prices.

The Agricultural Adjustment Act of May 1933 incorporated many of the lessons learned from the reform proposals of the 1920s. Through the Domestic Allotment Plan, a subsidy for farmers who reduced their production, the act attempted to raise farm prices. The money for these subsidies was to come from taxes on the processors of farm products. To administer these programs, the act established the Agricultural Adjustment Administration.

When the Supreme Court overturned the AAA in 1936 on the grounds that the tax on processors was unconstitutional, FDR pushed through the Soil Conservation and Domestic Allotment Act of 1936 to replace it. This act provided benefit payments to farmers who practiced soil conservation in cooperation with a federal program. The funds came from the general revenue, not a special tax, but its effects were similar.

The New Deal farm program worked reasonably well. It did not bring about the farmers' hoped-for millennium, but during FDR's first term gross farm income rose 50 percent, crop prices climbed, and rural debts fell sharply. Not all of these gains can be attributed to the New Deal because part of the price rise was caused by the great Dust Bowl droughts of the mid-1930s in the plains states. The New Deal was, however, a giant step forward in the effort to establish a prosperous rural economy.

ALGER HISS

The onslaught of the depression made such an impact on me and my immediate friends that it seemed to us that we had to try to help right the wrongs that had befallen the country. All during the period of Roosevelt's campaign, and for some time before, those of us who'd been under the influence of Felix Frankfurter thought of Roosevelt as a great man. We also knew some of the professors at Columbia, the Brain Trusters, and Roosevelt became our hero.

In early 1933 I got a telegram from Jerome Frank, who was general counsel for the new Agricultural Adjustment Administration in the Department of Agriculture under Henry Wallace. I was invited to be one of his two chief assistants. I delayed. I wanted to go to Washington and believed anyone who had the opportunity would want to serve the President, but I was a little embarrassed at leaving my New York law firm so soon after starting. Then I got a telegram from Felix saying, "On basis national emergency, you must accept Jerome Frank's offer." This was enough to settle it for me. When I went to the senior partners, to my pleasure and surprise they thought I should go to Washington. I left immediately.

The Triple-A legislation hadn't been passed yet. It was still being drafted, so I helped on that for some time. A vacant office in the Department of Agriculture was turned over to us. I felt I was a volunteer; the spirit was rather as though we were going to fight for the country. We were like a militia in mufti, and we had enlisted for the duration. The depression was the greatest crisis the country had faced since the Civil War. We were romantic and a little smug to think we were quite that important. But we had opportunities that would not have come our way for years in the practice of a big firm.

I was then twenty-eight. The first job I was given was drafting the cotton contract.[1] The theory of the AAA was that farmers' prices were ruinously low. There was a glut not only of cotton but also of wheat and

1. The Cotton Acreage Reduction Contract of 1933 included a Cotton Benefits Program which paid cotton farmers approximately six to eight cents per pound for the 25 to 50

other commodities, which kept depressing prices. Therefore actual production should be reduced because that would tend to raise prices. The farmers could not reduce production without economic injury to themselves unless they were helped by the government, so benefit payments, as they were called, were given to them as an incentive to reduce production.

Since cotton was already in the ground and coming up, they couldn't be paid not to plant. They had to be paid to plow up every third row, and the first cotton contract provided precisely for that. We had to find out what the cotton experts wanted, and we had to learn something about cotton. When we went down to the Government Printing Office to correct proofs of the first cotton contracts, we worked as fast as if we had been in a big corporate office getting out an indenture. That print order was for some millions of copies. The figure that sticks in my mind is something like 9 million; that sounds huge, but there were small cotton farms and big cotton farms, and they were spread all over the South from Texas to Virginia. It was heady stuff to be in charge of the final draft of a contract of that magnitude. Then we drafted contracts for wheat, for corn, and for hogs. Then peanuts, rice, and sugar were added. It was the busiest of times, and most of us felt that we were helping save the country from collapse.

Every department was full of bright young people. We were a very happy band of brothers, all helping each other. The National Labor Relations Board got started, Social Security, the SEC. It was an extraordinarily vital time for young people. We acquired a considerable amount of arrogance, because much of what we believed in was opposed by conservative forces. A large percentage of the press eventually came to oppose Roosevelt, but the public didn't. So we had the gratification of feeling we were on the side of a great leader who had the confidence of the people.

After the first year of the cotton program, it was clear that, for all its idealism, it was hurting and might further hurt the tenants because if a landowner was going to reduce production by a third, he had a third too many tenants or sharecroppers. Most of them depended on the little huts that were supplied and the garden patches where they were allowed to raise vegetables for themselves. In the new contract, in which we called for a reduction of planting, this became a basic issue. What do you do about tenants? Section 7 of the second cotton contract was the

---

percent of the planted crop that they plowed under. It required them to split the money equally with their sharecroppers and 75 percent to 25 percent in favor of their tenant farmers.

one that provided the answer.[2] It became a hot issue because the land-owners had always been free to get rid of tenants any time they wanted. Of course they'd never before had a problem of major reduction. They hadn't liked the fact that in the first contract we had insisted on payments going directly to tenants for their share of the crop that was plowed up. Senator Ellison Smith of South Carolina came to my office when he heard that checks were going out to tenants. A senator coming to see a young bureaucrat shows how things were turned upside down by the New Deal. Normally, he would have called, and someone would have rushed to his office. He came to see me and said, "Young fella, you can't do this to my niggers, paying checks to them. They don't know what to do with money. The money should come to me. I'll take care of them. They're mine." That attitude, much less kindly expressed, was widespread. The second cotton contract was thought to be too radical, and the cotton section of Congress had to get along with the planters. The program would be a failure unless the owners of the plantations agreed to sign. So there was real conflict.

Those of us in charge of cotton contracts felt we were representing Secretary Wallace's view. The terms, slightly diluted, seemed to be the best that we could get. They provided that no signer of a contract, no owner of land, could get rid of his tenants. He had to retain the same number of tenants. There were clauses that indicated they should be the same individuals, unless a tenant behaved in such a way that threatened property or safety. If they were thieves the planter could get rid of them, but they could not be gotten rid of lightly. They had a right to live in the huts that they'd been living in and to continue to have use of work animals and garden plots. This caused real turmoil, and not just within the Triple-A. There was tremendous excitement and tension, and the members of Congress, members of the cotton section, felt that this would impair the whole program.

As a result of this, Chester Davis, who was the administrator of the Triple-A, insisted that Wallace fire Jerome Frank, who was first in the general counsel's office. Francis Shea, Jerome Frank, three or four other people like Gardner (Pat) Jackson were all discharged and the general counsel's office was put under the solicitor of the Department of Agri-

2. Section 7 of the Cotton Acreage Reduction Contract of 1934–35, which had to be signed by every cotton planter in the South as a condition of receiving benefit payments, required the landlord to make a good faith effort "insofar as possible" to protect the jobs of those tenants and sharecroppers no longer needed to produce the reduced crop. The planters argued that this was only a moral obligation and not legally enforceable. The legal opinion section of the AAA attempted to insist that it was a legal requirement and planters had to keep all their tenants to get their payments. The new contract also changed the landlord-tenant benefit distribution ratio in favor of the landlords.

culture. From then on my interest in the Triple-A lessened and the fire went out of the whole thing. We felt that Wallace had backed down from his own principles. It was a terrible shock to Jerome, who was very close to Wallace. Tugwell was away at the time, and when he came back it was too late to do anything. I was also acting as counsel to the Nye Munitions Committee[3] then, so my supervision of this opinion had been done at night. I was trying to do two jobs at once, and I spent most of my time on the Nye Committee.

Shortly after, when Triple-A's constitutional case came up, Stanley Reed, Solicitor General, asked me to go to the Department of Justice to write the brief because of my experience in the Department of Agriculture. In September 1935, therefore, I joined the Solicitor General's staff to help write the brief in the Triple-A case, *U.S. v. Butler* (1936).

TELFORD TAYLOR

At the end of my clerkship with Judge Augustus Hand, I landed in Interior because my friend Mel Siegel, who was clerking for Justice Cardozo, introduced me to the solicitor, Nathan Margold. Interior was an old stick-in-the-mud department, and Ickes was trying to churn it up. It was rather dull, not what I'd expected, but I got very much involved with public lands, especially the Elk Hills case, which involved properties in California. The question was did they belong to the United States or to the Southern Pacific Railway? That hinged on whether they were known to be oil lands in 1903. I wrote an opinion saying that the land belonged to the government. Ickes signed the opinion and that settled that.

A lot of other things were brightening up life. Ike Stokes and I were taken on by Corcoran, Cohen, Max Lowenthal, and Landis as two young dogsbodies to do the donkey work on the drafting of the Securities Exchange Act of 1934. It was a lot of fun and got me involved in legislative drafting, which I did a great deal of and enjoyed.

Felix Frankfurter was into the life of almost every *Law Review* student who passed through Harvard for those years. He was an elitist, but there were exceptions. Francis Shea is a good example. As far as grades

3. The Nye Munitions Committee, established by the Senate on 12 April 1934, was an inquiry into the manufacture and traffic in arms chaired by Senator Gerald P. Nye, a Democrat from North Dakota. The committee's hearings stressed the heavy profits made by munitions-makers during World War I and tried, inconclusively, to show their influence on U.S. entry into the war.

were concerned, he did not do well at law school, but for some reason he made a dent on Felix. He went on to make a huge success of his professional life.

Felix was good to me in every professional material way. He was ultimately responsible for persuading Larry Fly to make me general counsel of the Federal Communications Commission. I have to thank Felix for everything. But we never had any real rapport.

I lived with a group of bachelors in a house on 18th Street. Francis Shea liked to sit up late and drink and talk. Tom Eliot would be up there trying to sleep. We'd hear him coughing and slamming doors. In the daytime we got along well. Shea worked in the Triple-A legal opinion section under Jerome Frank. Jerome Frank and I hit it off very well. He invited me to come over to the legal opinion section. The writing of the opinions covered a multitude of things, including benefit contracts having to do with sharecroppers and the way the benefit payments would be divided between the owner and the sharecropper. These pro-sharecropper opinions led to the so-called "purge" in which Jerome Frank and Francis Shea were fired.[4] Alger was so disaffected that he soon left. I hadn't been involved in the political fracas—I'd just barely come—so I became chief of the legal opinion section in Jerome Frank's place. He had assembled a very good staff, among them the young lady he subsequently married, Hilda Groshnikoff.

When Alger Hiss left to go with the munitions investigation, I held his job. In his last few months, he had been representing the department for the congressional committees that drafted the agricultural legislation. I took over; it was just fascinating. I got acquainted with the Hill, with committee methods and staffs.

During the discussion of the amendments to the Agricultural Adjustment Act, I sat on the floor with the senior senator, old Cotton Ed Smith of South Carolina, who headed the Agriculture Committee. He was antique and early nineteenth century in his attitudes. All he ever talked about on the floor was southern womanhood and cotton. He was a great shot with tobacco juice. I remember one committee meeting John Abt and I attended; it was hot, and John had on lovely white pants and white sport shoes. His foot kept dangling close to the spittoon, waving back and forth. Cotton Ed looked down and noticed John's foot. He sat back; then he leaned forward and let fly. It went right past the shoe and into the spittoon. He was a dead shot.

The Agricultural Adjustment Act was the law under which the Sec-

---

4. David L. Kreeger drafted the opinion in favor of the sharecroppers. Though not affected by the purge, within a few months he followed Shea to the Puerto Rico Reconstruction Administration. Kreeger went on to serve a year with the Public Works Administration, a year with the Bituminous Coal Commission, and six years in the Justice Department.

retary of Agriculture launched the benefit program, which paid benefits to farmers to reduce acreage so prices would go up. Farmers who owned all their own land and farmed it got the whole benefit payment, but sharecroppers had only a proprietary interest. So they would share with the owner in payments but the question was on what basis. There was no court battle. The fight was all within the department; they just changed the interpretation of the law.

My experience in Congress was very good for me, but it came to an end in the summer of 1935 when I became assistant counsel to the Senate Committee on Interstate Commerce under Max Lowenthal, who was the counsel. Burton K. Wheeler of Montana was the chairman. That was a good show. Wheeler's relation to the Administration, which never was very good because he hated the Attorney General, Homer Cummings, became bad. He stayed with FDR on the Public Utility Holding Company Act, which he was largely responsible for putting through the Senate. But then came the Court-packing plan, on which he led the opposition, and later on the war, when he became a leader of the isolationists. Relations with the Administration became bad. I was with that committee for four years, 1935 to 1939, when this big change took place.

The purpose of the Interstate Commerce Committee was to investigate railroad finances. As a result of the depression, there was a wave of railroad bankruptcies; then railroads really counted, everybody rode them, and widows had their money in railroad bonds. Max Lowenthal had written a book called *The Investor Pays,* a critical analysis of the reorganization of the Chicago, Milwaukee and St. Paul Railroad.[5] I was put in charge of the New York office of the committee and lived there for four years.

The committee looked into the financial activities of the railroads, such as purchases of stock in other roads to make big combinations. The Van Sweringens, who built most of downtown Cleveland, came very close to putting together a transcontinental railroad.[6] The crash and the depression had pretty well wiped them out as well as bondholders and a lot of the railroads. So we investigated railroad financing.

We went through files and held hearings at which Wheeler presided; when he got very busy on the Court-packing plan, the number two Democrat on the committee, Harry S. Truman, then a freshman senator, took over. Wheeler, Wallace White of Maine, and Truman

5. Max Lowenthal, *The Investor Pays* (New York: Knopf, 1933).
6. Mantis and Oris Van Sweringen were real estate operators, railroad managers, and speculators who developed the Shaker Heights suburb of Cleveland. In 1916, they gained control of the New York, Chicago and St. Louis Railroad, and later added the Lake Erie and Western, the Toledo, Peoria and Western, and the Wheeling and Lake Erie railroads. Their holding company pyramid collapsed after their deaths in 1935 and 1936.

were the three active senators on the committee. Gradually, Truman took over more of the running of the committee. I got to know Truman quite well, much better than Wheeler. He left things to the staff. A number of us got a lot of work examining witnesses, bankers from the big Wall Street and Chicago firms. That meant travel. I was all over the main financial centers. By then we'd all gotten pretty much the idea that business and bankers were a dangerous lot. It became too much of a stereotype. It became a fixed and not a selective attitude. One had to grow out of that knee-jerk reaction to bankers and businessmen.

We all found Truman a very nice man. We became very fond of him, and we found his heart was in the right place. But he showed no signs of leadership.

Senator Wheeler, on the other hand, was a man of enormous personal force, but he was not highly educated; his grammar occasionally fell down. In a curious way he was like an English barrister. He could pick up anything with very little preparation. We used to worry a great deal about the hearings when he examined witnesses. We'd go around the night before, and he would sit back in the chair and pull a handkerchief out of his pocket and drape it on his head. He would sit, apparently asleep, while we talked. But the next day he would murder the witnesses. He was a real power. I had great admiration for him; he was an old rogue. Most of those leaders, like Lyndon Johnson, pulled strings and made deals and were rough and tough operators.

Wallace White was pleasant, reasonably able, but a creature of the business interests. Then there were McAdoo, Cotton Ed Smith, Borah, Joe Robinson, Huey Long—you certainly couldn't get together a crew like that nowadays. There were times when they engaged in a great fracas on the floor. When the agriculture bill was going through, the Court struck down the National Industrial Recovery Act as unconstitutional. Should they withdraw the amendments? Were they to be held unconstitutional? I remember Joe Robinson saying, "Don't let it go, Ed. Keep going. We don't really know what that decision means." Robinson was a real leader. On another occasion—the Court-packing plan—whether he believed in it or not, he handled it as a matter of loyalty, and it led to his death. During the debate on the plan, Wheeler was leading the opposition. Robinson keeled over right on the floor from a heart attack. Wheeler said that was the finger of God pointing at the man who was on the evil side of the thing.

It's hard to say whether the New Deal succeeded or not. I'm inclined to think the regulatory measures like the Securities Exchange Act were more successful than things like Triple-A, which was based on economic theories of dubious validity. The National Industrial Recovery

Act and the NRA came to dismal ends and accomplished little. The Public Utility Holding Company Act was a bit more successful, but it was designed to prevent fraud and other bad practices, not to bring prosperity. The prime purpose of the statute was to police the industry. The TVA was a very lasting improvement of a regional nature.

JOHN C. DREIER

I came to Washington enthused about the New Deal and interested in land and farming. I met with Secretary Ickes and told him of my interest in a program called Subsistence Homesteads.[7] The program helped people acquire small tracts of land to engage in part-time farming in order to overcome the limitations of the part-time cash income they earned. This was thought to be a form of security, particularly in small towns where there was seasonal employment. The plan was to improve income by producing food. I worked with an expert from Montana, and Mrs. Roosevelt helped initiate one of our first projects in West Virginia.[8] She persuaded architects and planners to work on this particular project as a model. Unfortunately, there were all kinds of practical problems; it proved to be very costly and of limited success. We did, however, develop projects in the East, South, and Middle West; we helped people move and to work out small farms which we financed.

Later, we dealt with the purchase of submarginal farms. The Department of Agriculture over the years had shown that there were a great many farms in areas that were no longer economically farmable. They varied from forty to hundreds of acres. Many of them were in hilly land that had badly eroded. They also included large acreages in the Dust Bowl, which at that time enveloped large sections of the Great Plains, and a lot of farms in cutover areas of poor soil. This land could be used for forestry, conservation, and recreation. In the Plains, it could be restored to grazing with grass cover. In the 1930s the government could buy such land for low prices, as low as $5.00 an acre. (Land bought in Florida at that price would cost $1,000 an acre today.) The

7. The Subsistence Homesteads projects were provided for in the National Industrial Recovery Act of 1933, which allocated $25 million for them. Initially, FDR placed the program in the Interior Department. It languished there until FDR transferred it to the Agriculture Department in 1935.
8. Mrs. Roosevelt took a special proprietary interest in the communities planned for West Virginia, Reedsville and Arthurdale. She even helped decide the details of interior decoration for the homes.

federal government would buy the land and turn it over either to the U.S. Forest or the Park Service, or create state forest or state recreational areas and wildlife refuges.

During the reorganization of government departments, I found myself in the new Resettlement Administration established in 1935, whose chief was Rex Tugwell. I wrote an article for him that he liked, and speeches that provided information on the new Resettlement program. Tugwell was interesting, warm, and friendly. He made a good impression, although he always had the air of the academic, a scholarly person who differed from the local people. He was very intelligent about the way he addressed people, and he did well.

On a trip into the deep South we visited Mound Bayou in Mississippi, a community of blacks who were Republicans and descendants of the slaves of Jefferson Davis's brother. He had given them land in the rich delta cotton areas. They told us a story about an incident in 1928 when Al Smith was a presidential candidate. The Mississippi Democrats were worried so they resorted to extreme stories about the other side. When the Republican candidate, Herbert Hoover, came through Mound Bayou on his train, the local Democrats put out a statement saying that Mr. Hoover had danced on the station platform with the black Republican committeewoman, Mary Booze. In those days it was an unpardonable sin. Republicans denied the story. They retorted that the train just slowed down and Hoover stood on the back platform and waved; the train then moved on. The Democrats persisted. "Just tell us: If the train had stopped and the people were dancing, would Mr. Hoover have danced with Mary Booze?" We got beyond such tales and observed that so much of that rich delta land never was well managed and consequently folded up.

The function of the Resettlement Administration was to raise the poorer sector of the rural population. They loaned funds to poor farmers and gave them technical assistance. They recognized that farmers were not well-informed, so they made up plans for individual farm management. They would finance the necessary fertilizer, machinery, seeds, or animals. That program was successful. They also had the Farm Tenancy Act of 1937, under which loans were made to farm tenants so they could purchase the farms they were renting. During that period the whole of southern agriculture changed. The old sharecropping cotton farm in the Southeast turned into livestock and other crops. Cotton farming moved west to the big flatlands where they could use heavy machinery. The program also eased the adjustment of people to the new economic picture. In this job I traveled all over the country. I got to know the rural landscape all the way from Maine to California, from Florida to the Pacific Northwest. Many Americans don't really know where all the states are, but if you're an agriculturalist you even know where the principal counties are.

Tugwell's Resettlement Administration also included the Green-belt towns.[9] I had something to do with one at Greenbelt, Maryland. The President came to the dedication. I saw him close enough to admire that extraordinarily jaunty way of his, that gracious informality. He had that rare combination of a man who enjoys power and yet considers everything in the light of the public good. He recreated hope in people.

I then moved into the Soil Conservation Service, in the Department of Agriculture. I visited the Dust Bowl at the height of the storms. There were two big centers of the worst wind erosion, one around the Panhan-dle in Northwest Texas and parts of Oklahoma, New Mexico, and Colo-rado, and the other in North and South Dakota. Even in Washington we could visualize the clouds of dust. I remember reading about dust falling on snow in Vermont in the spring; it had dried out and started blowing in the Great Plains while there was still snow on the ground in Vermont.

I went to the Dust Bowl with Morris Llewellyn Cooke of Philadel-phia, a marvelous person of great ability, an engineer who was the first head of the Rural Electrification Administration. Also on this trip were Dr. Lewis C. Gray, a land use expert, and Kendall Foss, one of Cooke's aides. We held public hearings and visited the actual ruination of places. (Later, Cooke submitted the report recommending action to aid the Great Plains.)

Our mission was to discourage people from plowing up prairies and sowing wheat where the land was poor and had dried out; we recom-mended restoring it as grazing area. Large tracts of land were turned into cattle pastures. Roosevelt's pet project, however, was called the Shelter Belt, the planting of trees. At first there was to be a whole strip of forest from Canada to Mexico along the Great Plains. In actuality, the plan helped farmers to plant windbreaks on their farms to prevent the wind from being so destructive. Fortunately, there was a change in the climatic cycle. Soon, little dams were built along with little farm ponds to help with the cattle and conserve water.

9. The Greenbelt towns were one of the Resettlement Administration's programs to estab-lish suburban communities for low-income city workers. They included Greenbelt (near Washington, D.C.), Greenhills (near Cincinnati), Greendale (near Milwaukee), and Greenbrook (near New Brunswick, N.J.).

CHAPTER 18

The Curmudgeon: Harold Ickes

Harold L. Ickes was a member of FDR's "inner cabinet" from 1933 until the President's death in 1945. During all that time he was FDR's Secretary of the Interior, but because of the number of other official duties he performed, he was sometimes referred to as the "secretary of things in general." Energetic, courageous, incorruptible, "Honest Harold" was ideally suited to the task of developing a solid nationwide public works program.

He was, however, also vain, quarrelsome, suspicious of everyone, cynical, and extremely conservative with money. He would have been a poor choice to head a major relief operation that required fast spending of money to succeed. FDR recognized his limitations, calling him a good administrator but too slow, and the President periodically diverted funds to Hopkins's relief efforts. Ickes hoped to revive the economy by large public works projects that would "prime the economic pump" through heavy capital expenditures; Hopkins aimed at putting as many men to work as fast as possible. This led to a long-term feud between Ickes and Hopkins. Ickes's ultimate weapon in these struggles—to threaten resignation—greatly irritated his Cabinet colleagues. In May 1936, for instance, Hopkins recorded in his diary: "All day planning the work program—which would be a great deal easier if Ickes would play ball—but he is stubborn and righteous, which is a hard combination— he is also the 'great resigner'—anything doesn't go his way, threatens to quit." Ickes was an old-time Bull Moose Republican Progressive, who had earned his battle scars in fierce struggles with the Republican Old Guard. He had as little love for most of the New Dealers as they had for him.

As Secretary of the Interior, Ickes was a dedicated conservationist in the mold of Theodore Roosevelt and Gifford Pinchot. He also significantly reformed the department's Indian policy. He expanded the National Parks and federal grazing lands. As head of the Public Works Administration after 1933, he controlled the spending of more than $9 billion for federal and nonfederal public works ranging from great hydroelectric dams in the West to small-town post offices and parks. He managed to keep the PWA's enterprises free from graft and corruption, but in so doing his care sometimes produced delays that defeated the pump-priming purposes of the agency. At the same time, his long-term construction plans proved a godsend in fighting the 1937–38 recession.

Ickes continued as Secretary of the Interior Department until February 1946, when he resigned in a dispute with President Truman. From then until his death in 1952, he lived in retirement on his Maryland farm, contributing articles to periodicals and writing a syndicated newspaper column, "Man to Man."

ARTHUR GOLDSCHMIDT

The first time I heard about Harold Ickes was in the winter of 1934, when my wife and I went to a dinner party. Some top Democratic politicals were there, and they were complaining about Ickes being afraid someone would swipe a cigar off his desk and about the difficulties they were having with him because he wasn't getting on with the Public Works Administration. I was working in Harry Hopkins's office at that time, so I rather enjoyed all these complaints about Mr. Ickes.

He was very much a figure in Washington, partly because of his reputation as a difficult person and partly because he liked the limelight and sought it. He was, in his own words, a curmudgeon. One of my favorite stories is that he took the doors off the booths in the men's room so people couldn't sit and read the newspaper too long. Another is rather good. Ickes complained about the vast numbers of dockets that came in, proposals for public works from states and municipalities that were supposed to go through the legal division, the finance division, and the engineering division of Public Works. He felt that many of them were approved without adequate review by the heads of the divisions. So with the help of his secretary he cooked up a fake docket that started out and ended up perfectly soundly, but in the middle a large section of *Alice in Wonderland* had been typed in. When that particular docket went through all three divisions with approval, he raised hell with his staff. He ran his office largely through fear. I've always felt public administration was divided between those people who ruled by love and those who ruled by fear, and he obviously was in the latter category.

I came into Public Works in late 1938, in the office of the power division under Clark Foreman. He had been Ickes's adviser on race relations before he became head of the power division and had had a lot to do with Ickes's rather good record on the problem of race. Ickes was the first man to integrate a public cafeteria, a government cafeteria, in Washington, and Clark Foreman was the first man in Washington to have a black secretary, despite the fact that it caused him all kinds of problems because he was working very actively with southerners.

Ickes was fun to work for because he was very active and he liked to fight. I sometimes think he liked to fight more than he liked any principle, although he was a man of great principle and enjoyed being called "Honest Harold." In the liberal community he was something of a hero because he always took the right positions on the big things like race, civil liberties, and the coming war in Europe. Ickes was very, very good on all the big things, and one was very proud of him for that. On the other hand, on all the little things he wasn't very good at all. He was crotchety, opinionated, and often liked to fight for the sake of fighting more than for a cause. His broad principles didn't always carry over into his personal behavior. For instance, there was a lot of bugging going on, many quite improper personnel procedures. I think he never made the connection between the means he frequently used and the ends that he felt strongly about. So there was a dichotomy between his broad and strongly held convictions and his behavior.

We were all concerned about not having any conflicts of interest. We had to disclose all of our stock holdings. We were enjoined from accepting any gifts which, of course, we wouldn't do anyway. I think the rule was that you couldn't accept anything you couldn't eat within a couple of days. That might include a Christmas box of grapefruit from Texas or the Lyndon Johnson turkeys. One Christmas when Lyndon was a congressman, he shipped a carload of turkeys up and sent them around to all his friends in the Cabinet and subcabinet. They even trickled down to people like me. I think ours weighed forty pounds dressed. There was no way of cooking a turkey that big in our house, so we had to send it to the local Chinese restaurant to have it cooked for Christmas day. But the worst of it was that everybody else had these turkeys, and between Christmas and New Year's we were constantly invited out to eat turkey hash or turkey this or turkey that. We just had turkey coming out of our ears. The whole Georgetown set was loaded down with Lyndon Johnson turkeys.

There was a story that John Carmody, who by that time had become head of Public Works, refused the turkey on the grounds that he didn't want to accept a bribe from a congressman. Lyndon was furious about that. "If John Carmody can be bought for one turkey, he must be a pretty poor administrator. He could have done what the White House did: accept the turkey and turn it over to the local hospital or the orphans' home or something like that, but he didn't have to make a federal case that I was attempting to bribe him with a turkey."

Ickes's threats to resign were rather famous around the place, and if you read his diaries you find on every third or fourth page he's sending his resignation because of this or that issue. I never was close enough to him personally to have been in on any of this soul-searching about resignation. I certainly heard about it from people like Tom Corcoran and Ben Cohen or Abe Fortas and others who were closer to him.

One of his pet fights was to get the Forest Service into the Interior Department. He never was successful in that endeavor, but he was successful in a lot of other empire-building. He was very strong on western power development, but he was challenged by David Lilienthal, who felt that what was needed was a series of autonomous river-basin developments throughout the country. Ickes was very strong for having all of those river-basin developments in the Interior Department. At that time TVA was enormously successful, and one of the reasons it was successful was because Harold Ickes had supported TVA's effort to get into the power business. Lilienthal never would have been able to pull off what he did with TVA if it hadn't been for the support of the Public Works Administration in providing cities and municipalities with resources to build power systems to use TVA power. This was a very complicated, very controversial subject. Cities could apply for public works loans and grants and get a public power project. The result was that some of the big power companies were threatened in city after city by a possible competing line. Ickes stood very firm and developed a policy that called for elections. If an election went in favor of public power, Ickes required that a good faith offer be made by the city for the power lines of the company involved. If the offer was refused, the city could go ahead with the project.

This was what made the TVA power area successful. In the late thirties TVA was able to buy out a number of large power systems and develop its own program in the Tennessee Valley. Ickes wanted this type of development in the other river basins. There was a purely bureaucratic fight about how it should be done. I'm inclined to think that Ickes was right in holding that the complete independence of TVA, which Lilienthal made so much of, divorced it from any kind of adequate control by the federal government. We might have had a lot of competing regional programs that had no truly federal policy behind them. This was the great battle between Ickes and Lilienthal. In a sense, nobody won the battle. TVA remained independent. The Bonneville Power Administration was made part of Interior and so were several other agencies. But the whole scheme never went through. The war came and the idea of a federal program that would provide public power and public transmission throughout the country died. But if we hadn't had Bonneville and Grand Coulee we never could have produced the aluminum that was needed for the war.

I worked on the aluminum issue for Ickes, in relation to the war agencies and the Defense Plant Corporation, which financed many of the aluminum plants. But again, Ickes was very insistent that not all the power from these western projects be simply channeled to the Aluminum Company of America, which at that time held a monopoly of aluminum production in the country. Ickes insisted that that monopoly was bad for the country, and I think he made a good case for it. Before Pearl Harbor the efforts of ALCOA to produce aluminum were pretty picayune. They didn't want too much aluminum production and they were only willing to consider increments that they themselves could handle. The case against ALCOA brought by the Justice Department had not succeeded in requiring any kind of divestiture, so ALCOA was one of the true monopolies in this country. I went through four volumes of Justice Department briefs, and they had done a beautiful job of showing up ALCOA. I kept feeding that stuff to Ickes. His fight was based on the fact that Congress had strengthened the Bonneville Power Act in a manner that would prevent monopolies by limited groups. He was not going to let Bonneville and Grand Coulee power be almost entirely channeled to ALCOA. There was a bitter battle, and a lot of people felt that he was not adequately concerned about the war effort because he'd insisted on bringing unknown groups into producing something as technically complicated as aluminum, which is a lot of nonsense. You can make aluminum in your back yard if you have the power. But fortunately he stuck to his guns. So there was a lot of competition in the field, with the result that a lot of aluminum was produced, and much of it through the federal power program.

In a fight like that Ickes was absolutely unshakeable and fearless. He just insisted. And he would write letters to the press. He called a meeting on aluminum, and Thurman Arnold from Justice, Robert P. Patterson from the Army, Frank Knox from the Navy, and others came. I was there, and he just laid it down with them. He wasn't going to be pushed into selling power to ALCOA. They had a big row with him about it. Thurman Arnold was on his side; Knox was sort of wishy-washy; Patterson was worried. But most of these people believed that only ALCOA could produce aluminum.

Ickes's impulses were good. He was antimonopoly, he was pro the little guy, he was supportive of things like the Rural Electrification Administration, anything that would help the little fellow.

His own lifestyle was not modest. He had money, so he never suffered the pangs of hunger or deprivation. He lived rather well. We had a little executives' dining room in the Interior Department. The only decoration in it was a framed sampler saying, "It Is Better to Die of Hunger than to Season Your Victuals with the Cares of Office." Signed: Harold L. Ickes. I remember taking a young lady to lunch there. She looked at that motto and said, "You know, anyone who's ever been hungry couldn't have written that." And of course that was true.

Ickes loved to write a mean letter. If you were working with him on it, it was great fun. He'd spend all night thinking up a letter to write to Jesse Jones that would raise his hackles. Jones was head of the Reconstruction Finance Corporation, and Ickes despised him.

Hopkins and Ickes were notorious enemies at the early stages of the New Deal. Hopkins was responsible for quick, labor-intensive jobs, and Ickes was trying to justify large investments in dams and bridges that had a long lead time before they could be constructed. Each found the other's procedures unacceptable. If you had to put people to work quickly, you couldn't wait until all the drawings for a huge project were finished. On the other hand, if you were thinking in terms of resource development like a dam on the Columbia River, you couldn't put people to work without blueprints. So there was a natural antagonism between the two. Both of them had a lot of flair, both of them were good for the newspapers, both of them were good at coining phrases. The curious thing was that I never knew how real this battle through newspaper comments was, because when Hopkins's wife died in 1937, Ickes invited him up to his place and they spent the weekend together. He reached out to Hopkins during the period when Hopkins was in trouble. I remember that these two, both having gone through the same experience, were together at that particular time.[1]

I had a problem with Ickes when I was working with Homer T. Bone and others, trying to develop the Columbia Valley Authority project.[2] It would cover not only Bonneville and Coulee but also the

1. Harold Ickes's first wife, Anna Wilmarth Thompson, whom he had married in 1911, was killed in an automobile accident in 1935.
2. The Columbia River Valley Authority was a proposed regional public power agency modeled on the TVA. It was never approved, giving way to the more modest Bonneville Power Administration proposal.

many additional power sites that have since been built on the Columbia River and its tributaries. It's one of the biggest collections of hydro power in the world. Homer T. Bone was a man of very strong convictions himself, and he and Ickes didn't always see eye to eye. Homer occasionally slipped off into the Lilienthal camp on the question of whether the Columbia Valley Power Authority should be an autonomous agency or be part of the Interior Department. Abe Fortas and I tried very hard to keep Bone on the track and to keep Ickes from blasting Bone for getting off the track. We wrote a speech for Ickes to make in the state of Washington, Homer Bone's home state, in which we tried to get Ickes to make some kindly comments about the senior senator from Washington. We sent the draft in. He sent for us, and we walked down his huge Mussolini-like office that intimidated you even if you'd done it a hundred times. As we walked shoulder-to-shoulder from the door to the desk, he stuck out his chin and said, "What are you two trying to make out of me, a love bird?"

I once worked very hard on a letter to Jesse Jones, written in the typical Ickes manner, very blunt and very tough. I had said something about his divisive manner in paragraph one, and I didn't want to use "divisive" again in paragraph two. So I said he was being "schistic." I figured there was such a word. I looked in my dictionary, and sure enough, there was "schistic." I left it and sent the letter to Ickes. It was late Friday, and the letter had to get out before Ickes left. He called me in and went through the letter, humphed a couple of times, and asked a couple of questions. "Mr. Goldschmidt, is this word 'schistic' spelled correctly?" "Yes, sir, I looked it up." He had his dictionary behind his desk at a window. He got up from his desk, went to the window, and looked it up. "It's not in the dictionary." I saw he had a different dictionary. "Mr. Secretary, it's late and this letter has to get out. Otherwise you're losing one of the beats in this controversy. I assure you that that word is in my dictionary." "Can you show it to me?" I padded back to my office, carried my huge dictionary back, slammed it down in front of him, and pointed out the word. He didn't say "I'm sorry" or anything. He signed the letter and off it went. It was a letter to Jesse Jones. That's why it was important.

I had the feeling that from time to time Roosevelt got as impatient with Ickes as Truman finally did. But someone like Tom Corcoran, who was very good at straightening out personality problems, probably joshed the Old Man into putting up with Ickes. Ickes must have been a hell of a guy to have working for you, because he was constantly kibitzing, constantly involving himself in fields that were not his own—often, I thought, because Roosevelt used him to launch trial balloons. As the war came closer and Ickes got involved in helping Britain, helping the Allies, his public statements were frequently used to see how the public would react. The famous destroyer deal was done under Ickes's roof. Whether Ickes had anything to do with it, I don't know, but Ben Cohen certainly worked that out.

Ickes was used frequently to take unpopular positions, and I always thought he did so with the President's consent. Ickes was very good at taking on controversy. He took on Martin Dies, for instance. When some of us in the Interior Department, including myself, were accused of being radicals, Communists, crackpots, and whatnot by Martin Dies, Ickes took on that guy at a time when it wasn't a very popular thing to do. Dies, like Joe McCarthy later on, was playing to a rather noisy and fairly large class. Ickes immediately jumped into the fray in defense of people on his own staff, although he himself was very strongly anti-Communist and not in any way a leftist.

Ickes had a very strong personality. He was a real person, but I'm not sure the legend has survived. The other day I told a young person that I had worked in Interior under Ickes, and he said, "Ickes, Ickes, what is that an acronym for?" Then I realized how old I was. He certainly was a colorful character. He could make the headlines with a phrase. I remember his line about Dewey throwing his diaper into the ring.

One of the sad things about Ickes's monument is that his diaries, which are important source books of the period, are so terribly dull. They're so terribly dull because they were badly edited, and they were badly edited, apparently, because Ickes's widow didn't want them to be edited in any other way. The result is that when you read the diaries, it's like reading the stage directions of an important play without reading the play itself. Ickes goes on and on about some speech he'd made which was very important at the moment because it was a policy trial balloon for the New Deal. All you get are angry reactions to criticism or comments on some rather ephemeral issue, whereas the speech itself was history-making.

LEONA B. GERARD

When I met Harold Ickes a few years before the New Deal, he had not yet begun to refer to himself as a curmudgeon. We met as a result of my interest in Muscle Shoals, a small town on the Tennessee River in Alabama that eventually became the nucleus of the TVA. During World

War I, the government constructed dams, powerhouses, and nitrate plants at Muscle Shoals to prove to private utility companies that hydroelectric power could be profitably sold at much lower rates than they were charging. Some people thought it should be converted into a grand regional development by the federal government, and the League of Women Voters made it a major item on their national agenda. At that time I was speaking for the League before local chapters and giving radio addresses on the subject, encouraging members to write their congressmen to ask them to approve the proposed project. Partly because of these talks, Professor Paul Douglas, who had taught me labor economics at the University of Chicago, asked if I would join the board of a small, nonprofit economics group in Chicago known as the Utility Consumers' and Investors' League and there I met lawyer Harold Ickes.

For many years Ickes had been active in Republican circles. Next to politics, his great love was conservation, including what remained to be rescued of the American Indian. He did not project a glamorous image: short, stocky, gray, middle-fiftyish, a hard worker, but one who at times could smile. There was nothing bland about his views.

Shortly after the election of 1932, to his surprise, he received a letter from the President: "Mr. Ickes, you and I have been speaking the same language for the last twenty years. I am having difficulty finding a Secretary of the Interior. I want a man who can stand on his own feet. Above all, I want a man who is honest, and I have about come to the conclusion that the man I want is Harold L. Ickes of Chicago." Ickes soon changed his address to Washington, D.C.

I sent him a letter of congratulations and told him I was free to work in the capital if he thought I could be of use to him. Several months later he telegraphed the offer of a job, nature unspecified, at $2,600 per annum, the professional entrance level pay. Within a month, my two children and I settled in a pleasantly furnished apartment on 16th Street.

The morning in October when I reported for work, I saw Ickes in shirt sleeves and vest at an enormous desk, conferring with Assistant Secretary E. K. Burlew. They seemed miles away and the scene was like an early Charlie Chaplin film where he had a great distance to overcome before reaching the throne. After greeting me, they resumed their conversation—as though I weren't there—on how I could be of most use to Ickes.

Soon after Ickes became Secretary of the Interior, the President also appointed him administrator of PWA. We were in the depths of the depression. Congress had appropriated the largest sum ever funded for a single project, in excess of $3 billion, to put people back to work. Ickes had no administrative experience; now, besides overall responsibility for the bureaus in the Department of the Interior, he had to recruit thousands of lawyers, fiscal experts, engineers, and managerial and service staff for PWA. He turned to me. "I am besieged by governors, state and municipal officials, lobbyists, descending en masse, who want to convince me that the PWA applications submitted by their constituencies for schools, hospitals, low-cost housing projects, and so on are the most badly needed out of all the hundreds of thousands of other appeals for loans and grants. What do you think of sitting at a table inside the entrance so you can head off these people, talk with them in my stead, and assure them you will report their interest to me? How does that strike you?"

I was dumbfounded. I could not imagine that any of those seeking the administrator would settle for a young woman representative. I feared such a plan would make trouble for Ickes, the department, and the PWA and I said so. He smiled and shook his head. "I guess you're right." He told Burlew to see that I had a desk in his outer office. "She will handle special assignments for me."

He worked a full seven days. He had a massage twice a week in his office that may have saved his life, but he must have had the right genes to start with. He was extremely irritated by employees straggling in ten to twenty minutes late, so he instructed the guards to lock the outside doors at 8:35, five minutes after opening time, and leave them locked for a couple of hours. His telephone started ringing. There were jibes by newspaper columnists, so the brief experiment ceased. To relieve the crick in his neck, he would take an occasional stroll past the portraits of his predecessors, especially Albert Fall, the disgraced Teapot Dome culprit, where he would pause to renew his vow to restore the department's honor.

But his life was not all work. He enjoyed attending state dinners at the White House in honor of foreign heads of state. For relaxation he worked on his stamp collection, an interest he shared with FDR.

During the first eighteen months, despite increasingly heavy responsibilities, Ickes was probably closest to the President. There were direct phone calls from 1600 Pennsylvania Avenue, invitations to the White House for small poker parties, and easy personal access to the President. Together they smiled over the pleas of economic Bourbons now beseeching government to take over areas that historically were sacred to private enterprise. Besides the ill-housed, ill-fed, and ill-clothed, there were citizens disenfranchised by poll taxes and farmers battling with stones and pitchforks against foreclosures of their mortgaged farms.

But later there were new favorites among Cabinet members, snipings at Ickes appeared in the press, and the critics of PWA mounted at the same time the depression extended in all directions. PWA, despite its fine sewers, schools, bridges, and power plant projects, had put few people to work. Unemployment remained in the millions. Conflict erupted between Harold Ickes and social worker Harry Hopkins over the methods best calculated to put people to work.

In November 1933, like the rest of us, Ickes read in the newspapers that the President had given Hopkins millions of PWA dollars to set up projects not only for hardhats but also for writers, dancers, artists, seamstresses, teachers, and research historians, under a new agency named CWA, the Civil Works Administration. By January 1934, Hopkins had 4 million people at work in communities all over the country. Leaf-raking and graft were alleged, but money was put into circulation. The enmity between Ickes and Hopkins increased.

After the first six months Ickes appointed me an executive assistant for PWA, the only woman among six men. I assisted the secretary on many occasions, but there is one I will not forget. We drove to the Hill to a meeting of the subcommittee that had oversight of the proposed Florida Ship Canal. The senator asked searching questions; Ickes referred to me for relevant material. As we left, the senator remarked that if Interior ever found it no longer required my services, he would like to add me to his staff. As we rode back in the long black Interior limousine, the secretary told me I had done well. It was the only time he said so in the seven years I worked with him. It helped me when the going got rough.

One day in 1935, a letter arrived from the White House informing Ickes that all future applications for PWA funds were to be submitted to a new committee on allotments. Ickes regarded this as only one of a number of betrayals. But there were so many complaints that the order was revoked after three days. Then began a series of threats to resign and personal tragedy as well, for his wife, Anna, was killed in an automobile accident. But personal bitterness never affected his decisions. He understood the political facts of life. "As I was leaving, the President called me to urge me to plan for a real vacation. He was most friendly and touching about it," he once told me. Or there would be a call about a speech Ickes had made. He had become the foremost speaker among his Cabinet colleagues.

I will never forget the Marian Anderson affair in 1939. The Daughters of the American Revolution had built an auditorium seating 4,000. The great Marian Anderson was to sing until the DAR ladies suddenly found out she was black. They had made a mistake in the date, they said, but they would refund the money for tickets purchased. Ickes immediately asked the National Park Service director if there was any district ordinance that might prohibit her from singing on the steps of the Lincoln Memorial. There was none. In the late afternoon of the scheduled day an audience of about 75,000 people sat on folding chairs or sprawled on rugs, newspapers, and the bare grass along the reflecting pool and the slopes of the Memorial, awaiting the singer's appearance. Ickes led her forward, merely saying, "I give you Marian Anderson." Applause cracked out like a thunderbolt and just as suddenly stopped when she lowered her head to sing. It was like being in church. I overheard a man say, "Ickes's not making a speech, that was true eloquence."

Early in December 1936, Ickes appointed me to PRRA, the Puerto Rico Reconstruction Administration and I sailed for San Juan.

In 1929 violent earthquakes had practically destroyed Puerto Rico's principal crops, sugar, coffee, and citrus fruit. Sugar production recovered somewhat, but in order to assist the new American beet sugar industry, Congress passed a law drastically reducing the amount of duty-free cane sugar that Puerto Rico could export to the mainland.[3] Then came the Great Depression.

During the famous First Hundred Days Roosevelt did not overlook the island. Various planning groups there and on the mainland met to see what could be done to alleviate Puerto Rico's distress. Dr. Carlos Chardon, a scientist and chancellor of the University of Puerto Rico, had a plan that became the basis of the PRRA program. A year later, the President appointed Dr. Ernest Gruening as administrator of PRRA and Dr. Chardon became the assistant administrator in Puerto Rico. Toward the end of 1936, charges began flying about San Juan accusing PRRA of favoritism in hiring its supervisory employees from one particular political party and ignoring the others. Violence erupted in some parts of the island. Chardon resigned.

I arrived with a letter of instructions from the secretary. My first survey was made in a two-seater single-engine plane. Many projects had barely begun; others were in the early stages of development on drawing boards. They included rural and urban public health dispensaries, community centers, hydroelectric and cement plants, canning and sewing centers, schools and other public buildings, malaria control, and rural housing.

Much of this truly excellent program had bogged down primarily because there were two competing authorities. Every decision of Dr.

3. The Tariff Act of 1931 (Smoot-Hawley Act) sought to stabilize the price of sugar in the United States and thus protect American sugar producers by raising tariffs on all sugar imports, including those from Puerto Rico.

Chardon, the regional administrator, who was well versed in Spanish law and custom, had to push its way through the bottleneck of the legal division, most of whose mainland members were unfamiliar with the local scene. Matters were reaching a stalemate. The obvious first step seemed to be to remove Dr. Gruening. PRRA had become a political liability. Some months later Gruening became governor of Alaska.

The good name of Honest Harold Ickes was put to good use by making him the PRRA administrator with the clear understanding that the program must emanate from the Puerto Rican assistant administrator. Ickes asked me to run the new PRRA liaison office in Washington, and I stayed there three years as his special assistant.

I continued to visit the island once or twice a year, sometimes on assignments not always immediately connected with PRRA. One of the assistant administrators wrote a small book in which he said, "No unusable bridge or group of incompleted houses marred the landscape with their emptiness or deterioration." Lots of people in Puerto Rico did live somewhat better for a while because of PRRA.

Ickes continued to hold weekly staff meetings in his even larger office in the new Interior Building. There were only two other women who attended the meeting regularly, a lawyer in the solicitor's office and the head of personnel. For several years the Congress had declined to appropriate more funds to continue PWA and PRRA. The meaning of this decline finally hit home. In the thirties, most of us associated with exciting government work were merely emergency employees. We had no status. We could be dismissed at any time. I had two children who had to be fed and clothed, and some day they would be going to college. But I liked Washington. I began looking into the civil service system and got on the rolls as an administrative analyst. At my last staff meeting I walked up to Ickes to say good-bye. He wished me well and then asked me what I regarded as the most important thing I had learned while working for him. I must say I hesitated. A rush of feeling engulfed me as I recalled pride, anger, and enthusiasm. "The most important thing," I smiled—"I learned to depend on myself." Ickes found his own feelings too. "I'm glad you said that. I always want my people to grow more self-reliant. Good luck." I thanked him and wished him well.

CHAPTER 19

The Black Cabinet

Blacks were not easily won over to the New Deal. Even the depression did not loosen their loyalty to the party of Lincoln and they voted for Hoover in 1932. The early New Deal aroused sharp criticism from black leaders as they attacked the NRA for displacing black industrial workers and raising prices more than wages. One black writer described the Blue Eagle as a "predatory bird," and said the NRA really stood for Negroes Ruined Again. Blacks also protested the Triple-A for proposing policies that would drive black tenant farmers and sharecroppers from their lands while benefitting white landlords.

There were forces in the New Deal, however, that were striving to aid blacks. Roosevelt took every opportunity to appoint blacks to important posts in the Administration and New Deal policies did attempt, frequently, to break up old Jim Crow patterns. Eleanor Roosevelt and Harold Ickes, in particular, identified themselves with the needs of blacks. Ickes, who had been president of the Chicago NAACP, created a new position in the Interior Department—the Director of Negro Economics—and appointed blacks to jobs in the department and in the Works Progress Administration. He also made sure they had a share of the new apartments in his subsidized housing projects. All these efforts began to turn blacks from the Republican party, but for the most part, it was the all-encompassing economic relief program that finally made them New Dealers.

One New Deal agency that assisted influential and middle-class blacks was the National Youth Administration, where Mary McLeod Bethune saw that vital resources were directed to thousands of young blacks for continuing their education. Many black intellectuals felt that the New Deal offered blacks only half a loaf, but the great mass of the black population rallied to the Democrats in gratitude for federal aid and sympathetic treatment.

The switch of blacks from the Republican to the Democratic party began in 1934. By mid-1938, a *Fortune* magazine poll revealed that 84.7 percent of black respondents supported FDR. The movement of blacks into the Democratic party—along with union members, Jews, Catholics, urban voters, and other minorities—provided a crucial element of the liberal New Deal coalition. The leadership was supplied, in part, by a small group of black government officials who met together frequently to coordinate strategy. Calling themselves the Black Cabinet, they helped move the New Deal toward civil rights and inspired the great mass of blacks to hope for total equality.

ROBERT C. WEAVER

The Black Cabinet evolved from Negro participation in the New Deal, and that participation can be traced to two events that took place in 1933. One was the Second Amenia Conference at the summer home in New York of Joel E. Spingarn, chairman of the board of the National Association for the Advancement of Colored People, where the Roosevelt Administration was discussed. That group conducted an extensive analysis of the desirability of having black advisers in federal agencies, and though not too optimistic about their effectiveness, agreed it would be worse not to have them. The second event was a Rosenwald Fund meeting in Washington to discuss the economic status of the Negro.[1] At that meeting it was also agreed that the special problems of blacks needed special attention and the Fund became committed to the need for racial advisers. It quickly moved to implement this resolution in August 1933 by recommending Clark Howell Foreman, a white southerner and an associate of the Fund, to Harold L. Ickes, Secretary of Interior and administrator of the Public Works Administration, as the first New Deal racial adviser. To expedite the appointment, the Rosenwald Fund paid Foreman's salary.

Foreman's designation was predicated on the assumption by the Fund, supported by Robert Mussa Moton, president of Tuskegee Institute, and Kelley Miller, a professor at Howard University, that a white

1. The Julius Rosenwald Fund, established in 1919 by Julius Rosenwald, president of the Sears, Roebuck Company, provided financial aid to many black organizations.

would be more effective in the job than a black. Ickes agreed. The appointment, however, did not set well with an articulate segment of black America. Walter White and Roy Wilkins, spokesmen for the NAACP, objected to having a white adviser for Negroes because such action symbolized a paternalistic approach to race relations. To counter this, I was named Foreman's associate in November 1933, becoming the first black adviser on Negro affairs, and I too was paid by the Rosenwald Fund.

Foreman and I, with the approval of Secretary Ickes, set up four meetings of the Interracial Interdepartmental Group composed of those concerned with the special problems of blacks. It was an official body, its members were designated by Cabinet members and agency heads, and its minutes were duly recorded and preserved. The first meeting was convened in February 1934 and eighteen persons from fifteen departments and agencies participated. Seven were black, two of whom were career appointees and five were Roosevelt appointees. The Interracial Interdepartmental Group had its final meeting in June 1934.

During those months an increasing number of black racial advisers were appointed. (By 1937, all but five of the New Deal agencies had Negro advisers on their payrolls.) The most significant appointment was that of Mary McLeod Bethune, educator and president of the National Council of Negro Women.[2] She was a dynamic personality who quickly took center stage and knew how to dramatize issues by using flattery and shame to elicit favorable responses to her appeals. Joseph P. Lash, in *Eleanor and Franklin,* quotes a male colleague's admiring appraisal of her when he said she had "the most marvelous gift of affecting feminine helplessness in order to attain her ends with masculine ruthlessness."[3] In 1935, she was appointed director of Negro Affairs in the National Youth Administration, becoming one of the new breed of black appointees. These persons were chosen more for themselves and their ability to define issues relevant to the black community than to pay off political debts.

It was Mrs. Bethune who convened the Black Cabinet in 1935. The name of the group seems to have originated with a reporter in the black press. The group was not a cabinet in the usual sense of the word, since none of its members save Mrs. Bethune had more than sporadic, if any, contact with the President. Actually, she had direct access to Mrs. Roosevelt, and through her to the President, but only occasional direct ac-

2. The National Council of Negro Women, a federation of major black women's clubs, was organized by Mary McLeod Bethune in 1935. She served as its first president from 1935 to 1949.
3. Joseph P. Lash, *Eleanor and Franklin* (New York: Norton, 1971), p. 523.

cess to him. Members of the Black Cabinet were responsible to various agencies of government, and some of them transmitted information and recommendations to the President through their bosses on the White House staff, through Mrs. Bethune, or, as in my case, through all three.

In contrast to the earlier Interracial Interdepartmental Group, the Black Cabinet did not have white participants; it had no official standing and kept no minutes. The meetings of the group continued on an irregular schedule, but we were always subject to being called in an emergency. At the beginning, they were usually held in Mrs. Bethune's apartment; as the group increased in size, larger accommodations were secured.

A picture of the 1937 Black Cabinet's ten members was published in the black press. In the center of the front row is Mrs. Bethune. Three of those who surround her, Henry A. Hunt, Charles E. Hall, and I, attended the first meeting of the Interracial Interdepartmental Group three years earlier. Others in the picture are Joseph H. B. Evans (Farm Security Administration), Laurence A. Axley (Department of Labor), Edgar G. Brown (CCC), N. Robinson (Agriculture), Alfred E. Smith (WPA), and a now unidentified individual. Mrs. Bethune was chairman and I was vice-chairman.

The Black Cabinet provided a forum where problems could be discussed and potential solutions developed. The members often made concrete decisions and carried out assignments concerning matters such as preparing memoranda for future meetings, presenting ideas to government officials or black leaders, and assembling information for release to the press. Early in the functioning of the group, these latter activities were delegated to the rather highly trained younger members, and an interesting relationship developed between them and the more mature Mrs. Bethune. In 1974 on the occasion of the unveiling of a memorial to that venerable lady in Washington I noted: "My younger associates and I developed analyses and program proposals. She articulated and dramatized them. The division of labor evolved with little or no dissent. To us she was Mrs. Bethune, or in terms of researchers, Mother Superior. We were her boys. There was no generation gap since all of us were concerned with a common cause." That common cause was to maximize the participation of blacks in all phases of the New Deal.

Increasingly over time, those remaining active in the Black Cabinet became relatively close. Its composition fluctuated, but Mrs. Bethune, Frank Horne, and I were constant participants. William Hastie was a significant member during his tours of duty in the federal government in Washington. Others such as Alfred E. Smith, who succeeded Forrester Washington as administrative assistant for racial problems in FERA and WPA, played sustained roles. Some who had been associated with me in Interior, PWA, the U.S. Housing Authority, and other agencies, such as Henry Lee Moon and William J. Trent, Jr., who succeeded me as adviser in Negro affairs in the Department of Interior, also functioned as long-time members of the group. As the composition of the Black Cabinet constantly changed, there was a consistent tendency toward ascendancy of nonpolitical personalities. With this development I became the leader and convener of a subgroup composed exclusively of younger black federal officials. We met frequently in my recreation room at home for all-night bull sessions which, in the words of a later article in the *New York Times Magazine,* "swung from feverish rounds of poker to even more feverish discussions of how faster progress could be made in achieving equal opportunities for Negroes."[4]

CHARLOTTE MOTON HUBBARD

During my childhood many people touched my life and left something of themselves that, over the years, shan't be forgotten. The women I especially remember are Mary S. Booth, Jennie Booth Moton, Miss Nannie Burroughs, Mrs. Julius Rosenwald, Mrs. George Mason, Mrs. Charlotte Hawkins Brown, Mrs. Jessie Daniel Ames, Mrs. William J. Schieffelin, and—perhaps most of all—Mary McLeod Bethune.

It is difficult to recall the first time "Ma Bethune," as she was frequently and fondly called, visited our home on the campus at Tuskegee Institute where my father, Robert Mussa Moton, had followed Booker T. Washington as head of the institution.[5] It is not difficult to remember my impressions of her, for even as a child I was aware of the exuberant, forceful vitality of her personality. As a matter of fact, I became quite good at mimicking her, which amused and amazed both my parents and brings to mind Robert Burns's "Oh wad some power the giftie gie us to see oursels as ithers see us!" quoted often by Father. I cannot imagine anyone who met Mrs. Bethune forgetting her. Our paths crossed often as I grew older and she never failed to welcome me warmly because of her respect for my parents.

4. A. A. Raskin, "Washington Gets 'The Weaver Treatment,' " *New York Times Magazine* (14 May 1961), p. 33.
5. Booker T. Washington served as the first principal of the recently chartered Negro Normal School at Tuskegee, Alabama, from 1881 to 1915. Robert Mussa Moton succeeded Washington as principal and served from 1915 to 1935.

Her visits to our home and her conversations with Father and Mother dealt primarily with fund-raising for her school in Florida and the work of the women's clubs in the state of Alabama. Father was a member of the Bethune-Cookman Trustee Board[6] and a master at raising funds for Tuskegee and Hampton,[7] and Mother was active in civic and campus affairs and women's organizations.

One summer while I was at the Chellis School of the Dance at Boston University, the National Association of Colored Women's Clubs held their national convention at Symphony Hall.[8] Serving my mother as her driver, I attended a few of the meetings to watch her hold forth as president. When asked by the delegates what she as president would make her major projects, Mother turned to Mrs. Bethune, who was attending the convention as a previous president (1924–1928), and said with compelling confidence, "I plan, with your cooperation, to complete two excellent projects started by Mrs. Bethune when she served as our president, to complete paying for our national headquarters in Washington, D.C. (on 11th Street) and to try to complete our commitment to the Fred Douglass Home."

It was at this meeting that Mrs. Bethune told the delegates of her plan to organize the National Council of Negro Women to serve as a national voice for Negro women. She said too that she would therefore not be able to give any more time to the Association. Many of the delegates gasped in shocked surprise and disapproval, and others rose from their seats expressing their feelings against her plans. Mother, not waiting for the ladies to calm down, used her gavel with determination and in a not too gentle voice confronted the delegates. "We will not allow Mrs. Bethune to give up her support of the Association, will we ladies? We do not plan to block her plan to join the National Council of Negro Women, do we ladies? We need her support and we will get it, won't we delegates?" The delegates shouted their approval of Mother's questions, and Mrs. Bethune accepted their cheers with pleasure and satisfaction.

Mrs. Bethune did not, however, abandon her own plan. In 1935 she organized the National Council of Negro Women in order to make it

6. Bethune-Cookman College is a primarily black institution of higher education created in 1923 by the merger of Daytona (Florida) Normal and Industrial Institute and the Cookman Institute of Jacksonville, Florida. The name was changed to Bethune-Cookman College in 1929 to commemorate the founder of the Daytona Normal and Industrial Institute and the instigator of the merger, Mary McLeod Bethune.
7. The Hampton Institute in Virginia is a primarily black institute of higher education attended by many of the post-Civil War generation of black leaders, including Booker T. Washington.
8. The National Association of Colored Women's Clubs was a national federation of black women's organizations. One of its main activities in the 1920s was to raise money to preserve the Washington, D.C., home of Frederick Douglass as a national memorial.

the voice nationally for Negro women while the Association remained a voice on local and state levels. Unavoidably, some conflicts arose between the two organizations, but differences were kept to a low key by those who recognized the importance and value of cooperation among women working to promote the plight of American citizens whose complexions are dark. They knew that Mrs. Bethune's contribution was invaluable to the progress of all Negroes trying to survive under a blanket of hatred. The Association of Colored Women's Clubs continued to work on its many projects, as they fought along with white women to abolish lynching—practiced by terrorist KKKs dressed in their sheets and hoods—and to develop schools to educate delinquent girls to be better homemakers. It is important that young people today not forget that had it not been for Mary McLeod Bethune and others like her, with their ability to inspire both young and old, many Americans identified as "Negroes," "colored," and "black" would still be totally ignored.

While teaching at Hampton Institute in Virginia, I was asked to represent Boston University during Dr. Frederick D. Patterson's inauguration as the third president of Tuskegee Institute. Mrs. Bethune was one of the principal speakers. I recall vividly her closing remarks as she turned to Dr. Patterson, saying with compelling force, "Frederick Douglass Patterson, put your hand in God's, keep your feet on the ground, and all will go well with you."

She inspired others in her various projects and plans. She demanded their talents and time with ruthless assurance. She had the charisma of a Baptist preacher, the self-discipline of a soldier, and the cleverness and strength to survive. She had a talent for manipulating people, events, and political situations in order to reach her goals. With a never-wavering recognition of the value of power and a keen sense of humor, she faced her tasks with courage and assurance, gaining the confidence and respect of thousands of Americans from all walks of life. Mary McLeod Bethune will never be forgotten for her contribution to America's continuing quest for human growth and reachable goals.

CHAPTER 20

The Economists

Franklin Roosevelt was not an economist. He had little of the specialized knowledge of the academic, but he was not simply a tool in the hands of his advisers and specialists. He did have a clear economic philosophy of his own. That philosophy grew from the same influences that shaped his political philosophy: the tradition of noblesse oblige as practiced by the Hudson River gentry; the courses he took in economics at Harvard and his own readings while recovering from polio; his practical experience in dealing with diverse economic groups, individuals, and schools of thought throughout his career; and his experience in applying progressive economic ideas as a state senator, Assistant Secretary of the Navy, vice-presidential candidate, and governor of New York. The result was a very definite set of views on the economy, particularly in areas such as labor, big business, welfare legislation, conservation, power development, and regional planning. In formulating the New Deal, therefore, Roosevelt suited his advisers and his administrators to his ideas and not the other way around. In his campaign speech in Chicago on 1 October 1932 he put these ideas concisely.

"As I have often made clear, underneath my economic policies is an attitude toward economic life. I have tried to set forth what I conceive to be a reordered relationship among all the factors in the economic scale . . .

"I pointed out in San Francisco that our task is to meet the problem of underconsumption, of adjusting production to consumption, of distributing wealth and products more equitably . . .

"The way to distribute wealth and products more equitably is to adjust our economic legislation so that no group is unduly favored at the expense of any group or section. Where our laws assist or permit any group to exploit other groups, the exploited ones can no longer buy. Government must systematically eliminate special advantages, special favors, special privileges, wherever possible, whether they come from tariff subsidies, credit favoritism, taxation, or otherwise."

Throughout his presidency, FDR continued to insist on these guidelines. Historians may debate whether he followed a traditional or a Keynesian or an eclectic policy. The fact remains: the New Deal was very much a product of FDR's personal economic philosophy.

WALTER S. SALANT
EDWARD M. BERNSTEIN
JOHN W. PEHLE

SALANT: I went to Washington in September 1934. I had just returned from a year at Cambridge University, where I studied economics and was exposed to Keynes's vigorous discussion of his new ideas two years before publication of his book.[1] To get into the activities of the New Deal was part of my motivation, but I also felt that if I was to become a professional economist I had to overcome my innocence about sources of statistical information. I therefore worked at the Treasury Department for about a year and a half and then for a stockbroker for part of a year. Then I went to Harvard to resume graduate work, but I returned to Washington in 1938.

Treasury was still an old-line institution in 1934. I was in the research division, which had a staff of about twelve. In prior years its main duty seemed to be preparing the Annual Report of the Secretary and appraising the business outlook. Nobody who came to the Treasury a few years later could have recognized it as the same organization I joined. Henry Morgenthau, who had become Secretary when William Woodin, the first appointee, died in May 1934, brought with him some people from the Farm Credit Administration.[2] The research division

1. John Maynard Keynes, *General Theory of Employment, Interest and Money* (New York: Harcourt, Brace, 1936).
2. The Farm Credit Administration was created by Executive Order on 27 March 1933 to consolidate in a single agency the functions of all existing federal units dealing with agricultural credit (for example, the Federal Farm Board and the Federal Farm Loan Board). Congress then passed the Farm Credit Act on 16 June 1933, which greatly facilitated agricultural credits. In 1939, the FCA became part of the Agriculture Department.

gradually took on more duties. It did some economic forecasting, mainly on government tax revenue, and appraised the market for government bonds. It had worked chiefly by calling in people from private business who were regarded as experts on the business outlook and on the government bond market. After 1934 it expanded its own staff and the scope of its activities and was broken up into several divisions. There were the division of research and statistics, the division of tax research, and the division of monetary research, which did the international financial work.

BERNSTEIN: It was Morgenthau who brought in the economists. Harry Dexter White had been in an early group, which had come with Profesor Jacob Viner. Later, Morgenthau brought George Haas in from the Farm Credit Administration. Haas established the division of research and statistics, and Harry White became one of his principal assistants. White, because of his imagination, became more influential with Morgenthau. The division of monetary research was set up for him.

PEHLE: I went to the Treasury Department in June 1934, just after I graduated from Yale Law School. It was a fascinating experience because a lot was going on. One of the things about Treasury was that, under Morgenthau, the ordinary jurisdictional bounds were not regarded as applicable. So the staff felt free to start developing programs in any field Treasury was interested. The staff had numerous clashes with other agencies, especially the State Department because Treasury wanted to get into the international field.

    The general counsel was Herman Oliphant, a professor from Columbia who was a very imaginative and forceful person. He hired a lot of young lawyers, who like me were given responsibilities far beyond those they would get in private practice. We felt that we were working for something above and beyond what we were being paid to do.

BERNSTEIN: One of the big achievements was to transfer finance and power from New York to Washington. An amendment to the Federal Reserve Act made the Federal Reserve Board more important, restructuring the powers of the Board.[3] Until then, the Federal Reserve Bank

3. The Federal Reserve Act of 1913 (Owens-Glass Act), which established the Federal Reserve Board to regulate the nation's banking system, was amended by the Emergency Bank Relief Act of 1933 (Glass-Steagall Act). It created the Federal Deposit Insurance Corporation (FDIC), extended the open-market functions of the Federal Reserve Board to enable it to prevent excessive speculation on credit, permitted branch banking, divorced deposit from investment banking, and widened membership in the Federal Reserve System to include savings and industrial banks.

of New York had been the dominant element in the Federal Reserve system. Power was shifted within this system from the New York Board to the Bank in Washington and to the Treasury.

SALANT: The Glass-Steagall Act of 1933 changed the composition of the Federal Reserve Board (in addition to changing its name to Board of Governors of the Federal Reserve System). Under the original Federal Reserve Act the Secretary of the Treasury and Comptroller of the Currency were members of the Board. Under the new legislation, they ceased to be members. That is of interest now, in view of the present discussion about reducing the Federal Reserve's independence from the Administration and the proposals to put the Secretary back on the Board.

BERNSTEIN: Taking the Secretary of the Treasury and the Comptroller of the Currency off the Board was simply an attempt to further the Board's independence. But, in fact, the Board was less independent of the Treasury. The Federal Reserve system could engage in foreign operations on its own account, but after this, all operations on foreign accounts were in a sense subject to the Treasury. The Treasury and the Federal Reserve took over the power to make policy decisions that were formerly made in the Federal Reserve Bank of New York, although most operations, as distinguished from decision-making, continued to be in the New York Fed.

SALANT: For a long time there seemed to be no one who held the final authority on financial policy in the Roosevelt Administration. In the early years of the New Deal, all sorts of ideas about monetary policy were floating around officially. It's indicative of the spirit of the times that both sensible and wild ideas were also floating around outside the government. One task of the Treasury's division of research was to answer letters from the general public, which were coming in at a tremendous rate on what should be done about economic policy, especially monetary policy. Everybody seemed to have ideas.

BERNSTEIN: The question of the monetary system was not a new one. The United States had gone off gold and silver during the Civil War, and there was plenty of experience from that period. The legislation the United States adopted during the Civil War and/or in the 1870s gave the Secretary of the Treasury the power to buy and sell gold at prices in the public interest. He had this power when the 1933 crisis on gold resulted in our going off the gold standard.[4] In 1933 the Treasury did not have the power to change the official monetary price, only the price at which the Treasury bought and sold in the market. Strange as it sounds, the interest on the public debt was payable in gold during the period when the dollar was a greenback. The customs duties were payable in gold. The Federal Reserve note that we had before 1933 said on the front, "This is legal tender for all debts, public and private, except interest on the public debt and customs duties."

SALANT: I think the most interesting aspect of gold policy was the casting about for people who knew something and the complete inability of the President or anybody very close to him to distinguish somebody who knew something from somebody who knew nothing. That is part of the truth in what has been said about FDR's being open to anything. That openness was not accompanied by any ability to discriminate.

One example is the decision to have the government buy gold to raise its price but to confine the purchases at first to domestically mined gold. That was done under the influence of a book by George Warren and Frank Pearson, a statistician and an agricultural economist who found a close relationship between agricultural prices and the dollar price of gold.[5] The Administration wanted to raise farm prices that had fallen drastically during the depression, and thought that raising the price of gold would do it. Warren and Pearson observed that a change in the dollar price of gold, when other gold-standard countries did not change the price in their currencies, changed the exchange rate between the dollar and those other major currencies. The effect depended on America's purchasing foreign exchange to buy gold abroad at the price prevailing there so they could sell it to the Treasury at the increased U.S. price. Now monetary economists knew that the prices of farm products, which are set in world markets, would not be affected if the rise in the price the Treasury paid for gold did not apply to foreign gold and therefore did not affect the exchange rate. But Warren and Pearson and the Administration did not seem to know it. Of course, the limitation of the higher purchase price to domestically mined gold was soon dropped when it was recognized that it was only a gravy train for domestic miners. So much for economic innocence in the early days of the New Deal.

4. The Emergency Bank Relief Act of 1933 also gave the President broad discretionary powers over transactions in credit, currency, and gold and silver, including foreign exchange, and authorized the Treasury to call in all gold money and gold certificates in the country. By abandoning its promise to exchange paper money for gold, the act allowed the United States to go off the gold standard.

5. George F. Warren, Frank A. Pearson, and H. Stoker, *Wholesale Prices, 1720–1932* (Ithaca: Cornell University Press, 1932).

BERNSTEIN: The Administration not only confined the initial gold buying to domestic gold but also appointed a committee in New York headed by Fred Kent, an officer of the Bankers' Trust Company, to supervise exchange transactions. It wanted to prevent people from making a profit by a kind of arbitrage[6] that would have helped to achieve a desired effect on the exchange rate. New Dealers weren't sophisticated enough to realize that anybody could engage in an exchange transaction by buying, say, wheat in New York and selling it in Liverpool, thereby indirectly exchanging dollars for pounds sterling. The point is that the Administration went off the gold standard in order to raise prices, mainly farm prices, and this required that the price of the dollar in terms of other currencies be reduced. A rise in the price of gold could not accomplish that if it didn't change the price of dollars in other currencies. That is to say, a change in the exchange rate for the dollar was needed. Raising the price of domestically mined gold alone showed a failure to understand that.

SALANT: Another illustration of monetary naïveté, still not sufficiently appreciated, was lack of concern about the effect of the purchase of silver on the Chinese economy. China was on a silver standard, and the United States, by bidding up the world price of silver, forced up the price of Chinese currency, exerting a deflationary effect on the Chinese economy. This was done at the behest of the silver bloc, which had great influence, and partly because one leading member of it, Senator Key Pittman, was chairman of the Senate Foreign Relations Committee.

PEHLE: I recall the conflict between Marriner Eccles, the head of the Federal Reserve Board, and Secretary Morgenthau, who was very sensitive about the role and the jurisdiction of the Treasury. Despite his going into other departments' business, Morgenthau didn't want other people getting into Treasury Department affairs. And Marriner Eccles was an activist who had his own views about tax policy. Morgenthau asked the general counsel, Ed Foley, to write a memo about the historical responsibilities of the Treasury in the tax field. He sent it over to the President saying, "The Treasury has always done this and if the Treasury isn't going to be the spokesman for the Administration on tax policy, I'll resign." Morgenthau was human enough to show the top staff the reply he got back from FDR, which said, "Ah, Hen! Ah, Hen." That was the end of that. The President just brushed it off.

The most important thing to Morgenthau, and he made this very

6. Transactions in bills of exchange, stocks, or commodities designed to take advantage of price differences between various markets.

clear, was his relationship with the President. The President did approve the memo. Nevertheless, there was always a battle. Later as head of the War Refugee Board,[7] I went to see the President, at Eleanor Roosevelt's suggestion. I hadn't cleared it with Morgenthau. The next morning he called me in and really gave me a bad time. He said I must understand the most important thing in his life was his relationship with the President. Nobody in the Treasury was going to have direct contact with the President except with his approval.

PEHLE: In the Treasury, everybody called everybody, except Secretary Morgenthau, by his first name. Secretary Morgenthau was only called Henry by Herbert Gaston, someone who had worked at the *New York World*. He was the public relations man. Everybody else in the Treasury called Secretary Morgenthau Mr. Secretary.

BERNSTEIN: There's a story of how committee meetings would be held and the chairman would call somebody "John" or "Jim." Finally someone came up and said to the chairman, "Who is this fellow you've been calling John? What's his last name?" He said, "I'm sorry; I don't know him that well." The informality was shocking to me, a young man from North Carolina.

Harry White had made me his chief assistant and sent me to a meeting at Dean Acheson's office. Acheson said "Stay behind." The possibility of such a thing had never occurred to me, and I don't think it could have happened in the government before, that a youngster be asked by an assistant secretary of another department to stay because he wanted to chat. This informality had an enormous effect in generating ideas.

The budget problem during the New Deal days troubled the President. He was elected saying he was going to balance the budget, and he was running a deficit. If he had done the accounting on the basis of the present method—we used to exclude trust funds from the budget—the budget deficit wouldn't have been very great. Nevertheless, it worried Morgenthau and the debt was climbing. Mr. Morgenthau always had the same line: of course the dollar was the strongest currency and he wasn't troubled about the public debt, but if ever it rose to $75 billion, it would disturb him. At that time, the debt probably was around $40 or $45 billion. The debt is now over $1,000 billion. We now, in a single year, add more to the debt than the aggregate debt of the United States in 1940.

7. The War Refugee Board was established by Executive Order on 22 January 1944 to assist the immediate rescue and relief of the Jews of Europe and other victims of the Nazis. Its members included the Secretaries of Treasury, War, and State.

SALANT: The annual interest on the deficit approximates that figure.

BERNSTEIN: The annual interest is over that and exceeds the debt that we had before World War II began. The Administration was sensitive about its deficit, though we would now say that it was extremely small. The President once presented the budget to a press conference. Walter Trohan of the *Chicago Tribune* hefted the budget, which was like the telephone directory, and said, "Some budget! What's making it so heavy is the deficit."

SALANT: I think it's well to remember that during the period we're talking about, from 1933 to 1939 or 1940, there were changes in attitude and spirits. One important change was caused by the sharp recession from September 1937 to the middle of 1938. It was a great disillusionment to most New Dealers, who had been feeling pretty good about the extent of recovery. Even though now the recovery is referred to as a failure because we didn't get to full employment, the period 1933 to 1937 should not be characterized as one of no recovery. The increase in output from 1933 to 1937 was enormous. It put total national output back to the 1929 level, and despite a rise in the labor force it decreased the unemployment rate substantially, even though it didn't bring it down to full employment. But in September 1937 there was a collapse of business activity. Industrial production, in fact, declined by more than it had ever done before or has done since in four or five months. That was a terrible shock to the economists of the New Deal, who by then were a better assorted group than the original group. It was discouraging, and it caused a lot of ferment and a lot of questioning about what had occurred. There was a change in spirit which I don't know how to characterize. It was more than mere discouragement; there was more introspection after that. In 1938 and early 1939 the Administration was struggling for ways to restore the recovery when war broke out and there was an expansion of defense orders.

PEHLE: Secretary Morgenthau would go to Cabinet meetings and when he came back he would call together his "9:30 group" of about thirty people. He would tell them everything that had happened at the Cabinet meeting. This was the way you made a department work because everyone felt he was a participant in what was going on at the top level. What it did for the esprit de corps in the Treasury Department was extraordinary.

BERNSTEIN: The spirit of innovation and experimentation was what made the New Deal click.

SALANT: All of it emanated from the President. That spirit was what brought in young people. It also generated ideas, fermentation, energy, a feeling that something was being done, that there was leadership when leadership was needed, that there was a relationship between the government and the people in which the government was the citizen's friend. That was not the public's perception of the preceding Administration. I would doubt that such a perception of the relation between government and the people had ever existed before.

PEHLE: One of the things that illustrates Roosevelt's relation with the people in government was the effect of the President's death. When word came that the President had died, something went out. He was the father, and in spirit the friend, of all the people. The President as the imaginative person open to suggestion—the feeling that the government was something beyond imagination—all of this went out.

BERNSTEIN: For the generation that lived with Roosevelt, whenever you spoke of "the President," it meant Roosevelt. When you meant any other President, it was always President Truman, President Eisenhower. Before the New Deal, the only business a citizen had with the government was through the Post Office. No doubt he saw a soldier or a sailor now and then, but the government had nothing to do with the general public. After Roosevelt, the public felt that government was then an active part of everyday life.

WILLARD L. THORP

The American Statistical Association was invited by Frances Perkins—presumably speaking on behalf of the President—to send a group of statisticians to Washington to advise the new Administration on what should be done to recoup statistical records. I was assigned to the Commerce Department, a key place because it was one of the main collectors of statistics. It included the Census Bureau and the Bureau of Foreign and Domestic Commerce. I had worked at this job for about a month, when the Assistant Secretary, John Dickinson, asked whether I would take the directorship of the Bureau of Foreign and Domestic Commerce. I had never directed more than two people, and this was an agency employing over 2,000. The Department of Commerce had never represented industry in the government the way the Labor Department represented labor, or Agriculture represented the farmer. It was more a service agency, most of it being made up of services like the Lighthouse Agency or the Patent Office.

I became the director in July 1933. The Bureau was in shambles. It had been Mr. Hoover's favorite. Washington was flooded with people asking for jobs. They were going to their representatives, who were almost automatically giving them support. I worked out an arrangement with the Democratic National Committee whereby I would allow three nominations for any important position. If I felt one of the nominees was competent for the job, I would give it to the person. After three tries, I would feel free to fill the post myself. Most of us operated in a nonpartisan way. We were frightened because we thought the country was on the verge of collapse. Huey Long or Father Coughlin might take over. It was terribly important to get things moving.

I think we improved working relations with other departments considerably. Various things didn't fit exactly into the role of the Bureau. There was the question of the Smoot-Hawley Tariff of 1931, the highest tariff there had ever been. We worked on the problem and came up with two alternatives. One was that industries should be judged according to their efficiency, and inefficient industries should have no protection. An efficient industry should have it, if there was a reason for it, but the tariff should be used as a way of improving the productivity and efficiency of American industry. The other was to recognize that trade was a two-way street, and therefore reciprocal tariff cuts would be the appropriate way to go. That legislation became the Reciprocal Trade Agreements Act.

Prohibition had come to an end. The Bureau supplied information about what the foreign trade situation would be under the continuing legislation. The legislation had never been struck from the books; it was just inoperative during Prohibition. I was very impressed with the President at this particular session. He looked at our report and said, "That isn't what I want. A new industry is being born. Should it be controlled by the federal government? Or should the government be an intermediary and buy liquor from the manufacturers and pass it on to the distributor? Or should we merely step in at the distribution point? Or should we just set up a lot of rules and regulations? I want a different report." We left, our tails between our legs. We came up with a program under the Federal Alcohol Control Administration created in 1933 that did only two things. No one who had been a bootlegger was allowed in the industry; people had to be licensed as individuals. Second, labeling on bottles had to be clear about age.

The Export-Import Bank was created in early 1934 at the time of the recognition of Russia. It was felt that substantial trade with Russia would worry the commercial banks. The federal government, therefore, should have a bank that would finance exports to Russia. The legislation was passed, but the bank never made a loan because Russia would never give the information a banker wants to have. Actually, the Export-Import Bank turned to financing Latin American trade.

In 1934 I was hired by the Department of Labor to help with some studies on the behavior of prices. Soon I was told Mary Rumsey wanted to see me. She was a mover and a shaker, Averell Harriman's sister, and a great friend of the Roosevelts. Despite her wealth, she built up strong support for the consumer. The National Recovery Administration had a Consumer Advisory Board, and the Department of Agriculture had a consumer adviser. Mrs. Rumsey asked me to serve on the National Emergency Council and take over the consumer division, a coordinating agency for various consumer activities.

What was needed was not coordination among different groups, but some kind of backstopping for them. Our division spent its time trying to build up consumer groups around the country. I never counted the many places I went to and the people I met. We tried to persuade them how much better off we would be if consumers were more effectively represented.

Later, I was asked to work for the National Recovery Administration. The Consumer Advisory Board had decided that there were so many policy problems they needed an advisory board. I was made chairman and Milton Katz was our general counsel. Individual industry groups could bring in a policy issue, or the Board could send a policy issue down. We had all kinds of questions. For example, "Should a code require every person in an industry to publish his prices?" It was not general practice then to publish manufacturers' prices.

The NRA had turned things around. People felt something was happening. Wages had gone far down and the NRA had set a floor under them. There was no minimum wage law, so the codes were used to stop the drop in wages. The consumers' groups were comprised of lawyers or professors. They were more articulate than the businessmen or the labor leaders. The net result showed a major change in the treatment of consumers. That was accomplished by the NRA. When Averell Harriman came as administrator of the NRA, Mrs. Rumsey asked me to use my experience to fill him in on government operations.

One also learned a lot of economics working for the NRA. For instance, one of the problems was what to do about electrical appliances. There are lots of different small electrical appliances, and they're sold through jobbers or directly. How should a code deal with this? I think one of the real contributions I made to economic literature was writing about the variety of elements that played a part in fixing prices in the electrical industry: the quantity discounts, the jobber discounts, and various other things that made it a very interesting and complicated business.

The NRA was a rather revolutionary bureau in relation to past American history, even though its provisions ultimately were declared unconstitutional. I felt that the NRA was a major factor in eliminating hopelessness and fear. I don't know how the chain reactions of falling prices and wages and profits, which are interrelated, could have been stopped without this kind of assurance to people.

Well, the NRA came to an end and I was left there with two or three other people. A man was brought down from one of the New York banks to devise some sort of successor to the NRA. We worked there, trying to figure out what might be done, and we finally worked out a program which had some similarity to the second foreign trade program. In other words, treatment of industries according to their performances.

It was a great period, one of tremendous concern, where there was a lot of improvisation, all the way from things like the Tennessee Valley Authority to recording for the first time the real property situation in the United States. As I look back, I don't know that I regard it as being a great revolution, except for the entrance of the government into a responsible position on the economy. That basic change has been with us ever since, and it ought to be with us, there's no doubt about it. This is a unified country. Many of its problems cannot be settled provincially and the government must deal with them. The first time that this ever happened was during the New Deal.

ROBERT R. NATHAN

In the summer of 1933 I became an employee in the Department of Commerce. Dr. Simon Kuznets, my former professor, had been asked to set up and direct the first official national income study this country ever undertook. Previously there had not been any official estimates of gross national product or gross national income. Kuznets asked that I be assigned to him.

In 1934 I was made chief of the national income section. Working there, I met a great many top officials, people like Marriner Eccles of the Federal Reserve, Henry Morgenthau and his top Treasury officials, Henry Wallace and his Agriculture officials, and Harry Hopkins, then in the Works Progress Administration of the Federal Emergency Relief Administration. National income data played an important role in providing information for solving the problems the country faced. We were concerned about how much unemployment there was. There had never been any figures from any source in the government. The awareness of what it meant was unbelievably low. Some thought national income was the total of all transactions that took place, others thought it referred to government revenues. A young senator, Claude Pepper, asked me to come down to discuss national income. People were groping and wrestling with the aggregate of the economy's performance. From 1933 to 1945, reliable, quality data were assembled and developed and analyzed. In the early days of World War II, we had to deal with a great many new problems: the needs of the military, our capacity to produce, setting goals. Almost nothing was available from World War I in quantitative terms. It was the New Deal that started all kinds of new censuses, surveys and analyses. National accounts was one of the most important; it was possible to see what progress the country was making.

I met Henry Wallace, a very curious person; he had an almost unquenchable desire to have a conceptual grasp of measures and events. Wallace was also in many ways a mystic. He was tremendously conscientious and dedicated. Often, he was more interested in philosophical aspects than results. He was never considered a first-rate manager.

Agriculture was more important to the country and the economy then than it is today. Now only about 4 percent of our labor force is in agriculture, in contrast to about 30 percent in the 1930s. I remember having lunch with Henry Wallace between Roosevelt's death and his funeral. As we talked about Roosevelt, I was impressed that Wallace truly felt that everything tends to happen for the best. He didn't reveal any bitterness that he was no longer Vice-President.

Henry Morgenthau was never a man of humor or of charm. There was a sort of inner warmth about him, but it never surfaced, and he was always dour-looking. Marriner Eccles was pretty strong-willed, and in many ways more articulate and tougher than Morgenthau. I worked rather closely also with Harry Dexter White on many matters, and I thought he was tremendously competent. Without him, Morgenthau could not have made the contribution that he did. The Treasury helped the country to move with an expansive fiscal policy.

Harry Hopkins had an exceedingly keen mind, and although he was restricted to relief and job creation he knew that relief was not distinct from the total economy. Harry Hopkins's amazing commitment to the job impressed me, but his physical frailty was disturbing. He was fairly tall and rather gaunt. After any extended period of time you could sense his fatigue, and also some kind of inner determination. When he was doing research for writing a book he didn't just say, "Well, what are the numbers?" he would say, "How did you get these?" When Hopkins autographed a copy of his book for me, he remarked, "I hope your estimates on unemployment will hold up, because I will hold you responsible if they don't."

When Hopkins asked me to do an article for him, he insisted on giving me the check. I didn't want it. I'm sure Hopkins was not a man of great means, but I finally took it. I enjoyed Hopkins and was tremendously impressed with the quality of his performance at the FERA and the WPA.

One thing about Hopkins that differentiated him from many others was his absolutely devoted loyalty. By the time I was chief of the national income division, Hopkins had become the Secretary of Commerce. It was a strange appointment, because he certainly didn't represent business. He brought in Richard Gilbert from Harvard, one of the most creative minds of the last half century. Dick made it possible for Hopkins to advance valuable creative ideas to the White House.

Had Hopkins been a healthy man, Roosevelt might have chosen him instead of Wallace as the vice-presidential candidate in 1940. Hopkins and Mrs. Roosevelt had parallel views on so many fronts. I always thought that Mrs. Roosevelt was unbelievably imaginative and creative.

The NRA was stationed right in the Department of Commerce. We had opportunities to work with people like Averell Harriman and William L. Batt. I was impressed with Harriman from the beginning because he was interested in concepts almost more than performance. I found him formal and formidable; he wasn't interested in petty matters. He didn't play with unimportant events, and he doesn't to this day. He was extremely useful to Roosevelt with business, but even then I sensed Harriman was more concerned with people and government and policies than with business.

The NRA couldn't help but intervene because of the way it was set up. Businessmen to this day have the same feeling: "We don't want the government to get involved. If we have to get together, we'll try to do it legally. We have to watch out for the antitrust division, and we can't get together too actively." The economists teach one that when you produce something, you also produce the income to buy it, and that's true. Wages, salaries, interest, and dividends add up to the mean generated by a company, the contribution to the national income and national purchasing power. What Roosevelt and the New Deal did was to try to stimulate that income by providing government jobs and some spending, not all of which was highly efficient, but it couldn't have been. It helped create demand, which business responded to. But businesses didn't want to be told when to invest and how to invest.

All the talk about Roosevelt being an enemy of business is just nonsense. If the recession and the depression had gone on much longer, we probably would have moved to socialism or Communism.

CHAPTER 21

The Anonymous
White House Assistants

During his first term in office, FDR created an enormous number of new federal agencies in his efforts to promote economic recovery and social reform. The result was a rapid and often undisciplined expansion of the executive branch. After the 1936 election, FDR responded to the growing management crisis by appointing the President's Committee on Administrative Management, whose task it was to plan the reorganization of the executive branch. When the Administration introduced the committee's proposal into Congress in early 1937, it seemed to have widespread support. Unexpectedly, however, the reorganization bill failed to pass, mostly because the Court-packing plan embroiled Congress and the President. When the management bill came up again in April 1938, more than 100 Democratic congressmen deserted the President to defeat the measure, charging that it would make him a dictator. FDR effectively replied to his critics: "History proves that dictatorships do not grow out of strong and successful governments, but out of weak and helpless governments."

Following the 1938 elections, FDR resubmitted a watered-down measure that passed easily through Congress. The Administrative Reorganization Act of 1939 established the Executive Office of the President and transferred to it the Bureau of the Budget, the National Resources Planning Board, and several other agencies. It also gave the President the power to shift certain existing agencies and to reorganize them, if Congress did not counteract his proposals within a certain number of days. Under this provision, FDR established the Federal Security Agency, the Federal Works Agency, and the Federal Loan Agency and placed twenty-four existing units under them. Finally, the act also established the office of administrative assistant to the President—the origin of the White House staff—and permitted the President to appoint six such assistants to help him run the executive branch. In the years to come, the presidential assistants—men with "a passion for anonymity"—grew in number and influence. By the time of FDR's death, the White House staff had grown to number in the hundreds. The Administrative Reorganization Act of 1939 was one of FDR's most lasting contributions to the modernization of the federal government.

JAMES H. ROWE, JR.

The story of how I got to the White House is rather long. In 1935 I was with Justice Holmes up to the time he died. Then I went to work for Tom Corcoran on the RFC. Ben Cohen was in Interior, but he and Tom both worked for the President. There was a group—Joe Rauh, Henry Herman, Ambrose Doskow—five or six lawyers all working for Ben and Tom, helping them draft speeches, getting around on the Hill to make sure everybody knew about FDR's interests. We looked for material. There was a lot of drafting in Ben's and Tom's work, and we'd sit around while they were doing it or we'd go out and roam around the Hill.

It was a mixed group. Not everyone was young. Some were old Wilsonians, some were Teddy Roosevelt Bull Moosers, and a few were Norman Thomas socialists. The senior men were all young when FDR was Assistant Secretary of the Navy under Wilson, and then the young men who had not believed in anything became ardent New Dealers.

In 1938, I was at the SEC. Jimmy Roosevelt had come down from Massachusetts to be secretary to the President, and he ran certain functions of the government. However, he also had ambitions to be governor of Massachusetts, and from time to time would go up to Massachusetts to make a speech. He would close down his office in the White House while he wrote the speech in Massachusetts, which infuriated a number of people. Tommy Corcoran went in and raised hell with him and said, "You just can't do this. The federal government's more important than Massachusetts. I'll get you a fellow who can write speeches." So he got me, and I wrote a speech, then another speech. Jimmy said, "Why don't you come to the White House?" When he mentioned the salary, it was a great improvement. So in January 1938 I said I would. Not long after, Jimmy went out to the Mayo Clinic to have an operation for his ulcer.

He fell in love with his nurse and left his wife, Betsey Cushing Roose-velt, who later married John Hay Whitney. Jimmy did not come back to the White House. He went into the motion picture business in Holly-wood, so I started doing his work.

In 1936, Louie Brownlow had started to plan the reorganization of the government, taking the Budget Bureau out of Treasury and putting it in the White House, doing this, doing that, and also creating six new assistants to the President.[1] They were called "administrative assistants to the President" and they were patterned, Louie Brownlow said, after the British system of assistants with a passion for anonymity. Roosevelt appointed three or four immediately, but I was appointed first. I stayed with that job from 1939 until just before Pearl Harbor.

In 1938, when Jimmy was there, I had an office in the White House itself. He had a lovely big office. It was the best office except for the President's, and we divided it. He took two-thirds, I had a third. When I became administrative assistant the next year, we all moved to the Exec-utive Office Building, then called the State-War-Navy Building. We had trouble getting in because Cordell Hull, the Secretary of State, was still there. The President told Hull he wanted to move some of his people over there, and Secretary Hull said, "Mr. President, it's impossible. I haven't got any space." Well, the President said, "Why don't I just come look?" So he went over one day in his wheelchair and started going down the corridor, stopped, and said, "Let's go in here, Cordell." It was a great big room. He said, "What are in those files?" And Cordell said, "I'm not too sure, Mr. President." The President opened one, pulled a couple of memoranda out, and said, "White Horses in China, 1920. Cordell, you have just lost." I had a beautiful office there, about the size of a house.

We worked mostly by memoranda. Almost every night after din-ner, the President dictated to Grace Tully, and I would find three or four memoranda on my desk in the morning saying, "Go do this" or "I hear something about this. Will you please find out." My replies were usually memoranda, only occasionally personal. I would see him sometimes five or six times a week. Then a week might go by and I wouldn't see him at all, depending on what he thought was urgent.

For his assistants Roosevelt picked Lauchlin Currie, because some-body told him he needed an economist, and William H. McReynolds, the civil service expert. (Most of the personnel in the White House and in the government were part of the civil service.) I handled the political

1. Louis Brownlow was chairman of the President's Committee on Administrative Man-agement from 1936 to 1937. It was this committee's study that eventually led to the Ad-ministrative Reorganization Act of 1939.

appointments. When Roosevelt appointed me he said, "Now I want you to be a bird dog. I want you to sniff around all over town." That's what I did mostly, sniff and report back. I was the Hill lobbyist. I handled the independent agencies. When I came back after the war, David D. Lloyd, a college friend, was working for Truman. I said, "Dave, who's doing what in the White House these days under Mr. Truman? Who's doing all that?" And he told me. "My God," I said, "you've got nine people doing what I used to do." Nowadays they must have 300 or 400 doing what I used to do. I had a broad brush.

James V. Forrestal came in and was there briefly before he went into the Navy. Sherman Minton was there briefly. He'd been a very liberal senator from Indiana but wasn't reelected. Roosevelt liked him for he had always been a great supporter, so he put him in the White House to wait for a judgeship, and the judgeship did turn up. He was a circuit judge in the Middle West for several years, and then Truman appointed him to the Supreme Court. He became the most conservative judge the Court had had in many years. So how can you tell? He was still relatively young when he became conservative. I don't know why he did it, but he did. He was a nice man.

Roosevelt always knew everything. I don't know how the hell he knew it, but he did. I can remember once going in with a problem that he'd given me. I gave him all the answers, and he looked at the ceiling. "You know, there was some fellow in here the other day—I can't remember his name—about this thing. He's been working on it. Did you find out about that?" I realized I hadn't turned that stone over. This happened to me twice before I learned better. He delighted in letting you know that he knew something about the problem that you didn't. Therefore, you became more careful the next time.

He had great powers of assimilation. I don't know how he got all the facts. Lyndon Johnson got them on the telephone, but Roosevelt didn't telephone that much. He did get a lot of information from Missy LeHand and Grace Tully who got around town pretty much. His regular secretaries, Stephen T. Early, Marvin McIntyre, and Colonel Edwin "Pa" Watson, were all Virginians and very conservative. I don't know what the hell they were doing there in the first place, except they all started with him when he ran for Vice-President. They were not happy with the New Dealers. I never sent a paper through Pa Watson; I didn't think it would ever get there. Missy LeHand and Grace Tully were sympathetic, so you always had a corridor to the President. Missy would slip me in the back way.

Roosevelt created a feeling of confidence in everybody he talked to; we all thought we had a special relationship. This could cause some mix-ups. Roosevelt didn't understand farm issues, nor did I. One day he said, "Go down and see Senator Lister Hill and ask him to vote yes on this farm bill." Lister was an old friend so I trotted down and said, "Senator, the President would like you to vote yes on this bill." "Well, Jimmy, I'd love to. I have only one problem. Your colleague Eugene Casey was in here half an hour ago telling me the President wanted me to vote no. Will you go back and tell the President I'll vote either way, but which way does he want." That happened occasionally. You got your signals, and you'd find that two or three people were doing the opposite of what you were doing.

Quite often Roosevelt would say, "If you do that again, you're going to need another job." I came in one day to see him and he said, "Didn't I see your name in the society column, going to a cocktail party? If I read that too often, you're going to need another job."

I remember another conversation, about Leon Henderson. Leon was then at the SEC and was raising hell. The President said, "I think I ought to move him some place. I'm not quite sure how to do it, because I'll antagonize a lot of people. You go find out." So I went plodding around town, came back, and said, "Yes, Mr. President, you should move Leon, and this is the way you should do it." He listened and he said, "I think you're right. I have to move him, but I'm not going to do it your way. I'm going to do it my way." And I, at the age of twenty-nine, said, "Mr. President, your way won't work, and I think you'd better do it my way." "No, I think I'll do it mine." Since I was twenty-nine, I came back the third time and said, "Mr. President, your way will not work. I think you ought to do it my way." He smiled almost beatifically as he said, "No, Jim, we're going to do it my way and I'll tell you why. The American people may have made a mistake, but they elected me President, not you." So he would clip you on the turns.

He had problems, as we all do, making up his mind, but once he made it up, he didn't want some fellow telling him he had to rethink what he had just decided to do. Presidents can't afford the time. When you saw him, he would socialize and take all the time you wanted for work. We'd get a lot of appointments to clear, and I would harass Pa Watson about them. Poor Pa was harassed by everybody in the United States who wanted to see the President. One time he said, "All right, Jim, you've been a nuisance, but you can have lunch with the President tomorrow and get 'em all cleared so you won't be bothering me." So I went in to lunch. I remember it was a lovely day, and we ate outside on the grounds, and I was there for two and three-quarters hours. I got one appointment cleared. The rest of the time he told me about life in Hyde Park, and I couldn't get a damned word in. He was fond of talking. The thing you have to remember about Roosevelt is that he could not move, he had polio. The only way he could really socialize was by talking with people. He was noted as a filibusterer. You'd come in with your fifteen minutes and he'd talk for fourteen and a half, and he was relaxed about it. This is the way he took time off. Otherwise, he worked all day and most of the night.

All the staff adored him, and that's not true of any other President I know of. That complete charm was always there. I remember the first time I met him. I'd just gotten to the White House and he had twice-a-week press conferences. Steve Early said, "Jim, have you met the President?" "No, I haven't." "Well, you stay after the press conference and I'll introduce you." So when the press conference was over, Steve Early brought me up: "This is Jim Rowe. He's working with Jimmy, Mr. President." The President looked up. I can still remember this as though it happened yesterday. He said, "Jim, I knew you were here and all week I've been wanting to get you in because I want to ask you about two or three real problems I've got and I want your advice. And I'll get to them." It took me two days to realize he didn't mean it. He did that with everyone all the time.

Tommy Corcoran made a point about him once, and I think it's probably valid. I asked, "Why is it FDR's so good?" Tommy said, "Look, there you are. You have to work for a living. Here I am. I have to work for a living. This fellow had nothing to do all his life except politics. He's spent the bulk of his life in politics. He got to know every wrinkle of politics. He got to know how to handle anybody, and he worked at it 100 percent. You work at it 5 percent, and I work at it 7." There's something to that. All his life he was dealing with political people.

He rarely got caught. I can remember when he put all the lawyers under civil service. The lawyers raised hell so I went in: "Mr. President, you just can't do this. You just won't get competent lawyers." He asked, "Well, how can I get out of it? Civil service is good politics. I did it for purely political reasons." I replied, "Well, maybe we can create a new committee to handle it," which we did. A fellow named Samuel Ordway, who was on the civil service, called me to say, "I gather you're going to take the lawyers out of civil service again." "I think the President is, yes." "Well," he said, "you tell him if he does that I'll have to resign." I told the President, who said, "Good. I haven't accepted a resignation for the last few months. Call him and tell him I've accepted it."

It was a much smaller government and more manageable. You knew everybody and the young lawyers all knew everybody. If I wanted to find out something in agriculture, I'd call a fellow like Tel Taylor.

He'd say, "Well, I don't know but I'll find somebody who does." And the fellow would call me back in five minutes. Today, you have to go through the secretary and you might get an answer in three weeks or you might not. Today, the government's too damned big. FDR got things done in a hurry. I remember Mike Mansfield, the Senate leader, once telling me, "We've passed too much legislation, and it is indigestible. We will never be able to handle it all." And Mike was right.

Roosevelt saw a great number of senators, a great number of congressmen. I'm speaking of the period before the war because when we started rearming he didn't have much time.

I remember one of my favorite stories. It was right after the 1940 election. C. Benham "Beanie" Baldwin was Assistant Secretary of Agriculture. Certain people on the House Agriculture Committee had been defeated. Beanie said to me, "We've got to get Sam Rayburn to make some decent appointments. He won't do this unless the President puts the pressure on him to get some liberals on it." "Well," I said, "Beanie, in ten minutes I'm going out the door, and I'm going to the Caribbean with my wife for a vacation. However, you can dictate a memorandum to Kitty, my secretary, and she'll get it over to Grace Tully and the President will see it." When I came back I got a memorandum from the President saying, "Beanie Baldwin is persona non grata on the Hill. Why? Find out." So I went off on my little feet asking subtle questions but I couldn't find anybody. Finally I got to Lyndon Johnson. I said, "What do you know about Beanie Baldwin? He's persona non grata." Johnson said, "It's not only Beanie Baldwin; it's you and Beanie Baldwin. Do you remember a memorandum that you dictated? This is the way it began: 'Mr. President, Jim Rowe and I have been discussing this matter, and we've decided that Rayburn is absolutely impossible and you must do something about him.' " And I said, "How do you know?" "Well," he said, "I happened to go with the Speaker to see the President. This was while you were loafing, as usual. After they had their discussion, the President said to Rayburn, 'Anything else, Sam?' Rayburn reached in his pocket and pulled out this memorandum and said, 'Yes, Mr. President.' Roosevelt read it, and his face went absolutely red. He said, 'I don't know anything about it, but I'll find out about it.' " Then Johnson said, "I fixed you up with Rayburn. You're not in trouble, but Baldwin's in real trouble."

Lyndon was in the business of making friends. Unlike most young congressmen, he cultivated the New Dealers because he had a good sense of where the power was. In those days the executive branch had the power. The young New Dealers were really running things. Lyndon got on his bicycle and got to know them all. He got to know Abe Fortas and was a great friend of his right from the beginning.

When Wayne Morse ran for the Senate he gave Johnson a lot of trouble. He said he needed money. Wayne was the greatest money collector that ever hit the Senate; he could raise more money than anybody else even though everybody expected him to be defeated. He would say, "I haven't any money and my opponent is spending all this," and later reports would show he outspent his opponent about three to one. So Johnson said, "Where are we going to get Wayne Morse some money?" I came up with a brilliant idea. "You know, he's on the District of Columbia Committee and these people in Washington never give money. What we ought to do is create a committee that will collect money from Washington." Lyndon said, "Who should run it?" I said, "Ganson Purcell is a big Home Rule type. Make him chairman." So Johnson made Ganson chairman and he did a very fine job. In the middle of it Ganson said, "I'm writing a fund-raising letter and I've got to have something in it about what Wayne Morse has done for the city. Will you get it?" So I called Morse's assistant. He said, "I'll call you back tomorrow." He never called. I called him several times and finally a week later he called and said, "This is Wayne Morse's assistant. I can't find anything he's done for the city." Despite this, Ganson managed to raise about $20,000, a lot of money in those days. Lyndon said, "Tell Ganson to bring the check. I don't want him giving it to Wayne Morse. I want him to bring it down to me." Ganson and I went down with the check and Wayne Morse. Just as Ganson was about to hand the check to him, Johnson said, "This is against the law. You can't give money to people in the Senate Office Building." So we all marched outside and got under a tree and the transaction was made. We also had a big luncheon for Morse and Johnson made a famous remark: "Wayne, you have problems out there. I'll come out and campaign for or against you, whichever one you think will help most."

When he was a young congressman, Johnson used to come to our house to dinner. Ten or twelve people would be there, I guess. He was a big, tall, rangy, good-looking Texan, and he would dominate. Eventually, no matter how interesting he was, people would sort of fade off and have their own conversations. As soon as he saw that, he'd just go to sleep. Lady Bird Johnson would be a little embarrassed, and she'd get up after a while and shake him. He'd start right off on another thing and hold everybody's attention all over again. When he lost 'em he'd go back to sleep.

When I'd been in the White House almost four years, I told the President I thought it was a great job, but it had fit me only to be President. I didn't think I was going to be President, so could I leave? Francis Biddle wanted me to go over to be deputy attorney general at the Department of Justice. Roosevelt grumbled somewhat, but not too much, and off I went. I went on vacation with my good wife, and while we were away Pearl Harbor was bombed. I came back, worked briefly in the White House, then went over to Justice. I stayed in the Justice Department until 1943, when I joined the Navy, went off to sea, and never went back into government.

CHAPTER 22

Speaker Rayburn

Samuel Taliaferro Rayburn, born in 1882 in Roane County, Tennessee, graduated from East Texas State Normal School in 1903 with a Bachelor of Science degree and a teaching certificate. In 1906 he won a seat in the Texas House of Representatives and was reelected three times, serving as Speaker in his last term. In 1912 Rayburn won election to Congress and served continuously in the House until his death in 1961. He quickly won a reputation for hard work, effectiveness, and shrewdness and by World War I was a well-respected junior member of the Democratic leadership. His political rise was reflected in the names given him by his friends and the press: Mr. Democrat, Mr. Speaker, Mr. Congress, and, his own favorite, Mr. Sam.

When the Democrats took over Congress in 1931, Rayburn became chairman of the House Interstate and Foreign Commerce Committee. Two years later, he used this position to shepherd much of FDR's vital legislation through Congress. He coauthored the Railroad Holding Company Act of 1933, the Securities Act of 1933, the Securities Exchange Act of 1934, the Federal Communications Act of 1934, the Public Utility Holding Company Act of 1935, and the Rural Electrification Act of 1936. From 1937 to 1940 Rayburn was Democratic majority leader. He served as Speaker of the House from 1940 to 1947, from 1949 to 1953, and from 1955 to 1961, twice as long as any other Speaker in history. During the interim periods of Republican ascendancy, he served as minority leader.

Perhaps his most critical moment as Speaker occurred on the vote to extend the Selective Service Act in August 1941. When the last vote had been called and Rayburn saw that the bill had passed by only one vote, he immediately took the tally sheet from the clerk and announced the results. According to House rules no one can change his or her vote after it is announced, so the results stood, and Rayburn saved Selective Service and helped prepare the nation for World War II.

During the 1940s and 1950s, Rayburn was one of the most powerful men in Congress. His short, stocky, bald figure dominated the capital city. The powerful and the famous sought his favor, but always the professional, he avoided personal publicity. On an average day, he did business with a hundred or more members of Congress. When he supported Presidents against his own instincts, he did so in the national interest. He was an equal to Presidents—as he put it, "I didn't serve *under* eight Presidents, I served *with* eight." Although in failing health at the age of seventy-nine and suffering from excruciating back pains, he won his greatest parliamentary victory in 1961 in the bitter fight to enlarge the crucial House Rules Committee and thereby make possible the liberal social legislation of the New Frontier and the Great Society.

RICHARD W. BOLLING

By the time President Franklin D. Roosevelt took office, Sam Rayburn not only had had considerable experience as a forceful personality in the Wilson Administration, he also had had the opportunity, being in the minority, to read an enormous amount of history and biography. He was a learned man when it came to the biography of American political figures. He and Truman were very much alike; they read a great deal more than the average politician, both before they got to be politicians and afterward. There's a story that when Rayburn first came to Washington in 1912 he asked Champ Clark, the erudite Speaker from Missouri, for a reading list.

Rayburn was an incredible person to work with. Of all the Speakers, he was the outstanding legislator, the finest ever. He handled a great deal of the early New Deal legislation. Things moved fast in those First Hundred Days. Virtually everything that went through Congress, from REA to the Public Utility Holding Company Act, went through Sam Rayburn's Interstate and Foreign Commerce Committee. Despite the excellence of the legislation that Roosevelt sent up, it always needed changes in order to get it through the House of Representatives.

By the time I knew Rayburn, he was in the last dozen years of his life. He was an enormously vigorous, committed person. The House was his whole life. Curiously enough, even at that youthful age I was commissioned to go see him. Both Harry Truman and Adlai Stevenson, the ex-President and the President who never was elected, asked me to talk to Mr. Rayburn about staying on. For the first time I had an opportunity to visit him in his home on a private, personal basis. From then on, we were very close.

He never told me that he wanted me to be Speaker, but whenever I was doing some tough job for him like knocking a few heads together, he'd say, "Dick, you've got to remember that you've got to be popular." I would always reply the same way. "Well, Mr. Sam, I know what I'm doing and I understand the consequences and I will keep right on doing it." He'd just shake his head and move away.

One of the many things I learned from Rayburn was how to preside in the House. There's a small story there that's sort of fun. Once when I was brand new at the chair I said, "People tease me for giving an accurate count. Isn't it proper to give an accurate count?" Mr. Sam looked at me and twinkled. "Absolutely, except in very great emergencies." He had perfect, complete integrity, with the exceptions that are essential in crises in democratic societies. They can occur in legislatures or in conventions. I never saw a man who managed always to keep his convictions as to what was good for the country, good for the party, good for the House, and so on down. It took a while to get to what was good for Sam Rayburn. He always had something that was more important than his own personal ego or profit.

You could argue with him, and I did. That was one of the privileges of intimacy. When he finally decided that we'd finished the subject, that was the end.

I wasn't in the House for those First Hundred Days of the New Deal, but there are many stories and anecdotes about them. He was very proud of his role. He would say—and I won't try to imitate his words—that of course there were the Hundred Days, and of course there was a great emergency, and of course the Congress wanted to go along, but there was legislative work to be done also and there was this interaction of which most people never seem to be aware. Nothing's similar. The bill that comes from the President is not always just out of the White House. Sometimes the ideas in the bill were invented on the Hill and the message got through that this is a good idea. There's a great deal more complexity in the legislative process than the press acknowledges. A bill doesn't originate with the President and his men all the time. Sometimes, often, a bill evolves from a continuous interaction. Roosevelt was so finished a politician as to work this way.

One of the first things Roosevelt did when he came into office was to make the contacts he would need with those influential on the Hill. I'm absolutely sure that Tommy the Cork (Thomas Corcoran) and Ben Cohen—whenever they got to the White House where Raymond Moley and Rexford Tugwell and the rest were analyzing the dilemmas that they would have on the Hill—looked hard at those who would play significant roles.

I learned from Rayburn what a lot of Democrats have not learned: cne always passes legislation in the House of Representatives with the whole House, not just one party. At least one starts out attempting to do that. First as chairman of the Interstate and Foreign Commerce Committee, then as Speaker, he always understood where everybody on his committee stood politically. As Speaker he knew where everybody in the entire House was politically. I used to do the last count for Mr. Rayburn, the count after the whips had given an account. I would go in and talk to him about it, and he would take the fifteen to forty undecided voters and, never quite telling me how he did it, he would decide where they were going and what the result would be. He was almost always right. He would say: "You know, Dick, if you don't understand that, then you don't understand that you have to be able to feel things that you can neither see nor hear in the House of Representatives. If you don't understand that, you don't really belong here as a legislative leader."

There was a Board of Education in a room downstairs, one floor below the Speaker's office. That room was used first for many years by Nick Longworth and then by John Garner. It was not a large room, and it was very plainly furnished. It had a big desk and a big old-fashioned sofa and a couple of big black leather chairs. There were a few chests and a big icebox screened by a large wood cupboard. The ceilings had been preserved and were quite lovely. There were pictures of Texas, the Star of Texas, a tremendous pair of horns—a very heavy informal formality. Nobody came unless Mr. Rayburn personally okayed him. There were half a dozen regulars, and all kinds of other people came occasionally. Rayburn got to be Speaker in 1940, but he was the majority leader from 1937 to 1940. I'm sure he had something like a Board of Education somewhere else in the building. It was a place in which he gathered information, occasionally yarned about Texas, but most of the time figured out how to proceed with the legislative program.

Mr. Rayburn had a lot of friends in and out of Congress. I heard enough about his personal life to know that it was fairly active. He could get almost anybody to spend time with him when he wanted to, and he didn't have to do it very subtly because all kinds of people were trying to move in on him, friends and foes alike. He really cared about people. A lot of Republicans can get along without compassion, given their views, but the Democrats have to have it. Mr. Rayburn had real feeling for people. You could persuade him to support almost any bill if you could convince him it was good for "the folks."

I had an experience with him the last day he was in Washington that tells a lot about him. I'd been sitting with him in his back office, where he was on the sofa, obviously in terrible pain. I said, "Mr. Sam, why in the name of God did you stay?" "Oh," he said, "It's simple. We had this bill that I knew we were going to lose. It was an education bill.[1] It was a Kennedy bill, and I knew we were going to lose it, and I wanted to be the one to take the blame for it and not leave it on Kennedy's shoulders."

He was a selfless person in a very curious and interesting way, and he was very careful about his power, his legislative power. He never let that slip away, but he was an extraordinarily generous man. I once had a crucial matter that had to do with a dam that I needed. I mentioned it to him casually. We got to the crucial vote and I sensed a presence. He had come in silently and just sat down. He never said a word. We got to the vote. I thought I was going to do badly on the Democratic side, rather better on the Republican side. It was that kind of a local thing; the person who offered the amendment was a Republican. Pork-barrel matters are never partisan. Rayburn stood up with me for the amendment, so naturally almost all the Democrats voted for it and it passed. He'd do that kind of thing for other people, not just for me. He was always watching for other people's concerns. He once said to me, "Dick, you know, you could lead this institution from the Chair or the floor," which meant that you can do it as Speaker or as majority leader.

His commitment to Roosevelt was based not only on personality, which must have been tremendously strong, but also on the fact that FDR was doing things for the country that he believed in.

1. The Federal Aid to Education Bill of 1961 passed the Senate but was defeated by a coalition of Republicans and conservative Democrats in the House.

CHAPTER 23

The National Youth Administration

FDR created the National Youth Administration by Executive Order under the Emergency Relief Appropriation Act of 1935. He placed it under the Works Progress Administration and named Aubrey Williams as director. The main purpose of the NYA was to establish and run work relief and employment training programs for sixteen- to twenty-five-year-olds who had graduated from, or dropped out of, high school and whose families could not support them. The NYA also provided part-time jobs so young people could stay in high school or college, hoping that by keeping them in school it might also prevent them from further depressing the labor market. By the end of its first year, the NYA was providing aid to over half a million youths, and by 1939–40—the NYA's peak year—it was providing aid to over 750,000 students in 28,000 high schools and 1,700 colleges across the nation.

In 1939, after the passage of the Administrative Reorganization Act, FDR transferred the NYA to the Federal Security Agency. In 1942, he moved it again, this time to the War Manpower Commission, where it helped train workers for defense industries. As the wartime demand for manpower rose, however, the supply of unemployed and needy students declined, and with it the need for the NYA. In September 1943, after eight years of service, the NYA was terminated. It had worked itself out of a job.

As for the Great Depression, I must say that I was shielded and protected by a very able and caring father. It never dawned on me that I might suffer. I do remember being scared the day the banks closed. I took a look at my meal ticket. It was the custom when you were attending the University of Texas[1] to buy yourself a $5.00 meal ticket. I think it was 35¢ for lunch and 45¢ for dinner, or something like that. Anyhow, I took a look at my meal ticket and heaved a sigh of relief because it was a brand new one and I hadn't eaten one meal off of it. Then I really had a shock. I got a letter from my father saying, "The banks are closed. I hope you have cashed a check in the last day or two. Here is the last dollar out of the cash register."

I did not personally feel the pain of the depression, but I knew it through Lyndon's recital of the period when he was working for Representative Kleberg.[2] Lots of farms and ranches in Mr. Kleberg's district were being foreclosed. Lyndon was as mad as could be about it and just screaming for some kind of help. A lot of those people he was able to help became our lifelong friends and helped us later.

Lyndon was more intimately connected to the New Deal much earlier than I. In fact, I was always on the periphery. We went up there to Washington as young bride and groom in December of 1934. Lyndon was secretary to Congressman Dick Kleberg of Corpus Christi, Texas, and oh how seriously he took the job! The first thing he asked me to do was to learn the names of the ten counties that they represented—and I use "they" knowingly because he really felt that it was his job to help represent them—and the ten major towns in each one and the names of two or three of the most important, forceful people in the area. I just thought that was the funniest thing I ever heard of, but I set about doing it.

I shall always remember that first year because it was my earliest real acquaintance with snow. As soon as I had given Lyndon his breakfast and gotten him off to the office early in the morning, I would clean up our tiny apartment on Kalorama Road and then put on some boots and go out walking all over that section of town. There was a popular song at that time called "Walking in a Winter Wonderland." I would go along humming the words of that song, and I'm sure if anybody was passing me they thought I was a little dotty.

1. Lady Bird Johnson attended the University of Texas in Austin from 1929 to 1933.
2. Lyndon Baines Johnson was secretary to Representative Richard Kleberg from 1931 to 1935.

So came summertime and I wanted to go visit my daddy. I hadn't seen him in six or eight months and went to East Texas to visit him. While I was there, I got a call from Lyndon saying, "How would you like to live in Austin?" Well, to anybody who's lived in Austin that's like saying, "How would you like to go to Heaven?" So I said, "I would adore it." He told me that he had been offered the job of head of the National Youth Administration for the state of Texas. I think quite possibly he got that through Congressman Maury Maverick of San Antonio, who for a young congressman had made quite a place for himself in Washington. He was flamboyant and picturesque, a really lovable character and a longtime friend.

So Lyndon returned to Texas and set to work on the National Youth Administration, which ushered in perhaps one of the happiest times of our lives.[3] It was crammed with experiences and with people who became lifelong friends. We developed an understanding of the needy young people, boys and girls from about sixteen to twenty-five. It became a cram course in education for me. Lyndon already knew a great deal from his experience, his growing up.

Lyndon soon came to know Aubrey Williams. He went to Washington on very occasional trips. They didn't have conferences and think tanks in those days. Aubrey was quite a character, tweedy-looking and Lincolnesque and scholarly, but very warm. I liked him tremendously. We also had lots of visitors from Washington who came to see how our particular state was being handled in the National Youth Administration. Even Mrs. Roosevelt came. Mary McLeod Bethune, a prominent black leader, became involved. Her efforts were directed to raising the educational status of black people.

We had a system of giving aid to colleges. A small amount was paid to each student who worked in the library or provided janitorial or other services, and that was applied toward their tuition and living expenses. One of the aims of the NYA was to keep them in college. The other aim, if they weren't college material or didn't want to go to college, was to give them a skill—typing, beauty parlor training, cooking, sewing for the girls, or welding, automobile repair, and painting for the boys. So it was a busy and wonderful year and Lyndon learned a lot and made friendships that lasted all his life. In fact, if anybody asked me what a political machine was, I'd say in our case it was those Lyndon knew in the National Youth Administration and those he went to school with at Southwest State Teachers College.[4]

In that group I recall Jake Pickle, who, it turned out, was to succeed

3. Johnson was director of the NYA in Texas from June 1935 to April 1937.
4. Johnson attended Southwest Texas State Teachers College from 1927 to 1930.

Lyndon in Congress and is still there; Ray Roberts, who also went on to Congress, first as secretary to the Speaker, Mr. Rayburn, and then on to his own seat; and just a bevy of others. John Connally worked in the NYA. A whole generation later, when we dedicated a job-training corps at Camp Gary in San Marcos, I looked around the platform at the people who were doing the introductions. There was a judge who handled the guest of honor, the governor, and on up to the President. All of them had been with the National Youth Administration, either making very little per hour mending roads or buildings, or working in college libraries. So it was a breeding ground for learning and achievement, and it worked very well. I know Lyndon kept on thinking that the Job Corps could surely do as well in a later generation. I don't know whether he would have said it had done so or not. Either our generation of young folks had an enormous instinct for hard work and survival, or else I'm just looking at it favorably, through the lenses of time.

The NYA extended to all of the colleges—it was statewide. They tried to get the word to all the needy folks to come and try to qualify. It was a period of many late nights and early mornings. I don't think Lyndon ever worked harder or more joyfully because, in general, things did go right. It was one of his first associations with black people in an administrative fashion. The Latin Americans he knew well from having talked with them and having represented their district. But he didn't know much about blacks. There was a college named Prairie View, which was all black and belonged to Texas A and M University. He was very anxious that money be allotted to them to install programs as well as in Marshall where there were two black colleges.

When Congressman James P. Buchanan from our tenth district— who had been in office a very long time—died in February of 1937, Lyndon had calls immediately from his old schoolteachers, his old kinfolks, offering to do anything they could to help him run for office. I remember one of his roommates at school said, "I've got a new car. I'll just give it to you. You can travel all over the district in it." So we did. I'm afraid it was a wreck when we gave it back.

There were ten counties; Austin was the only town. Lyndon came from the smallest county, Blanco, and a very small town, Johnson City. He was the first to announce, but he was rapidly followed by many better-known people, including a best friend and inheritor of the congressman, a state senator, a respected local judge, and a marvelous, flamboyant lawyer who had kinfolks up and down the district. We had lots of competition.

The Democratic primary was where you won or lost in Texas in those days. You didn't think anything about the November election.

This was a special election because of the death of a congressman. So it was set for April, and high man won in a special election, although usually if you didn't get a majority, there would be a runoff. In any case, on the Thursday night before the election, standing in line at a great big rally, Lyndon began to have the sort of pains he couldn't ignore. As soon as the rally was over, he went to the hospital. Our own doctor came and looked at him and said he had to have his appendix removed immediately, and he called in one of the better-known doctors of the area. Together they all decided that Lyndon had to have the appendix out immediately, so they removed it early the next morning. He was pretty much out all that day, the last one before the election. He let me know how he hoped I would spend election day—that is, by taking friends and kinfolks and home-bound elderly citizens to the polls and telephoning, which I did. I finally wound up with one of our best friends eating peanut butter sandwiches about ten o'clock at night, the first real meal I'd had that day. Lyndon won and that ushered in a new chapter in our lives.

How Lyndon met the President was interesting. Actually it was in Texas right after his election, right after he emerged from the hospital in April of 1937. The governor of our state, Jimmy Allred, a marvelous, handsome, young, vital man, asked Lyndon to go with him down to Galveston to greet the President. I remember so well a photograph that we kept forever of FDR, a big, smiling Roosevelt with an oleander, a boutonniere, on his coat, and young, handsome Jimmy Allred, and a very young, beaming Lyndon Johnson between them, all of them with these oleanders, the Galveston flower.

I loved the trips across the country to Washington and I never got too many of them. I liked them best in a car, second best in a train, and least of all in a plane, but that did not become part of our lives for a while. Lyndon rented a lovely apartment on Connecticut Avenue. I drove up there with one of Lyndon's secretaries' wives and immediately fell in love with Washington all over again. It was a yeasty, exciting time. The lights burned long in those offices, and the people really felt that they could roll up their sleeves and make America great. Lyndon had an expression about that: "You feel like charging Hell with a bucket of water." This feeling, this enthusiasm, pushed them a long ways. There were very few times in our country's life when so many good minds gathered together in that city intent on raising the level of living and the safety of the American people. I'm so glad I got to be a part of it.

In each job Lyndon had there was a shaky period at first when he thought, "This is too much. I can't learn it all. I can't do what I want to do. There's so much to be done, I can't master it." There was a tense period of uncertainty and great effort, and then there would come a time when he would sort of have a sign of getting a grip on it. He had a very busy congressional office, and he worked there for tremendously long hours. It was years into our married life before he quit going down on Sundays for a couple of hours and, even then, he went half a day on Saturdays with his office staff.

The main thing that occupied Lyndon's time and brains for those first years was a series of dams on the lower Colorado River which had already been begun by the Insull interests but had been abandoned when they went bankrupt. Our dear friend and mentor, our Senator A. J. Wirtz, had been the lawyer for the Insulls, but he wanted to work with anybody who would build some dams. The dams became their joint interest. They would provide rural, cheap electricity for the farmers all over the tenth district, flood control—we had lost a good deal of property and a number of lives every year or so when that river would go on the rampage—and irrigation for the rice farmers downstream. Looking back, I see the difference in attitudes. We were not affluent and never considered recreation as a major use of the dams. During the sixties and seventies, recreation blossomed and everybody in that area along those six lakes now has a boat.

As a congressman, Lyndon had the good fortune to meet Grace Tully and Tom Corcoran, Jim Rowe and Ben Cohen, and to be initiated into the administrative branch. We enjoyed the camaraderie between them, particularly in the case of Jim Rowe. There was the marvelous exchange of letters with Tom Corcoran, full of banter and sometimes hot-headed disagreement; they are still fun to read. Lyndon had the good fortune to be put on a committee that was of special interest to President Roosevelt, naval affairs. It's amazing that, being so young and new, he would get asked to small meetings at the White House, sometimes just him and the President. I remember one time he came back looking very pensive and saying that he had seen the President in bed with a cape around his shoulders. He was chilly, but he still wanted to talk over the business that he had on his mind. It was one of the first times Lyndon recognized that his man was crippled. Lyndon was an early admirer of FDR and never ceased to be one. In fact, he even embraced what became known as the Court-packing plan. I expect Roosevelt was reelected in spite of that and not because of it.

Speaker Sam Rayburn early became one of our closest and dearest friends. Lyndon had known him all his life practically because Speaker Rayburn had been in the Texas House of Representatives along with Lyndon's father.[5] Lyndon's father had taken Lyndon to sit by him during the legislative sessions and introduced him to everyone. That's how

5. LBJ's father, Sam Ealy Johnson, served in the Texas House of Representatives from 1904 to 1908 and 1918 to 1924.

Lyndon came up as secretary to a congressman. Speaker Rayburn would keep track of him in a fatherly way and be nice to him. Very early on, Lyndon became a member of what they called the Board of Education, which met in a simple little room of the Speaker's where a few of his good friends would gather to have a drink at the close of the day and discuss the legislation passed and the legislation planned and who ought to do what. Frequently this would continue into dinner at some seafood place, or whatever was the Speaker's specialty. Frequently, he would come out and have dinner with us. Texas had a close-knit delegation.

As the years went by, we really enjoyed going to dinner with Speaker Sam Rayburn. He lived a very Spartan bachelor type of life, and yet he was a natural host. There was a good cafe across the street, and they would send over whatever the Speaker had ordered for dinner and serve it. He himself would be the bartender; Tom Corcoran came often, Ben Cohen occasionally, a group of young congressmen, some of them Texans but not by any means all of them because Rayburn made lots of friends. Being the Speaker, he knew the House like a well-read book, and he had a changing series of friends. The talk was so good. I contributed little, but I learned much as I soaked it up by osmosis. We would speak about Mr. Rayburn's interest in REA. He put it in a nutshell when he said, "Farm-to-market roads and REA changed the life of Texas farmers and ranchers." The roads were gradually building across Texas, the farm-to-market roads, or ranch-to-market roads, and REA put people to work. There was a little while when we in Blanco County had 13,000 connected paid-up customers due to REA.

We would also go out to dinner with Senator Wirtz and other good friends from home. Those were big times for me, because I was very wide-eyed and young. We lived in a series of apartments and I would yearn for a home. I kept on raising the subject and Lyndon kept on saying, "We can't do it because any congressman that buys a Washington home, his constituents will say—he's forgetting us." So we were diametrically opposed. I wasn't all that caring about what the constituents thought; I wanted a home. I think we had eight different apartments over four years because, you see, we would go home the day Congress adjourned. We'd go back to Texas, and it was Lyndon's custom to go over to what he called "every post office." A community large enough to have a post office was large enough to get a visit. He held a series of speeches to service clubs or just to the general public on the courthouse square because he was a dedicated believer in representative government. You told the people what you were doing and why, and they told you what they thought of it and why. You led them as far as you could lead them, and when you couldn't lead them you could express their wishes or get out. That was their choice.

I didn't become a mother until 1944, and I didn't become the owner of a house until the fall of 1942, so in those early years I did what most housewives did. I joined the Congressional Club and went to tea every Friday afternoon and listened to some ambassador or Cabinet member or head of a committee or some person from the stage or somebody who would tell us how to decorate a house. These lectures furnished us with some inspiration, as well as social chitchat. Then we had the 75th Club, which was all of the women whose husbands came to Congress at that time. Mrs. Margaret Chase Smith from Maine, whose husband was a congressman, was a member of that club. She later ran for senator after his death.

I attended only the big things at the White House that any other congressman's wife would attend, and I went to rented white tie and tails occasions. I insisted on renting a silk hat for Lyndon, because you needed it for about five minutes when you walked in and you checked it along with your overcoat. Big receptions were always given in wintertime. You went upstairs to a reception which probably had a thousand people, all of the congressmen, all of the senators. One of the great joys was when Rebecca Baines Johnson, Lyndon's mother, a widow and my good friend, was visiting us and the White House found out about it and included her in the invitation.

The biggest word in my vocabulary, the most important, was "constituency," which one spelled in capitals. That was one of the things you could do for your husband. You could take all these constituents to see the Capitol, Mount Vernon, the Custis Mansion, and the White House, all on the regular tours. My beat was really the Capitol and lunch in the Senate dining room. I tried to help Lyndon in that way, and I spent my hours going to innumerable weddings, gatherings, and in the first year or so paying calls. This is something that was wiped out of Washington life after the Second World War. But it was still alive then. We went and left cards at everybody's house—everybody who had preceded your husband in being elected, everybody on his committee, everybody in your state delegation, and the White House, at a minimum. It was an interesting custom. Every wife of a Supreme Court Justice was supposed to be at home at least once a season, maybe several times. I think the House's day to be at home was Tuesday, the Senate was Thursday, Sunday was the diplomatic day. Maybe it was Wednesday for the Court, and the Cabinet wives had a day. So you simply went around and dropped little white cards. Occasionally the lady would be at home and say, "Do come up." I made some interesting acquaintances that way.

Some member of the delegation handled instruction about the rules. Somebody gave me a little book that had all the rules. After going to a dinner party, within twenty-four hours, you went by and left a card. You weren't expecting to be received. You just dropped off your card. But that system even then was falling in favor and passed out of the picture before too long. People just got too busy to attend to such things.

Mrs. Roosevelt led us wives, one winter, through the drab, slumlike areas of Washington. I could not tell you now what streets we were on. I guess we were in the Southeast. I remember her striding along with our small group. I went out of curiosity. I wanted to know what was going on and what was to be learned from it. Accustomed as I was to rural poverty and poverty among blacks, I hadn't seen anything like this urban poverty. You usually kept off those streets, but that day we just walked right among them. I think she did everything she could to put the spotlight on these distressing places, especially with the President. We were always impressed by her concern and determination.

Then, of course, there was Frances Perkins, whom everybody respected, even if they made jokes about her hats. It was not until the war that Anna Rosenberg Hoffman came. Grace Tully was early a dear friend, and Missy LeHand, too.

I recall the first time Lyndon went eagerly panting down to the White House, having obtained an appointment with the President. He was so anxious to tell him all about the dams on the Colorado River and how much they were needed. After a few civilities, he just got down to the point of telling him the whole story when the President sort of neatly remarked, did Lyndon know something about—and then launched into a long monologue which you couldn't very well interrupt. After a while, Pa Watson or some other assistant stuck his head in the door and said, "Your next appointment's here, sir." That was the end of it, and Lyndon went out dismayed and disconsolate. Tom Corcoran—or it may have been Jim Rowe—told him that if he ever got in again, and Lyndon was determined to, the thing to do was to go armed with maps and charts and pictures of what the dams could do, what happened with the dams, to make a sort of visual presentation. Roosevelt liked maps and charts, and it would draw his interest.

So that really happened. The next time Lyndon went, he was well-supplied with maps and he did get the President's attention. He looked at them all. Then he picked up the phone and called somebody in the Interior Department who would handle the purse strings for dams—federal appropriations for them—and for beginning rural electrification. He called him by his first name very affably and said, "I want us to look into working on those dams down there where this new young congressman from Texas, Lyndon Johnson, is." And this officer apparently replied, "My gosh, he's been bothering us more than I want to hear about." Then he said, "Mr. President, they don't have but five households a mile," or one household a mile, or whatever it was. "There's not enough people down there to meet the criteria." Lyndon used to repeat what the President said, laughingly, "Don't worry, they'll breed fast."

CHAPTER 24

Eleanor Roosevelt

Anna Eleanor Roosevelt, born on 11 October 1884 in New York city, was the niece of Theodore Roosevelt and fifth cousin to Franklin Delano Roosevelt. Eleanor, like her husband, was born into an old and distinguished family. Much of her character was shaped by the fatal alcoholism of her beloved father, Elliott, the emotional rejection of her mother, Anna Hall, who referred to her as "granny," and their early deaths. From the age of nine she was raised by her grandmother and educated in private schools in the United States and Europe. Not surprisingly, she remembered herself as "a solemn child, without beauty. I seemed like a little old woman entirely lacking in the spontaneous joy and mirth of youth."

Eleanor and Franklin were married in 1905 and became the parents of six children. After FDR entered politics, her activities came to revolve more and more around his career. She became an expert hostess while he served as Assistant Secretary of the Navy, but she eagerly abandoned her social duties for wartime support activities. Following the Great War she devoted increasing time to political and social reform. When FDR was struck down by polio in 1921, she became his political representative as well as his nurse and morale builder. She organized women for the New York Democratic party, and from 1924 to 1928 she served as finance chairman. By 1928, when FDR won election as governor of New York, she was a political figure in her own right.

As First Lady, Eleanor Roosevelt set as many precedents as did her husband. She traveled extensively—40,000 miles during 1933 alone—to promote the New Deal. Beginning in 1935, she wrote a syndicated newspaper column, "My Day." She worked tirelessly on behalf of minorities, women, education, and social reform. She particularly supported the NAACP and the cause of racial equality.

During World War II, she served as assistant director of the Office of Civilian Defense and visited soldiers serving in the Southwest Pacific and the Caribbean. She was a member of the U.S. delegation to the United Nations and helped write the U.N. Declaration on Human Rights. When Eisenhower became President in 1953 she resigned, but served again during the Kennedy Administration when she chaired the President's Commission on the Status of Women. By the time of her death in 1962, she had become world famous. Adlai Stevenson summed up her contribution at her memorial service: "What other single human being has touched and transformed the existence of so many? . . . She walked in the slums . . . of the world, not on a tour of inspection . . . but as one who could not feel contentment when others were hungry."

CLAUDE D. PEPPER

All who knew anything about the Roosevelt Administration and what it meant to the United States and to the world appreciate the immeasurable contribution that Mrs. Roosevelt made. In the first place, she was absolutely necessary to the President, since he had a physical handicap and limitation. She brought him information that could come only from someone who could go out and *see.* She went into mines, down into coal mines, and the men at the bottom of the mine said, "My God, there's Mrs. Roosevelt!" She went into the schoolrooms, she went into the factories, she went *everywhere* (she went into war zones, of course, later on). Prodding, looking, seeking information, and coming back and disclosing that information to the President, she was his eyes, his ears, and his feet. Through her he got facts that were essential to him and to the proponents of his important program.

Mrs. Roosevelt also had an almost unparalleled compassion for other people. She, who was of patrician birth and upbringing, like President Roosevelt, somehow or other had the spiritual growth within her that made her compassionate and sensitive to the needs of people. There she was out doing more things than anybody ever tried to do before: to help people in every walk of life where there was a need, a genuine need for assistance. And she was so dedicated to this cause.

In the field of education, of course, she was especially active, for she realized the value of education. Jobs—she just went everywhere to try to help people get jobs, to try to help them grow, to do better work. She tried to help people get homes; she'd go into the shacks, into the slums, and see the state of the houses in which people lived. She'd try her best to get decent housing. And medical care was one of her primary concerns. Of course she supported national health insurance, or any kind of plan that would provide better health for the needs of people. She also was trying to help handicapped children. In other words, the scope of her interests was the scope of human need. And her compassion and her concern were as wide as the breadth of human need. That was what she was dedicated to.

Mrs. Roosevelt told me that she thought all of our people had basic rights—a right to live in decent housing, a right to have a decent diet, a right to wear decent clothes, a right to get decent medical care, and a right to get a decent education that would enable them to do something useful in life. She assumed that these were ordinary rights that the people of the United States had, and she discovered that these needs were not available to the people all over this country. She was aware of the acuteness of these needs and she was a wonderful advocate, a most persuasive advocate of the government's doing something.

Of course in the area of peace, in the area of international good will and harmony, she was like one of the famous minds, perhaps Francis Bacon, who took all knowledge as his sphere. She took all human need as her concern. She didn't want war to devastate a country that should be used otherwise, that is, to support people and peaceful pursuits. She didn't want people to be killed by war but to have a chance to live out their normal lives in good health. She didn't want people to be taken away from their ordinary pursuits and be put into service in war when it was not necessary.

There has never been another Mrs. Eleanor Roosevelt. She had indefatigable energy; she was keenly intelligent; she had enormous compassion and concern for fellow human beings. It didn't make any difference to her who they were, whether they were Indians, or blacks, or were from this land or that land, or what culture or religion they belonged to. She believed in the principle that we're all God's children, and she thought she was helping God's children when she was helping people. She defied an old custom, a tradition, way back before the civil rights laws ever took effect, in acting without prejudice.

She advocated the doing away with discrimination on account of race or sex. She was one of the first of the great advocates of equality for women. She didn't support the ERA, and I disagreed with her as I thought her premise was in error. She disagreed because she thought women might be drafted. But I don't think that's true; Congress determines whom the government should draft. All men are equal and they don't draft all men—they don't draft old men, they don't draft very young boys.

I saw Mrs. Roosevelt many times. Sometimes I'd go over and see her, to ask her to try to help with something that I was interested in. Then again, she'd call me about something, maybe some piece of legislation, or some administrative matter, or maybe something in Florida that she was interested in. I saw quite a lot of Mrs. Roosevelt. We had her come down to Florida State University in Tallahassee. Mrs. Pepper went down with her and introduced her to the local people. They wanted her to come because she had spoken at the Bethune-Cookman College, and back in those days civil rights matters were not of the same character as they are now. A lot of these white institutions got after Mrs. Pepper and me to get Mrs. Roosevelt to come to their place to speak, so she went to Florida State University too.

Mrs. Roosevelt sort of imposed on the President to do this, do that, or the other, often when he did not want to discuss the matter. But she didn't have too many times to talk to him; she was away a great deal, seeing, doing. I believe she was almost literally the co-President in the sense that she had an active part in a perfectly proper way. I don't think she tried to dominate the President, but she tried to urge him, to push to do things. He was like the rest of us; a lot of times he'd let something sort of stay on the back burner. She'd get after him again and again: "Franklin, we must do this, we must do that; you haven't done anything about that problem you were going to do something about."

Mrs. Roosevelt, to one degree or another, had a large part in nearly all of the welfare programs. She would come back and tell the President the need, and sometimes she'd go out to the agencies themselves and press for her programs. Take the NYA. I know she had a lot to do with the initiation of the National Youth Administration program for education. I know she was working very closely with Aubrey Williams and those who ran those programs. She worked very closely with Harry Hopkins when he was in charge of the WPA program, the Works Progress Administration. When he had problems, when he needed her to speak to the President, or to somebody else in Congress, he could go to her, get her help.

Everybody who was head of a big program tried to get Mrs. Roosevelt's help. Bernard Baruch told me many times about how he liked to talk to Mrs. Roosevelt. A lot of times he'd take advantage of an opportunity to talk to her when he didn't get a chance to talk to the President. Maybe he sometimes preferred to talk to Mrs. Roosevelt. A lot of other people talked to Mrs. Roosevelt as a way of getting ideas to the President. She had a lot more ideas even than President Roosevelt did. She was just full of them; she was calling for this and that.

We had dinner at the White House a good many times. Of course, she was always a very gracious hostess; she would always try to make good arrangements. But you know, although Mrs. Roosevelt was a lady of grace and charm and of the best manners and breeding, that was a minor side of life to her. The big thing in life was: What did you do for people? What did you do for the country? She took on all the duties of the hostess, but there's such a contrast between her and a good many other First Ladies. Mrs. Roosevelt did her job as First Lady with good grace; she poured tea with grace and charm, and she poured many millions of gallons of it I guess in her lifetime. But it was all incidental to leading a meaningful life. Being a hostess wasn't the important thing to her. Pouring tea was a way to bring people together so they could enjoy one another's company under pleasant circumstances. But she always rose above such events.

Another small matter to her was her clothes. She was always properly dressed, of course; she dressed very well. But clothes didn't mean too much to her. She liked running out there and seeing how children were clothed and cared for in some community, or she poked around in the poor housing conditions in another area, or she checked up on the health care of some other children. If they'd have given her a trip to Paris to see the new fashion gowns, she wouldn't have taken the time to do it.

On the running of the White House—the President is reputed not always to have liked the food that the housekeeper turned out—Mrs. Roosevelt didn't put in much time. She had a housekeeper, a Mrs. Henrietta Nesbitt, who ran the house. You had to have a house to live in and this was the beautiful home of the American people's President, and Mrs. Roosevelt looked after it very well, and kept it very well, but cared very little about housekeeping.

Eleanor Roosevelt's relationship with the President seemed to be a partnership where there was mutual respect and mutual cooperation. But it was basically a partnership. They worked together. The President, I think, was very much aware of what he owed her, not only for what she'd done for him when he was flat on his back—it was probably she who got him through with her indomitable will, her determination to survive that tragedy. Roosevelt is said to have remarked on one occasion, "Once you've spent two years lying on your back trying to move your big toe, after that anything is easy." It was that inimitable, indomitable Eleanor Roosevelt who never let him get it into his head that he was through. It was just like talking to a sick child—you never let him get the idea that he wasn't going to get well.

I credit Mrs. Roosevelt and her indomitable encouragement with a very, very large share in bringing about his recovery. She did everything to make things comfortable for him and to create the kind of environment that would keep him from succumbing to self-pity. She got him going again in politics. She probably was the one responsible for that, for without her encouragement just to jump back in he might not have reentered politics.[1] She was in a way a much stronger character than he was in personal characteristics. He had a lot of fight in him, a lot of determination, but it came and went, as it were. Hers was with her all the time.

There's no doubt that Mrs. Roosevelt, just by her encouragement and inspiration, was immeasurably responsible for the magnificent, affirmative life that the President lived. She was a great, gracious lady, a magnificent spirit, a supreme and superb human being, a lady of enormous compassion for her fellow man, and a truly great lady of the world. She loved mankind. She was one of the dynamic patriots who have moved across the earth among all the millions that have been the children of God.

1. Most historians believe that Mrs. Roosevelt was reluctant to see FDR run for the governorship in 1928 because she feared the impact on his health and doubted he could win. See, for example, Frank Freidel, *Franklin D. Roosevelt: The Ordeal* (Boston: Little, Brown, 1954), pp. 252–255.

BIOGRAPHIES OF CONTRIBUTORS

BIOGRAPHICAL NOTES

INDEX

Biographies
of Contributors

EDWARD M. BERNSTEIN was born in 1904 in Bayonne, New Jersey. He graduated from the University of Chicago in 1927 and received a Ph.D. in economics from Harvard in 1931. He taught economics at North Carolina State University from 1930 to 1935 and at the University of North Carolina from 1935 to 1940.

Bernstein went to Washington in 1940 at the invitation of the Treasury to prepare its answers to a questionnaire of the Senate Banking Committee on the monetary policies of the New Deal. The questions covered the measures taken between 1933 and 1940 on gold, silver, exchange rates, and banking legislation. He remained at the Treasury until 1946, serving in turn as principal economist, assistant director of the division of monetary research, and assistant to the Secretary of the Treasury. In 1944 he was executive secretary and chief technical adviser of the U.S. delegation at the Bretton Woods Monetary and Financial Conference.

RICHARD W. BOLLING was born in 1916 in New York City. He graduated from the University of the South in 1937 and received a master's degree there two years later; he also did graduate work at Vanderbilt University. He entered the House of Representatives in the 81st Congress and remained through the 97th Congress and until 1982. While serving from Missouri's Fifth District, he was chairman of the Select Committee on Committees and the Rules Committee. He was also a member of the Steering and Policy Committee of the Democratic Caucus. He was often mentioned as a possible Speaker of the House, but never succeeded to that office. Bolling served in the army from 1941 to 1946. He was a Chubb Fellow at Yale (1965) and a Fellow at the Center for Advanced Studies at Wesleyan University (1962–1964). He is the author of *House Out of Order* (1965) and *Power in the House* (1968).

WILBUR J. COHEN, born in Milwaukee in 1913, graduated from the University of Wisconsin in economics in 1934 and went to Washington at the ripe age

21. As research assistant to the executive director of FDR's cabinet-level Committee on Economic Security, he helped to draft the Social Security Act. In 1935 he joined the staff of the Social Security Board, where he remained until 1956, eventually becoming director of its division of research and statistics. In the 1960s he served as Assistant Secretary, Under Secretary, and Secretary of the Department of Health, Education, and Welfare and oversaw major social legislation passed as part of the Great Society program in the fields of health, education, and medical care. He is known as the father of Medicare and Medicaid.

After 1955 Cohen became professor of education and public welfare administration at the University of Michigan; he served as dean of the School of Education there from 1969 to 1978. He is the author of many books in his field, including *Social Security: Programs, Problems and Policies.* He is now Sid W. Richardson Professor of Public Affairs at the Lyndon B. Johnson School of Public Affairs, the University of Texas at Austin. He recalls: "Like many other young people, I was attracted to the New Deal by the dynamic challenge and experimentation which FDR offered. It was an exciting, thrilling experience."

THOMAS CORCORAN was born in 1900 in Pawtucket, Rhode Island,

a textile manufacturing community near Providence. His father, Patrick, son of an Irish immigrant, was Pawtucket's leading lawyer and Democratic politician.

Although well-to-do, Patrick insisted that his three sons work with their hands until prepared to work with their heads. From the age of twelve, Tom, the eldest, sold papers, worked in stores, and did other odd jobs while going to school and during summer vacations.

At Brown University he earned his way partly as a dance band pianist and partly as a winner of scholastic prizes. Finishing first in the class of 1922, he moved on to Harvard Law School, where he again led his class, winning his doctorate in law and a research fellowship under Felix Frankfurter. The following year he became secretary to Justice Holmes, who became his mentor and hero. The two read all of the Old Testament, Montaigne's essays, and much of Dante's *Inferno,* which Corcoran read aloud in English while the Justice followed in the Italian text. They also dipped into the Greek classics, Corcoran reading aloud in the original.

After the Holmes interlude, Corcoran went to New York to work in the law office of Cotton and Franklin, a Wall Street firm with an important corporate practice. He became skillful in the blue sky operations of the stock markets.

Corcoran moved on to work for the Reconstruction Finance Corporation, which became a model for several other government agencies. He and Ben Cohen were recommended by Felix Frankfurter to write the Securities Exchange Act. From then on they were partners: Cohen was the draftsman and Corcoran, whose talents were for persuasion and lobbying, convinced legislators to pass the New Deal legislation.

After his retirement from government in 1941, Corcoran plunged into corporate law, representing major concerns doing business with Washington departments and agencies before, during, and after World War II. The press referred to him as a lawyer lobbyist; he called himself a lawyer entrepreneur. He died in 1981.

KENNETH CRAWFORD was born in 1902 in Sparta, Wisconsin, and

grew up in Jefferson, Wisconsin. He graduated from Beloit College in 1924 and took his first big step in the newspaper world by joining the United Press in Chicago. The UP moved him around the Midwest, promoting him as he traveled. In 1927 he landed in Washington as bureau chief and covered Calvin Coolidge and the "sons of the Wild Jackass," as Senators George Norris, William Borah, Hiram Johnson, and Homer Capehart were then called.

When Ralph Ingersoll decided to publish an "adless" newspaper, *PM*, Crawford became bureau chief. On the side, he wrote a weekly column for the *Nation* and the *New Republic* under the name of TRB, a still extant column he handed over to Richard Strout. His book about lobbyists, *The Pressure Boys,* was a bestseller. He also found time to ghost-write George Allen's book *Presidents Who Have Known Me.*

When the war came Crawford went overseas, joining *Newsweek* as a war correspondent. After a hitch in North Africa, Italy, and Turkey, he landed in the first wave on the Normandy beaches with the Fourth Infantry. He went on to join Patton's Third Army for the assault on Paris. Shortly after the war he became *Newsweek*'s bureau chief. He retired in 1976, and died in December 1982.

JOHN C. DREIER was born in Brooklyn, N.Y., in 1906 and took his A.B. at Harvard in 1928. From 1929 to 1931 he taught at the Cranbrook School in Bloomfield Hills, Michigan. He became active in conservation and land use when he joined the Department of the Interior in 1933, later moving to the Farm Security Administration and Department of Agriculture. In 1941 he joined the Department of State, where he became chief of the Division of Special Inter-American Affairs. From 1951 to 1960 he represented the United States on the Council of the Organization of American States with the rank of ambassador; he served as chairman of the Council in 1951–1952. He also served as an adviser to the U.S. Delegation to the United Nations. Dreier later became a professor of Latin American studies, and director of the Inter-American Center at the School of Advanced International Studies of the Johns Hopkins University. Now retired, he is a trustee of College of the Atlantic, Bar Harbor, Maine, and a director of the Maine Coast Heritage Trust.

THOMAS H. ELIOT was born in Cambridge, Massachusetts, in 1907, and educated at Harvard, where he earned his law degree in 1932. He has had a varied career in law, government, politics, and education. As counsel to the President's Committee on Economic Security from 1934 to 1935, he was principal draftsman of the Social Security Act. From 1935 to 1938 he was counsel to the Social Security Board. He served a term as a congressman from Massachusetts from 1946 to 1948. In the House of Representatives he led the successful opposition to bills that would have legalized more wiretapping than the courts then allowed and would have set up detention camps for deportable aliens. He tried, unsuccessfully, to end the life of the House Un-American Activities Committee. After World War II he practiced law in Boston, then became a professor of political science at Washington University in St. Louis. In 1962 he was named chancellor of the university, a post he held until his retirement in 1971. After retiring he served five years as president of the Salzburg Seminar in American Studies. He now lives in Cambridge, Massachusetts, where since 1977 he has taught a course on constitutional issues at the Buckingham, Browne and Nichols school.

THOMAS I. EMERSON was born in 1907 in Passaic, New Jersey. He graduated from Yale College in 1928 and from Yale Law School three years later, then practiced law in New York with a small firm until 1933. He was always interested in public affairs and participated in political and social events, and his boyhood ambition was to be a senator from New Jersey.

In June 1933 Emerson went to Washington to work in the National Recovery Administration; later he served with the National Labor Relations Board. He also held legal posts at the Social Security Board and in the Department of Justice as special assistant to the Attorney General. His other government positions included associate general counsel and later deputy administrator for enforcement at the Office of Price Administration, general counsel of the Office of Economic Stabilization, and general counsel at the Office of War Mobilization and Reconversion.

Emerson became a professor at the Yale Law School in 1946 and was named Lines Professor there in 1955. His major field of research, writing, and teaching has been constitutional law, with particular emphasis on civil liberties and civil rights.

ABE FORTAS was born in Memphis, Tennessee, in 1910, the youngest of five children of a cabinetmaker. He worked his way through high school playing the violin; this instrument began as a source of pleasure but soon became a means of support. He won scholarships to Southwestern College in Memphis, from which he graduated in 1930, and to Yale Law School, where he soon came to the attention of Professor William O. Douglas. He became known as Bill Douglas's prize student.

For the first four years after law school Fortas commuted between a teaching job at Yale and his New Deal assignments. In 1933 he became assistant chief in the legal division of the Agricultural Adjustment Administration. In 1934 at Douglas's request he went to work for the Securities and Exchange Commission. By 1939 Douglas had to let him go to the Interior Department, where he later became Under Secretary (1942–1946).

In 1946 he turned to the private practice of law, forming the Washington firm of Arnold, Fortas, and Porter. From 1965 to 1969 he was an Associate Justice of the U.S. Supreme Court. Since 1970 he has practiced law in Washington with the firm of Fortas and Koven.

Fortas once remarked that the only thing he could not live without was his music. He will also be remembered for his free legal defense of those accused of disloyalty, and for his insistence that free legal defense be provided for the poor. He died in April 1982.

HENRY HAMILL FOWLER was born in 1908 in Roanoke, Virginia, graduated from Roanoke College in 1929, and four years later earned his law degree at Yale. Joe, as friends call him, has lived three different professional lives: as private practitioner of the law, political appointee, and international investment adviser.

While at the law firm of Covington, Burling, he was drawn to the challenge of the New Deal. As attorney for the Tennessee Valley Authority from 1934 to 1939, he became the successful defender of the TVA before the Supreme Court. Appointed chief counsel of the Senate Civil Liberties Subcommittee in 1939, Fowler worked to improve conditions for migrant workers. Later he participated in the negotiations for what would become known as the St. Lawrence Seaway project. At the outset of World War II he became assistant counsel to the Office of Production Management. After the war he served on the Allied Control Council, and then joined a law firm begun by former members of the War Production Board.

During the Korean War Fowler returned to the government when President Truman appointed him director of the Office of Defense Mobilization and the Defense Production Administration. After another interlude in private practice he again reentered government service, as Under Secretary of the Treasury from 1961 to 1964 and Secretary from 1965 to 1968. In 1969 he joined the investment firm of Goldman, Sachs. He now serves as cochairman of the Committee on the Present Danger.

MILTON V. FREEMAN, born in 1911 in New York City, graduated from City College in 1931 and from Columbia Law School in 1934. He worked for the New Deal in the Securities and Exchange Commission for almost twelve years, drafting regulations and forms, interpreting statutes, investigating violations, and trying and arguing court cases.

In 1946 Freeman went into practice with Thurman Arnold and Abe Fortas, and was later joined by Paul Porter. His work was principally in the corporate and securities fields, but also involved various international and constitutional issues. He took part in major controversies while with the SEC; for example, from 1948 to 1956 he represented Cyrus Eaton, the industrialist and investment banker of internationalist views and friend of high Soviet leaders. In the late 1940s and early 1950s he spent a good deal of his time, along with Arnold, Fortas, and Porter, defending victims of the government loyalty programs. He also carried out a successful challenge in the Supreme Court to provisions of the McCarran Act, which denied naturalized citizens the same rights to live abroad as native-born citizens.

PAUL A. FREUND was born in St. Louis in 1908 and educated in public schools there and at Washington University, from which he graduated in 1928. After taking his law degree at Harvard and completing a year of postgraduate work as research assistant to Professor Felix Frankfurter, he went to Washington in September 1932 to serve as law clerk to Justice Brandeis.

At the end of his term as clerk Freund joined a small group in the legal division of the Treasury, working on special assignments from Dean Acheson, who was then Under Secretary. In November 1933 Acheson was forced to resign over his opposition to the Administration's gold-buying program, and Freund moved to the Reconstruction Finance Corporation to assist Stanley Reed, its general counsel, in defending the validity of the government's devaluation of the dollar and abrogation of gold clauses in private and public bonds.

When Reed was appointed Solicitor General early in 1935, Freund transferred with him to the Department of Justice, where he participated in some major New Deal cases. He stayed at Justice until the summer of 1939 when he left Washington to teach law at Harvard, then returned to Justice in 1942 as an assistant to the Solicitor General Charles Fahy. In his two periods of service he argued about thirty cases before the Supreme Court.

Freund returned to Harvard in 1946. He declined an invitation to become Solicitor General in the Kennedy Administration. In one of his scholarly roles he served as editor of the multivolume History of the Supreme Court, which was funded by Justice Holmes's gift of his estate to his country. Freund is now Carl M. Loeb University Professor Emeritus at Harvard.

LEONA B. GERARD was born in 1899 and educated in the Chicago school system. In 1920 she graduated from the University of Chicago, where she was in Phi Beta Kappa.

Through her activities in the League of Women Voters she came to know early New Dealer Harold L. Ickes. Arriving in Washington in October 1933, she served as an aide to Ickes and as assistant division chief in a Labor Department agency. At age 74, after college, marriage, motherhood, and nearly a quarter of a century in the federal government, she discovered her true vocation, as a writer. She has published *Poems Mostly about Love and Other Benchmarks* (1977) and *Benchmarks,* II (1980). She lives in Eugene, Oregon.

GERHARD A. GESELL was born in Los Angeles in 1910 and grew up in New Haven, Connecticut, where his father was a physician on the Yale faculty. After graduating from Phillips Andover Academy and Yale College and taking his law degree at Yale Law School, he went to Washington in 1935 as a trial attorney at the Securities and Exchange Commission. He served as the trial attorney in the case of Richard Whitney.

In 1941 Gesell left the SEC and joined the Washington law firm of Covington, Burling. In December 1967 he was nominated by President Johnson as a federal judge on the United States District Court for the District of Columbia. He has served in that capacity ever since.

ARTHUR "TEX" GOLDSCHMIDT was born in San Antonio in 1910. He went to college at Columbia, but dropped his postgraduate work there in the summer of 1933 when he was offered a job with the new Federal Emergency Relief Administration under Harry Hopkins. He helped to create the Civil Works Administration, the Federal Surplus Property Corporation, the National Youth Administration, and the Works Progress Administration with its Federal Arts Project.

Later, Goldschmidt worked in the power division of the Public Works Administration and then in the division of power of the Department of the Interior. As Interior's representative to the State Department's interdepartmental committees, he helped plan such international programs as the Marshall Plan and Point Four. He went to the United Nations in 1950 to help set up its technical assistance programs, and left in 1966 when President Johnson appointed him to represent the United States in the U.N. Economic and Social Council. Since 1969 he has done consulting work for international organizations, primarily the U.N. Development Program. As U.N. representative of the Society for International Development, he chairs the development committee of the Conference of Non-Governmental Organizations at the United Nations.

FRANCIS THORNTON GREENE was born in 1908 in New York City. He graduated from the Virginia Military Institute in 1930 and earned his law degree from Harvard in 1933. In 1934 he went to Washington to join the staff of the general counsel's office of the Securities and Exchange Commission, and in 1937 he was appointed head of the opinion and brief writing section of that office. In this capacity he helped to prepare the argument upholding the constitutionality of the Securities Exchange Act of 1934. From 1938 until 1941 he was assistant director of the trading and exchange division of the SEC under chairman Ganson Purcell, working with the technical committees of the New York Stock Exchange and the New York Clearing House Banks.

Greene served as a commander in the Naval Reserve from 1941 to 1945, then went into the private practice of law in Richmond, Virginia. He returned to Washington in 1949 and worked for the Defense Department (1949–1950), the Federal Maritime Board (1950–1952), and the American Merchant Marine Institute (1953–1956). In 1956 he once again entered private practice.

PAUL M. HERZOG was born in New York City in 1906. He graduated from Harvard College in 1927 and took his law degree at Columbia in 1936. In the summer of 1933 he was appointed assistant to the secretary of the National Labor Board. For about two years, his principal jobs were to act as receptionist for the board members, who were often visited by people seeking to influence their decisions; to set up a file system for the mountains of correspondence; to help establish about twenty regional offices all over the United States; and to prepare draft opinions in which the board members announced their decisions in many controversial cases applying and interpreting Section 7a of the National Industrial Recovery Act. He was one of half a dozen staff members who worked for that board and for its successor.

Herzog left Washington in 1935 soon after the Wagner Act was passed, but returned exactly ten years later as chairman of the National Labor Relations Board (1945–1953), appointed by President Truman. In the interim, he served briefly in the Naval Reserve, practiced law in New York, and was a member, and later chairman, of the New York State Labor Relations Board.

ALGER HISS was born in Baltimore in 1904 and educated at Johns Hopkins and Harvard Law School. He was clerk to Justice Holmes in 1929, then practiced law in Boston and New York. In 1933 Judge Jerome Frank persuaded him to "hurry down" to Washington. Hiss established himself as assistant general counsel and a draftsman at the Agricultural Adjustment Administration (AAA).

Discouraged by the purge of Frank and others at the AAA, Hiss moved on to the Senate Munitions Committee investigating the munitions industry. With this assignment completed he moved to the Solicitor General's office. After that he became assistant to Assistant Secretary of State Francis B. Sayre, and later he covered the Far East for the State Department.

Hiss helped to inaugurate the United Nations, serving as executive secretary at the preparatory conference at Dumbarton Oaks and then as secretary general at the San Francisco conference that drafted the United Nations Charter. His next post was as president of the Carnegie Endowment for International Peace.

He is now a member of the Massachusetts Bar, and lectures at colleges and other institutions.

DONALD HISS was born in Baltimore in 1906. He graduated from Johns Hopkins in 1929 and took his law degree at Harvard in 1932, then spent a year as clerk to Justice Holmes. He joined the New Deal in 1933 at the termination of his clerkship, and was assigned to the housing division of the Public Works Administration under Harold Ickes.

The following year Hiss was transferred to the Office of Subsistence Homesteads set up in the Department of the Interior, an experimental project designed to encourage industries to locate in rural areas or small towns where workers could produce food on parcels of land. In 1935 he became assistant to the Solicitor General, Gerard Reilly, and in 1938 he moved to the State Department to become an assistant to the legal adviser to the Philippines.

From 1938 to 1953 Hiss taught law in the evenings at both Catholic University and Johns Hopkins University's School of Advanced International Studies. He left the State Department in 1945 and joined the Washington law firm of Covington, Burling. He is retired and lives with his wife in Southbury, Connecticut. Adhering to Voltaire's final admonition, he "cultivates his garden."

CHARLES A. HORSKY

CHARLES A. HORSKY was born in Helena, Montana, in 1910. He attended the University of Washington in Seattle and took his law degree at Harvard in 1934. After spending a year as clerk for Judge Augustus Hand in New York, he joined the office of the Solicitor General, and made his first court appearance before the Supreme Court. In 1937 he joined the Washington law firm of Covington, Burling, specializing in appellate litigation.

During his forty-odd years as a Washington lawyer, Horsky had the opportunity to join the staff of Justice Jackson in the War Crimes Trials at Nuremburg after World War II, and later to be adviser on the affairs of the District of Columbia for Presidents Kennedy and Johnson. He taught at the University of Virginia Law School and is the author of *The Washington Lawyer* (1952).

CHARLOTTE MOTON HUBBARD

CHARLOTTE MOTON HUBBARD was born in Hampton, Virginia, the daughter of Dr. Robert Russa Moton, the second president of Tuskegee Institute. She was educated at Tuskegee and at the Sargent College of Physical Education, in Boston, where she received her degree in 1934.

Mrs. Hubbard was assistant director of the Hampton Institute Dance Group and attended the Bennington School of the Dance Arts in Vermont. She taught courses in the elementary, high school, and college programs at Hampton Institute. During World War II she became a member of the national staff of the Girl Scouts and also worked in the national physical fitness program in Philadelphia and the Office of Community War Services in the recreation division of the Federal Security Agency in Washington.

Hubbard's career after the war included working as community relations director for WTOP-TV and in the department of public relations of the United Givers Fund. She also developed in-service training programs for recreation workers, under the sponsorship of the American Friends Service Committee, the Catholic Interracial Council of Washington, the Congress of Racial Equality, the Washington Urban League, the American Jewish Council, the Washington Council of Churches, and the Unitarian Fellowship for Social Justice.

In 1964 Mrs. Hubbard went to work for the Department of State, developing programs known as community meetings on foreign policy. Later President Johnson appointed her Deputy Secretary of State for Public Affairs, and she traveled in both Asia and Africa for the department. She retired in 1973.

LADY BIRD JOHNSON, born Claudia Alta Taylor in 1912 in Karnack, Texas, grew up in the serenity of an antebellum home in deep East Texas. Her vistas were widened at St. Mary's Hall, where an English teacher encouraged her gift of words, and later at the University of Texas, where she received a degree in journalism in 1934.

Mrs. Johnson described the New Deal years as "those yeasty days of doing." The shy, dark-eyed girl married the young New Dealer after a whirlwind three-month romance, and was startled when he asked her to memorize all the county seats in Texas. It did not take her long to master those, and later the alphabet soup of the New Deal—NYA, TVA, NRA—that would lift the country out of the depression.

Mrs. Johnson was both spectator and participant as a young congressional wife swept up in the excitement and hopes of the New Deal, married to a "tornado of a man" who allied himself and his political future with Franklin D. Roosevelt. In the late thirties the Johnsons were part of the group of young people around Washington whose political and social lives were full of heady conversation about ways to get the country moving again. In 1941 the young couple were invited to their first White House dinner, and Lady Bird recorded: "Tonight I went to my first (will it be the last?) lovely dinner at the White House. Everything managed with a watch-making precision!"

Lady Bird's keen perceptions enabled her as First Lady to rally people to the causes she loves best. She worked for a beautiful, clean environment, and she translated the poverty programs of her husband's Great Society into flesh and blood issues by visiting poor areas of the country and urging the public to look, see, and act. She remains today an influential voice in American life.

MILTON KATZ was born in New York City in 1906 and graduated from Harvard College in 1927 and Harvard Law School in 1931. He landed in the New Deal in 1935 and spent three years as executive assistant chairman and special counsel at the Securities and Exchange Commission. His later posts included special assistant attorney general and solicitor to the War Production Board.

During World War II Katz served in the Navy. After the war he became chief of the Marshall Plan in Europe with the rank of ambassador, and later joined the Ford Foundation as associate director in charge of its international program.

He returned to the Harvard Law School, where in 1954 he became the Henry L. Stimson Professor of Law and the director of international legal studies. Among his books are *Cases and Materials in Administrative Law* (1947), *The Things That Are Caesar's* (1966), and *The Relevance of International Adjudication* (1968).

CHARLES R. KAUFMAN was born in Chicago in 1908. He graduated from the University of Michigan in 1930 and received a law degree from Harvard in 1933. In 1933 he became legal secretary to Judge Learned Hand of the U.S. Court of Appeals. He went to Washington in 1934 and was appointed supervising attorney at the Securities and Exchange Commission, where he remained for three years.

Kaufman entered private practice with the firm of Pope and Ballard, where he stayed until 1952. He is currently a member of the Chicago firm of Vedder, Price, Kaufman and Kammholz. His friends describe him as enjoying fly fishing, tennis, and golf, in addition to his many private charities and civic activities.

LEON H. KEYSERLING was born in Charleston, South Carolina, in 1908. He received a B.A. from Columbia in 1928 and a law degree from Harvard three years later. He also completed the course requirements for a doctorate in economics before he interrupted his studies to work for the New Deal.

Keyserling went to Washington in March of 1933 and worked briefly as an attorney for the Agricultural Adjustment Administration. He soon became a legislative assistant to Senator Robert F. Wagner; in his four years in that position he was involved in such issues as legislation on public works, the wages and hours and collective bargaining provisions of the National Industrial Relations Act, the National Labor Relations Act of 1935, and the Housing Act of 1937. In 1937 he moved to the U.S. Housing Authority, where he remained until 1942. After World War II he assisted in drafting the Employment Act of 1946 and the Housing Act of 1949.

Keyserling's multifaceted career in Washington included the drafting of three convention platforms for FDR and membership on and chairmanship of the Council of Economic Advisers under President Truman. Later, as a private consultant, he advised the governments of France, India, Israel, and Puerto Rico. He is the author of many studies in economics. He retired a few years ago to work on voluntary efforts related to American economic problems, "all in the philosophy and practice of the New Deal."

DAVID A. MORSE was born in New York City in 1907 and educated in the Somerville, New Jersey, public school system, Rutgers College, and Harvard Law School. He went from private law practice to the New Deal in 1933, serving successively in the Interior Department, in the Justice Department, and with the National Labor Relations Board. He returned to private practice in New Jersey until Pearl Harbor, when he entered the armed forces and became a member of General Eisenhower's staff.

After the war he was general counsel of the National Labor Relations Board, held several high-ranking positions in the Department of Labor, then served as director general of the International Labour Organization in Geneva from 1948 to 1970. He returned to New York in 1970 to become a senior partner in the law firm of Surrey and Morse.

ROBERT R. NATHAN, born in Dayton, Ohio, in 1908, received his academic training in economics at the Wharton School of the University of Pennsylvania and his law degree from Georgetown Law School in 1938. He went to Washington in the early days of the New Deal to work on the first official national income study under Simon Kuznets. Among his positions were chief of the national income division of the Department of Commerce, assistant director of research in several defense agencies, chairman of the planning committee of the War Production Board, and deputy director of the Office of War Mobilization and Reconversion.

Nathan remained in the government until shortly after World War II, when he organized his own consulting firm. Since 1946 he has been engaged in development planning and implementation in the less developed countries and in consulting services to business, labor, and governments in the United States.

JOHN W. PEHLE was born in Minneapolis in 1909 and educated in public schools there and in Sioux Falls, South Dakota, and Omaha, Nebraska. He graduated from Creighton University in 1930 and was awarded a Doctor of Jurisprudence degree from Yale Law School in 1935. He was employed by the office of the general counsel at the Treasury from 1934 to 1940. He then served as assistant to Secretary of the Treasury Morgenthau and as director of the Foreign Funds Control. In 1944 he became executive director of the War Refugee Board. Two years later he resigned from the Treasury to enter private practice with several Treasury colleagues. In 1968 his firm was merged with Morgan, Lewis and Bockius, where he still practices law.

CLAUDE D. PEPPER was born on a farm near Dudleyville, Alabama, in 1900. He attended public schools and served in the Students' Army Training Corps. He graduated from the University of Alabama in 1921 and took his law degree at Harvard in 1924.

From 1929 to 1930 he served in the Florida Legislature, and in 1936 he was elected to the United States Senate. He served on the Senate Foreign Relations Committee from 1937 until 1950, when he was defeated for reelection. He was elected to the U.S. House of Representatives in 1962, and has been reelected every term since. He has served on the Subcommittee on Rules in both the 97th and 98th Congresses and is now chairman of the Rules Committee.

Pepper has attended every Democratic Convention since 1940. He holds many awards, including the Eleanor Roosevelt Humanities Award (1968) and the Veterans of Foreign Wars Award (1968). He is an active member of many civic clubs and organizations and the author of various articles in law reviews, magazines, and newspapers.

EDWARD F. PRICHARD, JR., was born in 1915 in Paris, Kentucky. He graduated from Princeton University in 1935 and received a law degree from Harvard Law School in 1938. He worked with the Senate Civil Liberties Subcommittee, and in 1939–1940 he was law clerk for Justice Frankfurter. In 1940 and 1941 he worked in the Attorney General's office as special assistant to Attorneys General Jackson and Biddle. From 1942 to 1945 he was general counsel of the Office of Economic Stabilization, working in the White House with James F. Byrnes and Fred Vinson. After 1945 he practiced law in Kentucky.

Prichard is active in local Democratic politics. He has been a delegate to several Democratic National Conventions, was a member of the Platform Committee in 1948, and served as general counsel of the Democratic National Committee from 1946 to 1948. He also was a member of the Council on Higher Education in Kentucky from 1966 until 1980.

WARNER B. "RAGS" RAGSDALE was born in Hiram, Georgia, one of those small southern towns where everyone knows everyone's secrets. After Harris College and a period at Georgia Tech, he went into the advertising department of the *Atlanta Journal* to polish up his education in newspaper work. Within four years he went on to the *Florida Metropolis,* the *Hendersonville News,* and the *Charlotte Observer.* He also worked for the Associated Press in Atlanta, the International News

Service in Birmingham, and the *Philadelphia Evening Ledger.* In 1926 the AP moved him to New Orleans and then to Washington.

After seventeen years with the AP Ragsdale joined *U.S. News and World Report,* where for twenty-seven years he covered every political event of importance. He met every President and attended every political convention, even the odd ones like the Townsendites in Cleveland in 1936, the Progressive party meeting in Philadelphia in 1948 that nominated Henry Wallace, and the Dixiecrat gatherings in Jackson, Mississippi, and Birmingham, Alabama.

Ragsdale's gentle southern speech, slow-paced questions, and reassuring mannerisms made an immediate impression on Sam Rayburn, the Speaker of the House. The two men became close friends, and Rags often traveled home with Rayburn to Bonham, Texas. When Rayburn realized that his back pain foretold a fatal illness, he sent for Rags, who did his best to comfort his friend. The Speaker gave him the last of a thousand and one interviews.

Now retired, Rags is writing a book about all the Presidents he has known.

JOSEPH L. RAUH, JR., born in Cincinnati in 1911, graduated from Harvard in 1932 and received his law degree from Harvard Law School in 1935. His Washington initiation occurred in 1935 when he was chosen by Felix Frankfurter as secretary to Justice Cardozo. He later served as secretary to Justice Frankfurter. These experiences led to his association with the master craftsmen of New Deal legislation, Ben Cohen and Tom Corcoran. From 1935 to 1942 he acted as assistant to this indomitable pair. If, as Rauh points out, Ben Cohen was the greatest draftsman of the New Deal, Rauh was the young "brains and believer" who waited on him day and night.

Rauh has been an attorney in Washington for two generations with the firm of Rauh and Silard, as well as being general counsel to the United Automobile Workers. He has also represented other labor groups, including the Brotherhood of Sleeping Car Porters and the American Federation of State, County, and Municipal Employees. Beyond his advocacy of labor unions, he has defended many persons accused of disloyalty, including Arthur Miller and Lillian Hellman.

Rauh was a chief lobbyist for the Civil Rights Act of 1964 and the Voting Rights Act of the next year, and he led the fight against the confirmation to the Supreme Court of Harold Carswell and Clement Haynesworth. For twenty years he was chairman or vice chairman of the local Democratic party of Washington, D.C. He was among the founders of the Americans for Democratic Action (ADA), and at the 1964 Democratic convention he helped get recognition for the Mississippi Freedom Democratic party.

GERARD D. REILLY was born in Boston in 1906, graduated from Harvard College in 1927, and received a law degree in 1933. He joined the New Deal in 1934 and worked in the Home Owners' Loan Corporation, helping distressed homeowners meet their mortgage payments. In the summer of 1934 the solicitor of the Labor Department offered Reilly a position on his staff, working on naturalization and immigration matters. When the National Industrial Recovery Act was declared unconstitutional, Reilly was assigned to draft bills that would protect labor standards. These resulted in amendments to the Davis-Bacon Prevailing Wage Law, and to the passage of the Walsh-Healy Act, the National Labor Relations Act, and the ill-fated Bituminous Coal Act. Reilly also helped Secretary of Labor Frances Perkins design procedures to expedite entry into the United States of German and Austrian victims of Hitler's persecution. The Labor Department was unable to persuade Congress to lift immigration quotas until 1939.

Reilly was appointed Solicitor General in 1937 and served until 1941. One of his major accomplishments was the passage of the Fair Labor Standards Act. He also helped to set up the wage and hour division to administer the new law. In the fall of 1941 he left the Labor Department and began serving on the National Labor Relations Board. He entered private practice in 1946, became a judge in the Court of Appeals in Washington in 1970, and served as Chief Judge from 1972 to 1976.

DAVID RIESMAN was born in Philadelphia in 1909. He attended William Penn Charter School, Harvard College (A.B. 1931), and Harvard Law School (LL.B. 1934). After holding a fellowship from Harvard and trying to work as a blue-collar laborer, he went to Washington in 1935 to serve as clerk to Justice Brandeis.

Riesman practiced law in Boston, taught at the University of Buffalo Law School, and worked with Ruth Benedict and Margaret Mead as a research fellow at Columbia Law School. He was deputy assistant district attorney of New York County, and during World War II he worked for Sperry Gyroscope Company. After the war he became a professor of social science at the University of Chicago. His most famous early book is *The Lonely Crowd* (coauthored). From 1958 until his retirement in 1980 he was Henry Ford II Professor of Social Sciences at Harvard. He continues to teach and to supervise graduate students. His major civic concern is the study of the dangers of uncontrolled nuclear weapons.

DOROTHY ROSENMAN was born in 1900 in New York City. After graduating from high school she studied with one of the first disciples of Madame Montessori and then held a Montessori class at the day nursery of the Emanuel Sisterhood Settlement House. She next studied with Miss Owens, the English originator of the concept of the nursery school, at Columbia University. She then changed the day nursery at the Emanuel Sisterhood to a nursery school. These experiences became her training ground in social work.

In the 1920s Mrs. Rosenman was elected a member of the housing committee of the Women's City Club. From then on she devoted herself to housing, not only in New York but also in the nation.

During the New Deal she became chairman of the United Neighborhood Houses. She took active part in developing and promoting new legislation, and later became chairman of the National Committee on Housing, working with all the housing agencies. She appeared before congressional committees to argue for improved housing legislation. She also wrote numerous articles for magazines and the book *A Million Homes a Year*. Since 1954 she has been a member of the board and of the executive committee of the NAACP Legal Defense and Educational Committee.

JAMES H. ROWE, JR., is well known for many reasons, but mainly for being the first person with a passion for anonymity ever to become an assistant to a President. He was born in Montana in 1909 and educated at Harvard College and Harvard Law School. After a stint as attorney to the National Emergency Council in 1934, he became the last clerk for Justice Holmes.

As many as four New Deal activities—the Reconstruction Finance Corporation, work on labor bills, the Public Works Administration, and the Securities and Exchange Commission—gave Rowe an overview of government and an early inclination for politics. In 1936, at the Democratic National Committee, he worked for the re-election of President Roosevelt, which in turn led him to that famous White House desk, where he remained from 1938 to 1941. He then went to the Department of Justice as what is now known as deputy attorney general.

During World War II Rowe served on naval aircraft carriers in the Pacific, returning with two presidential citations, a navy commendation, and eight battle stars. After the war he became a technical adviser at the international trials in Nuremberg. His private practice began in 1946 with the Washington firm of Corcoran, Youngman, and Rowe.

Over the years Rowe has served on many boards, beginning with the first Hoover Commission (1948–1949). He was a public member of the Foreign Service Selection Board (1949), chairman of the commission to reorganize the government of Puerto Rico (1949), and chairman of the U.S.–Puerto Rico Status Commission (1964–1967).

WALTER S. SALANT

WALTER S. SALANT was born in 1911 in New York City and went to private school there and then to Harvard, where he studied economics. He also attended Cambridge University and heard John Maynard Keynes lecture. In 1934 he joined the Treasury's division of research and statistics, where for two years he worked on analyses of currency proposals, the silver purchase program, exchange rates, fiscal matters, employment, and other macroeconomic problems.

Salant left the government to work on Wall Street and then returned to Harvard to complete his doctorate. In 1938 he returned to Washington to assist Raymond Goldsmith at the Securities and Exchange Commission in his pioneering work of estimating individual saving in the United States. A year later he joined a small advisory group formed in the Department of Commerce; in 1940 the group moved to what became the Office of Price Administration. As part of this group, Salant helped to devise the national economic strategy for price control during World War II. He became economic adviser to the Economic Stabilization Director in 1945 and economic adviser to the Price Decontrol Board in 1946. Later he was a member of the Council of Economic Advisers. He left the government in 1953, taught at Stanford, and became a senior fellow at the Brookings Institution.

ROBERT L. STERN

ROBERT L. STERN was born in New York City in 1908. He received his A.B. from Williams College in 1929 and his LL.B. from Harvard Law School in 1932. Stern arrived in Washington in 1933 and became attached to the Interior Department that first year working on what were known as "hot oil" cases in the petroleum division. In 1934 he moved to the Department of Justice, where he remained for twenty years. He spent his first thirteen years at Justice in the antitrust division, and wrote legal briefs for a variety of New Deal cases. He left Washington in 1954 and joined the Chicago law firm of Mayer, Brown, and Platt.

RICHARD LEE STROUT

RICHARD LEE STROUT was born in Cohoes, New York, in 1898. No sooner had he graduated from Harvard College in 1919 than he crossed the ocean to England to become a reporter for the *Sheffield Independent*. In World War I he was commissioned a second lieutenant in the infantry. Back on home ground he worked briefly on the *Boston Post* in 1921 and in the same year began his long association with the *Christian Science Monitor*. Before departing the Boston area, he managed to get an M.A. from Harvard in 1923.

In 1925 Strout went to the Washington bureau of the *Monitor,* where he remains, turning out a daily column, an occasional news story, and, until early 1983, his popular weekly TRB column for the *New Republic.*

He went abroad in World War II as war correspondent. In 1958 he won the George Polk award for national reporting. Many honors followed, including the University of Missouri Award for Journalism, the Sidney Hillman Award, and the National Press Club "Fourth Estate" recognition. In 1978 he received a Pulitzer Citation for *Farewell to Model T,* which he wrote with E. B. White. His own comments, entitled *Views and Perspectives on the Presidency,* were published in 1979. His eminence in the pecking order of White House press conferences is so secure that he has never claimed a front-row seat. He doesn't have to.

TELFORD TAYLOR was born in Schenectady, New York, in 1908. He

graduated from Williams College in 1928 and from Harvard Law School in 1932, then served for a year as clerk to Judge Augustus Hand of the Court of Appeals for the Second Circuit.

Taylor arrived in Washington in September of 1933 and went to work as an assistant solicitor in the Department of the Interior. A year later he transferred to the legal division of the Agricultural Adjustment Administration as assistant chief of the opinion section under Frank Shea and Jerome Frank. Early in 1935 the famous AAA "purge" occurred, in which Shea, Frank, and several others were fired. Taylor then became understudy to Alger Hiss, who was handling legislative liaison between the AAA and Congress, and when Hiss resigned a few weeks later Taylor took on that assignment.

In the fall of 1935 Taylor became assistant counsel to the subcommittee on railroad finance of the Senate Committee on Interstate Commerce. Put in charge of the subcommittee's New York office, he moved to New York. This assignment lasted until 1939, when he was appointed special assistant to the Attorney General and moved back to Washington. He next joined the staff of the claims division of the Department of Justice. In 1940 he was appointed general counsel of the Federal Communications Commission, a position he held until October of 1942, when he joined the Army. After the war he served as associate counsel and U.S. representative for the prosecution of war criminals. He has taught law at Yale, Columbia, and Cardozo law schools and is well known as a writer of books, articles, and reviews.

WILLARD L. THORP was born in Oswego, New York, in 1899. He

took his B.A. at Amherst College in 1920, his M.A. at the University of Michigan a year later, and his Ph.D. at Columbia in 1924. He taught economics at Amherst from 1926 to 1934 and was on the research staff of the National Bureau of Economic Research during the same period.

Thorp's Washington experience began in 1933. Working in various agencies, he found himself dealing with tariff issues, coping with the problems caused by the repeal of Prohibition, and helping to set up the Export-Import Bank. He also served for a time as chairman of the advisory council of the National Recovery Administration.

He left the government in 1935 and spent ten years as director of economic research at Dun and Bradstreet. At the end of World War II he was back in Washington, this time at the State Department, where he handled the two limited, short-term economic plans that formed the groundwork for the Marshall Plan. This task earned him five years in Paris "on loan" to the Development Assistance Committee.

Thorp returned to the academic life at Amherst in 1952 as professor of economics and director of the Merrill Center for Economics. He also rejoined the NBER and became affiliated with the Salzburg Seminar in American Studies. At present he is chairman of the finance committee of Pelham, Massachusetts, where he and his wife reside.

FRANK WATSON was born in Los Angeles in 1907. He graduated from the University of Redlands in 1928 and from Harvard Law School in 1932. After law school he began law practice with the Boston firm of Warner, Stockpole and Bradlee.

In 1933 he was appointed attorney for the Reconstruction Finance Corporation in Washington. That same year he also served as assistant solicitor for the Department of the Interior and the Treasury and in 1934 he became legal adviser to the housing committee of the National Emergency Council and general counsel for the Federal Housing Administration.

Watson moved to Indiana in 1935 to become director of the Purdue Housing Project at Purdue University. In 1937 he was president of the American Dwellings Corporation in Indianapolis. In 1938 he reentered government service, working for the Federal Housing Administration, where from 1939 to 1940 he directed the municipal housing division.

Beginning in 1941 Watson devoted himself to private business, and from 1965 to 1972 he taught at the California State University at Humboldt. Among his publications is *Housing Problems and Possibilities in the United States* (1935).

ROBERT C. WEAVER was born in Washington, D.C., in 1907. He attended Harvard University, where he received his B.S. degree in 1929, his M.A. in 1931, and his Ph.D. in economics in 1934. He entered government in 1933 and served in Washington for the next ten years, working in housing and labor recruitment. He was adviser to Secretary of the Interior Harold L. Ickes, special assistant to Nathan Straus of the Housing Authority, administrative assistant to Sidney Hillman of the National Defense Advisory Commission, and director of the Negro Manpower Service in the War Manpower Commission during World War II.

In 1944-1945 Weaver was executive secretary of the Mayor's Committee on Race Relations in Chicago. He taught at Columbia Teachers College and at N.Y.U., and from 1949 to 1954 he directed the Opportunity Fellowships Program of the John Hay Whitney Foundation. He held posts in the field of housing in New York City from 1955 to 1961, served as administrator of the Housing and Home Finance Agency from 1961 to 1966, and was Secretary of Housing and Urban Development from 1966 through 1968.

He became president of the Bernard M. Baruch College of the City University of New York in 1969 and resigned from that post in 1971 to become a member of the faculty at Hunter College. At present he is a Distinguished Professor Emeritus of Urban Affairs at Hunter College.

HERBERT WECHSLER, born in New York City in 1909, was educated in the New York public schools and at the City College of New York, where he received his A.B. in 1928. He graduated from Columbia Law School in 1931 and has been teaching and practicing law ever since.

Wechsler participated extensively in government service, including positions as law secretary to Justice Stone (1931–1932), special assistant to the Attorney General (1940–1944), and assistant attorney general in charge of the war division of the Department of Justice (1944–1946). He was also a member of the advisory committee to the Supreme Court on rules of criminal procedure (1941–1945), the President's Commission on Law Enforcement and the Administration of Justice (1965–1967), and the Commission on Revision of the Federal Appellate System (1973–1975).

From 1952 to 1962 Wechsler was the chief reporter for the model penal code of the American Law Institute, a work that stimulated the revision and modernization of criminal law throughout the country. He became executive director of the American Law Institute in 1963, and held the Harlan Fiske Stone Professorship of constitutional law at Columbia until his retirement in 1978.

ELIZABETH "WICKIE" WICKENDEN was the infallible rescuer of desperate drifters in those hectic early months of the New Deal. She became house-hunter, finder of doctors and dentists, and provider of transport. Harry Hopkins depended on her to accomplish the impossible, and she did.

After a series of executive positions in the social programs of the New Deal, including the Federal Emergency Relief Administration, the Works Progress Administration, and the National Youth Administration, she became a teacher and a consultant to a series of national agencies: director of the Field Foundation's study group on Social Security, adjunct professor at Fordham University Graduate School of Social Science, and member of the advisory committee of Save Our Security. She later served as a consultant to Yale University and on President Kennedy's task force on health and Social Security legislation.

At present, she is director of the study group of the National Monetary Reporting Agency, which interprets and reports on current Social Security policy in Washington. She also serves on the National Citizens Advisory Council on the Status of Women. She is the author of many articles and still writes about issues in the field of social welfare.

Biographical Notes

Listed below are some persons mentioned in the text, not identified elsewhere, for whom the reader may wish additional information.

ACHESON, Dean Gooderham   b. 1893 in Middletown, Conn., d. 1971. A lawyer, Acheson received his LL.B. from Harvard University, served as law clerk to Justice Louis D. Brandeis, and was a member of the law firm Covington, Burling. In May 1933 he became Under Secretary of the Treasury, but resigned in December in a dispute with FDR over the price of gold. From 1934 to 1941 he was a partner in Covington, Burling, Rublee, Acheson, and Shorb, and represented the New York Stock Exchange during the Richard Whitney hearings. He was Assistant Secretary of State, 1941–1945, Under Secretary of State, 1945–1947, and Secretary of State, 1949–1953.

ALTMEYER, Arthur Joseph   b. 1891 in DePere, Wis., d. 1972. An economist, he received his Ph.D. from the University of Wisconsin and he served as secretary of the Wisconsin Industrial Commission. He was chief of the compliance division of the National Recovery Administration, 1933–1934. From 1934 to 1935 he served as Assistant Secretary of Labor and as chairman of the Technical Board of the President's Committee on Economic Security. Altmeyer is frequently credited with getting the Social Security Act through Congress. He was a member of the Social Security Board, 1935–1945, becoming chairman in 1937, and was U.S. Commissioner of Social Security from 1946 to 1953. He also served as a member of the executive committee of the National Youth Administration.

ARNOLD, Thurman Wesley   b. 1891 in Laramie, Wyo., d. 1969. A lawyer and writer, he received his LL.B. from Harvard University, had a private practice in Laramie, and taught law at the University of Wyoming, the University of West Virginia, and Yale University. He was a special assistant to the U.S. Attorney General, 1937–1938, and served as the Justice Department's representative on the Temporary National Economic Committee, 1938–1941. From 1938 to 1942 he was an Assistant U.S. Attorney General in charge of the antitrust division of the Justice Department, and from 1943 to 1945 was an Associate Justice of the U.S. Circuit Court of Appeals for the District of Columbia.

BAKER, Jacob   b. 1895 in Costillo County, Col., d. 1967. A businessman and government official, he was a mine operator, plantation owner, and head of the Vanguard Press. From 1933 to 1934 Baker was an assistant administrator of the Federal Emergency Relief Administration and the Civil Works Administration. From 1935 to 1937 he was director of Federal Relief Project No. 1, the art, theater, and music projects. He was also chairman of the National Resources Planning Board, 1933–1937, and president of the United Federal Workers of America, 1937–1940.

BALDWIN, Calvin Benham   b. 1902 in Radford, Va., d. 1975. A railroad worker and businessman, he worked for the Norfolk and Western Railroad and was owner of Electric Sales and Service Co. From 1933 to 1935 he was an assistant to the Secretary of Agriculture, from 1935 to 1940, assistant administrator of the Resettlement Administration and of the Farm Security Administration, and from 1940 to 1943, administrator of the Farm Security Administration. In 1943 he served as coordinator of the State Department in Italy; from 1943 to 1945 he was assistant chairman of the Congress of Industrial Organizations' Committee on Political Action.

BEAMON, Middleton   b. 1877 in Rutland, Vt., d. 1951. A lawyer, he received his LL.B. from Harvard University. From 1919 to 1949, he was legislative counsel to the U.S. House of Representatives and participated in the drafting of all revenue bills, the Transportation Act of 1920, the Tariff Acts of 1920 and 1930, the Social Security Act, the Federal Food, Drug, and Cosmetic Act of 1938, and numerous other measures.

BETHUNE, Mary McLeod   b. 1875 near Mayesville, S.C., d. 1955. A noted black civil rights leader and educator, she was president of the Daytona (Florida) Normal and Industrial School, which merged with the Cookman Institute of Jacksonville and was renamed Bethune-Cookman College in her honor, from 1904 until 1942. Bethune also served as president of the National Association of Colored Women, 1924–1928. In 1935 she founded the National Council of Negro Women and served as its president from 1935 to 1949. She was also a member of the National Advisory Committee of the National Youth Administration, 1935, director of Negro affairs for the NYA, 1936–1939, and director of the Negro affairs division of the Interior Department, 1939–1944. She was the acknowledged leader of the unofficial Black Cabinet from 1936 to 1944.

BIDDLE, Francis Beverly   b. 1886 in Paris, d. 1968. A lawyer, he received his LL.B. from Harvard University, served as law clerk to Justice Oliver Wendell Holmes, and was special assistant U.S. district attorney for the Eastern District of Pennsylvania. From 1934 to 1935, he was chairman of the National Labor Relations Board. Biddle was also chief counsel of the joint committee to investigate the Tennessee Valley Authority, 1938–1939, judge of the U.S. Circuit Court of Appeals, 1939–1940, Solicitor General of the U.S., 1940, Attorney General of the U.S., 1941–1945, and judge at the Nuremberg trials, 1945–1946.

BLACK, Hugo La Fayette   b. 1886 near Ashland, Ala., d. 1971. A lawyer, he received his LL.B. from the University of Alabama. After a number of years in private practice and state office, he was elected Democratic senator from Alabama, 1927–1937, and was chairman of the Senate Labor Committee, 1933–1937. As Associate Justice of the U.S. Supreme Court from 1937 to 1971, he was noted as a great liberal.

BOETTIGER, Anna Roosevelt Dall   b. 1906 in New York City. She was the oldest child of Franklin and Eleanor Roosevelt. Her first marriage to Curtis Dall ended in divorce. In 1935 she married John Boettiger, publisher of the Seattle *Post-Intelligencer.*

BORAH, William Edgar   b. 1865 in Fairfield, Ill., d. 1940. A lawyer, he was a progressive Republican senator from Idaho, 1907–1940. A strong isolationist, Borah served as chairman of the Senate Foreign Relations Committee, 1924–1933, and was an unsuccessful candidate for the Republican presidential nomination in 1936.

BRANDEIS, Louis Dembitz   b. 1856 in Louisville, Ky., d. 1941. A lawyer, writer, and jurist, he received his LL.B. from Harvard University. In private practice in Boston, he frequently defended labor and radical causes for which he became known as the "people's attorney." He served as Associate Justice of the U.S. Supreme Court from 1916 to 1939. The first Jew to serve on the Court, he was noted for his liberal positions.

BROWN, James Douglas   b. 1898 in Somerville. N.J. An economist, he received his Ph.D. from Princeton University. He was a member of the President's Advisory Committee on Employment, 1930–1931, and of the Advisory Committee on Railroad Employment for the Federal Coordinator of Transportation, 1933–1935. He was also staff consultant to the President's Committee on Economic Security, 1934–1935, a consulting economist to the Social Security Board, 1936, and chairman of the Advisory Council on Social Security, 1937.

BURLING, Edward Burnham   b. 1870 in Hardin County, Iowa, d. 1966. A lawyer, he received his LL.B. from Harvard University and from 1895 to 1915 was in private practice. From 1917 to 1919 he served as counsel to the War Shipping Board. He was a founding partner in the Washington, D.C., law firm of Covington, Burling, Rublee, Acheson, and Shorb from 1919 to his death.

BURNS, John Joseph   b. 1901 in Cambridge, Mass., d. 1957. A lawyer, he received his LL.B. from Harvard University and was a professor of law at Harvard. From 1931 to 1934 he was an Associate Justice of the Massachusetts Superior Court. He resigned this position to become general counsel of the Securities and Exchange Commission from 1934 to 1937.

BUTLER, Pierce   b. 1866 in Dakota County, Minn., d. 1939. A lawyer and jurist, he received his A.B. from Carleton (Minnesota) College. After many years in private practice as counsel to railroads, he served as an Associate Justice of the U.S. Supreme Court, 1923–1939. He was noted for his strongly conservative positions.

BYRD, Harry Flood   b. 1887 in Martinsburg, W. Va., d. 1966. A publisher and Democratic politician, he was president of the Valley Turnpike Company, publisher of the Winchester *Star* and Harrison (Va.) *Daily News Record,* and apple grower. From

1915 to 1925 he was a member of the Virginia State Senate, from 1926 to 1930 he was governor of Virginia, and from 1933 to 1966 he was U.S. senator from Virginia.

BYRNES, James Francis   b. 1879 in Charleston, S.C., d. 1972. A journalist, lawyer, politician, and statesman, he was official court reporter for the Second Circuit of South Carolina, editor of the Aiken (South Carolina) *Journal and Review,* and solicitor for the Second Circuit of South Carolina. From 1911 to 1925 he was a Democratic congressman from South Carolina; from 1931 to 1941 he was senator from South Carolina, one of FDR's most trusted lieutenants in the Senate. From 1941 to 1942 he served as an Associate Justice of the U.S. Supreme Court, resigning to serve as director of the Office of Economic Stabilization, 1942–1943, and director of the Office of War Mobilization, 1943–1945. As Secretary of State from 1945 to 1947, he negotiated the peace treaties with the minor Axis powers. He then served as governor of South Carolina, 1951–1955.

CARDOZO, Benjamin Nathan   b. 1870 in New York City, d. 1938. A lawyer and jurist, he received his LL.B. from Columbia University and was in private practice from 1889 to 1913. He was elected to the New York State Supreme Court in 1913 and promoted to the New York Court of Appeals in 1914. He served there from 1914 to 1932, from 1927 to 1932 as chief judge. He was Associate Justice of the U.S. Supreme Court from 1932 to 1938, where he was noted for his liberal positions.

CARMODY, John Michael   b. 1881 in Bradford County, Pa., d. 1963. An industrial executive, he rose from clerk and bookkeeper to vice-president and general manager of the Davis Coal and Coke Company. In 1933 he served as chairman of the Bituminous Coal Labor Board. He was chief engineer for the Civil Works Administration and a member of the National Mediation Board from 1933 to 1935. From 1936 to 1939 he was a member of the National Labor Relations Board and administrator of the Rural Electrification Administration. He was also head of the Federal Works Agency for the Interior Department, 1935–1941, and a member of the U.S. Maritime Commission, 1941–1946.

CLARK, Joel Bennett   b. 1890 in Bowling Green, Mo., d. 1954. A lawyer, son of former Speaker of the House James B. Clark, he received his LL.B. from George Washington University. From 1913 to 1917 he served as parliamentarian of the House of Representatives. He was a Democratic senator from Missouri, 1933–1945, and introduced the Clark Amendment to exempt from the Social Security system those companies that already had proper old-age retirement systems. From 1945 to 1954 he was an Associate Justice of the U.S. Circuit Court of Appeals for the District of Columbia.

COHEN, Benjamin Victor   b. 1894 in Muncie, Ind. A lawyer, he received his J.D. from the University of Chicago and his S.J.D. from Harvard University. He was law clerk to Judge Learned Hand, an attorney for the U.S. Shipping Board, and Zionist counsel to the Paris Peace Conference. From 1921 to 1933, he was in private practice in New York City. He served as associate general counsel for the Public Works Administration, 1933–1934, and as counsel to the National Power Policy Committee of the Interior Department, 1934–1941. At the same time, he played an important but unpublicized role in the drafting and passage of the Securities Act of 1933, the Securities Exchange Act of 1934, the Public Utility Holding Company Act of 1935, and the Fair Labor Standards Act of 1938. From 1945 to 1947, he served as counselor to the Department of State.

COVINGTON, James Harry   b. 1870 in Easton, Md., d. 1942. A lawyer, he received his LL.B. from the University of Pennsylvania. After a number of years in private practice, he became state attorney for Talbot County, Maryland. As a Democratic congressman from Maryland, 1909–1914, he played an important part in the passage of the Federal Trade Commission Act of 1914. He was Chief Justice of the Supreme Court of the District of Columbia from 1914 to 1918, and from 1918 until his death he was a founding partner in the law firm Covington, Burling, Rublee, Acheson, and Shorb.

CUMMINGS, Homer Stillé   b. 1870 in Chicago, Ill., d. 1956. A lawyer, he received his LL.B. from Yale University. After a long career in local politics and elective office in Stamford, Conn., he became a floor leader for FDR at the 1932 Democratic convention. From 1933 to 1939 he served as U.S. Attorney General.

DAVIS, Chester Charles   b. 1887 near Linden, Iowa, d. 1975. A lawyer, journalist, and businessman, he received his A.B. from Grinnell (Iowa) College, was editor of *The Montana Farmer,* and served as executive vice-president of National Cornstalk Processing Co. and Maizewood Products Corp. Davis was administrator of the Agricultural Adjustment Administration and a member of the board of directors of the Commodity Credit Corporation, 1933–1936. While at the AAA, he was instrumental in forcing the dismissal of Frank Shea, Jerome Frank, Gardner Jackson, and Dave Kreeger on the issue of tenants' rights. From 1934 to 1936 he was a member of the Industrial Emergency Policy Committee of the National Emergency Council and of the board of trustees of the Export-Import Bank of Washington. He was also a member of the Board of Governors of the Federal Reserve System, 1936–1941, president of the Federal Reserve Bank of St. Louis, 1941–1951, and associate director of the Ford Foundation.

DAVIS, John William   b. 1873 in Clarksburg, W. Va., d. 1955. A lawyer, Democratic politician, and diplomat, he received his LL.B. from Washington and Lee University. From 1911 to 1913 he was a Democratic congressman from West Virginia. He was U.S. Solicitor General, 1913–1918, and ambassador to the Court of St. James's, 1918–1921. In 1924 he was the compromise Democratic nominee for President, but lost to Calvin Coolidge. A conservative whose clients included public utility holding companies, Davis was one of the founders of the anti-FDR American Liberty League in 1934.

DOUGHTON, Robert Lee   b. 1863 in Laurel Springs, N.C., d. 1954. A merchant, farmer, and banker, he was a member of the North Carolina State Board of Agriculture and a state senator. From 1911 to 1953 he was a Democratic congressman from North Carolina, serving as chairman of the House Ways and Means Committee from 1933 to 1947 and 1949 to 1953. Doughton was influential in obtaining the passage of the Social Security Act of 1935.

DOUGLAS, Paul Howard   b. 1892 in Salem, Mass., d. 1976. An economist and political economist, he received his Ph.D. from Columbia University and was professor of industrial relations and economics at the University of Chicago. He served as a member of the National Recovery Administration's Consumers' Advisory Board, 1933–1935. From 1937 to 1938 he was a member of the Advisory Committee to the U.S. Senate and the Social Security Board. He was Democratic senator from Illinois, 1949–1967, from 1959 to 1967 serving as chairman of the Joint Economic Committee.

EARLY, Stephen T.   b. 1889 in Crozet, Va., d. 1951. A journalist with United Press and with Associated Press, he served as advance man in FDR's campaign for the vice-presidency in 1920. He was also a publicity representative for the U.S. Chamber of Commerce and for the Paramount-Publix Corporation. From 1933 to 1937 he served as assistant secretary to FDR; from 1937 to 1945 he was secretary. From 1949 to 1950 Early was an Under Secretary of Defense.

ECCLES, Marriner Stoddard   b. 1890 in Logan, Utah, d. 1977. A businessman and banker, he served as Assistant Secretary of the Treasury in 1934. He was a member of the Board of Governors of the Federal Reserve System from 1934 to 1948, serving as chairman from 1936 to 1948. From 1942 to 1946 he was also a member of the Economic Stabilization Board.

FAHY, Charles   b. 1892 in Rome, Ga., d. 1979. A lawyer, he received his LL.B. from Georgetown University. From 1933 to 1934 he was first assistant solicitor for the Interior Department and served concurrently as a member of the National Recovery Administration's Petroleum Administrative Board. He was chairman of the PAB from 1934 to 1935. From 1935 to 1940 he served as general counsel to the National Labor Relations Board and argued the case before the Supreme Court that determined the NLRB's constitutionality. He was U.S. Solicitor General from 1941 to 1949, and from 1949 to 1979 was a judge of the U.S. Circuit Court of Appeals.

FARLEY, James Aloysius   b. 1888 in Grassy Point, N.Y., d. 1976. A bookkeeper by profession, from 1932 to 1940 he served concurrently as chairman of the New York State Democratic Committee, chairman of the Democratic National Committee, and U.S. Postmaster General. He was one of FDR's chief contacts with the Democratic party organizations. In 1940 he broke with FDR over the third term issue.

FLY, James Lawrence   b. 1898 in Seagoville, Tex. A lawyer, he received his LL.B. from Harvard University. From 1929 to 1934 he served as Special Assistant U.S. Attorney General for antitrust cases. He was general solicitor, then general counsel, for the Tennessee Valley Authority from 1934 to 1939. In 1939 he was appointed chairman of the Federal Communications Commission.

FOREMAN, Clark Howell   b. 1902 in Atlanta, Ga., d. 1977. A liberal white southerner who was a strong supporter of civil rights, he was assistant director of the Julius Rosenwald Fund. From 1933 to 1934 he was adviser to Interior Secretary Harold Ickes on the economic status of Negroes. In 1934 he became special counsel to the Secretary of the Interior and established the Interracial Interdepartmental Group. He was director of the power division of the public works division in the Interior Department, 1935–1940. In 1938 he edited the National Emergency Council's "Report on Economic Conditions in the South." From 1940 to 1941 Foreman was director of defense housing for the Federal Works Administration.

FRANK, Jerome N.,   b. 1889 in New York City, d. 1957. A lawyer and jurist, he received his J.D. from the University of Chicago and was in private practice in Chicago and New York. From 1933 to 1935 he served as general counsel to the Agricultural Adjustment Administration and to the Federal Surplus Relief Corporation. In 1935 he was dismissed from the AAA for his position on tenants' rights. In 1937 he was appointed a commissioner of the Securities and Exchange Commission. Frank later served as a judge of the Second Circuit (New York) of the U.S. Circuit Court of Appeals.

FRANKFURTER, Felix   b. 1882 in Vienna, Austria, d. 1965. A lawyer, professor of law, and jurist, he received his LL.B. from Harvard University. From 1911 to 1913 he served as assistant to the Secretary of War. He was professor of law at Harvard Law School from 1914 to 1939. From 1939 to 1962 he served as Associate Justice of the U.S. Supreme Court, where he was noted for his strong belief in judicial restraint.

GARNER, John Nance   b. 1868 in Red River County, Tex., d. 1967. A lawyer and Democratic politician, he was a judge of Uvalde County (Texas) Court and a member of the Texas House of Representatives. From 1903 to 1933 he served as Democratic congressman from Texas, from 1931 to 1933 as Speaker of the House. From 1933 to 1941 Garner was Vice-President of the U.S., but broke with the Administration over the third term issue and retired from public life.

GENNERICH, Augustus Adolph   b. 1886 in Yorkville, N.Y., d. 1936. A New York City policeman, he was assigned to guard FDR during his 1928 gubernatorial campaign. FDR liked him and arranged for him to go to Albany with him. When FDR became President, Gennerich joined the Secret Service and went to Washington, D.C., with the President. He served FDR as bodyguard, nurse, masseur, and companion.

GLASS, Carter   b. 1858 in Lynchburg, Va., d. 1946. A printer, reporter, editor, and publisher of the Lynchburg *Daily News* and *Daily Advance,* he was a member of the Virginia State Senate. From 1902 to 1918 he was Democratic congressman from Virginia. He was coauthor of the Federal Reserve Act of 1913 and, from 1918 to 1920, Secretary of the Treasury. He was Democratic senator from Virginia, 1920–1946, serving as chairman of the Senate Banking and Finance Committee from 1933 to 1946. He was also coauthor of the Securities Act of 1933 (Glass-Steagall Act).

GREEN, William   b. 1872 in Coshocton, O., d. 1952. A coal miner and labor leader, he was president of the Ohio district of the United Mine Workers of America. From 1911 to 1915 he was a Democratic member of the Ohio State Senate. He was also statistician of the UMWA, and from 1912 to 1924, he was their representative on the American Federation of Labor's executive council. He was the AF of L's seventh vice-president, and from 1924 to 1952 he served as president of the AF of L. From 1933 to 1934 he was a member of the National Labor Board.

HAND, Augustus Noble   b. 1869 in Elizabethtown, N.Y., d. 1954. A lawyer and jurist, brother of Learned B. Hand, he received his LL.B. from Harvard University and was in private practice from 1895 to 1914. He served as judge of the U.S. District Court for the Southern District of New York, 1914–1927, and as judge of the Second Circuit (New York) of the U.S. Circuit Court of Appeals, 1927–1953.

HAND, Learned Billings   b. 1872 in Albany, N.Y., d. 1961. A lawyer and jurist, brother of Augustus N. Hand, he received his LL.B. from Harvard University and was in private practice from 1897 to 1909. He served as judge of the U.S. District Court for the Southern District of New York, 1909–1924, and as judge of the Second Circuit (New York) of the U.S. Circuit Court of Appeals, 1924–1951. From 1939 to 1949 he was chief judge of the Second Circuit.

HARRIMAN, William Averell   b. 1891 in New York City. Businessman and chief owner of the Union Pacific Railroad, Harriman served as a member of the National Recovery Administration's Capital Goods Committee, 1933–1934, becoming NRA administrator in 1934. From March to August 1941 he was FDR's special Lend-Lease representative to Great Britain. In August 1941 he was appointed ambassador to the Soviet Union, a post he retained throughout the war. In 1946 he served as ambassador to the Court of St. James's and Secretary of Commerce. From 1955 to 1959 he was Democratic governor of New York. In 1961 he served as ambassador-at-large for the Kennedy Administration. He was Assistant Secretary of State for Far Eastern Affairs, 1961–1963, Under Secretary of State for Political Affairs, 1963–1965, and, again, ambassador-at-large, 1965–1968. From March 1968 to January 1969 he was U.S. delegate to the Paris peace talks to end the Vietnam war.

HARRISON, Byron Patton   b. 1881 in Crystal Springs, Miss., d. 1941. A teacher and lawyer, he was Democratic congressman from Mississippi, 1911–1919. From 1919 to 1941 he was Democratic senator from Mississippi, serving as chairman of the Senate Finance Committee from 1933 to 1941.

HENDERSON, Leon   b. 1895 in Millville, N.J. An economist, he taught at the Wharton School and the Carnegie Institute of Technology and was director of consumer credit research at the Russell Sage Foundation. In 1934 and 1935 he was economic adviser and director of the research and planning division of the National Recovery Administration. In 1935 he served as economic adviser to the U.S. Senate Committee on Manufactures, in 1936, as an economic adviser to the Democratic National Campaign Committee, and in 1937, as a consulting economist for the Works Progress Administration. From 1938 to 1941 he was executive secretary for the Temporary National Economic Committee, and from 1941 to 1943 he was administrator of the Office of Price Administration.

HICKOK, Lorena Alice   b. 1893 in East Troy, Wis., d. 1968. A veteran Associated Press journalist, she became a close friend of Eleanor Roosevelt after FDR won the gubernatorial election in 1928. From 1933 to 1937 she served as a roving chief investigator for Harry Hopkins. She worked as a publicist for the New York World's Fair, 1937–1939, and for the Democratic National Committee, 1939–1945.

HOWE, Louis McHenry   b. 1871 in Indianapolis, Ind., d. 1936. A journalist, he was employed as a reporter for the New York *Herald.* From 1915 to 1918 he served as secretary to Assistant Secretary of the Navy Franklin Roosevelt, and then as assistant to Assistant Secretary Roosevelt from 1918 to 1920. From 1920 until his death he was FDR's personal secretary.

HUGHES, Charles Evans   b. 1862 in Glens Falls, N.Y., d. 1948. A lawyer, Republican politician, and jurist, he received his LL.B. from Columbia University and taught law at Cornell University and New York University. From 1907 to 1910 he was Republican governor of New York. He was Associate Justice of the U.S. Supreme

Court from 1910 to 1916, when he resigned to become the Republican presidential nominee. He was Secretary of State from 1921 to 1923, and from 1930 to 1941, Chief Justice of the U.S. Supreme Court.

HULL, Cordell   b. 1871 in Pickett, Tenn., d. 1955. A lawyer, politician, and diplomat, he received his LL.B. from Cumberland University and was a judge of the Fifth Judicial Circuit of Tennessee. He was Democratic congressman from Tennessee, 1907–1921 and 1923–1931, and from 1931 to 1933, Democratic senator from Tennessee. He served as Secretary of State from 1933 to 1944 and in 1944 won the Nobel Peace Prize.

JACKSON, Robert Houghwout   b. 1892 in Spring Creek, Pa., d. 1954. He received his LL.B. from Albany Law School and was a corporation lawyer in New York. He served as general counsel for the Bureau of Internal Revenue, 1934–1936, and as Assistant U.S. Attorney General for the antitrust division, 1936–1938. He was U.S. Solicitor General from 1938 to 1941, and from 1941 to 1954 he served as Associate Justice of the U.S. Supreme Court.

JOHNSON, Hiram Warren   b. 1866 in Sacramento, Cal., d. 1945. A lawyer and Republican politician, he was Theodore Roosevelt's vice-presidential running mate on the 1912 Bull Moose Progressive party ticket. He served as governor of California from 1911 to 1917. From 1917 to 1945 he was Republican senator from California and frequently supported policies opposed by the Senate's Republican leadership. He was an unsuccessful candidate for the Republican presidential nomination in 1920 and 1924. In 1932 and 1936 he supported FDR for President. While he generally backed New Deal social policies, he broke with FDR over foreign policy, the Court-packing plan, and the third term issue.

JOHNSON, Hugh S.   b. 1882 in Fort Scott, Kan., d. 1942. A soldier, he graduated from the U.S. Military Academy and rose from second lieutenant to brigadier general. From 1933 to 1934 he was administrator of the National Recovery Administration. In 1935 he served as administrator of the Works Progress Administration in New York City. He was also an editorial commentator for the Scripps-Howard newspaper and radio interests.

JONES, Jesse Holman   b. 1874 in Robertson County, Tenn., d. 1956. A lumber manufacturer and banker in Texas, he was director and chairman of the board of the Texas Trust Company. In 1932 he was appointed director of the Reconstruction Finance Corporation and was its chairman from 1932 to 1939. From 1933 to 1939 he was also a member of the National Emergency Council. In addition, he was chairman of the First and Second Export-Import Banks of Washington, 1936–1943, administrator of the Federal Loan Agency, 1939–1945, Secretary of Commerce, 1940–1945, a member of the Economic Defense Board, 1941–1945, and a member of the War Production Board and the Economic Stabilization Board, 1942–1945.

KENNEDY, Joseph Patrick   b. 1888 in Boston, Mass., d. 1969. A banker, financier, government official, and diplomat, father of President John F. Kennedy, he received his A.B. from Harvard University. In 1932 he was a heavy financial supporter of FDR and the Democratic party. From 1934 to 1935 he served as chairman of the

Securities and Exchange Commission. He was U.S. ambassador to the Court of St. James's, 1937–1940, resigning in opposition to growing U.S. support for the Allies.

LA FOLLETTE, Robert Marion, Jr.   b. 1895 in Madison, Wis., d. 1953. A publisher and progressive Republican politician, he served as private secretary to his father, Senator Robert La Follette, Sr., and as chairman of the Wisconsin State Republican Central Committee. He was vice-chairman of the Progressive National Executive Committee during his father's presidential campaign in 1924. Following his father's death in 1925, he was appointed to fill his unexpired Senate term and continued to serve in the Senate until 1947. He was reelected in 1934 and 1940 as a Progressive.

LANDIS, James McCauley   b. 1899 in Tokyo, d. 1964. A lawyer and legal scholar, he received his LL.B. and S.J.D. from Harvard University and was law clerk to Justice Louis D. Brandeis. He taught at Harvard Law School from 1926 to 1934, taking over Felix Frankfurter's classes when he was in Washington engaged in New Deal activities. From 1933 to 1934 Landis was chairman of the Federal Trade Commission. He was a member of the Securities and Exchange Commission from 1934 to 1937, and its chairman from 1935 to 1937. From 1937 to 1947 he was dean of Harvard Law School. He was also director of the Office of Civilian Defense, 1942–1943, director of American economic operations and minister to the Middle East, 1943–1945, and chairman of the Civil Aeronautics Board, 1946–1947.

LANDON, Alfred Mossman   b. 1887 in West Middlesex, Pa. An oil company owner and progressive Republican politician, he served two terms as governor of Kansas, 1933–1937. In 1936, Landon was the unsuccessful Republican presidential nominee.

LE HAND, Marguerite Alice   b. 1898 in Potsdam. N.Y., d. 1944. Missy LeHand was President Roosevelt's stenographer and personal secretary from 1920 to 1942.

LEWIS, David John   b. 1869 in Nuttals Bank, Pa., d. 1952. A coal miner and entirely self-educated, he was admitted to the Maryland bar. From 1911 to 1917 and from 1931 to 1939 he was Democratic congressman from Maryland. He was a member of the U.S. Tariff Commission, 1917–1925, and coauthor of the Wagner-Lewis Social Security Bill, 1934. From 1939 to 1943 he was a member of the National Mediation Board.

LEWIS, John Llewellyn   b. 1880 in Lucas, Iowa, d. 1969. A labor leader, he was elected president of the United Mine Workers of America in 1919. He was a member of the National Recovery Administration's Labor Advisory Board and National Labor Board, 1933–1935. In 1935 he was the leading force behind the creation of the Committee (later Congress) of Industrial Organizations. Although a Republican, he supported FDR in 1936; he broke with Roosevelt over the third term issue in 1940.

LILIENTHAL, David Eli   b. 1899 in Morton, Ill., d. 1981. A lawyer, he received his LL.B. from Harvard University and was a member of the Wisconsin Public Service Commission. From 1933 to 1946 he was a member of the board of the Tennessee Valley Authority, serving as chairman from 1941 to 1946. From 1946 to 1950 he was chairman of the board of the Atomic Energy Commission.

LUBIN, Isador   b. 1896 in Worcester, Mass., d. 1978. An economist, he received his Ph.D. from the Robert Brookings Graduate School and taught at the University of Michigan, the University of Missouri, and the Brookings School. He was commissioner of the Bureau of Labor Statistics in the Labor Department from 1933 to 1946. He also served as chairman of the Labor Advisory Board of the Public Works Administration, as a member of the Advisory Committee of the Federal Coordinator of Railroads, and as a member of the Technical Board of the President's Economic Security Committee which planned the Social Security program. He was a delegate to the Economic and Social Council of the United Nations from 1946 to 1963.

Mc CARRAN, Patrick Anthony   b. 1876 in Reno, Nev., d. 1954. A farmer, rancher, and politician, he served as district attorney of Nye County, Nevada, and as Chief Justice of the Nevada Supreme Court. From 1933 to 1954 he was Democratic senator from Nevada. A strong supporter of the silver industry, he opposed several New Deal measures, including the Economy Act of 1933 and the National Industrial Recovery Act. He was the author of the Civil Aeronautics Authority Act of 1938 and the Anti-Poll Tax Bill of 1944 and served as chairman of the Senate Judiciary Committee.

Mc INTYRE, Marvin Hunter   b. 1878 in LaGrange, Ky., d. 1943. After a career as a business representative for railroads and journalist, he became a special assistant for public relations to the Secretary of the Navy. In 1932, he was business manager and publicity representative of FDR's presidential campaign. From 1933 to 1936 he was assistant secretary to FDR, and from 1936 until his death he was secretary to FDR.

Mc KELLAR, Kenneth Douglas   b. 1869 in Richmond, Ala., d. 1957. A lawyer, he received his LL.B. from the University of Alabama and was Democratic congressman from Tennessee. From 1917 to 1953 he was Democratic senator from Tennessee, serving as president pro tempore from 1945 to 1947 and 1949 to 1953.

Mc REYNOLDS, James Clark   b. 1862 in Elkton, Ky., d. 1946. A lawyer and jurist, he received his LL.B. from the University of Virginia. McReynolds served as Assistant U.S. Attorney General from 1903 to 1907 and Attorney General from 1913 to 1914. From 1914 to 1941 he was Associate Justice of the U.S. Supreme Court, a member of the Court's conservative bloc.

MADDEN, Joseph Warren   b. 1890 in Damascus, Ill., d. 1972. A lawyer, legal scholar, and jurist, he received his J.D. from the University of Chicago and was professor of law at the University of Pittsburgh. He was chairman of the National Labor Relations Board from 1935 to 1940. He later served as judge of the U.S. Circuit Court of Claims and as judge of the Ninth Circuit of the U.S. Circuit Court of Appeals.

MAGRUDER, Calvert   b. 1893 in Annapolis, Md., d. 1968. A lawyer, he received his LL.B. from Harvard University and was law clerk to Justice Louis D. Brandeis. He was an attorney with the U.S. Shipping Board and professor of law and vice-dean at Harvard Law School. From 1934 to 1935 he was general counsel of the National Labor Relations Board, and from 1938 to 1939, general counsel to the wage and hour division of the Labor Department. He was a judge of the U.S. Circuit Court of Appeals, 1939–1959.

MARGOLD, Nathan Ross   b. 1899 in Jassi, Rumania, d. 1947. A lawyer, he received his LL.B. from Harvard University, practiced law in New York City, and was Assistant U.S. Attorney for the Southern District of New York. He was special counsel to the National Association for the Advancement of Colored People, 1930–1933. From 1933 to 1942 he served as solicitor for the Interior Department. Concurrently, he was chairman of the Petroleum Administrative Board and the Labor Policy Board of the National Recovery Administration. He was also special assistant to the Attorney General, 1933–1935, and a judge of the Washington, D.C., Municipal Court, 1942–1947.

MARTIN, William McChesney, Jr.   b. 1906 in St. Louis, Mo. A lawyer, investment banker, and government official, he was graduated from Yale University and the Benton College of Law in St. Louis. A member of the New York Stock Exchange from 1931, he was elected its governor in 1935, served as chairman of the Constitution Committee, 1936–1937, was secretary of the Committee to Reorganize the Exchange, 1937–1938, and was elected president of the Exchange in 1938. A partner in the firm of A. G. Edwards and Sons, he was also publisher and editor of the *Economic Forum,* 1932–1934. From 1945 to 1949 he was director of the Export-Import Bank of Washington, and he served as Assistant Secretary of the Treasury from 1949 to 1951. From 1951 to 1970 he was chairman of the Board of Governors of the Federal Reserve System.

MATHEWS, George C.   b. 1886 in Northwood, Iowa, d. 1946. An expert in utility rate structures, he received his A.B. from the University of Wisconsin. He served on the Wisconsin Railroad Commission as a rate expert, as statistician for its Utility Rate Department, and as director of its Securities and Statistics Division. He was director and chief examiner of the Wisconsin Public Service Commission, 1931–1933, became vice-president of Middle West Utilities Company in 1933, and the same year, was appointed to the Federal Trade Commission. From 1934 to 1940 he was a member of the Securities and Exchange Commission.

MOLEY, Raymond Charles   b. 1886 in Berea, O., d. 1975. A journalist and professor of public law at Columbia University, Moley became an early member of FDR's Brain Trust. He was a speech writer for FDR's 1932 campaign and recruited academic advisers for the New Deal. He served as Assistant Secretary of State in 1933 and as a member of the Advisory Council to the Committee on Economic Security in 1934.

MORGENTHAU, Henry, Jr.   b. 1891 in New York City, d. 1967. Publisher of *American Agriculturalist,* 1922–1933, he was a friend and neighbor of President Roosevelt. He served as chairman of the Federal Farm Board in 1933 and as administrator of the Farm Credit Administration from 1933 to 1934. In 1934 he was appointed Under Secretary of the Treasury. From 1934 to 1945 he served as Secretary of the Treasury.

MURPHY, Frank   b. 1890 in Harbor Beach, Mich., d. 1949. A lawyer, politician, and jurist, he received his LL.B. from the University of Michigan, was chief assistant U.S. district attorney for the Eastern District of Michigan, taught law at the University of Detroit, and was judge of Detroit's Recorder's Court. He was Democratic mayor of Detroit from 1930 to 1933, governor-general of the Philippines from

1935 to 1936, governor of Michigan from 1937 to 1938, and U.S. Attorney General from 1939 to 1940. Murphy was an Associate Justice of the U.S. Supreme Court from 1940 to 1949, a member of the Court's liberal bloc.

NORRIS, George William   b. 1861 near Clyde, O., d. 1944. A teacher and a lawyer, he was graduated from Valparaiso University, served as district judge for the Fourteenth District of Nebraska, and was Republican congressman from Nebraska. He served as Republican senator from Nebraska from 1913 to 1937 and as an Independent Republican from 1937 to 1943. Norris was one of the Senate's strongest progressive voices. He voted against U.S. entry into World War I and was a consistent supporter of labor and public power. He endorsed Al Smith in 1928 and FDR in all four of his presidential campaigns.

O'BRIAN, John Lord   b. 1874 in Buffalo, N.Y., d. 1973. A prominent Republican lawyer, he received his LL.B. from the University of Buffalo, was a member of the New York State Assembly, served as U.S. Attorney for the Western District of New York, and was special assistant to the U.S. Attorney General for war work, in charge of interning enemy aliens. From 1929 to 1933 he served as Assistant Attorney General in charge of the antitrust division of the Justice Department, and as special counsel to the Justice Department, he argued the *Ashwander* case before the U.S. Supreme Court. He returned to private practice as a member of the law firm Covington, Burling. During World War II, he served as an assistant general counsel for the Office of Production Management and as general counsel for the War Production Board, 1941–1944.

PATMAN, Wright   b. 1893 near Hughes Springs, Tex., d. 1976. A farmer and lawyer, he was graduated from Cumberland University Law School, served as assistant county attorney of Cass County, Texas, was a member of the State House of Representatives, and was district attorney of the Fifth Judicial District of Texas. Patman served as Democratic congressman from Texas from 1929 to 1976 and was coauthor of the Robinson-Patman Act on Price Discrimination.

PECORA, Ferdinand   b. 1882 in Nicosia, Italy, d. 1971. A lawyer, he received his LL.B. from New York Law School and was assistant district attorney for New York County. From 1933 to 1934 he served as counsel to the U.S. Senate Committee on Banking and Currency's investigation of the stock market (Pecora Committee). He was a member of the Securities and Exchange Commission from 1933 to 1935, when he was appointed a justice of the New York Supreme Court. In 1950 he resigned to run for mayor of New York City.

PITTMAN, Key   b. 1872 in Vicksburg, Miss., d. 1940. A lawyer, he practiced in Seattle until 1897, when he joined the Alaska gold rush. While in Alaska, he helped establish the government of the city of Nome. In 1902 he moved to Tonopah, Nevada, and continued his law practice. Unsuccessful as the Democratic Senate candidate in 1910, he was elected in 1913 to fill the vacancy caused by the death of George S. Nixon and continued in the Senate until 1940. From 1933 to 1940 he was chairman of the Foreign Relations Committee and president pro tempore of the Senate. A strong supporter of the silver industry, he was also a leading isolationist. He opposed the Treaty of Versailles and the League of Nations in 1919 and 1920; in the 1930s he supported the Neutrality Acts and opposed aid to the Allies.

PRESSMAN, Lee A.   b. 1906 in New York City, d. 1969. A labor lawyer, he received his LL.B. from Harvard University. He served as counsel to the Agricultural Adjustment Administration from 1933 to 1935 and was among those dismissed in the controversy over tenants' rights. From 1935 to 1936 he was general counsel to the Works Progress Administration and the Resettlement Administration, from 1936 to 1948 he was general counsel to the Congress of Industrial Organizations and the United Steel Workers Union, and from 1937 to 1938 he was a member of the Advisory Committee on Social Security.

REED, Stanley Forman   b. 1884 in Mason County, Ky., d. 1980. A lawyer and jurist, he was counsel to the Burley Tobacco Growers Cooperative Association. He served as general counsel to the Federal Farm Board, 1929–1932, general counsel to the Reconstruction Finance Corporation, 1932–1935, and U.S. Solicitor General, 1935–1938. From 1938 to 1957 he was Associate Justice of the U.S. Supreme Court. Unpredictable in his decisions, he generally supported the New Deal and liberal policies.

RICHBERG, Donald Randall   b. 1881 in Knoxville, Tenn., d. 1960. A labor lawyer, he received his LL.B. from Harvard University and was in private practice in Chicago. In 1933 he was coauthor of the National Industrial Recovery Act. He served as general counsel to the National Recovery Administration from 1933 to 1935 and as executive director of the National Emergency Council from 1934 to 1935. In 1935 he also served as chairman of the NRA's Board and was appointed special assistant to the U.S. Attorney General. In 1936 he returned to private practice with the firm of Davies, Richberg, Beebe, Busick, and Richardson of Washington, D.C.

RIEFLER, Winfield William   b. 1897 in Buffalo, N.Y., d. 1974. An economist, he received his Ph.D. from the Brookings Graduate School and was a foreign trade officer with the Commerce Department stationed in Buenos Aires. He worked for the Federal Reserve Board, first in the division of research and statistics, then as executive secretary of the Committee on Bank Reserves, as economic adviser to the executive council, and as chairman of the Central Statistics Board. He was also an economic adviser to the National Emergency Council, 1934–1935, and a special assistant to the U.S. ambassador in London, 1942–1944. From 1948 to 1959 he was assistant to the chairman of the Board of Governors of the Federal Reserve System.

ROBERTS, Owen Josephus   b. 1875 in Philadelphia, Pa., d. 1955. A lawyer, legal scholar, and jurist, he received his LL.B. from the University of Pennsylvania, was a professor of law there, and was a corporation lawyer in Philadelphia. He served as Associate Justice of the U.S. Supreme Court from 1930 to 1945. Initially a member of the conservative bloc, he became a key swing vote in the late 1930s and early 1940s.

ROBINSON, Joseph Taylor   b. 1872 near Loake, Ark., d. 1937. A lawyer, he served as Democratic congressman from Arkansas, 1903–1913, and as senator, 1913–1937. In 1913 he also served as governor of Arkansas. From 1923 to 1933 he was Democratic minority leader of the Senate and from 1933 to 1937, majority leader. In 1928 Robinson was the unsuccessful Democratic candidate for the vice-presidency. He was coauthor of the Robinson-Patman Act on Price Discrimination.

ROOSEVELT, Anna Eleanor   *see* BOETTIGER, Anna Roosevelt Dall

ROOSEVELT, Elliott   b. 1910 in New York City. An advertising executive, he was the third son of Franklin and Eleanor Roosevelt. In the 1930s he was a vice-president of Kelly, Nason, and Roosevelt, account executive with the firm of Paul Cornell, Inc., and president of Hearst Radio, Inc.

ROOSEVELT, James   b. 1907 in New York City. The oldest son of FDR, he served as unofficial aide to his father in 1933 and was an administrative assistant to the President from 1937 to 1938. He was president of an insurance company, a motion picture executive, and a colonel in the military. An unsuccessful Democratic candidate for governor of California in 1950, he served as Democratic congressman from California from 1955 to 1967.

ROOSEVELT, John Aspinwall   b. 1916 in New York City, d. 1981. An investment executive, he was the youngest son of Franklin and Eleanor Roosevelt. He was employed by William Filene's Sons Company of Boston and by Grayson-Robinson Stores, Inc., of Los Angeles. He headed the firm of Roosevelt, Lee, Magee, Inc., of Beverly Hills, and was a senior vice-president and director of Bache Halsey Stuart Shields, Inc.

ROSENMAN, Samuel Irving   b. 1896 in San Antonio, Tex., d. 1973. A lawyer and jurist, he received his LL.B. from Columbia University and served as a Democratic member of the New York State Assembly. He was counsel to FDR while he was governor of New York, 1929–1932. From 1932 to 1943, while an Associate Justice of the New York Supreme Court, he continued to advise FDR and served as a speech writer. From 1943 to 1946 he was special counsel to the President.

SHEA, Francis Michael   b. 1905 in Manchester, N.H. A lawyer, he received his LL.B. from Harvard University. He was chief of the legal opinion section of the Agricultural Adjustment Administration from 1933 to 1935 and coauthored the controversial opinion on Section 7 of the Cotton Contract of 1934–35. Following his dismissal from the AAA, he became counsel for the Securities and Exchange Commission. From 1935 to 1936 he was general counsel of the Puerto Rico Reconstruction Administration in the Interior Department. He was dean and professor of law at the University of Buffalo, 1936–1941, and from 1939 to 1944 he was also Assistant U.S. Attorney General. He was an associate prosecuting attorney at the Nuremberg trials in 1945.

SMITH, Alfred Emanuel   b. 1873 in New York City, d. 1944. A Democratic politician, he began his career in 1895 when Tammany Hall appointed him investigator in the city Commissioner of Juries office. He was a member of the State Assembly, sheriff of New York County, and president of the New York City Board of Aldermen. From 1918 to 1921 and from 1925 to 1929 he served as governor of New York state. He was the unsuccessful Democratic presidential nominee in 1928. Embittered by his loss to FDR at the 1932 Democratic convention, he endorsed Republicans for President in 1936 and 1940.

SMITH, Ellison Du Rant   b. 1864 in Lynchburg, S.C., d. 1944. "Cotton Ed" Smith made his living in mercantile and agricultural businesses and was a member of the State House of Representatives from 1896 to 1900. He was one of the founders of the Southern Cotton Association in 1905. He served as Democratic senator from South Carolina from 1909 to 1944.

STONE, Harlan Fiske   b. 1872 in Chesterfield, N.H., d. 1946. A lawyer, legal scholar, and jurist, he received his LL.B. from Columbia University and entered private practice in New York City. He served as dean of Columbia Law School, 1910–1923, and as U.S. Attorney General, 1923–1925. From 1925 to 1941 he was Associate Justice of the U.S. Supreme Court. He was Chief Justice from 1941 to 1946 and a member of the Court's liberal bloc.

SUTHERLAND, George   b. 1862 in Buckinghamshire, Eng., d. 1942. A lawyer and jurist, he was a member of the Utah State Senate, 1896–1900, a Republican member of Congress, 1901–1903, and U.S. senator, 1905–1917. He was also president of the American Bar Association and counsel for the U.S. in the Norway-U.S. arbitration at the Hague in 1922. He served as Associate Justice of the U.S. Supreme Court from 1922 to 1938, and was a member of the Court's conservative bloc.

SWOPE, Gerard   b. 1872 in St. Louis, Mo., d. 1957. An engineer, he received his B.S. in electrical engineering from the Massachusetts Institute of Technology and, from 1893 to 1922, rose from the rank of helper to president of General Electric Corporation. He was chairman of the board of GE from 1922 to 1933. In 1933 he served as chairman of the Coal Arbitration Board and of the Business Advisory and Planning Council of the Commerce Department. He was also a member of the National Labor Board. In 1934 he served as a member of the President's Advisory Council on Economic Security and, from 1937 to 1938, he was a member of the Advisory Council on Social Security.

TUGWELL, Rexford Guy   b. 1891 in Sinclairville, N.Y., d. 1979. A political scientist and economist, he received his Ph.D. from the Wharton School of Finance and Commerce and was a professor of economics at Columbia University. From 1932 to 1934 he was a leading member of FDR's Brain Trust. In 1933 he served as Assistant Secretary of Agriculture. He was an Under Secretary of Agriculture from 1934 to 1936 and administrator of the Resettlement Administration from 1936 to 1938. He served as governor of Puerto Rico from 1941 to 1946.

TULLY, Grace G.   b. 1900 in Bayonne, N.J. FDR's assistant private secretary from 1928 to 1941, she was private secretary to FDR, 1941–1945, following Missy Le-Hand's illness and death. After FDR's death she became executive secretary of the Franklin D. Roosevelt Memorial Foundation.

VAN DEVANTER, Willis   b. 1859 in Marion, Ind., d. 1941. A lawyer and jurist, he received his LL.B. from Cincinnati Law School and served as Assistant U.S. Attorney General assigned to the Interior Department. He was a judge of the Sixth Circuit of the U.S. Circuit Court of Appeals, 1903–1910. From 1910 to 1937 he was Associate Justice of the U.S. Supreme Court, a member of the Court's conservative bloc.

VINSON, Frederick Moore   b. 1890 in Louisa, Ky., d. 1953. A lawyer, politician, and jurist, he received his LL.B. from Centre College Law School (Kentucky) and served as city attorney in Louisa, as commonwealth attorney for the Thirty-second Judicial District of Kentucky, and as Democratic member of Congress from 1924 to 1929 and from 1931 to 1938. In Congress he was a member of the Ways and Means Committee. He was appointed an Associate Justice of the U.S. Circuit Court of Appeals for the District of Columbia in 1938, and from 1942 to 1943 served concurrently as chief judge of the U.S. Emergency Court of Appeals. He resigned to become director of the Office of Economic Stabilization. He was also administrator of the Federal Loan Administration and director of War Mobilization and Reconversion. From July 1945 to June 1946 he served as Secretary of the Treasury. From 1946 until his death in 1953 he was Chief Justice of the U.S. Supreme Court.

WALLACE, Henry Agard   b. 1888 in Adair County, Iowa, d. 1965. An agricultural scientist and reformer, he published an agricultural journal and was the owner of a profitable seed hybridization business. Originally a progressive Republican, he joined the Democratic party in 1928. From 1933 to 1940 he was Secretary of Agriculture and administrator of the Agricultural Adjustment Administration. He served as Vice-President of the U.S. from 1941 to 1944 and as Secretary of Commerce from 1945 to 1946.

WALSH, David Ignatius   b. 1872 in Leominster, Mass., d. 1947. A lawyer, he received his LL.B. from Boston University, served as a member of the Massachusetts House of Representatives, and was lieutenant governor and governor of Massachusetts. He was Democratic senator from Massachusetts from 1919 to 1925. Defeated for reelection in 1924, he was elected to fill the vacancy caused by the death of Henry Cabot Lodge and served again from 1926 to 1947. He was chairman of the Senate Labor Committee and coauthor of the Walsh-Healey Act of 1936.

WATSON, Edwin Martin   b. 1883 in Eufala, Ala., d. 1945. A soldier, he graduated from the U.S. Military Academy in 1908 and rose from second lieutenant to brigadier general. From 1933 to 1934 "Pa" Watson was military aide and appointments secretary to FDR. He was assistant secretary, 1934–1936, and secretary, 1936–1945. He died aboard ship on the return voyage from the Yalta Conference.

WELLES, Sumner   b. 1892 in New York City, d. 1961. A diplomat, he was secretary of the U.S. Embassies in Tokyo and Buenos Aires, chief of the Latin American Affairs Division of the State Department, U.S. commissioner in the Dominican Republic, and a member of the Dawes Financial Mission to the Dominican Republic. He served as a Special Assistant Secretary of State and U.S. Ambassador to Cuba in 1933. From 1933 to 1937 he was Assistant Secretary of State. He was appointed Under Secretary of State in 1937. FDR usually operated through him rather than Secretary of State Cordell Hull.

WHEELER, Burton Kendall   b. 1882 in Hudson, Mass., d. 1975. Beginning as a stenographer, he received his LL.B. from the University of Michigan and began his practice in Butte, Montana. He was a member of the state legislature, U.S. district attorney for Montana, and unsuccessful Democratic candidate for governor in 1920. He was elected to the U.S. Senate in 1922 and served from 1923 to 1947. In 1924 he was the unsuccessful candidate for the vice-presidency on the LaFollette-Wheeler Conference for Progressive Political Action ticket.

WILLIAMS, Aubrey Willis   b. 1890 in Springfield, Ala., d. 1965. A social worker, he was director of the Wisconsin Conference of Social Work and field representative for the American Public Welfare Association. In 1933 he became field representative for the Federal Emergency Relief Administration. He was assistant administrator of the FERA and the Civil Works Administration from 1933 to 1935. From 1935 to 1938 he was deputy administrator of the Works Progress Administration. He was also executive director and administrator of the National Youth Administration, 1935–1943. Following the Senate's rejection of his nomination to be the administrator of the Rural Electrification Administration, he resigned to become director of organization for the National Farmers' Union.

WILLKIE, Wendell Lewis   b. 1892 in Elwood, Ind., d. 1944. A corporate lawyer and Republican politician, he received his LL.B. from Indiana University and was in private practice from 1916 to 1932. From 1933 to 1940 he was president of the Commonwealth and Southern Utility Corporation and a leading opponent of the Securities and Exchange Commission's actions against utility holding companies. In 1940 he was the unsuccessful Republican presidential candidate.

WINANT, John Gilbert   b. 1889 in New York City, d. 1947. The liberal Republican governor of New Hampshire from 1925 to 1926 and 1931 to 1934, he served as chairman of the Textile Inquiry Board in 1934. From 1935 to 1937 he was chairman of the Social Security Board. For a time in 1935, and from 1937 to 1940, he served as assistant director of the International Labor Organization in Geneva, Switzerland. In 1941 he was appointed U.S. ambassador to the Court of St. James's.

WITTE, Edwin Emil   b. 1887 in Jefferson County, Wis., d. 1960. An economist, he received his Ph.D. from the University of Wisconsin. He was chief of the Wisconsin Legislative Reference Library, acting director of the Unemployment Compensation Division of the Industrial Commission of Wisconsin, a member of the Wisconsin State Planning Board, a member of the Wisconsin Citizens' Committee on Public Welfare, a member of the Wisconsin Labor Relations Board, and chairman of the Economics Department at the University of Wisconsin. From 1936 to 1937 he served as executive director of the President's Committee on Economic Security. He was a member of the Advisory Committee on Social Security from 1937 to 1938, and in 1941 became a member of the Advisory Council on Unemployment Security and a Special Agent for the National Defense Mediation Board. He also served as a member of the National War Labor Board from 1944 to 1945.

WYZANSKI, Charles Edward, Jr.   b. 1906 in Boston, Mass. A lawyer, he received his LL.B. from Harvard University and was law clerk to Judge Augustus N. Hand and to Judge Learned B. Hand. From 1933 to 1935 he was a solicitor in the Labor Department. He was a special assistant to the U.S. Attorney General from 1935 to 1937 and delivered the oral arguments in the Social Security test case. In 1941 he became a judge of the U.S. District Court for Massachusetts.

Index